S0-AHT-695

WHO'S WHO IN DICKENS

WHO'S WHO IN DICKENS

A COMPLETE DICKENS REPERTORY IN DICKENS' OWN WORDS

COMPILED BY

THOMAS ALEXANDER FYFE

ONE OF H.M. JUDGES AT GLASGOW

AUTHOR OF "DICKENS AND THE LAW

HASKELL HOUSE PUBLISHERS LTD.

Publishers of Scarce Scholarly Books

NEW YORK. N. Y. 10012

1971

First Published 1913

HASKELL HOUSE PUBLISHERS LTD.
Publishers of Scarce Scholarly Books
280 LAFAYETTE STREET
NEW YORK, N. Y. 10012

Library of Congress Catalog Card Number: 75-152551

Standard Book Number 8383-1236-5

Printed in the United States of America

PREFACE

THIS book describes the Dickens creations, in the words of Dickens himself. But it is not a mere Dickens Dictionary. It presents, not *names* only, but *portraits*.

No author is so frequently quoted, on the platform and in the Press, as Charles Dickens. But even those most familiar with his works are often, at the moment, unable to locate the reference. The idea of this book is to recall the characters so referred to.

The book has another object. Its chief purpose is to illustrate the marvellous word-power which Dickens possessed. In a few words, or a terse sentence, or at most in a short paragraph, he presents a vivid portrait, which stamps upon the reader's mind, not only the individuality of the particular character, but the type of humanity which it portrays.

My hope is that the book may not only be useful to the Dickens student, but may entertain the general reader.

T. A. F.

Adams.—Head boy at Dr. Strong's school.—" One Adams, who was the head boy, then slipped out of his place and welcomed me. He looked like a young clergyman in his white cravat, but he was very affable and good-humoured."—*David Copperfield.*

Adams, Colonel.—Lord Verisopht's second at the duel with Sir Mulberry Hawk.—" Meanwhile the two seconds, as they may be called now, after a long conference each with his principal, met together in another room. Both utterly heartless; both men about town; both thoroughly initiated in its worst vices; both deeply in debt; both fallen from some higher estate; both addicted to every depravity for which society can find some genteel name, and plead its most depraving conventionalities, as an excuse; they were naturally gentlemen of unblemished honour themselves; and of great nicety concerning the honour of other people."—*Nicholas Nickleby.*

Adams, Jack.—An acquaintance of Lord Feenix, of whom he related an anecdote at dinner at Mr. Dombey's. —" Jack—little Jack—man with a cast in his eye, and slight impediment in his speech. Man who sat for somebody's borough. We used to call him in my Parliamentary time W. P. Adams, in consequence of his being Warming Pan for a young fellow who was in his minority."—*Dombey and Son.*

Adams, Jane.—Housemaid of Mr. and Mrs. Harvey, the young couple.—*Sketches of Young Couples.*

Adams, Mr.—A clerk in an Insurance Office.—*Hunted Down.*

Affery.—Maid to Mrs. Clennam. Married Jeremiah Flintwich.—" Lived in terror of her husband and Mrs. Clennam, the clever ones."—*Little Dorrit.*

African Knife-Swallower, The.—A member of Mr. Crummles' company of actors.—*Nicholas Nickleby.*

Aged P.—Wemmick's old father, who lived with him

at the Castle at Walworth, was very deaf, but very proud of his son, who playfully referred to him as " the aged P." —*Great Expectations.*

Agnes.—Maid to Mrs. Bloss, a boarder at Mrs. Tibbs'. —" Mrs. Bloss, and Agnes, the latter in a cherry-coloured merino dress, openwork stockings, and shoes with sandals, like a disguised columbine."—*Sketches by Boz* (The Boarding House).

Agnew, Sir Andrew, M.P.—Introducer of a Sabbath Observance Bill.—*Sunday under Three Heads* (Reprinted Pieces).

Akershem, Sophronia.—" Mature young lady; raven locks; and complexion that lights up well when well powdered—as it is." Married Mr. Alfred Lammle, believing him to be a man of property; but was deceived. —*Our Mutual Friend.*

Akerman, Mr.—The head jailer at Newgate, who refused to open the doors to the rioters.—*Barnaby Rudge.*

Allen, Benjamin.—A medical student.—" Mr. Benjamin Allen was a coarse, stout, thick-set young man, with black hair cut rather short, and a white face cut rather long; he was embellished with spectacles, and wore a white neckerchief. He presented altogether rather a mildewy appearance, and emitted a fragrant odour of full-flavoured cubas."—*Pickwick Papers.*

Allen, Arabella.—Sister of Ben. Allen.—" A black-eyed young lady, in a very nice little pair of boots, with fur round the top."—*Pickwick Papers.*

Alice.—The only daughter of the Bowyer to whom Hugh Graham was apprenticed.—" Thus it came to pass that Mistress Alice, his only daughter, was the richest heiress in all his wealthy ward. Young Hugh had often maintained with staff and cudgel that she was the handsomest; to do him justice I believe she was."—*Master Humphrey's Clock.*

Alice.—The youngest of the five sisters of York, the tale of whom was told by the inside passenger, when the coach overturned, and Mr. Squeers, Nicholas, and the other passengers spent the night at a roadside inn.—*Nicholas Nickleby.*

Alicia, Princess.—Eldest daughter of King Watkins the First.—*Holiday Romance.*

Alicumpaine, Mrs.—A friend of Mrs. Orange who gave a juvenile party.—*Holiday Romance.*

Alicumpaine, John.—Husband of Mrs. Alicumpaine.—*Holiday Romance.*

Alphonse.—Page to Mr. Wititterly.—" A little page; so little indeed, that his body would not hold, in ordinary array, the number of small buttons which are indispensable to a page's costume, and they were consequently obliged to be stuck on four abreast, but, if ever an Alphonse carried plain Bill in his face and figure, that page was the boy."—*Nicholas Nickleby.*

Amelia.—A young lady visitor at Ramsgate.—" Daughter of a stout lady with four girls."—*Sketches by Boz* (The Tuggses at Ramsgate).

Amelia.—A housemaid at Dr. Blimber's School who took a kindly interest in little Paul Dombey.—" Paul couldn't dress himself easily, not being used to it. . . . He went down, when he was otherwise ready, to the next storey, where he saw a pretty young woman in leather gloves cleaning a stove. The young woman seemed surprised at his appearance, and asked him where his mother was. When Paul told her she was dead, she took her gloves off and did what he wanted, and furthermore rubbed his hands to warm them, and gave him a kiss; and told him whenever he wanted anything of that sort—meaning in the dressing way—to ask for 'Melia, which Paul, thanking her very much, said he certainly would."—*Dombey and Son.*

Amelia (the wife of Bill, one of Mr. Jaggers' clients).—" A knot of three men and two women were standing at a corner. One of the women was crying in her dirty shawl and the other comforted her by saying, as she pulled her own shawl over her shoulders, ' Jaggers is for him, 'Melia, and what more *could* you have.' "—*Great Expectations.*

Analytical Chemist, The.—Veneering's butler.—" Meantime the retainer goes round, like a gloomy analytical chemist; always seeming to say—after Chablis, sir—you wouldn't if you knew what it's made of."—*Our Mutual Friend.*

Anderson, Mr. and Mrs. John.—Tramps whom the Uncommercial Traveller met on the road.—" You may find another kind of tramp, embodied in the persons of a most exemplary couple, whose only improvidence appears to have been that they spent the last of their little All on soap. They are a man and woman spotless to behold,—John Anderson, with the frost on his short smock frock instead of his pow, attended by Mrs. Anderson."—*The Uncommercial Traveller* (Tramps).

Anglo-Bengalee Disinterested Loan and Life Assurance Company.—The Company started by Montague Tigg.—" It started into existence one morning, not an infant institution, but a grown-up Company, running alone at a great pace, and doing business right and left."—*Martin Chuzzlewit.*

Anne.—Housemaid at Mr. Dombey's town house, who married Towlinson, the footman.—*Dombey and Son.*

Anny.—One of the two old pauper women who attended Agnes Fleming in the workhouse.—*Oliver Twist.*

Antonio.—A musical Spanish sailor, whom the Uncommercial Traveller met at the house of Meggisson, a Liverpool crimp.—" If Antonio has brought any money in with him, I am afraid he will never take it out; and it even strikes me that his jacket and guitar may be in a bad way; but the look of the young man, and the tinkling of his instrument, so change the place in a moment to a leaf out of *Don Quixote*, that I wonder where his mule is stabled, until he leaves off."—*The Uncommercial Traveller* (Poor Mercantile Jack).

Apparition, The.—A loafer of whom the Uncommercial Traveller asked his way.—" I found myself on a swing bridge, looking down at some dark locks, in some dirty water,—over against me stood a creature, remotely in the likeness of a young man, with a puffed sallow face, and a figure all dirty, and shiny, and slimy, who may have been the youngest son of his filthy old father Thames, or the drowned man about whom there was a placard on the granite post, like a large thimble, that stood between us. I asked this apparition what it called the place."—*The Uncommercial Traveller* (Wapping Workhouse).

Appearance, The.—A ghost, visible only to the foreman

of the Jury.—" The murdered man never lost one trace of his distinctness in my eyes, nor was he at any moment less distinct than anybody else. I must not omit, as a matter of fact, that I never once saw the Appearance, which I call by the name of the murdered man, look at the murderer."—The Trial for Murder (*Christmas Stories*).

Appollers, The Glorious.—A society of which Dick Swiveller was President.—" A select convivial circle, called The Glorious Appollers, of which I have the honour to be Perpetual Grand."—*The Old Curiosity Shop*.

Apprentices, The Two Idle.—" Two idle apprentices, exhausted by the long hot summer, and the long hot work it had brought with it, ran away from their employer. Actuated by the low idea of making a perfectly idle trip they took to themselves (after Hogarth) the names of Mr. Thomas Idle and Mr. Francis Goodchild, but there was not a moral pin to choose between them, and they were both idle in the last degree."—The Lazy Tour of Two Idle Apprentices (*Christmas Stories*).

Artful Dodger, The.—(*See* **Dawkins.**)—*Oliver Twist.*

Ashford, Nettie (aged six and a half).—The heroine of the *Holiday Romance.*—" Nettie Ashford is my bride; we were married in the right-hand closet, in the corner of the dancing school, where first we met, with a ring (a green one) from Wilkingwater's toy shop. I owed for it out of my pocket money."—*Holiday Romance.*

Atherfield, Mrs.—A passenger on the ship *Golden Mary.*—" A bright-eyed blooming young wife, who was going out to join her husband in California, taking with her their only child, a little girl of three years old, whom he had never seen."—The Wreck of the *Golden Mary* (*Christmas Stories*).

Atherfield, Lucy.—Child of Mrs. Atherfield, a passenger on the *Golden Mary.*—" As the child had a quantity of shining fair hair, clustering in curls all about her face, and as her name was Lucy, Steadman gave her the name of the Golden Lucy."—The Wreck of the *Golden Mary* (*Christmas Stories*).

Atkinson.—A London perfumer in the holiday season. —" Even the few solitaries left on guard at Mr. Atkinson's, the perfumer round the corner, (generally the most inexorable gentleman in London and the most scornful of three and sixpence) condescend a little, as they drowsily bide, or recall, their turn for chasing the ebbing Neptune on the ribbed sea sand."—*The Uncommercial Traveller* (Arcadian London).

Aunt, Mr. F.'s.—An aunt of Mr. Finching, left to the care of his widow.—" An amazing little old woman, with a face like a staring wooden doll, too cheap for expression, and a stiff yellow wig, perched unevenly on the top of her head, as if the child who owned the doll had driven a tack through it anywhere, so that it only got fastened on. A further remarkable thing in this little old woman was that she had no name but Mr. F.'s Aunt."—*Little Dorrit.*

Avenger.—Pip's name for Pepper, his page-boy.—*Great Expectations.*

Ayresleigh, Mr.—A prisoner for debt.—" A middle-aged man, in a very old suit of black, who looked pale and haggard, and paced up and down the room incessantly."—*Pickwick Papers.*

B., Master.—A former resident at The Haunted House.—" One of these bells was labelled, on a black ground in faded white letters, Master B. This they told me was the bell that rang the most. . . . Following Master B.'s bell to its source, I found that young gentleman to have had but indifferent third class accommodation, in a triangular cabin under the cock loft, with a corner fireplace, which Master B. must have been exceedingly small if he were ever able to warm himself at, and a corner chimney-piece, like a pyramidal staircase to the ceiling for Tom Thumb."—The Haunted House (*Christmas Stories*).

Boanerges, Boiler.—A ranting preacher.—" I have in my day been caught in the palm of a female hand by the crown, have been violently scrubbed from the neck to the roots of the hair, as a purification for the temple, and have then been carried off, highly charged with saponaceous electricity, to be steamed like a potato in the unventilated breath of the powerful Boanerges Boiler and his congregation."—*The Uncommercial Traveller* (City Churches).

Babley, Richard.—(*See* **Dick, Mr.**)—*David Copperfield.*

Babley, Miss.—A sister of Mr. Dick.—" He had a favourite sister, said my aunt, a good creature, and very kind to him. But she did what they all do—took a husband—and he did what they all do—made her wretched."—*David Copperfield.*

Bachelor, The.—A friend of the clergyman of the parish where Mr. Marton was school-master.—" The little old gentleman was the active spirit of the place; the adjuster of all differences; the promoter of all merry-makings; the dispenser of his friends' bounty, and of no small charity of his own besides; the universal mediator, comforter, and friend. None of the simple villagers had cared to ask his name, or when they knew it to store it in their memory. Perhaps from some vague rumour of his college honours, which had been whispered abroad on his first arrival; perhaps because he was an unmarried, unencumbered gentleman; he had been called The Bachelor."—*The Old Curiosity Shop.*

Badger, Bayham.—A doctor with whom Richard Carstone studied medicine.—" Mr. Bayham Badger was a pink, fresh-faced, crisp-looking gentleman, with a weak voice, white teeth, light hair, and surprised eyes."—*Bleak House.*

Badger, Mrs. Laura.—Wife of Dr. Bayham Badger.—" She was a lady of about fifty I should think, youthfully dressed, and of a very fine complexion. She was surrounded in the drawing-room by various objects indicative of her painting a little, playing the piano a little, playing the guitar a little, playing the harp a little, singing a little, working a little, reading a little, writing poetry a little, and botanising a little; if I add to the list of her accomplishments that she rouged a little, I do not mean that there was any harm in it."—*Bleak House.*

Bagnet, Matthew.—A comrade of George Rouncewell. —" Mr. Bagnet is an ex-artilleryman, tall and upright, with shaggy eyebrows, and whiskers like the fibres of a cocoanut, not a hair upon his head, and a torrid complexion."—*Bleak House.*

Bagnet, Mrs.—Wife of Mr. Bagnet.—" Mrs. Bagnet is not at all an ill-looking woman; rather large-boned, a little coarse in the grain, and freckled by the sun and wind, which have tanned her hair upon the forehead, but healthy, wholesome and bright-eyed; a strong, busy, active, honest-faced woman, of from forty-five to fifty; clean, hardy, and so economically dressed (though substantially) that the only article of ornament of which she stands possessed appears to be her wedding ring, around which the finger has grown to be so large since it was put on, that it will never come off again, until it shall mingle with Mrs. Bagnet's dust. The old girl, says Mr. Bagnet in reply, is a thoroughly fine woman, consequently she is like a thoroughly fine day, gets finer as she gets on; I never saw the old girl's equal; but I never own to it before her; discipline must be maintained."—*Bleak House.*

Bagnet.—Misses Quebec and Malta, daughters of Mr. and Mrs. Bagnet.—" Those young ladies—not supposed to have been actually christened by the names applied to them, though always so called in the family, from the places of their birth in barracks—are respectively employed on three-legged stools; the younger (some five or six years old) in learning her letters out of a penny primer; the elder (some eight or nine perhaps) in teaching her, and sewing with great assiduity."—*Bleak House.*

Bagnet, Woolwich.—Son of Mr. and Mrs. Bagnet.—" Young Woolwich is the type and model of a young drummer."—*Bleak House.*

Bagstock, Major.—A choleric retired army officer, who flattered Mr. Dombey, and cultivated his society.—" A wooden-featured, blue-faced Major, with his eyes starting out of his head, in whom Miss Tox recognised, as she herself expressed it, something so truly military . . . it being as it were the Major's stronghold and Donjon-Keep of light humour to be on the most familiar terms with his own name.—Joey B., sir, the Major would say, with a flourish of his walking stick, is worth a dozen of you . . . notwithstanding his very liberal laudation of himself however, the Major was selfish. It may be doubted whether there ever was a more entirely selfish person at heart—or at stomach is perhaps a better expression, seeing that he was more decidedly endowed with that latter organ than with the former."—*Dombey and Son.*

Bailey Junior.—Page at Mrs. Todgers' boarding-house. —" Benjamin was supposed to be the real name of this young retainer, but he was known by a great variety of names. At the period at which we write he was generally known among the gentlemen as Bailey Junior, a name bestowed upon him in contradistinction, perhaps, to Old Bailey. If any piece of crockery, a dish or otherwise, chanced to slip through his hands, he let it go with perfect good breeding, and never added to the painful emotions of the company by exhibiting the least regret; nor did he, by hurrying to and fro, disturb the repose of the assembly, as many well-trained servants do; on the contrary, feeling the hopelessness of waiting upon so large a party, he left the gentlemen to help themselves to what they wanted, and seldom stirred from behind Mr. Jinkins' chair, where, with his hands in his pockets, and his legs planted wide apart, he led the laughter, and enjoyed the conversation."—*Martin Chuzzlewit.*

Bailey, Captain.—An officer whom David Copperfield met at the Larkins Ball, and regarded as a rival.—" I do waltz (pretty well too as it happens) and I take Miss Larkins out. I take her sternly from the side of Captain Bailey. He is wretched no doubt, but he is nothing to me. I have been wretched too."—*David Copperfield.*

Baker, Mr.—District Coroner in London.—When " The Apparition " pointed out to The Uncommercial Traveller a place where suicide frequently occurred.—" I asked this apparition what it called the place, unto which it replied with a ghastly grin and a sound like gurgling water in its throat, ' Mr. Baker's trap.' "—*The Uncommercial Traveller* (Wapping Workhouse).

Balderstone, Thomas.—Brother of Mrs. Gattleton.—" Uncle Tom was very rich, and exceedingly fond of his nephews and nieces; as a matter of course, therefore, he was an object of great importance in his own family. It was his pride that he remembered all the principal plays of Shakespeare from beginning to end, and so he did."—*Sketches by Boz* (Mrs. Joseph Porter).

Baldwin, Robert.—The testator in the tale of the lost will which Mr. Boffin found in " the wonderful museum." —*Our Mutual Friend.*

Balim, Mr.—The young ladies' young gentleman.—" This young gentleman has several titles . . . he has usually a fresh colour, and very white teeth . . . he must wear an under waistcoat, and smile continuously."—*Sketches of Young Gentlemen.*

Bamber, Jack.—One of the company of law clerks whom Mr. Pickwick met at The Magpie and Stump tavern. —" A little, yellow, high-shouldered man; there was a fixed grim smile perpetually on his countenance; he leant his chin on a long skinny hand, with nails of extraordinary length; and, as he inclined his head to one side, and looked keenly out from beneath his ragged grey eyebrows, there was a strange wild slyness in his leer, quite repulsive to behold."—*Pickwick Papers.*

Bamber, Jack.—Proposed by Mr. Pickwick as a member of the Clock Circle.—" A very extraordinary and remarkable person, living, and talking, and looking, like some strange spirit, whose delight is to haunt old buildings."—*Master Humphrey's Clock.*

Banger, Captain.—A vestryman.—" Captain Banger of Wilderness Walk."—*Our Vestry* (Reprinted Pieces).

Bangham, Mrs.—A charwoman present at the birth of Little Dorrit in the Marshalsea Prison.—" In the Debtors confined chamber Mrs. Bangham, Charwoman and Messenger, who was not a prisoner (though she had been once) but was the popular medium of communication with the outer world, had volunteered her services as fly catcher and general attendant."—*Little Dorrit.*

Banjo Bones, Mr. and Mrs.—Vocalists at a sailors' public-house visited by the police superintendent and the Uncommercial Traveller.—" Dotted among the audience, in snug and out of snug, the Professionals—among them the celebrated comic favorite Mr. Banjo Bones, looking very hideous with his blackened face and lump sugar loaf hat; beside him Mrs. Banjo Bones, in her natural colours, —a little heightened."—*The Uncommercial Traveller* (Poor Mercantile Jack).

Banks, Major.—A name assumed by Meltham.—*Hunted Down.*

Bantam, Mr. Angelo Cyrus.—The Master of Ceremonies at the Bath Pump Room.—" A charming young man, of not much more than fifty; dressed in a very bright blue coat, with resplendent buttons, black trousers, and the thinnest possible pair of highly polished boots. A gold eyeglass was suspended from his neck by a short black ribbon; a gold snuff-box was lightly clasped in his left hand; gold rings innumerable glittered on his fingers; and a large diamond pin, set in gold, glistened in his shirt frill. He had a gold watch, and a gold curb chain with large gold seals; and he carried a pliant ebony cane with a heavy gold top. His linen was of the very whitest, finest and stiffest; his wig of the glossiest, blackest and curliest. His snuff was prince's mixture; his scent boquet du roi. His features were contracted into a perpetual smile; and his teeth were in such perfect order that it was difficult at a small distance to tell the real from the false."—*Pickwick Papers.*

Baps, Mr.—A dancing master who conducted the breaking-up party at Dr. Blimber's Academy.—" Mr. Baps was a very grave gentleman, with a slow and measured manner of speaking."—*Dombey and Son.*

Baps, Mrs.—Present at the breaking-up party at Dr. Blimber's.—" Mr. Baps the dancing master came, accompanied by Mrs. Baps, to whom Mrs. Blimber was extremely kind and condescending."—*Dombey and Son.*

Baptista, Giovanni.—A Genoese courier at St. Bernard Convent, who told the tale of the English Bride.—*To be Read at Dusk* (Reprinted Pieces).

Baptiste.—A soldier billeted in a French town.—" Was there not Baptiste, billeted on the poor water-carrier, at that very instant sitting on the pavement in the sunlight, with his martial legs asunder, and one of the water-carrier's spare pails between them, which he was painting bright green outside, and bright red within."—Somebody's Luggage (*Christmas Stories*).

Barbara.—Mrs. Garland's maid; married Kit.—" Downstairs therefore Kit went, and at the bottom of the stairs there was such a kitchen as was never before seen or heard of out of a toy shop window; with everything in it as bright and glowing, and as precisely ordered, as Barbara herself."—*The Old Curiosity Shop.*

Barbara's Mother.—The mother of Mrs. Garland's maid who married Kit.—" Barbara's mother came in with astonishing accounts of the fineness of the weather out of doors, but with a very large umbrella notwithstanding; for people like Barbara's mother seldom make holiday without one."—*The Old Curiosity Shop.*

Barbary, Captain.—A friend of Captain Maroon.—*Little Dorrit.*

Barbary, Mrs.—Wife of Captain Barbary.—*Little Dorrit.*

Barbary, Miss.—Aunt of Esther Summerson who brought her up, and caused Lady Dedlock, her mother, to believe that she had died in infancy.—" She was a good, good woman; she went to Church three times every Sunday, and to morning prayers on Wednesdays and Fridays, and to lectures whenever there were lectures; she was handsome, and if she had ever smiled would have been (I used to think) like an angel; but she never smiled; she was always grave and strict."—*Bleak House.*

Barbox Brothers.—The name under which Jackson carried on business.—" The firm of Barbox Brothers had been some offshoot, or irregular branch, of the Public Notary and bill broking tree. It had gained for itself a griping reputation before the days of young Jackson, and the reputation had stuck to it, and to him."—Mugby Junction (*Christmas Stories*).

Bardell, Mrs. Martha.—Mr. Pickwick's landlady.—" Mrs. Bardell—the relict and sole executrix of a deceased custom-house officer—was a comely woman, of bustling manners, and agreeable appearance; with a natural genius for cooking, improved by study and long practice into an exquisite talent."—*Pickwick Papers.*

Bardell, Mr.—The deceased husband of Mrs. Bardell.—" The late Mr. Bardell, after enjoying for many years the esteem and confidence of his Sovereign, as one of the Guardians of his royal revenues, glided almost imperceptibly from the world, to seek elsewhere for that repose and peace which a custom-house can never afford. At this pathetic description of the decease of Mr. Bardell; who had been knocked on the head with a quart pot in a public-house cellar; the learned Serjeant's voice faltered, and he proceeded with emotion."—*Pickwick Papers.*

Bardell, Master Tommy.—Son of Mrs. Bardell.—" Clad in a tight suit of corderoy spangled with brass buttons of considerable size."—*Pickwick Papers.*

Bark.—A receiver of stolen property.—" Bark is a red villain, and a wrathful; with a sanguine throat, that looks very much as it were expressly made for hanging, as he stretches it out in pale defiance over the half door of his hutch. Bark's parts of speech are of an awful sort—principally adjectives."—*On Duty with Inspector Field* (Reprinted Pieces).

Barker, Fanny.—Niece of Mr. Flamstead, the scientific old gentleman.—*The Lamplighter* (Reprinted Pieces).

Barker, William.—(Also known as Bill Boorker or Aggerawatin Bill).—Originally a waterman, afterwards an omnibus cad.—" Mr. William Barker was born—but why need we relate where Mr. William Barker was born, or when—why scrutinise the entries in parochial ledgers, or seek to penetrate the Lucinian mysteries of lying-in-hospitals? Mr. William Barker *was* born, or he had never been. There is a son, there was a father. There is an effect, there was a cause . . . Mr. Barker acquired a high standing and no inconsiderable reputation among the members of that profession to which he more particularly devoted his energies; and to them he was generally known either by the familiar appellation of Bill Boorker, or the flattering designation of Aggerawatin Bill, the latter being a playful and expressive sobriquet, illustrative of Mr. Barker's great talent in aggerawatin and rendering wild such subjects of Her Majesty as are conveyed from place to place through the instrumentality of omnibuses."—*Sketches by Boz* (The First Omnibus Cad).

Barker, Phil.—One of Fagin's gang of thieves.—*Oliver Twist.*

Barkis.—The Yarmouth carrier. A silent reserved man, who sent by David to Clara Peggotty the brief message " Barkis is willin'," and who ultimately married her.—" The carrier's horse was the laziest horse in the world I should hope, and shuffled along with his head down. . . . The carrier had a way of keeping his head down, like his horse, and of drooping sleepily forward as he drove, with one of his arms on each of his knees. I say drove, but it struck me that the cart would have gone to Yarmouth quite as well without him, for the horse did all that; and as to conversation, he had no idea of it but whistling."—*David Copperfield.*

Barley, Bill.—The gruff, gouty old father of Clara, whom Herbert Pocket christened " Old Gruffandgrim."—*Great Expectations.*

Barley, Clara.—The daughter of old Bill Barley. Married Herbert Pocket.—*Great Expectations.*

Barnacle Family.—" The Barnacles were a very high family, and a very large family. They were dispensed all over the Public Offices, and held all sorts of public places. Either the nation was under a load of obligations to the Barnacles; or the Barnacles were under a load of obligations to the nation; it was not quite unanimously settled which; the Barnacles having their opinion, the nation theirs."—*Little Dorrit.*

Barnacle, Lord Decimus.—A cabinet minister.—" There was Lord Decimus Tite Barnacle himself in the odour of circumlocution—with the very smell of Dispatch Boxes upon him."—*Little Dorrit.*

Barnacle, Mr. Tite.—A permanent official at the Circumlocution Office.—" Mr. Tite Barnacle was a buttoned-up man, and consequently a weighty one. All buttoned-up men are weighty. All buttoned-up men are believed in. Whether or no the reserved and never exercised power of unbuttoning fascinates mankind; whether or no wisdom is supposed to condense and augment when buttoned-up, and to evaporate when unbuttoned; it is certain that the man to whom importance is accorded is the buttoned-up man. Mr. Tite Barnacle never would have passed for half his current value, unless his coat had been always buttoned-up to his white cravat."—*Little Dorrit.*

Barnacle, Mrs. Tite.—Wife of Mr. Tite Barnacle.—" The expensive Mrs. Tite Barnacle, née Stiltstalking, who made the quarter days so long in coming."—*Little Dorrit.*

Barnacle, Clarence.—Son of Mr. Tite Barnacle.—" He had a youthful aspect, and the fluffiest little whisker perhaps that ever was seen. Such a downy lip was on his callow chin, that he seemed half fledged, like a young bird. He had a superior eyeglass dangling round his neck, but unfortunately had such flat orbits to his eyes, and such limp little eyelids, that it wouldn't stick in when he put it up, but kept tumbling out against his waistcoat buttons, with a click that discomposed him very much."—*Little Dorrit.*

Barnacle, The Misses.—Daughters of Mr. Tite Barnacle.—"The three expensive Miss Tite Barnacles; double-loaded with accomplishments, and ready to go off; and yet not going off with the sharpness of flash and bang that might have been expected, but rather hanging fire."—*Little Dorrit.*

Barnacle, Ferdinand.—Private Secretary to Lord Decimus Tite Barnacle.—"The sprightly young Barnacle whose name was Ferdinand."—*Little Dorrit.*

Barnacle, William, M.P.—A guest at the wedding of Minnie Meagles.—*Little Dorrit.*

Barney.—A waiter at The Three Cripples public-house; a Jew.—"Younger than Fagin but nearly as vile and repulsive in appearance."—*Oliver Twist.*

Barronneau, Henri.—The landlord of the Cross of Gold Hotel at Marseilles, whose widow Rigaud married.—"I put up at the Cross of Gold, kept then by Monsieur Henri Barronneau, sixty-five at least, and in a failing state of health. I had lived in the house some four months, when Monsieur Henri Barronneau had the misfortune to die."—*Little Dorrit.*

Barronneau, Madame.—The young widow of Henri Barronneau, whom Rigaud married, and whom he was charged with murdering, but escaped.—"Monsieur Barronneau left a widow; she was two-and-twenty; she had gained a reputation for beauty, and (which is often another thing) was beautiful. I continued to live at the Cross of Gold. I married Madame Barronneau."—*Little Dorrit.*

Barsad, John.—Whose real name was Solomon Pross. A French spy in England's pay, afterwards a turnkey in a French prison. Assisted Carton to effect Darnay's escape. —*A Tale of Two Cities.*

Barton, Jacob.—Brother of Mrs. Malderton, and a guest at the dinner at Oak Lodge.—"Mr. Jacob Barton was a large grocer, so vulgar, and so lost to all sense of feeling, that he actually never scrupled to avow that he wasn't above his business."—*Sketches by Boz* (Horatio Sparkins).

Bates, Charley.—One of Fagin's gang of thieves, afterwards reformed and became a farmer.—" Charley Bates exhibited some very loose notions concerning the rights of property. . . . Master Charles Bates, appalled by Sikes' crime, fell into a train of reflection whether an honest life was not after all the best. Arriving at the conclusion that it certainly was, he turned his back upon the scenes of the past, resolved to amend it in some new sphere of action. He struggled hard, and suffered much, for some time; but, having a contented disposition, and a good purpose, succeeded in the end, and from being a farmer's drudge, and a carrier's lad, he is now the merriest young grazier in all Northamptonshire."—*Oliver Twist.*

Bates, Miss Belinda.—One of the guests at The Haunted House.—" Belinda Bates, bosom friend of my sister, and a most intellectual, amiable and delightful girl, got the Picture Room. She has a fine genius for poetry, and goes in—to use an expression of Alfred's—for woman's mission; woman's rights; woman's wrongs; and everything that is woman's with a capital W; or is not, and ought to be; or is, and ought not to be."—The Haunted House (*Christmas Stories*).

Bathe, Mr.—Landlord of a London tavern.—*Births—Mrs. Meek of a Son* (Reprinted Pieces).

Battens, Mr.—The oldest male resident in Titbull's Almshouses in the East of London.—" This old man wore a long coat, such as we see Hogarth's chairmen represented with, and it was of that peculiar green-pea hue without the green which seems to come of poverty. It had also that peculiar smell of cupboard which seems to come of poverty."—*The Uncommercial Traveller* (Titbull Almshouses).

Bayton.—The husband of a woman who having died of starvation was buried by the parish.—*Oliver Twist.*

Bazzard, Mr.—Clerk to Mr. Grewgious.—" A pale puffy-faced, dark-haired person of thirty, with big dark eyes that wholly wanted lustre, and a dissatisfied, doughy complexion that seemed to ask to be sent to the baker's." —*Edwin Drood.*

Beadle, Harriet.—Maid to Minnie Meagles.—(*See* **Tattycoram.**)—*Little Dorrit.*

Bear, Prince.—The enemy of Prince Bull.—*A Fairy Tale* (Reprinted Pieces).

Beauty, The.—The name of Capt. Boldheart's schooner. —" It were tedious to follow Boldheart through the commencing stages of his story; suffice it that we find him, bearing the rank of Capt. Boldheart, reclining in full uniform on a crimson hearthrug, spread out upon the quarter deck of his schooner *The Beauty* in the China Seas."—*Holiday Romance.*

Beaver, Nat.—One of the guests at The Haunted House.—" Jack Governor had also volunteered to bring with him one Nat Beaver, an old comrade of his, Captain of a Merchantman. Mr. Beaver, with a thick-set wooden face and figure, and apparently as hard as a block all over, proved to be an intelligent man, with a world of watery experiences in him, and great practical knowledge."—The Haunted House (*Christmas Stories*).

Bebelle.—The pet name of Gabrielle, a foundling.—" A mere mite of a girl stood on the steps of the Barber's shop, looking across the Place; a mere baby one might call her; dressed in the close white linen cap which small French country children wear (like the children in Dutch pictures); and in a frock of homespun blue, that had no shape, except where it was tied round her little fat throat, so that, being naturally short and round all over, she looked behind as if she had been cut off at her natural waist, and had had her head neatly fitted on it."—Somebody's Luggage (*Christmas Stories*).

Becky.—The barmaid of the inn at Hampton where Sikes and Oliver rested.—*Oliver Twist.*

Beckwith, Alfred.—The assumed name of Meltham.—*Hunted Down.*

Bedwin, Mrs.—Housekeeper to Mr. Brownlow.—" A motherly old lady very neatly and precisely dressed." —*Oliver Twist.*

Belinda.—An unknown correspondent of Master Humphrey's.—" Master Humphrey has been favoured with the following letter, written on strongly scented paper, and sealed in light-blue wax with the representation of two very plump doves interchanging beaks."—*Master Humphrey's Clock.*

Bell, Doctor.—A member of the medical section of the Mudfog Association.—"Mr. Knight Bell, M.R.C.S., exhibited a wax preparation of the interior of a gentleman, who in early life had inadvertently swallowed a door key." —*The Mudfog Sketches.*

Bella.—Housemaid at Miss Pupford's School.—Tom Tiddler's Ground (*Christmas Stories*).

Bella.—The younger of two sisters removed in a prison van.—"The door again opened, and the two first prisoners appeared. They were a couple of girls, of whom the elder could not be more than sixteen, and the younger of whom had certainly not attained her fourteenth year. That they were sisters was evident. . . . They were both gaudily dressed, the younger one especially. These two girls had been thrown upon London streets, their vices and debauchery by a sordid and rapacious mother."—*Sketches by Boz* (The Prisoner's Van).

Belle.—A girl who had been engaged to Scrooge when he and she were both poor, but whom he had renounced when he became wealthy, and whom the Ghost of Christmas Past showed him happily married.—"Scrooge looked on more attentively than ever, when the Master of the house, having his daughter leaning fondly on him, sat down with her and her mother at his own fireside,—and when he thought that such another creature, quite as graceful and full of promise, might have called him father, and been a spring time in the haggard winter of his life, his sight grew very dim indeed."—*A Christmas Carol.*

Beller, Henry.—A case mentioned in the Report upon Converts by the Committee of the Brick Lane Branch of the United Grand Junction Ebenezer Temperance Association.—"Henry Beller was for many years toastmaster at various Corporation dinners, during which time he drank a great deal of foreign wine; may sometimes have carried a bottle or two home with him; is not quite certain of that, but is sure, if he did, that he drank the contents; feels very low and melancholy; is very feverish, and has a constant thirst upon him, thinks it must be the wine he used to drink (cheers); is out of employ now; and never touches a drop of foreign wine by any chance (tremendous plaudits)."—*Pickwick Papers.*

Belling, Master.—A pupil at Dotheboys Hall.—*Nicholas Nickleby.*

Bellows, Mr.—A barrister—a guest at Mr. Merdle's dinner-party.—*Little Dorrit.*

Belltott, Mrs.—Maid to Miss Maryon.—" This young woman was the widow of a non-commissioned officer in a regiment of the line. She had got married, and widowed, at St. Vincent, with only a few months between the two events. She was a little saucy woman, with a bright pair of eyes, rather a neat little foot and figure, and rather a neat little turned-up nose; the sort of young woman, I considered at the time, who appeared to invite you to give her a kiss, and who would have slapped your face if you accepted the invitation."—Perils of Certain English Travellers (*Christmas Stories*).

Bellvawney, Miss.—An actress in Mr. Crummles' company.—" There was Miss Bellvawney, who seldom aspired to speaking parts, and usually went on as a page, in white silk hose, to stand with one leg bent and contemplate the audience, or to go in and out after Mr. Crummles in stately tragedy."—*Nicholas Nickleby.*

Ben.—The guard of the London Mail Coach whom Sikes overheard at Hatfield telling the tale of the murder of Nancy.—*Oliver Twist.*

Ben.—Waiter at a Rochester inn.—" Ben whose touch on all convivial instruments is perfect."—The Seven Poor Travellers (*Christmas Stories*).

Benjamin, Thomas.—The plaintiff in a divorce suit.—" The husband, whose name was Thomas Benjamin, had taken out his marriage licence as Thomas only, suppressing the Benjamin in case he should not find himself as comfortable as he expected. Not finding himself as comfortable as he expected, or being a little fatigued with his wife, poor fellow, he now came forward by a friend, after being married a year or two, and declared that his name was Thomas Benjamin, and therefore he was not married at all; which the Court confirmed, to his great satisfaction."—*David Copperfield.*

Benton, Miss.—Housekeeper to Master Humphrey, who entertained Tony Weller, Senior, and Tony Weller, Junior, to tea.—" On the evening in question, the housekeeper's room was arranged with particular care, and the housekeeper herself was very smartly dressed. The preparations, however, were not confined to mere showy demonstrations, as tea was prepared for three persons, with a small display of preserves, and jams, and sweet cakes which heralded some uncommon occasion. Miss Benton (my housekeeper bears that name) was in a state of great expectation."—*Master Humphrey's Clock.*

Berinthia (Miss Berry).—" Mrs. Pipchin's middle-aged niece, her good-natured and devoted slave, but possessing a gaunt and iron-bound aspect, and much afflicted with boils on her nose."—*Dombey and Son.*

Bet.—A companion of Nancy.—" A couple of young ladies called to see the young gentlemen; one of whom was named Bet, and the other Nancy. They wore a good deal of hair, not very neatly turned up behind, and were rather untidy about the shoes and stockings. They were not exactly pretty perhaps, but they had a great deal of colour in their faces, and looked quite stout and hearty. Being remarkably free and agreeable in their manners, Oliver thought them very nice girls indeed, as there is no doubt they were."—*Oliver Twist.*

Betley, Mr.—A boarder at Mrs. Lirriper's.—" Mr. Betley which at that time had the parlours and loved his joke."—Mrs. Lirriper's Lodgings (*Christmas Stories*).

Betsey.—Maid to Mrs. Raddle, Bob Sawyer's landlady. —" A dirty slipshod girl, in black cotton stockings, who might have passed for the neglected daughter of a superannuated dustman in very reduced circumstances."—*Pickwick Papers.*

Betsey, Mrs.—Nursemaid to Mrs. Britain.—" The two Master Britains were playing in the coach house under the superintendence of one Betsey."—*The Battle of Life.*

Betsy Jane.—Daughter of Mrs. Wickam's uncle.—" My uncle's child took on just as Master Paul do. My uncle's child made people's blood run cold sometimes, she did. I wouldn't have sat up all night alone with Betsy Jane, said Mrs. Wickam—not if you'd have put Wickam into business next morning for himself."—*Dombey and Son.*

Bevan, Mr.—An American doctor who befriended

Martin.—" A middle-aged man, with a dark eye and a sunburnt face. There was a cordial candour in his manner, and an engaging confidence that it would not be abused; a manly bearing on his own part; and a simple reliance on the manly faith of a stranger; which Martin had never seen before."—*Martin Chuzzlewit.*

Bianchini.—A scientific writer on spontaneous combustion.—*Bleak House.*

Bib, Mr. Julius.—One of the interviewers of Elijah Pogram.—*Martin Chuzzlewit.*

Biddy.—The granddaughter of Mr Wopsle's great-aunt, who ultimately became Joe Gargery's second wife. She was Pip's first teacher and his lifelong friend.—*Great Expectations.*

Bigby, Mrs.—Mother of Mrs. Meek.—" I have the greatest respect for Maria Jane's mama. She is a most remarkable woman. I honour Maria Jane's mama. In my opinion she would storm a town single-handed, with a hearth broom, and carry it. I have never known her to yield any point whatever to mortal man."—*Births—Mrs. Meek of a Son* (Reprinted Pieces).

Bigwig Family.—Officious intermeddlers.—" The Bigwig Family (composed of all the stateliest people thereabouts, and all the noisiest) had undertaken to save him the trouble of thinking for himself, and to manage him and his affairs."—*Nobody's Story* (Reprinted Pieces).

Bilberry, Lady Jemima.—Wife of Lord Decimus Barnacle.—*Little Dorrit.*

Biler.—The family nickname of Robin Toodle.—" The eldest, known in the family by the name of Biler, in remembrance of the steam engine."—*Dombey and Son.*

Bill.—The Parish Gravedigger.—*Oliver Twist.*

Bill, Uncle.—The wit of a Sunday tea-garden party.—*Sketches by Boz* (London Recreations).

Billickin, Mrs.—Landlady of the apartments where Rosa Bud resided in London.—" This lady's name, stated in uncompromising capitals of considerable size on a brass door-plate, and yet not lucidly as to sex or condition, was Billickin. Personal faintness, and an overpowering personal candour, were the distinguishing features of Mrs. Billickin's organisation."—*Edwin Drood.*

Billsmethi, Master.—Son of Signor Billsmethi.—" Master Billsmethi, when everybody else was breathless, danced a hornpipe, with a cane in his hand, and a cheese plate on his head, to the unqualified admiration of the whole company."—*Sketches by Boz* (The Dancing Academy).

Billsmethi, Miss.—Daughter of Signor Billsmethi.—" A young lady with her hair curled in a crop all over her head, and her shoes tied in sandals all over her ankles."—*Sketches by Boz* (The Dancing Academy).

Billsmethi, Signor.—A dancing master.—" Of all the dancing academies that ever were established, there never was one more popular in its immediate vicinity than Signor Billsmethi's of the King's Theatre. There was public tuition, and private tuition—an assembly room and a parlour. Signor Billsmethi's family were always thrown in with the parlour, and included in parlour price; that is to say a private pupil had Signor Billsmethi's parlour to dance *in*, and Signor Billsmethi's family to dance *with*; and when he had been sufficiently broken in in the parlour he began to run in couples in the Assembly Room."—*Sketches by Boz* (The Dancing Academy).

Bilson and Glum.—The employers of Tom Smart, the hero of The Bagman's Story.—" The great house of Bilson and Glum, Cateaton Street, City."—*Pickwick Papers* (The Bagman's Story).

Bintry, Mr.—A London solicitor.—" A cautious man, with twinkling beads of eyes, in a large overhanging bald head."—No Thoroughfare (*Christmas Stories*).

Birmingham, Mr. and Mrs.—Of the Lord Warden Hotel, Dover.—" Mr. and Mrs. Birmingham, host and hostess of 'the Lord Warden Hotel,' are very much esteemed friends, but they are too conceited about the comforts of the establishment when the night mail is starting."—*The Uncommercial Traveller* (The Calais Night Mail).

Bitherstone, Master.—A boarder at Mrs. Pipchin's house at Brighton.—" Paul had enough to do for the rest of that day in surveying Master Bitherstone from head to foot, and watching all the workings of his countenance, with the interest attaching to a boy of mysterious and terrible experiences."—*Dombey and Son*.

Bitzer.—Model boy at school, who was always able to answer Mr. Gradgrind's questions, afterwards became the confidential house porter at Bounderby's Bank.—"He held the respectable office of general spy and informer in the establishment, for which volunteer service he received a present at Christmas, over and above his weekly wage." —*Hard Times*.

Black.—A London constable.—*On Duty with Inspector Field* (Reprinted Pieces).

Black, Mrs.—One of Mrs. Lemon's pupils.—*Holiday Romance*.

Black Bill (a client of Mr. Jaggers).—A prisoner in Newgate awaiting trial, whom Pip met when he visited the prison with Wemmick.—*Great Expectations*.

Black Lion, The.—A London tavern, where Joe Willet met a recruiting sergeant, and enlisted for a soldier.—"The creaking lion over the house door was therefore, to say the truth, rather a drowsy, tame, and feeble lion; and as these social representatives of a savage class are usually of a conventional character (being depicted for the most part in impossible attitudes, and of unearthly colours) he was frequently supposed by the more ignorant and uninformed among the neighbours, to be the veritable portrait of the host, as he appeared on the occasion of some great funeral ceremony, or public mourning."—*Barnaby Rudge*.

Blackboy.—The mythical owner of Mr. Barkis's strong box.—"For years and years, Mr. Barkis had carried this box on all his journeys every day. That it might the better escape notice, he had invented a fiction that it belonged to Mr. Blackboy, and was to be left with Barkis till called for; a fable he had elaborately written on the lid, in characters now scarcely legible."—*David Copperfield*.

Blackey.—A street impostor.—"Where's Blackey who has stood near London Bridge these five-and-twenty years, with a painted skin to represent disease."—*On Duty with Inspector Field* (Reprinted Pieces).

Blackpool, Stephen.—A factory hand in Bounderby's Mills. Loved Rachel, a factory worker, but could not marry her because he was chained to a worthless wife who had become a drunkard and had wrecked his home life. Life's experience to him was "aw a muddle." He was misunderstood, and falsely accused of being concerned in a bank robbery. Ultimately was killed by falling into an unfenced pit shaft.—"A rather stooping man with a knitted brow, a pondering expression on his face, and a hard-looking head sufficiently capacious, on which his iron grey hair lay long and thin. Stephen bent over his loom, quiet, watchful, and steady, a special contrast, as every man was in the forest of looms where Stephen worked, to the crashing, smashing, tearing piece of mechanism at which he laboured."—*Hard Times.*

Blackpool, Mrs.—The drunken and dissipated wife of Stephen Blackpool, who disgraced herself, and ruined her home, and made life for Stephen well-nigh unendurable, but who was all through compassionated by Rachel.—"Such a woman—a disabled, drunken creature, barely able to preserve her sitting posture by steadying herself with one begrimed hand on the floor, while the other was so purposeless in trying to push away her tangled hair from her face, that it only blinded her the more with the dirt upon it."—*Hard Times.*

Bladwood, Ned.—A forgetful man referred to by Miss Mowcher.—"Have I got all my traps. It seems so. It won't do to be like long Ned Bladwood, when they took him to church—to marry him to somebody as he says—and left the bride behind."—*David Copperfield.*

Blake, Mr. Warmint.—The out-and-out young gentleman.—"Out-and-out young gentlemen may be divided into two classes, those who have something to do, and those who have nothing."—*Sketches of Young Gentlemen.*

Blank, Mr.—A member of the Mechanical Science Section of the Mudfog Association.—"Mr. Blank exhibited a model of a fashionable animal, composed of copperplates, gold leaf, and silk boards, and worked entirely by milk and water."—*The Mudfog Sketches.*

Blanquo, Pierre.—A Swiss mountain guide.—*Our Bore* (Reprinted Pieces).

Blathers.—One of the Bow Street officers who called at Mrs. Maylie's to investigate the burglary.—" A stout personage, of middle height, aged about fifty, with shiny black hair cropped pretty close, half whiskers, a round face, and sharp eyes."—*Oliver Twist.*

Blaudois.—(*See* **Rigaud.**)—*Little Dorrit.*

Blaze and Sparkle.—Fashionable London jewellers.—" If you want to address our people, sir, say Blaze and Sparkle, the Jewellers,—meaning by our people Lady Dedlock and the rest—you must remember that you are not dealing with the general public."—*Bleak House.*

Blazo, Sir Thomas.—Mentioned by Mr. Jingle as taking part in a cricket-match in the West Indies.—" Played a match once—single wicket—friend the Colonel—Sir Thomas Blazo—who should get the greatest number of runs."—*Pickwick Papers.*

Bligh.—The hero of a tale told by Captain Ravender in the long-boat after the wreck of the *Golden Mary.*—" As a means of beguiling the time, and inspiring hope, I gave them the best summary in my power of Bligh's voyage of more than three thousand miles, in an open boat, after the Mutiny of the *Bounty*, and of the wonderful preservation of that boat's crew."—The Wreck of the *Golden Mary* (*Christmas Stories*).

Bligh, Captain.—The master of the ship *Bounty.*—" A worse man to be entrusted with arbitrary power there could scarcely be."—*The Long Voyage* (Reprinted Pieces).

Blight, Young.—Mortimer Lightwood's office-boy.—" Whosoever had gone out of Fleet Street into the Temple, at the date of this history, and had wandered disconsolate about the Temple, until he stumbled on a dismal churchyard, and had looked up at the dismal windows commanding that churchyard, until, at the most dismal window of them all, he saw a dismal boy, would in him have beheld, at one grand comprehensive swoop of the eye, the managing clerk, junior clerk, common law clerk, conveyancing clerk, chancery clerk, every refinement and department of clerk, of Mr. Mortimer Lightwood, erewhile called in the newspapers eminent solicitor."—*Our Mutual Friend.*

Blimber, Doctor.—Principal of the school at Brighton where Paul was placed.—" The Doctor undertook the charge of ten young gentlemen, but he had always ready a supply of learning for a hundred on the lowest estimate; and it was at once the business and delight of his life to gorge the unhappy ten with it. The Doctor was a portly gentleman, in a suit of black, with strings at his knees and stockings below them. He had a bald head, highly polished, a deep voice, and a chin so very double that it was a wonder how he ever managed to shave into the creases. He had likewise a pair of little eyes that were always half shut up, and a mouth that was always half expanded into a grin, as if he had that moment posed a boy, and were waiting to convict him from his own lips."—*Dombey and Son.*

Blimber, Mrs.—Wife of Doctor Blimber.—"Mrs. Blimber was not learned herself, but she pretended to be, and that did quite as well. She said at evening parties that if she could have known Cicero she thought she could have died contented. It was the steady joy of her life to see the Doctor's young gentlemen go out walking, unlike all other young gentlemen, in the largest possible shirt collars, and the stiffest possible cravats. It was so classical, she said."—*Dombey and Son.*

Blimber, Miss Cornelia.—Daughter of, and assistant to, Doctor Blimber. Married Mr. Feeder.—"Miss Blimber, too, although a slim and graceful maid, did no soft violence to the gravity of the house. There was no light nonsense about Miss Blimber. She kept her hair short and crisp, and wore spectacles. She was dry and sandy, with working in the graves of deceased languages,—none of your living languages for Miss Blimber; they must be dead—stone dead—and then Miss Blimber dug them out, like a ghoul."—*Dombey and Son.*

Blinder, Bill.—A friend of Tony Weller who made his will on the lid of a corn chest.—"They opens the corn chest, and finds that he'd been and chalked his vill inside the lid; so the lid was obligated to be took off the hinges, and sent up to Doctors' Commons to be proved."—*Master Humphrey's Clock.*

Blinder, Mrs.—Neckett's landlady.—"A good-natured-looking old woman, with a dropsy, or an asthma, or perhaps both."—*Bleak House.*

Blinkins, Mr.—The Latin master at our school.—"Our

remembrance of our school presents the Latin Master as a colorless, doubled-up, near-sighted man, with a crutch; who was always cold; and always putting onions into his ears for deafness; and always disclosing ends of flannel under all his garments; and almost always applying a ball of pocket handkerchief to some part of his face, with a screwing action round and round."—*Our School* (Reprinted Pieces).

Blockitt, Mrs.—The nurse who attended Mrs. Dombey at the birth of Paul.—"A simpering piece of faded gentility."—*Dombey and Son.*

Blockson, Mrs.—A temporary servant at Mr. Knags'. —"A charwoman employed in the absence of the sick servant, and remunerated with certain eighteenpences to be deducted from her wages due."—*Nicholas Nickleby.*

Blogg.—The parish beadle who placed Sloppy with Mrs. Betty Higden.—"I made interest with Mr. Blogg the Beadle to have him as a minder, seeing him by chance up at church, and thinking I might do something with him." —*Our Mutual Friend.*

Bloss, Mrs.—A boarder at Mrs. Tibbs' of Great Coram Street. Married Mr. Gobler.—"There arrived a single lady with a double knock, in a pelisse the colour of a damson pie; a bonnet of the same with a regular conservatory of artificial flowers; a white veil, a green parasol with a cobweb border. . . . The lady whom we have hitherto described as Mrs. Bloss is no more. Mrs. Gobler exists; Mrs. Bloss has left us for ever. In a secluded retreat in Newington Butts, far far removed from the noisy strife of that great boarding house the world, the enviable Gobler and his pleasing wife revel in retirement; happy in their complaints, their table, and their medicine; wafted through life by the grateful prayers of all the purveyors of animal food within three miles around."—*Sketches by Boz* (The Boarding House).

Blotton, Mr.—A member of The Pickwick Club who called Mr. Pickwick a humbug.—"The Chairman felt it his imperative duty to demand of the honourable gentleman whether he had used the expression which had just escaped him in a common sense. Mr. Blotton had no hesitation in saying that he had not,—he had used the word in its Pickwickian sense; he was bound to acknowledge that personally he entertained the highest regard and esteem for the honourable gentleman; he had merely considered him a humbug in a Pickwickian point of view."—*Pickwick Papers.*

Blowers, Mr., K.C.—A London barrister.—"Jarndyce and Jarndyce has passed into a joke; that is the only good that has ever come of it. The last Lord Chancellor handled it neatly when, correcting Mr. Blowers, the eminent silk gown, who had said that such a thing might happen when the sky rained potatoes, he observed—or when we get through Jarndyce and Jarndyce, Mr. Blowers."—*Bleak House.*

Blubb, Mr.—A member of the Mudfog Association.—*The Mudfog Sketches.*

Blunderum, Mr.—A member of the Zoology and Botany Section of the Mudfog Association.—"Mr. Blunderum delighted the Section with a most interesting and valuable paper on the last moments of the learned pig."—*The Mudfog Sketches.*

Bobster, Miss Cecilia.—A young lady whom Newman Noggs took Nicholas to visit, under the mistaken belief that she was the young lady with whom Nicholas had fallen in love.—*Nicholas Nickleby.*

Bobster, Mr.—Father of Miss Cecilia Bobster.—*Nicholas Nickleby.*

Bocker, Tom.—A boy suggested by Rev. Frank Milvey for adoption by Mr. and Mrs. Boffin.—"But I doubt, Frank, Mrs. Milvey hinted after a little hesitation, if Mrs. Boffin wants an orphan quite nineteen, who drives a cart and waters the roads."—*Our Mutual Friend.*

Bodgers, Mr.—A deceased parishioner to whose memory a tablet had been erected in the church which David Copperfield attended in his youth.—"I look up at the monumental tablets on the wall, and try to think of Mr. Bodgers late of this parish, and what the feelings of Mrs. Bodgers must have been when affliction sore long time Mr. Bodgers bore and physicians were in vain."—*David Copperfield.*

Boffer.—A stockbroker who became bankrupt.—"I am very sorry he has failed, said Wilkins Flasher, Esquire; capital dinners he gave."—*Pickwick Papers.*

Boffin, Nickodemus (Noddy).—An unlettered, but warm-hearted man, to whom his master old Harmon left his property, failing his son complying with the matrimonial directions of the will.—" A broad, round-shouldered, one-sided old fellow. . . . Both as to his dress and to himself he was of an overlapping rhinoceros build, with folds in his cheeks, and his forehead, and his eyelids, and his lips, and his ears; but with bright, eager, childishly-inquiring grey eyes, under his ragged eyebrows and broad-brimmed hat."—*Our Mutual Friend.*

Boffin, Mrs. Henrietta.—Wife of Mr. Boffin.—" A stout lady of a rubicund and cheerful aspect . . . a smiling creature, broad of figure and simple of nature, with her hands folded in her lap and with buxom creases in her throat."—*Our Mutual Friend.*

Bogles, Mrs.—Landlady of a London boarding-house, who was arrested for debt.—" That celebrated evening party given at Mrs. Bogles' boarding house when I was a boarder there, on which occasion Mrs. Bogles was taken in execution, by a branch of the legal profession, who got in as the harp, and was removed (with the keys and subscribed capital) to a place of durance, half an hour prior to the commencement of the festivities."—*The Uncommercial Traveller* (Refreshments for Travellers).

Bogsby, James George.—The landlord of The Sols Arms.—" A well-conducted tavern, licensed to a highly respectable landlord, Mr. James George Bogsby."—*Bleak House.*

Bokum, Mrs.—Friend of Mrs. MacStinger's introduced to Captain Cuttle at the marriage of Jack Bunsby to Mrs. MacStinger.—" As he became less agitated, he learned from this lady that she was the widow of a Mr. Bokum, who had held an employment in the Custom House; that she was the dearest friend of Mrs. MacStinger, whom she considered a pattern for her sex; that she had often heard of the Captain, and had hoped he had repented of his past life; that she trusted Mr. Bunsby knew what a blessing he had gained, but that she feared men seldom did know what such blessings were till they had lost them; with more to the same purpose."—*Dombey and Son.*

Bolder.—Pupil at Dotheboys Hall.—" 'Come here, Bolder,' said Squeers. An unhealthy-looking boy, with warts all over his hands, stepped from his place to the master's desk, and raised his eyes imploringly to Squeers' face, his own quite white from the rapid beating of his heart."—*Nicholas Nickleby.*

Boldheart, Capt. (aged nine).—" It seems that our hero, considering himself spited by a Latin Grammar Master, demanded the satisfaction due from one man of honour to another; not getting it he privately withdrew his haughty spirit from such low company; bought a second-hand pocket pistol; folded up some sandwiches in a paper bag; made a bottle of Spanish liquorice water; and entered on a career of valour."—*Holiday Romance.*

Boldwig, Captain.—A neighbour of Sir Geoffrey Manning.—" Captain Boldwig was a little fierce man, in a stiff black neckerchief, and blue surtout. Captain Boldwig's wife's sister had married a Marquis, and the Captain's house was a villa, and his land 'grounds,' and it was all very high and mighty and great."—*Pickwick Papers.*

Bolo, Miss.—Mr. Pickwick's partner at whist, at Bath. —" If he played a wrong card Miss Bolo looked a small armoury of daggers . . . then, at the end of every hand, Miss Bolo would enquire, with a dismal countenance and reproachful sigh, why Mr. Pickwick had not returned that diamond; or led the club; or roughed the spade; or finessed the heart; or led through the honour; or brought out the ace; or played up to the King; or some such thing; and in reply to all these grave charges Mr. Pickwick would be wholly unable to plead any justification whatever, having by this time forgotten all about the game."—*Pickwick Papers.*

Bolter, Mr. and Mrs.—The name assumed by Noah Claypole and Charlotte when they eloped after robbing Mr. Sowerby.—*Oliver Twist.*

Boni, Signora.—A singer to whom Mr. Rodolph compared Miss Martin, the milliner ambitious of being a singer.—" Don't you think, Miss Martin, with a little cultivation, would be very like Signora Marra Boni me dear, asked Mr. Jennings Rodolph. Just exactly the very thing that struck me, my love, answered Mrs. Jennings Rodolph."—*Sketches by Boz* (The Mistaken Milliner).

Bonney, Mr.—Promoter of the United Metropolitan

Improved Hot Muffin and Crumpet Baking and Punctual Delivery Company.—" A pale gentleman in a violent hurry, who, with his hair standing up in great disorder all over his head, and a very narrow white cravat tied loosely round his throat, looked as if he had been knocked up in the night, and had not dressed since."—*Nicholas Nickleby.*

Boodle, Lord.—A guest at Chesney Wold.—" There is my Lord Boodle, of considerable reputation with his party, who has known what office is, and who tells Sir Leicester Dedlock, with much gravity, after dinner, that he really does not see to what the present age is tending."—*Bleak House.*

Boots and Brewer.—Two men about town, cultivated by the Veneerings, who in the election campaign took cabs and went about.—" Many vast reputations have been made solely by taking cabs and going about. This particularly obtains in all Parliamentary affairs. Whether the business in hand is to get a man in, or to get a man out, or get a man over, or promote a railway, or jockey a railway, or what else, nothing is understood to be so effectual as scouring nowhere in a violent hurry—in short, as taking cabs and going about."—*Our Mutual Friend.*

Boozey, William.—Captain of the foretop on Captain Boldheart's ship *The Beauty.*—*Holiday Romance.*

Bore, Our.—" It is unnecessary to say that we keep a bore; everybody does; our bore is admitted on all hands to be a good-hearted man; he may put fifty people out of temper, but he keeps his own; he preserves a sickly solid smile upon his face when other faces are ruffled, by the perfection he has attained in his art."—*Our Bore* (Reprinted Pieces).

Borrioboola-gha.—The African Mission conducted by Mrs. Jellyby.—*Bleak House.*

Borum, Augustus.—One of the six children of Mrs. Borum.—" At the next house they visited they were in great glory; for there resided the six children who were so enraptured with the public actions of the phenomenon, and who being called down from the nursery to be treated with a private view of that young lady, proceeded to poke their fingers into her eyes, and tread upon her toes, and show her many other little attentions peculiar to their time of life."—*Nicholas Nickleby.*

Borum, Charlotte.—Daughter of Mr. and Mrs. Borum. —*Nicholas Nickleby.*

Borum, Emma.—Daughter of Mr. and Mrs. Borum.—*Nicholas Nickleby.*

Borum, Mrs.—An art patroness at Portsmouth upon whom Nicholas called to solicit support for the benefit night of Miss Snevellicci.—*Nicholas Nickleby.*

Bottles.—The deaf stableman at The Haunted House.—"A phenomenon of moroseness not to be matched in England. . . . Bottles talks to nobody, and hears nobody, unless he is absolutely roared at."—The Haunted House (*Christmas Stories*).

Bouclet, Madam.—Keeper of a lodging-house at a French watering-place.—"A compact little woman of thirty-five or so. . . . Madam Bouclet let all her house, giving on the place, in furnished flats or floors; and lived up the yard behind, in company with Monsieur Bouclet her husband."—Somebody's Luggage (*Christmas Stories*).

Bouclet, Monsieur.—Husband of Madam Bouclet, "great at billiards."—Somebody's Luggage (*Christmas Stories*).

Bounderby, Josiah.—The self-made man of Coketown, who married Louisa Gradgrind.—"He was a rich man, banker, manufacturer, merchant, and what not, a big loud man with a stare and a metallic laugh; a man made out of a coarse material, which seemed to have been stretched to make so much of him. Mr. Bounderby threw on his hat—he always threw it on, as expressing a man who had been far too busily employed in making himself to acquire any fashion of wearing his hat—and with his hands in his pockets sauntered out into the hall. I never wear gloves, it was his custom to say; I didn't climb up the ladder in *them.* Shouldn't be so high up if I had."—*Hard Times.*

Bounderby, Mrs.—Imaginary mother of Josiah Bounderby, to whom he referred (his real mother being a decent old lady known as Mrs. Pegler).—"She kept a chandler's shop, pursued Bounderby, and kept me in an egg box. That was the cot of my infancy—an old egg box; as soon as I was big enough to run away of course I ran away; then I became a young vagabond; and instead of one old woman knocking me about and starving me everybody of all ages knocked me about and starved me."—*Hard Times.*

Bower, The.—Formerly known as Harmony Jail, the residence of old Harmon, but which Mrs. Boffin re-named The Bower.—" A gloomy house the Bower—with sordid signs of having been through its long existence as Harmony Jail in miserly holding . . . a certain leanness falls upon houses not sufficiently imbued with life (as if they were nourished upon it) which was very noticeable here." —*Our Mutual Friend.*

Bowley, Lady.—Wife of Sir Joseph Bowley, M.P.—" A stately lady in a bonnet."—*The Chimes.*

Bowley, Master.—Son of Sir Joseph and Lady Bowley. —*The Chimes.*

Bowley, Sir Joseph.—A gentleman to whom Trotty Veck carried a letter from Alderman Cute.—" Another, and an older, and a much statelier gentleman, whose hat and cane were on the table, walked up and down, with one hand in his breast, and looked complacently from time to time at his own picture; a full length—a very full length—hanging over the fireplace."—*The Chimes.*

Bowyer, The.—A London tradesman to whom Hugh Graham was apprenticed.—" This Hugh was apprenticed to an honest Bowyer, who dwelt in the ward of Cheype, and was rumoured to possess great wealth. His trade had been a profitable one in the time of King Henry the Eighth, who encouraged English archery to the utmost, and he had been prudent and discreet."—*Master Humphrey's Clock.*

Boxer.—John Peerybingle's dog.—" Everybody knew him all along the road, especially the fowls and pigs, who, when they saw him approaching, with his body all on one side, and his ears pricked up inquisitively, and that knob of a tail making the most of itself in the air, immediately withdrew into remote back settlements, without waiting for the honour of a nearer acquaintance."—*The Cricket on the Hearth.*

Boyleston School.—A Boston industrial school for boys. —" Boyleston School is an asylum for neglected and indigent boys, who have committed no crime; but who in the ordinary course of things would very soon be purged of that distinction, if they were not taken from the hungry streets, and sent here."—*American Notes.*

Boythorn, Lawrence.—A friend of Mr. John Jarndyce. —" I went to school with this fellow Lawrence Boythorn, said Mr. Jarndyce, more than five-and-forty years ago; he was then the most impetuous boy in the world, and he is now the most impetuous man; he was then the loudest boy in the world, and he is now the loudest man; he was then the heartiest and sturdiest boy in the world, and he is now the heartiest and sturdiest man; he is a tremendous fellow."—*Bleak House.*

Brandley, Mrs.—The lady with whom Estella resided at Richmond.—" Mrs. Brandley was a widow with one daughter, several years older than Estella. The mother looked young, and the daughter looked old; the mother's complexion was pink, and the daughter's was yellow; the mother set up for frivolity, and the daughter for theology. They were in what is called a good position, and visited, and were visited by, numbers of people."—*Great Expectations.*

Brass, Miss Sally.—Sister to Sampson Brass.—" His clerk, assistant, housekeeper, secretary, confidential plotter, adviser, intriguer, and bill of costs increaser,—a kind of Amazon at common law. . . . Miss Sally Brass was a lady of thirty-five or thereabouts, of a gaunt and bony figure, and a resolute bearing. In face she bore a striking resemblance to her brother Sampson; so exact indeed was the likeness between them, that, had it consorted with Miss Brass's maiden modesty and gentle womanhood to have assumed her brother's clothes in a frolic, and sat down beside him, it would have been difficult for the oldest friend of the family to determine which was Sampson and which Sally."—*The Old Curiosity Shop.*

Brass, Sampson.—Mr. Quilp's solicitor.—" This Brass was an attorney, of no very good repute, from Bevis Marks in the City of London. He was a tall, meagre man, with a nose like a wen, a protruding forehead, retreating eyes, and hair of a deep red. He had a cringing manner, but a very harsh voice, and his blandest smiles were so extremely forbidding, that to have had his company under the least repulsive circumstances, one would have wished him to be out of temper that he might only scowl."—*The Old Curiosity Shop*.

Bravassa, Miss.—An actress in Mr. Crummles' company.—"The beautiful Miss Bravassa, who had once had her likeness taken in character by an engraver's apprentice, whereof impressions were hung up for sale."—*Nicholas Nickleby*.

Bray, Madeline.—A young lady with whom Nicholas fell in love at first sight, when he saw her at the general agency office, and whom he ultimately married, after he had discovered and defeated the scheme of her selfish father, aided by Ralph Nickleby, to marry her to the old miser, Arthur Gride, a moneylender, who had Walter Bray in his power.—*Nicholas Nickleby*.

Bray, Walter.—The selfish invalid father of Madeline Bray, who, to secure an annuity and discharge of his debts to Arthur Gride and Ralph Nickleby, arranged to give his daughter in marriage to old Gride, a plot which was discovered and prevented by Nicholas.—"Walter Bray was scarce fifty, perhaps, but so emaciated as to appear much older. His features presented the remains of a handsome countenance, but one in which the embers of strong and impetuous passions were easier to be traced than any expression which would have rendered a far plainer face much more prepossessing."—*Nicholas Nickleby*.

Bridgman, Laura.—A girl blind, deaf and dumb.—"There she was before me; built up as it were in a marble cell, impervious to any ray of light or particle of sound; with her poor white hand peeping through a chink in the wall, beckoning to some good man for help, that an Immortal Soul might be awakened."—*American Notes*.

Briggs.—A dull pupil at Dr. Blimber's.—"Briggs sat looking at his task in stony stupefaction and despair."—*Dombey and Son*.

Briggs, Alexander.—Articled clerk to his brother Samuel, the attorney. Attended the committee meeting at Mr. Percy Noakes' chambers on behalf of his brother.—"As the party was known to have originated however remotely with Mrs. Taunton, the female branches of the Briggs family had arranged that Mr. Alexander should attend instead of his brother; and as the said Mr. Alexander was deservedly celebrated for possessing all the pertinacity of a Bankruptcy Court attorney, combined with the obstinacy of that useful animal which browses on the thistle, he required but little tuition."—*Sketches by Boz* (The Steam Excursion).

Briggs, Miss Julia.—One of the three daughters of Mrs. Briggs, guests at the Steam Excursion.—" The Misses Briggs asked for their guitars, and several gentlemen seriously damaged the cases in their anxiety to present them. Then there was a very interesting production of three little keys for the aforesaid cases, and a melodramatic expression of horror at finding a string broken; and a vast deal of screwing and tightening and winding and tuning; during which Mrs. Briggs expatiated to those near her on the immense difficulty of playing a guitar; and hinted at the wondrous proficiency of her daughters in that mystic art; Mrs. Taunton whispered to a neighbour that it was quite sickening; and the Misses Taunton looked as if they knew how to play, but disdained to do it."—*Sketches by Boz* (The Steam Excursion).

Briggs, Miss Kate.—One of the three Misses Briggs.—(*See* **Briggs, Julia.**)—*Sketches by Boz* (The Steam Excursion).

Briggs, Mr.—Father of Briggs (a pupil at Dr. Blimber's), who made his son work at lessons during vacation.—" As to Briggs, his father made no show of artifice about it. He never would leave him alone. . . . Briggs therefore was not at all sanguine on the subject of holidays."—*Dombey and Son.*

Briggs, Mrs.—The rival in society of Mrs. Taunton.—" Between the Briggses and Tauntons there existed a degree of implacable hatred quite unprecedented. The animosity between the Montagues and the Capulets was nothing to that which prevailed between these two illustrious houses. Mrs. Briggs was a widow, with three daughters and two sons; Mr. Samuel, the eldest, was an attorney; and Mr. Alexander, the youngest, was under articles to his brother. They resided in Portland Street, Oxford Street, and moved in the same orbit as the

Tauntons, hence their mutual dislike."—*Sketches by Boz* (The Steam Excursion).

Briggs, Samuel.—Nominated as one of the committee of ten who managed the steam excursion.—" Mr. Samuel Briggs was a mere machine, a sort of self-acting legal walking-stick. . . . Eight members of the committee were punctual in their attendance. Mr. Loggins, the solicitor, of Boswell Court, sent an excuse; and Mr. Samuel Briggs, the ditto of Furnival's Inn, sent his brother; much to his (the brother's) satisfaction, and greatly to the discomfiture of Mr. Percy Noakes."—*Sketches by Boz* (The Steam Excursion).

Brick, Mr. Jefferson.—The war correspondent of the *New York Rowdy Journal*.—" A small young gentleman, of very juvenile appearance, and unwholesomely pale in the face; partly perhaps from intense thought; but partly, there is no doubt, from the excessive use of tobacco, which he was at that moment chewing vigorously."—*Martin Chuzzlewit.*

Brick, Mrs. Jefferson.—Wife of Mr. Jefferson Brick.—*Martin Chuzzlewit.*

Brimer, Mr.—The fifth mate of the *Haleswell* East Indiaman.—*The Long Voyage* (Reprinted Pieces).

Britain, Benjamin.—Dr. Jeddler's blunt-spoken serving-man—afterwards married Clemency Newcome, and became the landlord of The Nutmeg Grater Inn.—" A small man with an uncommonly sour and discontented face. . . . It was comfortable to Mr. Britain to think of his own condescension in having married Clemency. She was a perpetual testimony to him of the goodness of his heart, and the kindness of his disposition, and he felt that her being an excellent wife was an illustration of the old precept that virtue is its own reward."—*The Battle of Life.*

Britain, Clem.—Daughter of Mr. and Mrs. Britain.—*The Battle of Life.*

Britain, Master.—Son of Mr. and Mrs. Britain.—*The Battle of Life.*

Brittles.—A servant at Mrs. Maylie's.—" Brittles was a lad of all work, who, having entered her service a mere child, was treated as a promising young boy still, though he was something past thirty."—*Oliver Twist.*

Brogley.—A sworn broker and appraiser, who took possession of Sol Gills' shop for a creditor.—" Mr. Brogley himself was a moist-eyed, pink-complexioned, crisp-haired man, of bulky figure and an easy temper,—for that class of Caius Marius who sits upon the ruins of other people's Carthages can keep up his spirits well enough."—*Dombey and Son.*

Brogson, Mr.—A guest at the dinner given by Mr. Budden in honour of his cousin, Mr. Minns.—" An elderly gentleman in a black coat, knee breeches, and long gaiters, who, under pretence of inspecting the prints in an annual, had been engaged in satisfying himself on the subject of Mr. Minns' general appearance by looking at him over the top of the leaves."—*Sketches by Boz* (Mr. Minns and his Cousin).

Brooker.—A returned convict who had in youth been a clerk to Ralph Nickleby, and who ultimately disclosed the secret domestic history of Ralph Nickleby, and revealed him as the father of Smike.—" A spare, dark, withered man of about his own age, with a stooping body and a very sinister face, rendered more ill-favoured by hollow and hungry cheeks deeply sunburnt, and thick black eyebrows, blacker in contrast with the perfect whiteness of his hair; roughly clothed in shabby garments of a strange and uncouth make; and having about him an indefinable manner of depression and degradation."—*Nicholas Nickleby.*

Brooks.—A friend of Sam Weller's.—" I lodged in the same house with a pieman once, and a wery nice man he was—regular clever chap too—make pies out o' anything he could—what a number o' cats you keep, Mr. Brooks, says I, when I'd got intimate with him. Ah, says he, I do —a good many—says he. You must be wery fond o' cats, says I. Other people is, says he, a winkin' at me; they ain't in season till the winter though, says he. Not in season, says I. No, says he, fruits is in, cats is out."—*Pickwick Papers.*

Brooks of Sheffield.—The name by which Mr. Murdstone and his friends, Mr. Quinion and Mr. Passnidge, referred to David, when talking of his mother in his presence.—" Quinion, said Mr. Murdstone, take care, if you please, somebody's sharp;—who is, asked the gentleman;—only Brooks of Sheffield—said Mr. Murdstone. There seemed to be something very comical in the reputation of Mr. Brooks of Sheffield, for both the gentlemen laughed heartily when he was mentioned, and Mr. Murdstone was a good deal amused also."—*David Copperfield.*

Browdie, John.—A Yorkshire contractor, bluff in manner but kind in heart. Married Matilda Price, the miller's daughter, and friend of Fanny Squeers. First met Nicholas at Miss Squeers' tea-party.—"The expected swain arrived with his hair very damp from recent washing, and a clean shirt, whereof the collar might have belonged to some giant ancestor, forming, together with a white waistcoat of similar dimensions, the chief ornament of his person."—*Nicholas Nickleby.*

Brown.—An acquaintance of Lord Feenix.—"Four bottle man at the Treasury Board."—*Dombey and Son.*

Brown.—One of Mrs. Lemon's pupils.—*Holiday Romance.*

Brown, Captain John.—The master of the ship *Polyphemus*, the story of the wreck of which was one of Sol Gills' favourite yarns.—"The *Polyphemus*, private West India trader, burden three hundred and fifty tons, Captain John Brown of Deptford, owners Wiggs & Co."—*Dombey and Son.*

Brown, Emily.—The young lady who, by arrangement between her father and Mr. Alexander Trott's father, was destined to marry Mr. Alexander Trott, but who preferred his rival, Mr. Horace Hunter, and eloped with him to Gretna Green.—*Sketches by Boz* (The Great Winglebury Duel).

Brown, Henry.—Brother of the three Miss Browns, who prepared the address for delivery at the meeting of The Child's Examination Society.—"The eldest boy fell forward and delivered a propitiatory address from behind his collar. It was from the pen of Mr. Henry Brown."—*Sketches by Boz* (Our Parish—The Ladies' Societies).

Brown, Mr.—A friend of Mrs. Nubbles.—"One Mr. Brown, who was supposed to be then a Corporal in the East Indies, and who could of course be found with very little trouble."—*The Old Curiosity Shop*,

Brown, Mr.—Passenger in Thames steamer.—"Girls who have brought the first volume of some new novel in their reticule become extremely plaintive, and expatiate to Mr. Brown or young Mr. O'Brien, who has been looking over them, on the blueness of the sky and brightness of the water."—*Sketches by Bŏz* (The River).

Brown, Mr.—One of the orchestra at the private theatricals at Rose Villa.—(*See* **Jenkins, Miss.**)—*Sketches by Boz* (Mrs. Joseph Porter).

Brown, Mrs.—The name by which Mrs. Marwood called herself when she found Florence Dombey in the street and stole her clothing.—"She was a very ugly old woman, with red rims round her eyes, and a mouth that mumbled and chattered of itself when she was not speaking."—*Dombey and Son.*

Browndock, Miss.—One of Mrs. Nickleby's examples of success.—"Bless my soul, Kate, said Mrs. Nickleby,—I've been thinking all day what a delightful thing it would be for Madame Mantalini to take you into partnership. Such a likely thing too, you know. Why, your poor dear papa's cousin's sister-in-law,—a Miss Browndock—was taken into partnership by a lady that kept a school at Hammersmith, and made her fortune in no time at all."—*Nicholas Nickleby.*

Brownlow, Mr.—An old gentleman whose pocket the Artful Dodger picked, and diverted the blame to Oliver, afterwards discovered to have been a friend of Oliver's father.—"The old gentleman was a very respectable-looking personage, with a powdered head and gold spectacles. He had taken up a book from the stall and there he stood reading away as hard as if he were in his elbow chair in his own study. . . . What was Oliver's horror and alarm, as he stood a few paces off, looking on with his eyelids as wide open as they would possibly go, to see the Dodger plunge his hand into the old gentleman's pocket, and draw from thence a handkerchief; to see him hand the same to Charley Bates; and finally to behold them both running away round the corner at full speed."—*Oliver Twist.*

Browns, The Three Miss.—Ardent admirers of the curate.—"When the young curate was popular, and all the unmarried ladies in the parish took a serious turn, the charity children all at once became objects of peculiar and especial interest. The three Miss Browns (enthusiastic admirers of the curate) taught and exercised, and examined and re-examined the unfortunate children, until the boys grew pale and the girls consumptive with study and fatigue."—*Sketches by Boz* (Our Parish—The Ladies' Societies).

Bucket.—A detective officer.—"A stoutly-built, steady-looking, sharp-eyed man in black, of about the middle age. Thoughtful Mr. Bucket is, as a man with weighty work to do, but composed, sure, confident."—*Bleak House.*

Bucket, Mr., Senr.—Father of Detective Bucket.—"My father was first a page; then a footman; then a butler; then a steward; then an innkeeper; lived universally respected, and died lamented."—*Bleak House.*

Bucket, Mrs.—Wife of Detective Bucket.—"A lady of a natural detective genius, which, if it had been improved by professional exercise, might have done great things, but which has paused at the level of a clever amateur."—*Bleak House.*

Bud, Rosa.—A pupil at Nuns' House, betrothed to Edwin Drood.—"The pet pupil of the Nuns' House is Miss Rosa Bud; of course called Rosebud; wonderfully pretty, wonderfully childish, wonderfully whimsical. An awkward interest (awkward because romantic) attached to Miss Bud, in the minds of the young ladies, on account of its being known to them that a husband has been chosen for her by will and bequest; and that her guardian is bound down to bestow her on that husband, when he comes of age."—*Edwin Drood.*

Budden, Mr. Octavius.—Of Amelia Cottage, Poplar Walk, Stamford Hill. Cousin of Mr. Augustus Minns.—"Mr. Budden, having realised a moderate fortune by exercising the trade of a corn chandler, and having a great predilection for the country, had purchased a cottage in the vicinity of Stamford Hill, whither he retired with the wife of his bosom, and his only son, Master Alexander Augustus Budden."—*Sketches by Boz* (Mr. Minns and his Cousin).

Budden, Mrs. Amelia.—Wife of Mr. Budden.—"Mr Minns's servant put into his hand a particularly small card on which was engraven in immense letters—Mr. Octavius Budden, Amelia Cottage (Mrs. B.'s name was Amelia), Poplar Walk, Stamford Hill."—*Sketches by Boz* (Mr. Minns and his Cousin).

Budden, Master Alexander.—Son of Mr. and Mrs. Budden; godson of Mr. Augustus Minns.—" The servant, in compliance with a significant look from Mrs. B., brought down Master Alexander, habited in a sky-blue suit with silver buttons, and possessing hair of nearly the same colour as the metal."—*Sketches by Boz* (Mr. Minns and his Cousin).

Budger, Mrs.—A guest at the Rochester Charity Ball. —" A little old widow, whose rich dress and profusion of ornament bespoke her a most desirable addition to a limited income."—*Pickwick Papers.*

Buffer, Doctor.—A member of the Mudfog Association. —*The Mudfog Sketches.*

Buffle, Mr.—A tax collector.—" It cannot be denied that Mr. Buffle's manners when engaged in his business were not agreeable. To collect is one thing, and to look about as if suspicious of the goods being gradually removed in the dead of the night by a back door is another."—Mrs. Lirriper's Legacy (*Christmas Stories*).

Buffle, Mrs.—Wife of Mr. Buffle, the tax collector.— " Mr. Buffle's family were not liked in the neighbourhood, for when you are a householder, my dear, you'll find it does not come by nature to like the Assessed, and it was considered besides that a one-horse phæton ought not to have elevated Mrs. Buffle to that height, especially when purloined from the taxes, which I myself did consider uncharitable."—Mrs. Lirriper's Legacy (*Christmas Stories*).

Buffle, Miss Robina.—Daughter of Mr. and Mrs. Buffle.—" It was whispered that Miss Buffle would go either into a consumption or a convent, she being so very thin and off her appetite, and two close-shaved gentlemen with white bands round their necks peeping round the corner whenever she went out, in waistcoats resembling black pinafores."—Mrs. Lirriper's Legacy (*Christmas Stories*).

Buffum, Mr. Oscar.—One of the interviewers of Elijah Pogram.—*Martin Chuzzlewit.*

Buffy, Mr., M.P.—A guest at Chesney Wold.—" The Right Honourable William Buffy, M.P., contends across the table with some one else that the shipwreck of the country—about which there is no doubt, it is only the manner of it that is in question—is attributable to Cuffy. If you had done with Cuffy what you ought to have done, when he first came into Parliament, and had prevented him going over to Duffy, you would have got him into alliance with Fuffy; you would have had with you the weight attaching as a smart debater to Guffy; you would have brought to bear upon the elections the wealth of Huffy; you would have got in for three Counties Juffy Kuffy and Luffy; and you would have strengthened your administration by the official knowledge and the business habits of Muffy; all this instead of being as you now are dependent upon the mere caprice of Puffy."—*Bleak House.*

Bulder, Colonel, and Family.—Guests at the Rochester Charity Ball.—" Colonel Bulder, Mrs. Colonel Bulder, and Miss Bulder were the next arrivals."—*Pickwick Papers.*

Bule, Miss.—One of the pupils at Miss Griffin's school, the favourite Sultana in the Seraglio.—" Miss Bule, whom I judge to have attained the ripe age of eight or nine, took the lead in Society."—(*See* **Zobeide**).—The Haunted House (*Christmas Stories*).

Bullamy.—The hall porter at the Anglo-Bengalee Company's offices.—" There was a porter on the premises—a wonderful creature in a vast red waistcoat and short-tailed pepper-and-salt coat—who carried more conviction to the minds of sceptics than the whole establishment without him. When he sat upon a seat erected for him in a corner of the office, with his glazed hat hanging on a peg over his head, it was impossible to doubt the respectability of the concern . . . whether he was a deep rogue, or a stately simpleton, it was impossible to make out."—*Martin Chuzzlewit.*

Bull, Prince.—The hero of a fairy tale.—" A powerful Prince whose name was Bull. He had gone through a great deal of fighting in his time, about all sorts of things, including nothing; but had gradually settled down to be a steady, peaceable, good-natured, corpulent, rather sleepy Prince."—*Prince Bull* (A Fairy Tale) (Reprinted Pieces).

Bull's Eye.—Bill Sikes' Dog.—" A white shaggy dog, with his face scratched and torn in twenty different places." —*Oliver Twist.*

Bulph, Mr.—Mr. Crummles' landlord at Portsmouth. —" Mr. Crummles lived in Saint Thomas Street, at the house of one Bulph, a pilot, who sported a boat-green door, with window frames of the same colour, and had the little finger of a drowned man on his parlour mantel shelf; with other maritime and natural curiosities. He displayed also a brass knocker, a brass plate, and a brass bell handle, all very bright and shining; and had a mast, with a vane on the top of it, in his back yard."—*Nicholas Nickleby.*

Bumble, Mr.—A self-important parish beadle—afterwards master of the workhouse.—" Mr. Bumble was a fat man and a choleric."—*Oliver Twist.*

Bumple, Michael.—The plaintiff in the suit Bumple *v.* Sludberry.—*Sketches by Boz* (Doctors' Commons).

Bung.—Formerly a broker's man, afterwards beadle of our parish.—" The life of this gentleman has been one of a very chequered description; he has undergone transitions—not from grave to gay, for he never was grave—not from lively to severe, for severity forms no part of his disposition; his fluctuations have been between poverty in the extreme, and poverty modified; or, to use his own emphatic language, between nothing to eat, and just half enough."—*Sketches by Boz* (The Broker's Man).

Bunsby, Jack.—Captain of the ship *Cautious Clara*, a friend of Captain Cuttle,—married Mrs. MacStinger.— " They stood upon the deck of the *Cautious Clara*. . . . Immediately there appeared, coming slowly up above the bulk head of the cabin, another bulk head—human and very large—with one stationary eye in the mahogany face, and one revolving one, on the principle of some lighthouses. This head was decorated with shaggy hair like oakum, which had no governing inclination towards the North East West or South, but inclined to all four quarters of the compass, and to every point upon it. The head was followed by a perfect desert of chin, and by a shirt collar and neckerchief, and by a dreadnought pilot coat, and by a pair of dreadnought pilot trousers, whereof the waistband was so very broad and high that it became a succedaneum for a waistcoat, being ornamented near the wearer's breast bone with some massive wooden buttons like backgammon men. As the lower portions of the pantaloons became revealed, Bunsby stood confessed."—*Dombey and Son.*

Burgess and Co.—A firm of tailors patronized by Mr. Toots.—" My tailors Burgess and Co., said Toots. Fash'nable but very dear."—*Dombey and Son.*

Burton, Thomas.—A case mentioned in the Report upon Converts by the committee of The Brick Lane Branch of The United Grand Junction Ebenezer Temperance Association.—" Thomas Burton is purveyor of cats' meat to the Lord Mayor and Sheriffs, and several members of the Common Council (the announcement of this gentleman's name was received with breathless interest); has a wooden leg; finds a wooden leg expensive going over the stones; used to wear second-hand wooden legs, and drink a glass of hot gin and water every night—sometimes two (deep sighs); found the second-hand wooden legs split and rot very quickly; is firmly persuaded that their constitution was undermined by the gin and water (prolonged cheering); buys new wooden legs now, and drinks nothing but water and weak tea; the new legs last twice as long as the others, and he attributes this solely to his temperate habits (triumphant cheers)."—*Pickwick Papers.*

Bury, George.—Brother-in-law of old John the Inventor.—" My wife's brother George Bury of West Bromwich (his wife unfortunately took to drinking, made away with everything and seventeen times committed to Birmingham Jail before happy release in every point of view)."—*A Poor Man's Tale of a Patent* (Reprinted Pieces).

Butcher, William.—A friend of old John the Inventor.—" A friend of mine by the name of William Butcher, is a Chartist—moderate—he is a good speaker." —*A Poor Man's Tale of a Patent* (Reprinted Pieces).

Butler, The Chief.—Manservant at Mr. Merdle's.— " The chief Butler was the next magnificent institution of the day. He was the stateliest man in company. He did nothing, but he looked on as few others could have done." —*Little Dorrit.*

Butler, Theodosius.—Cousin of the Misses Crumpton of Minerva House, who eloped from their school with Miss Dingwall Brooks.—" Mr. Theodosius Butler was one of these immortal geniuses who are to be met with in almost every circle. They have usually very deep, monotonous voices. They always persuade themselves that they are wonderful persons, and that they ought to be very miserable, though they don't precisely know why. They are very conceited, and usually possess half an idea; but, with enthusiastic young ladies, and silly young gentlemen, they are very wonderful persons."—*Sketches by Boz* (Sentiment).

Button, William.—A tailor of Tooley Street, impersonated at the circus by Jupe.—(*See* **Jupe.**)—*Hard Times.*

Buzfuz, Serjeant.—Counsel for Mrs. Bardell.—" Then there entered two or three more Serjeants; and among them one with a fat body and a red face, who nodded in a friendly manner to Mr. Serjeant Snubbin, and said it was a fine morning."—*Pickwick Papers.*

Callow, Docter.—A medical man consulted by Our Bore.—" He naturally thought of Callow, at that time one of the most eminent physicians in London, and he went to Callow. Callow said liver; and prescribed rhubarb and calomel; low diet and moderate exercise. Our Bore went on with this treatment, getting worse every day, until he lost confidence in Callow and went to Moon."—*Our Bore* (Reprinted Pieces).

Calton, Mr.—A boarder at Mrs. Tibbs'.—" Mr. Calton was a super-animated beau—an old boy—he used to say of himself that, although his features were not regularly handsome, they were striking; they certainly were; it was impossible to look at his face without being reminded of a chubby street door knocker, half lion half monkey; and the comparison might be extended to his whole character and conversation."—*Sketches by Boz* (The Boarding House).

Camilla, Mrs. (a sister of Matthew Pocket).—One of

the toadies of Miss Havisham.—"They somehow conveyed to me that they were all toadies and humbugs, but that each of them pretended not to know that the others were toadies and humbugs; because the admission that he or she did know it, would have made him or her out to be a toady and a humbug."—*Great Expectations.*

Camilla, Mr.—The husband of Miss Pocket, one of Miss Havisham's toadies.—*Great Expectations.*

Cape, Mr.—One of the orchestra at the private theatricals at Rose Villa.—(*See* **Jenkins, Miss.**)—*Sketches by Boz* (Mrs. Joseph Porter).

Capper, Mr.—The host who entertained Mr. Mincin, the very friendly young gentleman at dinner.—*Sketches of Young Gentlemen.*

Capper, Mrs.—Wife of Mr. Capper.—*Sketches of Young Gentlemen.*

Captain, The.—A patron of Bellamy's.—*Sketches by Boz* (A Parliamentary Sketch).

Captain, The.—Master of an American mail steamer. —"What have we here—the Captain's boat; and yonder the Captain himself. Now by all our hopes and wishes the very man he ought to be; a well-made, tight-built, dapper little fellow; with a ruddy face which is a letter of invitation to shake him by both hands at once; and with a clear blue honest eye that it does one good to see one's sparkling image in."—*American Notes.*

Carker, Harriet.—Sister of the brothers Carker, who on John's falling into disgrace devoted herself to him, and thereby incurred the displeasure of her brother James.—"This slight, small, patient figure, neatly dressed in homely stuffs, and indicating nothing but the dull household virtues, that have so little in common with the received idea of heroism and greatness—unless indeed any ray of them should shine through the lives of the great ones of the earth, when it becomes a constellation, and is tracked in Heaven straightway—this slight, small patient figure, leaning on the man still young, but worn and grey, is she, his sister, who of all the world went over to him in his shame, and put her hand in his, and, with a sweet composure and determination, led him hopefully upon his barren way."—*Dombey and Son.*

Carker, James.—Manager for Dombey and Son. Committed the firm to speculations which ruined the firm and enriched himself. Eloped with the second Mrs. Dombey.—" Mr. Carker was a gentleman thirty-eight or forty years old, of a florid complexion, and with two unbroken rows of glistening teeth, whose regularity and whiteness were quite distressing. It was impossible to escape the observation of them, for he showed them whenever he spoke; and bore so wide a smile upon his countenance (a smile however very rarely indeed extending beyond his mouth) that there was something in it like the snarl of a cat. He affected a stiff white cravat, after the example of his principal, and was always closely buttoned up and tightly dressed."—*Dombey and Son.*

Carker, John.—A junior clerk in Dombey and Son's counting-house, elder brother of James Carker, the manager; but, owing to an episode in his early career a broken-spirited man occupying a subordinate position.—" The younger brother's post was on the top of the official ladder; the elder brother's at the bottom. The elder brother never gained a stave, or raised his foot to mount one. Young men passed above his head, and rose and rose; but he was always at the bottom. He was quite resigned to occupy that low condition, never complained of it, and certainly never hoped to escape from it. . . . He was not old, but his hair was white; his body was bent or bowed, as if by the weight of some great trouble; and there were deep lines in his worn and melancholy face. The fire of his eyes, the expression of his features, the very voice in which he spoke, were all subdued and quenched, as if the spirit within him lay in ashes."—*Dombey and Son.*

Carlavero, Giovanni.—Keeper of an Italian wine shop who had, as a political offender, been a galley slave, and was rescued by an Englishman.—*The Uncommercial Traveller* (The Italian Prisoner).

Carlo.—One of Jerry's performing dogs.—" Now gentlemen, said Jerry, looking at them attentively, the dog whose name's called eats; the dogs whose names ain't called keep quiet. Carlo—the lucky individual whose name was called snapped up the morsel thrown towards him, but none of the others moved a muscle."—*The Old Curiosity Shop.*

Carolina.—Maid to Clara, the English bride.—*To be Read at Dusk* (Reprinted Pieces).

Caroline.—The wife of a debtor of Scrooge whom the Ghost of Christmas Yet to Come showed to Scrooge.—*A Christmas Carol.*

Carriwini, the Marquis.—Referred to by Mrs. Waters on the Ramsgate boat.—" Walter, my dear, said the black-eyed young lady, after they had sat chatting with the Tuggs's some half hour—Don't you think this gentleman (with an inclination of the head towards Mr. Cymon Tuggs) is very like the Marquis Carriwini."—*Sketches by Boz* (The Tuggs's at Ramsgate).

Carstone, Richard.—A ward in Chancery, married Ada Clare.—" A handsome youth, with an ingenuous face, and a most engaging laugh."—*Bleak House.*

Carter, Mr.—President of the Mechanical Science Section of the Mudfog Association.—*The Mudfog Sketches.*

Carton, Captain.—The commander of the expedition against the pirates who attacked Silver Store Colony; married Miss Maryon.—" We marines were now drawn up here under arms. The *Chace* party were drawn up separate. The men of the *Columbus* were drawn up separate. The officers stepped out into the midst of the three parties, and spoke so as all might hear. Captain Carton was the officer in command."—The Perils of Certain English Travellers (*Christmas Stories*).

Carton, Sydney.—A barrister, with a singular physical resemblance to Charles Darnay—a man of both brain and heart, but an idler, and a drunkard. Loved Lucie Manette, and for her sake personated Darnay, and effected his escape from prison, he himself going to the scaffold in his place.—" Sydney Carton, idlest and most uncompromising of men, was Stryver's great ally . . . at least it began to get about among such as were interested in the matter that, although Sydney Carton would never be a lion, he was an amazingly good jackal, and that he rendered suit and service to Stryver in that humble capacity. . . . Sadly, sadly, the sun rose; it rose upon no sadder sight than the man of good abilities and good emotions, incapable of their directed exercise, incapable of his own help, and his own happiness, sensible of the blight on him, and resigning himself to let it eat him away."—*A Tale of Two Cities.*

Casby, Flora (Mrs. Finching).—Daughter of Mr. Casby who in her youth had been a sweetheart of Clennam.—" Flora, always tall, had grown to be very broad too, and short of breath; but that was not much. Flora, who had seemed enchanting in all she said and thought, was diffuse and silly. That was much. Flora who had been spoiled and artless long ago, was determined to be spoiled and artless now. That was a fatal blow."—*Little Dorrit.*

Casby, Mr. Christopher.—A rack-renting proprietor of slum property in Bleeding Heart Yard.—" Mr. Casby lived in a street in the Gray's Inn Road. Patriarch was the name many people delighted to give him . . . so grey, so slow, so quiet, so impassionate, so very bumpty in the head, Patriarch was the word for him. His smooth face had a bloom upon it like ripe wall fruit. What with his blooming face, and that head, and his blue eyes, he seemed to be delivering sentiments of rare wisdom and virtue. In like manner his physiognomical expression seemed to teem with benignity. He had a long wide-skirted bottle-green coat on, and a bottle-green pair of trousers, and a bottle-green waistcoat. The Patriarchs were not dressed in bottle-green broadcloth, and yet his clothes looked patriarchal."—*Little Dorrit.*

Caswell, Oliver.—An inmate of Boston asylum for the blind.—*American Notes.*

Cat, le.—A French surgeon who wrote an account of a case of spontaneous combustion.—*Bleak House.*

Catlin, Mr.—A missionary.—" There was Mr. Catlin some years ago, with his Ojibbeway Indians. Mr. Catlin was an energetic, earnest man, who had lived among more tribes of Indians than I need reckon up here, and who had written a picturesque and glowing book about them."—*The Noble Savage* (Reprinted Pieces).

Cavaletto, John Baptist.—An Italian refugee in London, employed by Arthur Clennam.—" A sunburnt, quick, lithe, little man, though rather thick-set; ear-rings in his brown ears; white teeth lighting up his grotesque brown face; intensely black hair, clustering about his brown throat; a ragged red shirt open at his brown breast; loose seamanlike trousers; decent shoes; a long red cap; a red sash round his waist, and a knife in it."—*Little Dorrit.*

Caveton, Mr.—The throwing-off young gentleman.—"There is a certain kind of impostor—a bragging, vaunting, puffing young gentleman—against whom we are desirous to warn the fairer part of creation."—*Sketches of Young Gentlemen.*

Cecilia.—A charity child.—(*See* **Joseph and Cecilia.**)—*The Uncommercial Traveller* (The City of the Absent).

Certainpersonio, Prince.—Alicia's bridegroom.—"Prince, said Grandmarina, I bring you your bride. The moment the Fairy said these words, Prince Certainpersonio's face left off being sticky; and his jacket changed to peach-bloom velvet; and his hair curled; and a cap and feather flew in like a bird and settled on his head . . . the marriage was beautiful beyond expression. Grandmarina gave a magnificent wedding feast afterwards, in which there was everything and more to eat; and everything and more to drink."—*Holiday Romance.*

Chadband, Mr.—A preacher.—"Mr. Chadband is a large yellow man, with a fat smile, and a general appearance of having a good deal of train oil in his system. Mr. Chadband moves softly and cumbrously, not unlike a bear who has been taught to walk upright; he is very much embarrassed about the arms, as if they were inconvenient to him, and he wanted to grovel; is very much in a perspiration about the head; and never speaks without first putting up his great hand, as delivering a token to his hearers that he is going to edify them."—*Bleak House.*

Chadband, Mrs.—(*See* **Rachel.**)—Wife of Mr. Chadband.—"A stern, severe-looking, silent woman."—*Bleak House.*

Chancellor, The Lord High.—The chief judge of the Chancery Court.—"Hard by Temple Bar, in Lincoln's Inn Hall, at the very heart of the fog, sits The Lord High Chancellor, in his High Court of Chancery—with a foggy glory round his head, softly fenced in with crimson cloth and curtains."—*Bleak House.*

Chancery Prisoner.—The debtor whose room Mr. Pickwick hired in the Fleet.—" The Chancery Prisoner had been there long enough to have lost friends, fortune, home, and happiness, and to have acquired the right of having a room to himself. . . . He was a tall gaunt cadaverous man, in an old great-coat and slippers, with sunken cheeks, and a restless eager eye; his lips were bloodless and his bones sharp and thin."—*Pickwick Papers.*

Channing, Rev. Dr.—A clergyman.—*American Notes.*

Charker, Harry.—A corporal in the Royal Marines—a comrade of Gill Davis.—" He was one of the best of men, and, in a certain sort of way, one with the least to say for himself. I qualify it, because, besides being able to read and write like a Quarter Master, he had always one most excellent idea in his mind—that was Duty."—The Perils of Certain English Prisoners (*Christmas Stories*).

Charles, Old.—A waiter.—" The well-known and highly respected old Charles, long eminent at the West Country Hotel, and by some considered the father of the waitering."—Somebody's Luggage (*Christmas Stories*).

Charley.—Affianced to Angela Leath; but believing her fickle, left London on Christmas Eve, and was snowed up at The Holly Tree Inn.—" It happened in the memorable year when I parted for ever from Angela Leath, whom I was shortly to have married, on making the discovery that she preferred my bosom friend. From our school days, I had freely admitted Edwin in my own mind to be far superior to myself; and though I was grievously wounded at heart, I felt the preference to be natural, and tried to forgive them both. It was under these circumstances that I resolved to go to America—on my way to the Devil."—The Holly Tree (*Christmas Stories*).

Charley.—A marine-store dealer in Chatham to whom David sold his jacket on his tramp to his aunt's.—" An ugly old man with the lower part of his face all covered with a stubbly grey beard."—*David Copperfield.*

Charlotte.—Daughter of old John the Inventor.—" The other (Charlotte) her husband run away from her in the basest manner."—*A Poor Man's Tale of a Patent* (Reprinted Pieces).

Charlotte.—A school-fellow of Miss Wade.—*Little Dorrit.*

Charlotte.—Servant to Mr. Sowerby. Eloped with Noah Claypole after assisting him to rob the Sowerbys' house.—*Oliver Twist.*

Cheeryble Brothers.—A firm of London merchants (the partners of which were the twin brothers Charles and Edwin Cheeryble) in whose counting-house Nicholas found employment after leaving Mr. Crummles' theatrical company.—" The only inscription on the doorpost was Cheeryble Brothers; but, from a hasty glance at the directions of some packages which were lying about, Nicholas supposed that the brothers Cheeryble were German merchants. Both the brothers it may be here remarked had a very emphatic and earnest delivery; both had lost nearly the same teeth, which imparted the same peculiarity to their speech; and both spoke as if, besides possessing the utmost severity of mind that the kindliest and most unsuspecting nature could bestow, they had, in collecting the plums from Fortune's choicest pudding, retained a few for present use, and kept them in their mouths."—*Nicholas Nickleby.*

Cheeryble, Charles.—One of the twin brothers Cheeryble.—" He was a sturdy old fellow, in a broad skirted blue coat, made pretty large, to fit easily, and with no particular waist; his bulky legs clothed in drab breeches and high gaiters, and his head protected by a low-crowned broad-brimmed white hat, such as a wealthy grazier might wear . . . with such a pleasant smile playing about his mouth, and such a comical expression of mingled slyness, simplicity, kind-heartedness, and good-humour, lighting up his jolly old face, that Nicholas would have been content to have stood there and looked at him until evening, and to have forgotten meanwhile that there was such a thing as a soured mind, or a crabbed countenance, to be met with in the whole wide world."—*Nicholas Nickleby.*

Cheeryble, Edwin.—One of the twin brothers Cheeryble.—" What was the amazement of Nicholas, when his conductor advanced, and exchanged a warm greeting with another old gentleman the very type and model of himself, the face of each lighted up by beaming looks of affection, which would have been most delightful to behold in infants, and which, in men so old, was inexpressibly touching."—*Nicholas Nickleby.*

Cheeryble, Frank.—Nephew of the brothers Cheeryble. Ultimately married Kate Nickleby.—" This Mr. Frank Cheeryble, although, to judge from what had recently taken place, a hot-headed young man (which is not an absolute miracle and phenomenon in nature) was a sprightly, good-humoured, pleasant fellow, with much both in his countenance and disposition that reminded Nicholas very strongly of the kind-hearted brothers."—*Nicholas Nickleby.*

Cheesman, Mr.—Latin-master at a grammar school. —" Of course old Cheesman used to be called by the names of all sorts of cheeses; Double Gloucesterman; Family Cheshireman; North Wiltshireman; and all that; but he never minded it; and I don't mean to say he was old in point of years—because he wasn't—only he was called from the first Old Cheeseman."—*The Schoolboy's Story* (Reprinted Pieces).

Cheggs, Miss.—Sister of Mr. Alick Cheggs.—*The Old Curiosity Shop.*

Cheggs, Mr. Alick.—A market-gardener, married Sophy Wackles.—" Mr. Swiveller's conduct in respect to Miss Sophy, having been of that vague and dilatory kind, which is usually looked upon as betokening no fixed matrimonial intentions, the young lady began in course of time to deem it highly desirable that it should be brought to an issue one way or other; hence she had at last consented to play off against Richard Swiveller a stricken market-gardener, known to be ready with his offer on the smallest encouragement."—*The Old Curiosity Shop.*

Cherub, The.—Bella Wilfer's name for her father.—" If the conventional cherub could ever grow up and be clothed, he might be photographed as a portrait of Wilfer. His chubby, smooth, innocent appearance was a reason for his always being treated with condescension, when he was not put down. . . . So boyish was he in his curves and proportions, that his old schoolmaster, meeting him in Cheapside, might have been unable to withstand the temptation of caning him on the spot; in short, he was the conventional cherub, after the suppositious shoot just mentioned, rather grey, and with signs of care on his expression, and in decidedly insolvent circumstances.—*Our Mutual Friend.*

Chesney Wold.—The country-seat of Sir Leicester Dedlock.—*Bleak House.*

Chester, Edward.—Son of Sir John Chester. In love with Emma Haredale, whom he ultimately marries despite the objections of his father and hers.—*Barnaby Rudge.*

Chester, Sir John.—An accomplished but heartless man of the world, the enemy of Geoffrey Haredale, who killed him in a duel forced upon him by Sir John, father of Edward Chester who married Emma Haredale; also father of Hugh, the wild rioter, by a gipsy woman who was hanged at Tyburn.—"He was a staid, grave, placid gentleman, something past the prime of life, yet upright in his carriage for all that, and slim as a greyhound . . . soft spoken, delicately made, precise and elegant. . . . A smooth man of the world."—*Barnaby Rudge.*

Chestle, Mr.—A hop grower who married the eldest Miss Larkins. He was introduced by her to David at the Larkins Ball.—"She comes to me again, with a plain elderly gentleman who has been playing whist all night upon her arm, and says—Oh! here is my bold friend. Mr. Chestle wants to know you, Mr. Copperfield. I feel at once that he is a friend of the family, and am much gratified."—*David Copperfield.*

Chib, Mr.—A vestryman.—"Mr. Chib of Tucket's Terrace, and father of the vestry."—*Our Vestry* (Reprinted Pieces).

Chick, George and Frederick.—Sons of Mrs. Chick, to whom she referred when Paul was ordered sea air.—"There is nothing to be made uneasy by in that, said Mrs. Chick. My George and Frederick were both ordered sea air when they were about his age."—*Dombey and Son.*

Chick, Mr. John.—Husband of Mrs. Chick.—" A stout bald gentleman, with a very large face, and his hands continually in his pockets, and who had a tendency in his nature to whistle and hum tunes."—*Dombey and Son.*

Chick, Mrs. Louisa.—Sister of Mr. Dombey.—" A lady rather past the middle age than otherwise, but dressed in a very juvenile manner, particularly as to the tightness of her bodice, with a kind of screw in her face and carriage expressive of suppressed emotion."—*Dombey and Son.*

Chickenstalker, Mrs. (afterwards Mrs. Tugby).—A creditor of Trotty Veck.—" I am afraid sir, faltered Trotty, that there's a matter of ten or twelve shillings owing to Mrs. Chickenstalker—a shop sir in the general line."—*The Chimes.*

Chicksey, Veneering and Stobbles.—The firm of which Mr. Veneering, M.P., was sole partner.—" Chicksey and Stobbles, his former masters, had both become absorbed in Veneering, once their traveller or commission agent, who had signalized his accession to supreme power by bringing into the business a quantity of plate glass window and French polished mahogany partition, and a gleaming and enormous door-plate."—*Our Mutual Friend.*

Chickweed, Conkey.—A publican, known to Mr. Blathers, the Bow Street Officer, who pretended that his home had been robbed.—" And consequently the name of Mr. Chickweed, Licensed Vitler, appeared in the Gazette, among the other bankrupts; and all manner of benefits, and subscriptions, and I don't know what all, was got up for the poor man, who was in a werry low state of mind about his loss; . . . and a good bit of money he had made by it too, and nobody would never have found it out, if he hadn't been so precious anxious to keep up appearances, said Mr. Blathers."—*Oliver Twist.*

Chiggle, Mr.—A sculptor who made a marble bust of Elijah Pogram.—*Martin Chuzzlewit.*

Childers, Kidderminster.—Son of E. W. B. Childers.—" This gentleman was mentioned in the Bills as E. W. B. Childers, so justly celebrated for his daring vaulting act as the wild Huntsman of the North American Prairies; in which popular performance a diminutive boy with an old face, who now accompanied him, assisted as his infant son, being carried upside down over his father's shoulder by one foot, and held by the crown of his head heels upwards in the palm of his father's hand, according to the violent paternal manner in which wild huntsmen may be observed to handle their offspring."—*Hard Times.*

Childers, Mr. E. W. B.—One of Sleary's circus troupe.—" His face, close-shaven, thin, and sallow, was shaded by a great quantity of dark hair, brushed into a roll all round his head, and parted up the centre. His legs were very robust, but shorter than legs of good proportions should have been. His chest and back were as much too broad as his legs were too short. He was dressed in a Newmarket coat and tight-fitting trousers; wore a shawl round his neck; smelt of lamp oil, straw, orange peel, horses' provender, and sawdust; and looked a most remarkable sort of Centaur, compounded of the stable and the playhouse."—*Hard Times.*

Chill, Mr.—Uncle of Michael the Poor Relation.—" Avarice was unhappily Uncle Chill's master vice; though he was rich, he pinched, and scraped, and clutched, and lived miserably."—*The Poor Relation's Story* (Reprinted Pieces).

Chillip, Doctor.—The medical man who attended Mrs. Copperfield at David's birth.—" He was the meekest of his sex, the mildest of little men. He carried his head on one side, partly in modest depreciation of himself, partly in modest propitiation of everybody else."—*David Copperfield.*

Chillip, Mrs.—Doctor Chillip's second wife.—" Mr. Chillip was married again, to a tall raw-boned, high-nosed wife; and they had a weazen little baby, with a heavy head that it couldn't hold up, and two weak staring eyes, with which it seemed to be always wondering why it had ever been born."—*David Copperfield.*

Chimes, The.—A peal of city bells, which had a fascination for Trotty Veck.—" Being a simple man he invested them with a strange and solemn character. They were so mysterious, often heard and never seen, so high up, full of such a deep strong melody, that he regarded them with a species of awe, and sometimes, when he looked up at the dark arched windows in the tower, he half expected to be beckoned to by something which was not a bell and yet was what he had heard so often sounding in the chimes." —*The Chimes.*

Chinaman, Jack.—Keeper of a rival opium-den to that of Princess Puffer.—*Edwin Drood.*

Chips.—The hero of one of the Nurse's tales, told to the Uncommercial Traveller in his childhood.—" There was something of a shipbuilding flavour in the following story, as it always recurs to me in a vague association with calomel pills, so I believe it to have been reserved for dull nights, when I was low with medicine. Chips the father had sold himself to the devil for an iron pot, and a bushel of tenpenny nails, and half a ton of copper, and a rat that could speak; so had Chips the Grandfather; and Chips the great Grandfather had disposed of himself in the same direction, on the same terms; and the bargain had run in the family for a long long time."—*The Uncommercial Traveller* (Nurse's Stories).

Chirrup, Mr. and Mrs.—The nice little couple.—" Mr. Chirrup has the smartness, and something of the brisk quick manner, of a small bird. Mrs. Chirrup is the prettiest of all little women, and has the prettiest little figure conceivable."—*Sketches of Young Couples.*

Chittling, Tom.—One of Fagin's gang of thieves.—" Mr. Chittling was older in years than the Dodger, having perhaps numbered eighteen winters. . . . He had small twinkling eyes, and a pockmarked face, wore a fur cap, a dark corduroy jacket, greasy fustian trousers, and an apron. His wardrobe was in truth rather out of repair, but he excused himself to the company by stating that his time was only out an hour before, and that, in consequence of having worn the regimentals for six weeks past, he had not been able to bestow any attention on his private clothes."—*Oliver Twist.*

Chivery, Bob.—A turnkey at the Marshalsea Debtors' Prison.—" There was native delicacy in Mr. Chivery—true politeness; though his exterior had very much of a turnkey about it, and not the least of a gentleman."—*Little Dorrit.*

Chivery, John.—Son of Bob Chivery, the turnkey at

the Marshalsea.—" Little Dorrit's lover however was not a Collegian. He was the sentimental son of a turnkey. His father hoped, in the fulness of time, to leave him the inheritance of the unstained key; and had from his early youth familiarised him with the duties of his office, and with an ambition to retain the prison-lock in the family. While the succession was yet in abeyance, he assisted his mother in the conduct of a snug tobacco business. Young John was small of stature, with rather weak legs, and very weak light hair. One of his eyes was also weak, and looked larger than the other, as if it couldn't collect itself. Young John was gentle likewise; but he was great of soul; poetical, expansive, faithful."—*Little Dorrit.*

Chivery, Mrs.—Wife of the Marshalsea turnkey.—" Mrs. Chivery was a comfortable-looking woman, much respected about Horsemonger Lane for her feelings and her conversation."—*Little Dorrit.*

Choakumchild, Mr.—Master of Mr. Gradgrind's school at Coketown.—" He, and some one hundred and forty other schoolmasters, had been lately turned at the same time, in the same factory, on the same principles, like so many pianoforte legs. He had been put through an immense variety of paces, and had answered volumes of head-breaking questions. . . . If he had only learned a little less, how infinitely better he might have taught much more."—*Hard Times.*

Choke, General Cyrus.—A member of the Eden Land Corporation.—" A very lank gentleman, in a loose limp white cravat, a long white waistcoat, and a black great-coat."—*Martin Chuzzlewit.*

Chollop, Hannibal.—An American settler at Eden.—" A lean person, in a blue frock and a straw hat, with a short black pipe in his mouth, and a great hickory stick, studded all over with knots, in his hand."—*Martin Chuzzlewit.*

Chopkins, Laura.—Daughter of a neighbour of the Kenwigs.—*Nicholas Nickleby.*

Chopper.—The great-uncle of William Tinkling.—*Holiday Romance.*

Chopper, Mrs.—Mother of Mrs. Merrywinkle.—" A

mysterious old lady, who lurks behind a pair of spectacles, and is afflicted with a chronic disease, respecting which she has taken a vast deal of medical advice."—*Sketches of Young Couples.*

Chops.—A dwarf in Toby Magsman's show.—" He was an uncommon small man, he really was; certainly not so small as he was made out to be, but where is your Dwarf as is. He was a most uncommon small man, with a most uncommon large 'ed, and what he had inside that 'ed nobody ever knowed but himself, even supposin' himself to have ever took stock of it, which it would have been a stiff job for even him to do. . . . He was always in love of course; every human nat'ral phenomenon is; and he was always in love with a large woman; I never knowed the Dwarf as could be got to love a small one; which helps to keep 'em the Curiosities they are."—Going into Society (*Christmas Stories*).

Chowser, Colonel.—A guest at Ralph Nickleby's dinner-party.—" Colonel Chowser of the Militia—and the race-courses."—*Nicholas Nickleby.*

Christian, Fletcher.—An officer on board the ship *Bounty.*—*The Long Voyage* (Reprinted Pieces).

Christian, Thursday October.—Son of Fletcher Christian.—*The Long Voyage* (Reprinted Pieces).

Christiana.—Sweetheart of Michael the Poor Relation. —" I had loved Christiana a long time; she was very beautiful and very winning in all respects."—*The Poor Relation's Story* (Reprinted Pieces).

Christina, Donna.—A Spanish lady referred to by Mr. Jingle.—" Don Bolaro Fizz-gig—Grandee—only daughter Donna Christina—splendid creature—loved me to distraction—jealous father—high-souled daughter—handsome Englishman—Donna Christina in despair—prussic acid—stomach pump in my portmanteau—operation performed—old Bolaro in ecstasies—consent to our union—join hands and floods of tears—romantic story—very."—*Pickwick Papers.*

Christmas Past, The Ghost of.—Scrooge's first monitor. —" It was a strange figure—like a child; yet not so like a child as an old man, viewed through some supernatural medium, which gave him the appearance of having receded from the view, and being diminished to a child's proportions."—*A Christmas Carol.*

Christmas Present, The Ghost of.—Scrooge's second monitor.—" Its dark brown curls were long and free; free as its genial face, its sparkling eye, its open hand, its cheery voice, its unconstrained demeanour, and its joyful air."—*A Christmas Carol.*

Christmas Yet to Come, The Ghost of.—Scrooge's third monitor.—" It was shrouded in a deep black garment, which concealed its head, its face, its form, and left nothing of it visible save one outstretched hand."—*A Christmas Carol.*

Christopher.—A head waiter.—" The good old-fashioned style is that whatever you want, down to a wafer, you must be olely and solely dependent on the head waiter for; you must put yourself a newborn child into his hands. . . . A head waiter must be either head or tail; he must be at one extremity or the other of the social scale; he cannot be at the waist of it, or anywhere else but the extremities; it is for him to decide which of the extremities."—Somebody's Luggage (*Christmas Stories*).

Chuckster, Mr.—Clerk to Mr. Witherden the notary.—" Mr. Chuckster was standing behind the lid of his desk, making such preparations towards finishing off for the night as pulling down his wristbands, and pulling up his shirt collar; settling his neck more gracefully in his stock; and secretly arranging his whiskers, by the aid of a little triangular bit of looking glass."—*The Old Curiosity Shop.*

Chuffey.—Clerk to Anthony Chuzzlewit and Son.—" A little, blear-eyed, weazen-faced, ancient man came creeping out. He was of remote fashion, and dusty, like the rest of the furniture; he was dressed in a decayed suit of black, with breeches garnished at the knees with rusty wisps of ribbon, the very paupers of shoe strings; on the lower portion of his spindle legs were dingy worsted stockings of the same colour. He looked as if he had been put away and forgotten half a century before, and somebody had just found him in the lumber closet."—*Martin Chuzzlewit.*

Chuzzlewit, Anthony.—Brother of old Martin.—"Then there were Anthony Chuzzlewit, and his son Jonas; the face of the old man so sharpened by the wariness and cunning of his life, that it seemed to cut him a passage through the crowded room."—*Martin Chuzzlewit.*

Chuzzlewit, Anthony, and Son.—Warehousemen in London.—"The old-established firm of Anthony Chuzzlewit and Son, Manchester Warehousemen, and so forth, had its place of business in a very narrow street, somewhere behind the Post Office; where every house was on the brightest summer morning very gloomy; and where light porters watered the pavement, each before his own employer's premises, in fantastic patterns, in the dog days."—*Martin Chuzzlewit.*

Chuzzlewit, Diggory.—An impecunious member of the family.—"Letters are yet in the possession of various branches of the family, from which it distinctly appears, being stated in so many words, that one Diggory Chuzzlewit was in the habit of perpetually dining with Duke Humphrey. We find him making constant reference to an uncle, in respect of whom he would seem to have entertained great expectations, as he was in the habit of seeking to propitiate his favour by presents of plate, jewels, books, watches, and other valuable articles. Thus he writes on one occasion to his brother, in reference to a gravy spoon, the brother's property, which he (Diggory) would appear to have borrowed, or otherwise possessed himself of—Do not be angry; I have parted with it—to my uncle."—*Martin Chuzzlewit.*

Chuzzlewit Family.—"There can be no doubt that at least one Chuzzlewit came over with William the Conqueror. It does not appear that this illustrious ancestor came over that monarch, to employ the vulgar phrase, at any subsequent period; inasmuch as the family do not seem to have been ever greatly distinguished by the possession of landed estate."—*Martin Chuzzlewit.*

Chuzzlewit, George.—A cousin of old Martin.—"Then there was George Chuzzlewit, a gay bachelor cousin, who claimed to be young, but had been younger, and was inclined to corpulency."—*Martin Chuzzlewit.*

Chuzzlewit, Jonas.—Son of Anthony.—"The son had

so well profited by the precept and example of the father, that he looked a year or two the elder of the twain. The education of Mr. Jonas had been conducted from his cradle on the strictest principles of the main chance. This fine young man had all the inclination to be a profligate of the first water, and only lacked the one good trait in the common catalogue of debauched vices—open-handedness—to be a notable vagabond."—*Martin Chuzzlewit.*

Chuzzlewit, Martin (the elder).—Grandfather of young Martin; cousin of Pecksniff; a rich and suspicious old man.—*Martin Chuzzlewit.*

Chuzzlewit, Martin (the younger).—Grandson of old Martin.—" He was young—one-and-twenty perhaps—and handsome; with a keen dark eye, and a quickness of look and manner, which made Tom sensible of a great contrast in his own bearing, and caused him to feel even more shy than usual."—*Martin Chuzzlewit.*

Chuzzlewit, Mrs. Ned.—A sister-in-law of old Martin.—" Then there was the widow of a deceased brother of Mr. Martin Chuzzlewit, who being almost supernaturally disagreeable, and having a dreary face, and a bony figure, and a masculine voice, was, in right of these qualities, what is commonly called a strong-minded woman."—*Martin Chuzzlewit.*

Chuzzlewit, The Misses.—Daughters of Mrs. Ned Chuzzlewit.—" Beside her sat her spinster daughters, three in number, and of gentlemanly deportment; who had so mortified themselves with tight stays, that their tempers were reduced to something less than their waists, and sharp lacing was expressed in their very noses."—*Martin Chuzzlewit.*

Chuzzlewit, Toby.—The grandson of an obscure Chuzzlewit.—" When he lay upon his deathbed, this question was put to him, in a distinct solemn and formal way,—Toby Chuzzlewit, who was your grandfather; to which he, with his last breath, no less distinctly solemnly and formally replied—The Lord No Zoo."—*Martin Chuzzlewit.*

Cicero.—A negro porter who had been a slave and bought his freedom.—" A grey-haired black man."—*Martin Chuzzlewit.*

Circassian Fair.—The name given to Miss Pipson in the Seraglio.—(*See* **Pipson, Miss.**)—The Haunted House (*Christmas Stories*).

Circumlocution Office, The.—A Government department presided over by Sir Tite Barnacle.—"The Circumlocution Office was (as everybody knows without being told) the most important Department under Government. No public business of any kind could possibly be done, at any time, without the acquiescence of the Circumlocution Office. This glorious establishment had been early in the field, when the one sublime principle, involving the difficult art of governing a country, was first distinctly revealed to statesmen. It had been foremost to study that bright revelation, and to carry shining influence through the whole of the official proceedings. Whatever was required to be done, the Circumlocution Office was beforehand with all the public departments in the art of perceiving—how not to do it"—*Little Dorrit.*

Clare, Ada.—A ward in Chancery to whom Esther Summerson became companion at Bleak House; married Richard Carstone.—"A beautiful girl, with such rich golden hair, such soft blue eyes, and such a bright, innocent, trusting face."—*Bleak House.*

Clark, Betsy.—One of two housemaids who neglected their morning work to flirt with Todd's young man.—"When the fire is lighted, she opens the street door, to take in the milk; when, by the most singular coincidence in the world, she discovers that the servant next door has just taken in her milk too; and that Mr. Todd's young man over the way, is by an equally extraordinary chance, taking down his master's shutters. The inevitable consequence is that she just steps, milk jug in hand, as far as next door, just to say good morning to Betsy Clark; and that Mr. Todd's young man just steps over the way, to say good morning to both of them."—*Sketches by Boz* (The Streets—Morning).

Clark, Mr.—A wharfinger's clerk to whom Florence Dombey appealed when she lost her way at the docks.—"She peeped into a kind of wharf or landing-place upon the river side, where there were a great many packages, casks and boxes strewn about; a large pair of wooden scales; and a little wooden house on wheels, outside of which, looking at the neighbouring masts and boats, a stout man stood whistling, with his pen behind his ear, and his hands in his pockets, as if his day's work were nearly done."—*Dombey and Son.*

Clark, Mrs.—A client of The General Agency, in want of a companion, to whom Tom the clerk sent Madeline Bray.—*Nicholas Nickleby.*

Clarke, Mrs.—A widow whom Tony Weller married.—*Pickwick Papers.*

Clarkson.—A London barrister.—*The Detective Police* (Reprinted Pieces).

Clarriker.—Partner in business with Herbert Pocket. —" A worthy young merchant or shipping broker, not long established in business, who wanted intelligent help, and who in due course of time and receipt would want a partner."—*Great Expectations.*

Clatter, Doctor.—A medical man consulted by Our Bore.—" The moment Clatter saw Our Bore he said—accumulation of fat about the heart."—*Our Bore* (Reprinted Pieces).

Claypole, Noah.—Assistant to Mr. Sowerby. A mean selfish bully who ultimately became a professional thief in Fagin's gang, but turned King's evidence against Fagin and got a free pardon for himself.—" A large-headed small-eyed youth of lumbering make and heavy countenance."—*Oliver Twist.*

Cleaver, Fanny (Jenny Wren).—A doll's dressmaker, a cripple girl, with whom Lizzie Hexham lodged.—" The little figure went on with its work of gumming or glueing together, with a camel's-hair brush, certain pieces of card-board and thin wood, previously cut into various shapes. . . . The dexterity of her nimble fingers was remarkable, and as she brought two thin edges accurately together by giving them a little bite, she would glance at the visitors out of the corners of her grey eyes, with a look that out-sharpened all her other sharpness. She had an elfin chin, that was capable of great expression, and whenever she gave this look she hitched this chin up, as if her eyes and her chin worked together on the same wires."—*Our Mutual Friend.*

Cleaver, Mr.—The drunken father of Miss Jenny Wren, the doll's dressmaker.—" The whole indecorous threadbare ruin, from the broken shoes to the prematurely grey scanty hair, grovelled . . . the very breathing of the figure was contemptible, as it laboured and rattled in that operation like a blundering clock."—*Our Mutual Friend.*

Clennam, Arthur.—Adopted son of Mrs. Clennam. Returned from China, ultimately married Little Dorrit.—" I am the only son of parents who weighed, measured, and priced everything; for whom what could not be weighed, measured and priced had no existence."—*Little Dorrit.*

Clennam, Gilbert.—Grand-uncle of Arthur Clennam.—*Little Dorrit.*

Clennam, Mr.—Deceased father of Arthur Clennam. —" He was an undecided irresolute chap, who had had everything but his orphan life scared out of him when he was young."—*Little Dorrit.*

Clennam, Mrs.—Supposed mother of Arthur Clennam —an austere woman.—" On a black bier-like sofa in this hollow, propped up behind with one great angular black bolster, like the block at a State execution in the good old times, sat his mother in a widow's dress. There was a smell of black dye in the airless room, which the fire had been drawing out of the crape and stuff of the widow's dress for fifteen months, and out of the bier-like sofa for fifteen years. She was always balancing her bargain with the Majesty of Heaven; posting up the entries to her credit; strictly keeping her set off; and claiming her due; she was only remarkable for this, for the force and emphasis with which she did it; thousands upon thousands do it, according to their varying manner, every day."—*Little Dorrit.*

Clergyman, The.—Of the parish where Mr. Marton was school-master.—" He was a simple-hearted old gentleman, of a shrinking, subdued spirit, accustomed to retirement, and very little acquainted with the world, which he had left many years before, to come and settle in that place. His wife had died in the house in which he still lived, and he had long since lost sight of any earthly cares or hopes beyond it."—*The Old Curiosity Shop.*

Clergyman, The, of Dingley Dell.—" A bald-headed old gentleman with a good-humoured benevolent face."—*Pickwick Papers.*

Clergyman's Wife of Dingley Dell.—" A stout blooming old lady, who looked as if she were well skilled, not only in the art and mystery of manufacturing home-made cordials, greatly to other people's satisfaction, but of testing them occasionally very much to her own."—*Pickwick Papers.*

Cleverly, Susannah.—An emigrant on board the *Amazon.*—" A young woman of business, hustling a slow brother."—*The Uncommercial Traveller* (Bound for the Great Salt Lake).

Cleverly, William.—An emigrant on board the *Amazon.* Brother of Susannah.—*The Uncommercial Traveller* (Bound for the Great Salt Lake).

Click.—A fellow lodger of Tom the artist.—" I found myself walking along the Waterloo Road, one evening after dark, accompanied by an acquaintance and fellow lodger in the gas-fitting way of life. He is very good company, having worked at the theatres, and indeed he has a theatrical turn himself, and wishes to be brought out in the character of Othello, but whether on account of his regular work always blacking his face and hands more or less I cannot say."—Somebody's Luggage (*Christmas Stories*).

Click.—A London thief.—*On Duty with Inspector Field* (Reprinted Pieces).

Clickett (The Orfling).—Mrs. Micawber's maid-of-all-work.—" A dark-complexioned young woman, with a habit of snorting, who was servant to the family, and informed me before half an hour had expired that she was a orfling, and came from St. Luke's workhouse, completed the establishment."—*David Copperfield.*

Clissold, Laurence.—A friend of the deceased Mr. Raybrook, who had borrowed money from him.—" One Laurence Clissold had borrowed of the deceased, at the time when he was a thriving young tradesman in the town of Barnstaple, the sum of five hundred pounds."—A Message from the Sea (*Christmas Stories*).

Clive, Mr.—An official of the Circumlocution Office.—*Little Dorrit.*

Clocker, Mr.—A grocer friend of the landsman.—" The landsman was narrating his experience of an accident. . . . I was walking up and down the wooden causeway, next the pier off where it happened, along with a friend of mine which his name is Mr. Clocker.—Mr. Clocker is a grocer over yonder—from the direction in which he pointed the bowl of his pipe, I might have judged Mr. Clocker to be a merman, established in the grocery trade in five-and-twenty fathoms of water."—*Out of the Season* (Reprinted Pieces).

Clubber, Sir Thomas, and Family.—Guests at the Rochester Charity ball.—" Sir Thomas Clubber, Lady Clubber, and the Miss Clubbers, shouted the man at the door in a stentorian voice. A great sensation was created throughout the room by the entrance of a tall gentleman in a blue coat and bright buttons; a large lady in blue satin; and two young ladies on a similar scale, in fashionably made dresses of the same hue."—*Pickwick Papers.*

Cluppins, Mrs.—A friend of Mrs. Bardell's.—" Mrs. Cluppins was a little brisk busy-looking woman."—*Pickwick Papers.*

Cly, Roger.—An old servant of Darnay, who became a spy.—*A Tale of Two Cities.*

Cobb, Tom.—A general chandler and Post Office keeper at Chigwell. One of John Willet's three cronies.—*Barnaby Rudge.*

Cobbey, Master.—A pupil at Dotheboys Hall.—*Nicholas Nickleby.*

Cobbs.—The Boots at the Holly Tree Inn, who kept Charley company when snowed up there.—" A desperate idea came into my head—under any other circumstances I would have rejected it; but in the strait at which I was I held it fast. Could I so far overcome the inherent bashfulness which withheld me from the Landlord's table, and the company I might find there, as to call up the Boots, and ask him to take a chair—and something in a liquid form—and talk to me. I could—I would—I did."—The Holly Tree (*Christmas Stories*).

Codger, Miss.—A literary lady introduced to Elijah Pogram by Mrs. Hominy.—" Sticking on her forehead, by invisible means, was a massive cameo, in size and shape like a raspberry tart which is ordinarily sold for a penny, representing on its front the Capitol at Washington."—*Martin Chuzzlewit.*

Codgers, Reverend Mr.—A divine whose portrait the idle apprentices found on sale at Carlisle.—The Lazy Tour of Two Idle Apprentices (*Christmas Stories*).

Codlin and Short.—Proprietors of a travelling Punch and Judy show.—" When they came to any town or village, or even to a detached house of good appearance, Short blew a blast upon the brazen trumpet, and carolled a fragment of a song, in that hilarious tone common to Punches and their consorts; if people hurried to the windows, Mr. Codlin pitched the temple."—*The Old Curiosity Shop.*

Codlin, Thomas.—Joint-proprietor with Short of a Punch and Judy show. Expecting a reward to be forthcoming for harbouring Little Nell and her grandfather, he desired to secure it for himself.—" After bidding the old man good-night, Nell retired to her poor garret, but had scarcely closed the door when it was gently tapped at. She opened it directly, and was a little startled by the sight of Mr. Thomas Codlin. Take my advice, said Codlin; don't ask me why, but take it; as long as you travel with us, keep as near me as you can. You needn't tell Short, you know, that we've had this little talk together. God bless you; recollect the friend; Codlin's the friend, not Short; Short's all very well, as far as he goes, but the real friend is Codlin—not Short."—*The Old Curiosity Shop.*

Coiler, Mrs.—A neighbour of Pocket's invited to dinner.—" Mr. and Mrs. Pocket had a toady neighbour, a widow lady of that highly sympathetic nature that she agreed with everybody, blessed everybody, and shed smiles and tears on everybody according to circumstances. . . . She had a serpentine way of coming close at me when she pretended to be vitally interested in the friends and localities I had left which was altogether snaky and fork-tongued."—*Great Expectations.*

Coleshaw, Miss.—A passenger on board the *Golden*

Mary.—" A sedate young woman in black (about thirty I shall say), who was going out to join a brother."—The Wreck of the *Golden Mary* (*Christmas Stories*).

Colonel, The.—A client of Mr. Jaggers' at Newgate.—" A portly upright man in a well-worn olive-coloured frock coat, with a peculiar pallor overspreading the red in his complexion, and eyes that went wandering about when he tried to fix them."—*Great Expectations.*

Commodore, The.—The name of the stage-coach by which Mr. Pickwick and his friends travelled to Rochester along with Mr. Jingle.—*Pickwick Papers.*

Compeyson.—An accomplished criminal of gentlemanly manners, partner with Magwitch.—" And what was Compeyson's business in which we was to go pardners? Compeyson's business was the swindling, handwriting, forging, stolen bank-note passing, and such like. All sorts of traps as Compeyson could set with his head, and keep his own legs out of, and get the profits from, and let another man in for, was Compeyson's business. He'd no more heart than an iron file, he was as cold as death, and he had the head of the devil."—*Great Expectations.*

Conway, General.—A member of Parliament who faced the mob when the rioters attacked the House of Commons.—" You may tell these people, my Lord, that I am General Conway of whom they have heard; and that I oppose this petition and all their proceedings and yours. I am a soldier you may tell them, and I will protect the freedom of this place with my sword."—*Barnaby Rudge.*

Coodle, Lord.—A party politician.—" England has been in a dreadful state for some weeks. Lord Coodle would go out; Sir Thomas Doodle wouldn't come in; and there being nobody in Great Britain (to speak of) except Coodle and Doodle, there has been no Government."—*Bleak House.*

Cooper, Augustus.—A pupil at Signor Billsmethi's Dancing Academy.—" Mr. Augustus Cooper was in the oil and colour line—just of age; with a little money; a little business; and a little mother; who, having managed her husband and his business in his lifetime, took to managing her son and his business after his decease; and so, somehow or other, he had been cooped up in the little back parlour behind the shop on week-days, and in a little deal box without a lid (called by courtesy a pew) at Bethel Chapel on Sundays, and had seen no more of the world than if he had been an infant all his days."—*Sketches by Boz* (The Dancing Academy).

Cooper, Mrs.—Mother of Augustus Cooper.—*Sketches by Boz* (The Dancing Academy).

Copperfield, Betsy Trotwood.—The daughter of David Copperfield and his second wife, Agnes Wickfield, named after his aunt.—*David Copperfield.*

Copperfield, David (the third).—Son of David Copperfield and his second wife, Agnes Wickfield.—*David Copperfield.*

Copperfield, David, the Elder.—David's father. Nephew of Miss Trotwood.—" My father had once been a favourite of hers, I believe; but she was mortally affronted by his marriage, on the ground that my mother was a wax doll. She had never seen my mother, but she knew her to be not yet twenty. My father and Miss Betsy never met again. He was double my mother's age when he married, and of but a delicate constitution. He died a year afterwards, and, as I have said, six months before I came into the world."—*David Copperfield.*

Copperfield, David, the Younger.—The narrator of the tale.—" Whether I shall turn out to be the hero of my own life or whether that station will be held by anybody else these pages must show. To begin my life with the beginning of my life I record that I was born (as I have been informed and believe) on a Friday at twelve o'clock at night. It was remarked that the clock began to strike and I began to cry simultaneously. . . . I was born at Blunderstone in Suffolk, or thereby as they say in Scotland. I was a posthumous child. My father's eyes had closed upon the light of this world six months, when mine opened on it."—*David Copperfield.*

Copperfield, Mrs.—Mother of David. Married a second time to Mr. Murdstone, a hard, cruel man, who broke her spirit. Died when David was aged six.—" The first objects that assume a distinct presence before me, as I look far back into the blank of my infancy, are my mother with her pretty hair and youthful shape, and Peggotty with no shape at all. . . . We are playing in the winter twilight, dancing about the parlour, when my mother is out of breath, and rests herself in an elbow chair. I watch her winding her bright curls round her fingers, and straightening her waist, and nobody knows better than I do that she likes to look so well, and is proud of being so pretty."—*David Copperfield.*

Coppernose, Mr.—A member of the Mechanical Science Section of the Mudfog Association.—*The Mudfog Sketches.*

Cornberry, Mr.—An old man who bequeathed his estate to Miss Julia Manners.—*Sketches by Boz* (The Great Winglebury Duel).

Corney, Mrs.—The matron of the workhouse where Oliver Twist was born. Married Bumble the Beadle.—*Oliver Twist.*

Corresponding Society.—" The following Resolutions were unanimously agreed to. That the Corresponding Society of the The Pickwick Club is hereby constituted; and that Samuel Pickwick, Esq.; Tracy Tupman, Esq.; Augustus Snodgrass, Esq.; and Nathaniel Winkle, Esq.; are hereby nominated and appointed members of the same."—*Pickwick Papers.*

Cour, Captain de la.—A military officer billeted at Madam Bouclet's.—Somebody's Luggage (*Christmas Stories*).

Cower, Mr.—Solicitor to Mr. Joseph Tuggs.—" A stranger dismounted from a cab, and hastily entered the shop. He was habitated in a black cloth, and bore with him a green umbrella and a blue bag. I come from the Temple, said the man with the bag,—from Mr. Cower's the Solicitor."—*Sketches by Boz* (The Tuggses at Ramsgate).

Crackit, Toby (Flash Toby Crackit).—A house-breaker, engaged with Bill Sikes in the burglary of Chertsey where Oliver was shot.—" Sikes pushed Oliver before him, and they entered a low dark room, with a smoky fire, two or three broken chairs, a table, and a very old couch; on which, with his legs very much higher than his head, a man was reposing at full length smoking a long clay pipe. He was dressed in a smartly-cut snuff-coloured coat, with large brass buttons; an orange neckerchief; a coarse staring shawl pattern waistcoat, and drab breeches. Mr. Crackit (for he it was) had no very great quantity of hair, either upon his head or his face; but what he had was of a reddish dye, and tortured into long corkscrew curls, through which he occasionally thrust some very dirty fingers, ornamented with large common rings."—*Oliver Twist.*

Craddock, Mrs.—Landlady of a boarding-house at Bath. —*Pickwick Papers.*

Craggs, Mrs.—Wife of Mr. Craggs.—(*See* **Snitchey, Mrs.**)—*The Battle of Life.*

Craggs, Thomas.—The silent partner of Snitchey and Craggs, Dr. Jeddler's solicitors.—" A cold, hard, dry man, dressed in grey and white, like a flint, with small twinkles in his eyes as if something struck sparks out of them. Craggs seemed to be represented by Snitchey and to be conscious of little or no separate existence or personal individuality."—*The Battle of Life.*

Cratchit, Belinda.—Second daughter of Bob Cratchit.—*A Christmas Carol.*

Cratchit, Bob.—Scrooge's poorly paid clerk, whose home the Ghost of Christmas Present showed to Scrooge. —" Bob had but fifteen bob a week himself; he pocketed on Saturdays but fifteen copies of his Christian name, and yet the Ghost of Christmas Present blessed his four-roomed house."—*A Christmas Carol.*

Cratchit Family (on Christmas Eve).—" Such a bustle ensued that you might have thought a goose the rarest of all birds—a feathered phenomenon to which a black swan was a matter of course,—and in truth it was something very like it in that house. Mrs. Cratchit made the gravy (ready beforehand in a little saucepan) burning hot; Master Peter mashed the potatoes, with incredible vigour; Miss Belinda sweetened up the apple sauce; Martha dusted the hot plates; Bob took Tiny Tim beside him in a tiny corner at the table; the two young Cratchits set chairs for everybody, not forgetting themselves, and, mounting guard upon their posts, crammed spoons into their mouths, lest they should shriek for goose before their turn came to be helped. . . . They were not a handsome family; they were not well dressed; their shoes were far from being waterproof; their clothes were scanty; and Peter might have known, and very likely did, the inside of a pawnbroker's; but they were happy, grateful, pleased with one another and contented with the time."—*A Christmas Carol.*

Cratchit, Martha.—Eldest daughter of Bob Cratchit. —" Martha, who was a poor apprentice at a milliner's, then told them what kind of work she had to do, and how many hours she worked at a stretch, and how she meant to lie abed to-morrow morning for a good long rest, to-morrow being a holiday she passed at home."—*A Christmas Carol.*

Cratchit, Mrs.—Wife of Bob Cratchit.—" Then up rose Mrs. Cratchit, Cratchit's wife, dressed out but poorly in a twice turned gown, but brave in ribbons, which are cheap, and make a goodly show for sixpence."—*A Christmas Carol.*

Cratchit, Peter.—Eldest son of Bob Cratchit.—" Bob told them how he had a situation in his eye for Master Peter, which would bring in, if obtained, full five and sixpence weekly. The two young Cratchits laughed tremendously at the idea of Peter's being a man of business; and Peter himself looked thoughtfully at the fire, from behind his collar, as if he were deliberating what particular investments he should favour, when he came into the receipt of that bewildering income."—*A Christmas Carol.*

Cratchit, Tim.—A lame boy, son of Bob Cratchit.—(*See* **Tiny Tim.**)—*A Christmas Carol.*

Crawley, Mr.—A visitor at Bath.—*Pickwick Papers.*

Creakle, Junior.—Son of Mr. Creakle, the head master of Salem House.—" I heard that Mr. Creakle had a son, who had not been Tungay's friend, and who assisting in the school, had once held some remonstrance with his father, on an occasion when its discipline was very cruelly exercised, and was supposed besides to have protested against his father's usage of his mother. I heard that Mr. Creakle had turned him out of doors in consequence, and that Mrs. and Miss Creakle had been in a sad way ever since."—*David Copperfield.*

Creakle, Miss.—Daughter of the head master of Salem House.—" I heard that Miss Creakle was regarded by the school in general as being in love with Steerforth."—*David Copperfield.*

Creakle, Mr.—The head master at Salem House.—" Mr. Creakle's face was fiery, and his eyes were small, and deep in his head; he had thick veins in his forehead, a little nose, and a large chin; he was bald on the top of his head, and had some thin wet-looking hair, that was just turning grey, brushed across each temple, so that the two sides interlaced on his forehead. . . . I should think there never can have been a man who enjoyed his profession more than Mr. Creakle did. He had a delight in cutting at the boys, which was like the satisfaction of a craving appetite. I am confident that he couldn't resist a chubby boy especially. . . . I was chubby myself and ought to know."—*David Copperfield.*

Creakle, Mrs.—Wife of Mr. Creakle, the head master of Salem House.—*David Copperfield.*

Creevy, John La.—Brother of Miss La Creevy, portrait painter and friend of Kate Nickleby.—*Nicholas Nickleby.*

Creevy, Miss La.—A miniature portrait painter; the friend of Kate Nickleby, ultimately married Tim Linkinwater.—" Miss La Creevy was a mincing young lady of fifty."—*Nicholas Nickleby.*

Crewler, Caroline, Louisa, Margaret, Lucy.—Sisters of Sophy who married Traddles.—*David Copperfield.*

Crewler, Mrs.—Wife of Rev. Horace Crewler.—Mother of the " ten down in Devonshire."—*David Copperfield.*

Crewler, Rev. Horace.—The father of Sophy who married Traddles.—*David Copperfield.*

Crewler, Sarah.—Second daughter of Rev. Horace Crewler. One of the " ten down in Devonshire."—*David Copperfield.*

Crewler, Sophy.—Fourth daughter of Rev. Horace

Crewler—affianced to Traddles—afterwards married to him.—" She's a curate's daughter, said Traddles, one of ten down in Devonshire. . . . Sophy arrives at the house of Dora's aunts in due course. She has the most agreeable of faces—not absolutely beautiful—but extraordinarily pleasant—and is one of the most genial, unaffected, frank, engaging creatures I have ever seen."—*David Copperfield.*

Crimple, David.—A pawnbroker's assistant, whom Mr. Tigg appointed Secretary of the Anglo-Bengalee Disinterested Loan and Life Assurance Company.—" This gentleman's name by the way had been originally Crimp; but as the word was susceptible of an awkward construction, and might be misrepresented, he had altered it to Crimple."—*Martin Chuzzlewit.*

Crinkles, Mr.—A member of the Mechanical Science Section of the Mudfog Association.—" Mr. Crinkles exhibited a most beautiful and delicate machine, of little larger size than an ordinary snuff-box, manfactured entirely by himself, and composed exclusively of steel, by the aid of which more pockets could be picked in one hour, than by the present slow and tedious process in four-and-twenty."—*The Mudfog Sketches.*

Cripple Corner.—The business premises of Wilding and Co.—" There was a pump in Cripple Corner; there was a tree in Cripple Corner; all Cripple Corner belonged to Wilding and Co., Wine Merchants; their cellars burrowed under it; their mansion towered over it; it really had been a mansion in the days when merchants inhabited the city." No Thoroughfare (*Christmas Stories*).

Cripples, Mr.—A school-master who kept a small night school in the house where Frederick Dorrit lived.—*Little Dorrit.*

Cripples, The Three.—A public-house used by Bill Sikes and Fagin.—" A low public-house in the filthiest part of Little Saffron Hill; a dark and gloomy den, where a flaring gas light burnt all day in the winter time, and where no ray of sun ever shone in the summer."—*Oliver Twist.*

Cripps, Mrs.—Mother of Bob Sawyer's shop boy.——*Pickwick Papers.*

Cripps, Tom.—Bob Sawyer's shop boy.—"The conversation was becoming general, when it was interrupted by the entrance into the shop of a boy in a sober grey livery, and a gold laced hat."—*Pickwick Papers.*

Crisparkle, Mrs.—Mother of Rev. Septimus Crisparkle. —"What is prettier than an old lady—except a young lady—when her eyes are bright; when her figure is trim and compact; when her face is cheerful and calm; when her dress is the dress of a china shepherdess, so dainty in its colours, so individually assorted to herself, so neatly moulded on her. Nothing is prettier, thought the good Minor Canon frequently, when taking his seat at table opposite his long widowed mother."—*Edwin Drood.*

Crisparkle, Rev. Septimus.—Minor Canon at Cloisterham Cathedral.—"Septimus, because six little brother Crisparkles before him went out one by one as they were born, like six weak little rushlights as they were lighted . . . early riser; musical; classical; cheerful; kind; good-natured; social; contented; and boy-like; Mr. Crisparkle, Minor Canon and good man, lately coach upon the chief Pagan high roads, but since promoted by a patron (grateful for a well-taught son) to his present Christian beat."—*Edwin Drood.*

Crocus, Doctor.—A medical man at Belleville.—"A tall fine-looking Scotchman, but rather fierce and warlike for a professor of the peaceful art of healing."—*American Notes.*

Crookey.—An attendant at Namby's, the sheriff officer. —"The Attendant, in dress and general appearance, looked something between a bankrupt grazier and a drover in a state of insolvency."—*Pickwick Papers.*

Crowl, Mr.—A neighbour of Mr. Newman Noggs.—"A hard-featured square-faced man, elderly and shabby."—*Nicholas Nickleby.*

Crummles, Charles.—Son of Mr. Vincent Crummles, a member of the players' company.—*Nicholas Nickleby.*

Crummles, Miss C.—Daughter of Mr. Vincent Crummles a member of the players' company.—*Nicholas Nickleby.*

Crummles, Miss Ninetta.—Daughter (aged ten) of Mr. Vincent Crummles.—" This, said Mr. Vincent Crummles, bringing the maiden forward, this is the infant phenomenon, Miss Ninetta Crummles, my daughter, the idol of every place we go into."—*Nicholas Nickleby.*

Crummles, Mr. Vincent.—Actor-manager of a company of strolling players which Nicholas and Smike joined.—" He saluted Nicholas, who then observed that the face of Mr. Crummles was quite proportionate in size to his body; that he had a very full under lip, a hoarse voice, as though he were in the habit of shouting very much, and very short black hair, shaved off nearly to the crown of his head—to admit (as he afterwards learnt) of his more easily wearing character wigs of any shape or pattern."—*Nicholas Nickleby.*

Crummles, Mrs.—Wife of Mr. Vincent Crummles.—" A stout portly female, apparently between forty and fifty, in a tarnished silk cloak, with her bonnet dangling by the strings in her hand, and her hair (of which she had a great quantity) braided in a large festoon over each temple."—*Nicholas Nickleby.*

Crummles, Percy.—Son of Mr. Vincent Crummles, member of the players' company.—*Nicholas Nickleby.*

Crumpton, The Misses.—Principals of a Ladies' Seminary at Minerva House.—" The Miss Cruptons were two unusually tall, particularly thin, and exceedingly skinny personages, very upright and very yellow. Miss Amelia Crumpton owned to thirty-eight; and Miss Maria Crumpton admitted she was forty; an admission which was rendered perfectly unnecessary, by the self-evident fact of her being at least fifty. They dressed in the most interesting manner—like twins; and looked as happy and comfortable as a couple of marigolds run to seed. They were very precise, had the strictest possible ideas of propriety, wore false hair, and always smelt very strongly of lavender."—*Sketches by Boz* (Sentiment).

Cruncher, Jerry.—During the day an out-door messenger at Tellson's Bank; at night a resurrectionist.—" Except on the crown, which was raggedly bald, he had stiff black hair, standing jaggedly all over it, and growing downhill almost to his broad blunt nose. It was so like smith's work, so much more like the top of a strongly-spiked wall than a head of hair, that the best of players at leap-frog might have declined him as the most dangerous man in the world to go over."—*A Tale of Two Cities.*

Cruncher, Jerry, Junior.—Son of Jerry Cruncher, and his assistant.—*A Tale of Two Cities.*

Cruncher, Mrs.—Wife of Jerry Cruncher.—" A woman of orderly and industrious appearance."—*A Tale of Two Cities.*

Crupp, Mrs.—The landlady of the Adelphi chambers, where David resided.—" The advertisement directed us to apply to Mrs. Crupp on the premises, and we rang the area bell, which we supposed to communicate with Mrs. Crupp. It was not until we had rung three or four times, that we could prevail on Mrs. Crupp to communicate with us, but at last she appeared, being a short lady with a flounce of flannel petticoat below a nankeen gown."—*David Copperfield.*

Crushton, Hon. Mr.—Friend of Lord Mutanhed.—" The other gentleman with him, in the red under waistcoat and dark moustache, is the Honourable Mr. Crushton, his bosom friend."—*Pickwick Papers.*

Curate, The, of our Parish.—" Our Curate is a young gentleman of such prepossessing appearance and fascinating manners that, within one month after his first appearance in the Parish, half the young lady inhabitants were melancholy with religion, and the other half desponding with love. He was about twenty-five when he first came to astonish the parishioners. He parted his hair on the centre of his forehead, in the form of a Norman arch; wore a brilliant of the first water on the fourth finger of his left hand (which he always applied to his left cheek when he read prayers); and had a deep sepulchral voice of unusual solemnity."—*Sketches by Boz* (Our Parish).

Curdle, Mr.—A dramatic critic at Portsmouth; husband of Mrs. Curdle.—" He had written a pamphlet of sixty-four pages, post octavo, on the character of the Nurse's deceased husband in Romeo and Juliet; with an inquiry whether he really had been a merry man in his lifetime, or whether it was merely his widow's affectionate partiality that induced her so to report him."—*Nicholas Nickleby.*

Curdle, Mrs.—An art patron at Portsmouth upon whom Nicholas called with Miss Snevellicci.—" Mrs. Curdle was supposed, by those who were best informed on such points, to possess quite the London taste in matters relating to literature and the drama."—*Nicholas Nickleby.*

Curiosity Shop, The Old.—The business premises of Mr. Trent, the grandfather of Little Nell.—" The place, through which he wound his way at leisure, was one of these receptacles for old and curious things, which seem to crouch in odd corners of this town, and to hide their musty treasures from the public eye, in jealousy and distrust. There were suits of mail, standing like ghosts in armour here and there; fantastic carvings, brought from monkish cloisters; rusty weapons of various kinds; distorted figures in china, and wood, and iron, and ivory; tapestry and strange furniture that might have been designed in dreams."—*The Old Curiosity Shop.*

Cute, Alderman.—A patron of Trotty Veck.—" Coming out of the house at that kind of light heavy pace—that peculiar compromise between a walk and a jog trot—with which a gentleman upon the smooth down-hill of life, wearing creaking boots, a watch-chain, and clean linen, may come out of his house; not only without any abatement of his dignity, but with an expression of having important and wealthy engagements elsewhere."—*The Chimes.*

Cutler, Mr. and Mrs.—Guests at the Kenwigs' supper-party.—" A newly-married couple who had visited Mr. and Mrs. Kenwigs in their courtship."—*Nicholas Nickleby.*

Cuttle, Captain.—Friend of Sol Gills. A warm-hearted old salt, who took charge of the instrument shop when Sol Gills went in search of Walter, and who sheltered Florence Dombey when she ran away from home.—" An addition to the little party now made its appearance, in the shape of a gentleman in a wide suit of blue, with a hook instead of a hand attached to his right wrist; very bushy black eyebrows; and a thick stick in his left hand, covered all over (like his nose) with knobs. He wore a loose black silk handkerchief round his neck, and such a very large coarse shirt collar, that it looked like a small sail. . . . He was usually addressed as Captain, this visitor, and had been a pilot; or a skipper, or a privateersman; or all three perhaps; and was a very salt-looking man indeed. . . . The Captain was one of these timber-looking men, suits of oak as well as hearts, whom it is almost impossible for the liveliest imagination to separate from any part of their dress however insignificant."—*Dombey and Son.*

Dadson, Mr. and Mrs.—Guests at the school ball at Minerva House.—"Another pull at the bell. Mr. Dadson, the writing master, and his wife; the wife in green silk, with shoes and cap trimmings to correspond; the writing master in a white waistcoat, black knee shorts, and ditto silk stockings, displaying a leg large enough for two writing masters. The young ladies whispered to one another, and the writing master and his wife flattered the Miss Crumptons, who were dressed in amber with long sashes, like Dolls."—*Sketches by Boz* (Sentiment).

Daisy, Solomon.—Parish-clerk of Chigwell, one of John Willet's three cronies.—"A little man, who had little round black shiny eyes, like beads; moreover this little man wore at the knees of his rusty black breeches, and on his rusty black coat, and all down his long flapped waistcoat, little green buttons, like nothing except his eyes; but so like them, as they twinkled and glistened in the light of the fire, which shone too in his bright shoebuckles, he seemed all eyes from head to foot."—*Barnaby Rudge.*

Damiens.—A prisoner who for attempting the life of Louis XV was torn limb from limb.—*A Tale of Two Cities.*

Dancer, Daniel.—A miser whose biography Mr. Boffin pretended to be interested in.—*Our Mutual Friend.*

Dando.—The head man at Searles' boat-yard.—"What can be more amusing than Searles' yard. The head man, with the legs of his trousers carefully tucked up at the bottom—to admit the water we presume—for it is an element in which he is infinitely more at home than on land—is quite a character, and shares with the defunct oyster-swallower the celebrated name of Dando."—*Sketches by Boz* (The River).

Danton, Mr.—A guest at the Kitterbells' Christening Party.—"Mr. Danton was a young man of about five-and-twenty, with a considerable stock of impudence, and a very small share of ideas; he was a great favourite, especially with young ladies of from sixteen to twenty-six years of age both inclusive. He could imitate the French horn to admiration; sang comic songs most inimitably; and had the most insinuating way of saying impertinent nothings to his doting female admirers. He had acquired, somehow or other, the reputation of being a great wit; and accordingly, whenever he opened his mouth, everybody who knew him laughed very heartily."—*Sketches by Boz* (The Bloomsbury Christening).

Darby.—A police constable.—*Bleak House.*

Darby, Mr.—Husband of Mrs. Darby.—*The Uncommercial Traveller* (Poor Mercantile Jack).

Darby, Mrs.—Keeper of a low lodging-house in Liverpool, visited by the Uncommercial Traveller.—"It was a dirty and offensive place, with some ragged clothes drying in it; but there was a high shelf over the entrance door (to be out of the reach of marauding hands possibly) with two large white loaves on it, and a great piece of Cheshire cheese."—*The Uncommercial Traveller* (Poor Mercantile Jack).

Darnay, Charles.—The name taken in England by Charles St. Evremonde, a voluntary exile from France, who had renounced his position. Tried in London as a French spy, but acquitted, afterwards became a tutor in London, and married Lucie Manette, but having been proscribed by the Citizen Committee was arrested on revisiting France, and condemned to death, but was rescued by Sydney Carton, who personated him and went to the scaffold in his place.—*A Tale of Two Cities.*

Dartle, Miss Rosa.—Companion of Mrs. Steerforth. In love with James Steerforth.—"She had black hair and eager black eyes, and was thin. . . . I concluded in my own mind that she was about thirty years of age and that she wished to be married. . . . It appeared to me that she never said anything she wanted to say outright; but hinted it, and made a great deal more of it by this practice."—*David Copperfield.*

Datchery, Dick.—A visitor to Cloisterham.—" A white-haired personage with black eyebrows. Being buttoned up in a tightish blue surtout, with a buff waistcoat and grey trousers, he had something of a military air; but he announced himself at the Crozier (the orthodox hotel where he put up with a portmanteau) as an idle dog who lived upon his means."—*Edwin Drood.*

David.—The sexton of the parish where Mr. Marton was school-master.—" The old sexton, leaning on a crutch, was taking the air at his cottage door."—*The Old Curiosity Shop.*

David.—The butler at the house of the brothers Cheeryble.—" An ancient butler, of apoplectic appearance, and with very short legs, took up his position at the back of brother Ned's arm chair; and, waving his right arm preparatory to taking off the covers with a flourish, stood bolt upright and motionless."—*Nicholas Nickleby.*

Davis, Gill.—A private in the Royal Marines.—" I was a foundling child, picked up somewhere or another, and I always understood my Christian name to be Gill. It is true I was called Gills, when employed at Snorridge Bottom, betwixt Chatham and Maidstone, to frighten birds; but that had nothing to do with the baptism wherein I was made etc., and wherein a number of things were promised for me by somebody, who let me alone ever afterwards as to performing any of them, and who I consider must have been the Beadle."—The Perils of Certain English Prisoners (*Christmas Stories*).

Davis, Mr.—One of a company of English tourists in Rome.—" Mr. Davis always had a snuff-coloured great coat on, and carried a great green umbrella in his hand; and had a slow curiosity constantly devouring him, which prompted him to do extraordinary things, such as taking the covers off urns in tombs, and looking in at the ashes as if they were pickles. His antiquarian habits occasioned his being frequently in the rear of the rest, and one of the agonies of Mrs. Davis and the party in general was an ever present fear that Davis would be lost." *Pictures from Italy.*

Davis, Mrs.—Wife of Mr. Davis the antiquarian.—" It was impossible not to know Mrs. Davis's name, from her being always in great request among her party, and her party being everywhere. . . . I don't think she ever saw anything, or ever looked at anything, and she had always lost something out of a straw hand basket, and was trying to find it with all her might and main, among an immense quantity of English halfpence, which lay, like sands upon the sea-shore, at the bottom of it."—*Pictures from Italy*.

Dawes.—Nurse in a family where Miss Wade was governess.—"A rosy-faced woman, always making an obtrusive pretence of being gay and good-humoured."—*Little Dorrit*.

Dawkins, John (The Artful Dodger).—One of Fagin's gang of thieves, who found Oliver destitute in the street and took him to Fagin's.—"Hullo my covey, what's the row? The boy who addressed this inquiry to the young wayfarer, was about his own age, but one of the queerest-looking boys that Oliver had ever seen. He was a snub-nosed, flat-browed, common-faced boy enough; and as dirty a juvenile as one would wish to see; but he had about him all the airs and manners of a man. He was short of his age; with rather bow-legs, and little sharp ugly eyes. His hat was stuck on the top of his head so lightly that it threatened to fall off every moment, and would have done so very often if the wearer had not had a knack of every now and then giving his head a sudden switch, which brought it back to its old place again. He wore a man's coat, which reached nearly to his heels. He had turned the cuffs back, half-way up his arm, to get his hands out of the sleeves, apparently with the ultimate view of thrusting them into the pockets of his corduroy trousers, for there he kept them. He was altogether as roystering and swaggering a young gentleman as ever stood four feet six, or something less, in his bluchers."—*Oliver Twist*.

Daws, Mary.—Kitchen-maid at Mr. Dombey's; present at the discussion in the servants' hall of the bankruptcy of Dombey and Son.—"There is only one interruption to this excellent state of mind, which is occasioned by a young kitchenmaid of inferior rank—in black stockings—who, having sat with her mouth open for a long time, unexpectedly discharges from it words to this effect—suppose the wages shouldn't be paid."—*Dombey and Son*.

Dawson, Doctor.—The surgeon who attended Mrs. Robinson.—" We fancied that Mr. Dawson, the surgeon etc., who displays a large lamp, with a different colour in every pane of glass, at the corner of the row, began to be knocked up at night oftener than he used to be."—*Sketches by Boz* (Our Parish).

Deaf Gentleman, The.—One of Master Humphrey's friends.—" He produced a little set of tablets and a pencil, to facilitate our conversation, on our first acquaintance; and I well remember how awkward and constrained I was in writing down my share of the dialogue, and how easily he guessed my meaning, before I had written half of what I had to say."—*Master Humphrey's Clock.*

Dedlock, Sir Leicester.—" Is only a baronet, but there is no mightier baronet than he; his family is as old as the hills, and infinitely more respectable; he has a general opinion that the world might get on without the hills, but would be done up without Dedlocks. Sir Leicester is generally in a complacent state, and rarely bored; when he has nothing else to do, he can always contemplate his own greatness; it is a considerable advantage to a man to have so inexhaustible a subject."—*Bleak House.*

Dedlock, Lady.—Wife of Sir Leicester Dedlock, Baronet; mother of Esther Summerson.—" A whisper still goes about that she had not even family; howbeit Sir Leicester had so much family that perhaps he had enough, and could dispense with any more. But she had beauty, pride, ambition, insolvent resolve, and sense enough to portion out a legion of fine ladies; wealth and station added to these soon floated her upward; and for years now my Lady Dedlock has been at the centre of the fashionable intelligence, and at the top of the fashionable tree . . . an exhausted composure, a worn-out placidity, and equanimity of fatigue not to be ruffled by interest or satisfaction are the chief trophies of her victory; she is perfectly well-bred; if she could be translated to Heaven to-morrow she might be expected to ascend without any rapture."—*Bleak House.*

Dedlock, Sir Morbury.—An ancestor of Sir Leicester Dedlock.—*Bleak House.*

Dedlock, Lady Morbury.—Wife of Sir Morbury.—The

lady whose step was supposed to be heard on the terrace of Chesney Wold, known as The Ghost's Walk.—*Bleak House.*

Dedlock, Miss Volumnia.—A poor cousin of Sir Leicester.—" A young lady (of sixty) who is doubly highly related, having the honour to be a poor relation, by the mother's side, of another great family. She retired to Bath where she lives slenderly, on an annual present from Sir Leicester, and whence she makes occasional resurrections in the country houses of her cousins." —*Bleak House.*

Deedles.—A banker, at whose house Sir Joseph Bowley and Alderman Cute met, and who ultimately shot himself in his own counting-house.—*The Chimes.*

Defarge, Ernest.—Keeper of a wine-shop in Paris, an old servant of Dr. Manette, dominated by his wife, an ardent revolutionist.—" This wine-shop keeper was a bull-necked, martial-looking man of thirty. . . . He was a dark man altogether, with good eyes and a good bold breadth between them. . . . Defarge, with his pipe in his mouth, walked up and down, complacently admiring (his wife) but never interfering; in which condition indeed, as to the business and his domestic affairs, he walked up and down through life."—*A Tale of Two Cities.*

Defarge, Madame Thérèse.—Wife of Ernest Defarge—a revolutionist—leader of the women, one of a family whom the Evremondes had wronged, and so pursued Charles (Darnay) with vengeance; accidentally shot in a struggle with Miss Pross trying to reach Lucie Manette's room.—" Madame Defarge was a stout woman, with a watchful eye that seldom seemed to look at anything, a large hand heavily ringed, a steady face, strong features, and great composure of manner."—*A Tale of Two Cities.*

Defresnier and Cie.—Wine merchants of Neuchâtel for whom Mr. Obenreizer was London agent.—No Thoroughfare (*Christmas Stories*).

Dellombra, Signor.—The ghost who haunted the man who abducted the English Bride.—" I turned my head to the Signor Dellombra and saw that he was dressed in black and had a reserved and secret air and was a dark, miserable-looking man with black hair and a grey moustache."—*To be Read at Dusk* (Reprinted Pieces).

Demple.—A pupil at Salem House whose father was a doctor.—*David Copperfield.*

Denham, Mr.—The name assumed by Edward Longford, a poor student at the Institution, who was nursed by Milly during an illness, but under the evil spell of Redlaw, the haunted man, he forgot her kindness.—*The Haunted Man.*

Denis, Ned.—The hangman, a leader in the Gordon riots who was executed with Hugh.—" A squat, thick-set personage with a low retreating forehead, a coarse shock head of hair, and eyes so small and near together that his broken nose alone seemed to prevent their meeting, and fusing into one of the usual size."—*Barnaby Rudge.*

Dentist's Servant, The.—" Is that man no mystery to us, no type of invisible power? The tremendous individual knows (who else does) what is done with the extracted teeth; he knows what goes on in the little room where something is always being washed or filed; he knows what warm, spicy infusion is put into the comfortable tumbler, from which we rinse our wounded mouth, with a gap in it that feels a foot wide. The conviction of my coward conscience, when I see that man in a professional light, is that he knows all the statistics of my teeth and gums, my double teeth; my single teeth; my stopped teeth, and my sound."—*The Uncommercial Traveller* (Arcadian London).

Deputy.—A boy employed at a travellers' lodging-house in Cloisterham.—" All us man-servants at Travellers' Lodgings is named Deputy. When we're chock full, and the Travellers is all abed, I come out for my 'elth."—(*See* **Winks.**)—*Edwin Drood.*

Darrick, John.—The manservant of the foreman of the jury.—" John Derrick, my trusty and attached servant for more than twenty years."—The Trial for Murder (*Christmas Stories*).

Devasseur, Loyal.—A French citizen.—" His own family name is simply Loyal; but as he is married, and as in that part of France a husband always adds to his own name the family name of his wife, he writes himself Loyal Devasseur."—*Our French Watering Place* (Reprinted Pieces).

Dibabs, Jane.—A lady referred to by Mrs. Nickleby who had married a man older than herself.—" Jane Dibabs, she married a man who was a great deal older than herself, and *would* marry him, notwithstanding all that could be said to the contrary, and she was so fond of him that nothing was ever equal to it."—*Nicholas Nickleby.*

Dibble, Mrs. Dorothy.—Wife of Sampson Dibble.—*The Uncommercial Traveller* (Bound for the Great Salt Lake).

Dibble, Sampson.—A blind emigrant on board the *Amazon.*—*The Uncommercial Traveller* (Bound for the Great Salt Lake).

Dick.—The guard of the coach which carried Mr. Squeers and Nicholas to Dotheboys Hall.—" All right behind there, Dick, cried the coachman. All right, was the reply, off she goes."—*Nicholas Nickleby.*

Dick.—One of the boarded-out pauper children. Friend of Oliver.—" The child was pale and thin; his cheeks were sunken; and his eyes large and bright; the scanty parish dress, the livery of his misery, hung loosely on his feeble body, and his young limbs had wasted away like those of an old man."—*Oliver Twist.*

Dick.—Hostler at Salisbury Inn.—*Martin Chuzzlewit.*

Dick, Mr.—A slightly crazed but harmless old gentleman who resided with Miss Betsy Trotwood and by his own desire was called Mr. Dick, although his real name was Babley, who occupied himself writing a memorial about his affairs.—" Mr. Dick, as I have already said, was grey-headed and florid; I should have said all about him in saying so, had not his head been curiously bowed—not by age—it reminded me of one of Mr. Creakle's boy's heads after a beating—and his grey eyes prominent and large, with a strange kind of watery brightness in them, that made me in combination with his vacant manner, his submission to my aunt, and his childish delight when she praised him, suspect him of being a little mad. . . . Every day of his life he had a long sitting at the Memorial which never made the least progress, however hard he laboured, for King Charles the First always strayed into it sooner or later, and then it was thrown aside and another one begun."—*David Copperfield.*

Diego, Don.—Inventor of a flying machine.—"Don Diego de—I forget his name—the inventor of the last new Flying Machine."—*A Flight* (Reprinted Pieces).

Digby, Mr.—The theatrical name of Smike.—*Nicholas Nickleby.*

Dilber, Mrs.—A customer of Joe, the receiver of stolen goods.—"Mrs. Dilber was next: sheets and towels, a little wearing apparel, two old-fashioned silver teaspoons, a pair of sugar-tongs, and a few boots."—*A Christmas Carol.*

Dingo, Professor.—The second husband of Mrs. Bayham Badger.—*Bleak House.*

Dingwall, Cornelius, M.P.—Father of Miss Brooks, a pupil at Minerva House.—"Cornelius Brooks Dingwall, Esq., M.P., was very haughty, solemn, and portentous. He had naturally a somewhat spasmodic expression of countenance, which was not rendered the less remarkable by his wearing an extremely stiff cravat. He was wonderfully proud of the M.P. attached to his name, and never lost an opportunity of reminding people of his dignity. He had a great idea of his own abilities, which must have been a great comfort to him, as no one else had."—*Sketches by Boz* (Sentiment).

Dingwall, Master Frederick.—Son of Mr. Brooks Dingwall, M.P.—"One of these public nuisances, a spoiled child, was playing about the room, dressed after the most approved fashion, in a blue tunic with a black belt a quarter of a yard wide, fastened with an immense buckle, looking like a robber in a melodrama, seen through a diminishing glass."—*Sketches by Boz* (Sentiment).

Dingwall, Miss Lavinia.—Daughter of Mr Brooks Dingwall, M.P.—"Miss Brooks Dingwall was one of that numerous class of young ladies who, like adverbs, may be known by their answering to a commonplace question, and doing nothing else."—*Sketches by Boz* (Sentiment).

Dingwall, Mrs. Brooks.—Wife of Mr. Brooks Dingwall, M.P.—*Sketches by Boz* (Sentiment).

Diogenes.—Dr. Blimber's dog; which, having been a pet of Paul's, Mr. Toots obtained and presented to Florence Dombey, after Paul's death.—"Though Diogenes was as ridiculous a dog as we could meet with on a summer's day; a blundering, ill-favoured, clumsy, bullet-headed dog, continually acting on a wrong idea that there was an enemy in the neighbourhood whom it was meritorious to bark at; and though he was far from good-tempered, and certainly was not clever, and had hair all over his eyes, and a comic nose, and an inconsistent tail, and a gruff voice, he was dearer to Florence in virtue of that parting remembrance of him, and that request that he might be taken care of, than the most valuable and beautiful of his kind."—*Dombey and Son.*

Dismal Jemmy.—A strolling player whom Mr. Pickwick met at Rochester.—"A careworn-looking man, whose sallow face and deeply sunken eyes were rendered still more striking than nature had made them, by the straight black hair which hung in matted disorder half way down his face."—*Pickwick Papers.*

Diver, Colonel.—Editor of the *New York Rowdy Journal.*—"A sallow gentleman, with sunken cheeks, black hair, small twinkling eyes, and a singular expression hovering about that region of his face, which was not a frown, nor a leer, and yet might have been mistaken at the first glance for either; indeed it would have been difficult, on a much closer acquaintance, to describe it in any more satisfactory terms than a mixed expression of cunning and conceit."—*Martin Chuzzlewit.*

Dixons, The.—In the audience at the private theatricals at Rose Villa.—(*See* **Glumper.**)—*Sketches by Boz* (Mrs. Joseph Porter).

Dobble, Junior.—Son of Mr. Dobble.—*Sketches by Boz* (The New Year).

Dobble, Miss Julia.—Daughter of Mr. Dobble.—*Sketches by Boz* (The New Year).

Dobble, Mr.—The host of the New Year Party at the

house with the green blinds.—" The master of the house with the green blinds is in a public office; we know that by the cut of his coat, the tie of his neckcloth, and the self-satisfaction of his gait—the very green blinds themselves have a Somerset House air about them."—*Sketches by Boz* (The New Year).

Dobble, Mrs.—Wife of Mr. Dobble.—*Sketches by Boz* (The New Year).

Dobbleton, The Dowager Duchess of.—Referred to by Mrs. Waters on the Ramsgate boat.—" When, in the course of further conversation, it was discovered that Miss Charlotta Tuggs was the facsimile of a titled relative of Mrs. Belinda Waters; and that Mrs. Tuggs herself was the very picture of the Dowager Duchess of Dobbleton; their delight in the acquisition of so genteel and friendly an acquaintance knew no bounds."—*Sketches by Boz* (The Tuggses at Ramsgate).

Doche, Madame.—A dealer at Poissy Cattle Market. —*A Monument of French Folly* (Reprinted Pieces).

Doctor's Servant, The.—" We all know the Doctor's Servant,—we all know what a respectable man he is; what a hard dry man; what a firm man; who knows minutely what is the matter with us but from whom the rack should not wring the secret."—*The Uncommercial Traveller* (Arcadian London).

Dodger, The Artful.—The nickname of Dawkins.—(*See* **Dawkins, John.**)—*Oliver Twist.*

Dodger, The Hon. Ananias.—An American financier.—" I had not then broken away from the American gentleman in the travellers' parlour of the Convent; who, sitting with his face to the fire, had undertaken to realize to me the whole progress of events which had led to the accumulation by The Honourable Ananias Dodger of one of the largest acquisitions of dollars ever made in our country." —*To be Read at Dusk* (Reprinted Pieces).

Dodgington, Vicar of.—Who granted Mr. and Mrs. Anderson a certificate of character.—" As you come up with this spectacle of virtue in distress, Mrs. Anderson rises, and, with a decent curtsey, presents for your consideration a certificate from a Doctor of Divinity, the

Reverend the Vicar of Upper Dodgington, who informs his Christian friends and all whom it may concern, that the bearers, John Anderson and lawful wife, are persons to whom you cannot be too liberal."—*The Uncommercial Traveller* (Tramps).

Dodson and Fogg.—Solicitors for Mrs. Bardell.—"In the ground-floor front of a dingy house, at the very furthest end of Freeman's Court, Cornhill, sat the four clerks of Messrs. Dodson and Fogg, two of His Majesty's Attorneys of the Courts of King's Bench and Common Pleas at Westminster; and Solicitors of the High Court of Chancery."—*Pickwick Papers.*

Dodson, Mr.—Partner of the firm of Dodson and Fogg, Solicitors.—" A plump, portly, stern-looking man, with a loud voice."—*Pickwick Papers.*

Dogginson, Mr.—A vestryman.—" Regarded in our vestry as a regular John Bull; we believe in consequence of his having always made up his mind on every subject, without knowing anything about it."—*Our Vestry* (Reprinted Pieces).

Dolloby.—A dealer in secondhand clothes, to whom David sold his waistcoat when he ran away from London. —" The master of this shop was sitting at the door, in his shirt sleeves, smoking; and as there were a great many coats and pairs of trousers dangling from the low ceiling, and only two feeble candles burning inside to show what they were, I fancied that he looked like a man of revengeful disposition, who had hung all his enemies and was enjoying himself."—*David Copperfield.*

Dolphin's Head.—An inn visited by the Uncommercial Traveller.—" The sign of the House was The Dolphin's Head,—why only head I don't know; for the Dolphin's effigy at full length, and upside down—as a dolphin is always bound to be when artistically treated, though I suppose he is sometimes right side upward in his natural condition—graced the sign-board."—*The Uncommercial Traveller* (An Old Stage Coaching House).

Dombey and Son.—Paul Dombey, the Elder, and Paul, the Younger.—" Dombey was about eight-and-forty years of age,—son about eight-and-forty minutes. Dombey was rather bald, rather red, and though a handsome, well-made man, too stern and pompous in appearance to be prepossessing. Son was very bald and very red, and though (of course) an undeniably fine infant, somewhat crushed and spotty in his general effect as yet."—*Dombey and Son.*

Dombey, Florence.—Daughter of Mr. Dombey, a sweet girl but unregarded by her father, for whom she nevertheless cherished a warm affection, and to whom she became reconciled after her father's fortunes became broken. Married Walter Gay, the nephew of Sol Gills.—" There had been a girl some years before . . . but what was a girl to Dombey and Son. In the capital of the house's name and dignity, such a child was merely a piece of base coin, that couldn't be invested—a bad boy—nothing more."—*Dombey and Son.*

Dombey, Mrs. Fanny.—First wife of Mr. Dombey, mother of Paul Dombey, the Younger, died at his birth.—" Of these years he had been married ten,—married as some said to a lady with no heart to give him, whose happiness was in the past, and who was content to bind her broken spirit to the dutiful and meek endurance of the present."—*Dombey and Son.*

Dombey, Paul, the Elder.—A London merchant, sole partner of Dombey and Son.—" He had risen, as his father had before him, in the course of life and death, from Son to Dombey, and for nearly twenty years had been the sole representative of the firm."—*Dombey and Son.*

Dombey, Paul, the Younger.—Son of Mr. Dombey, a delicate dreamy boy devotedly attached to his sister Florence; died in his early youth.—*Dombey and Son.*

Donny, Misses.—Principals of Greenleaf, the boarding-school where Esther Summerson was educated.—" We were twelve boarders; and there were two Miss Donnys—twins."—*Bleak House.*

Doodle, Sir Thomas.—A party politician.—" At last Sir Thomas Doodle has not only condescended to come in, but has done it handsomely, bringing in with him all his nephews, all his male cousins, and all his brothers-in-law. so there is hope for the old ship yet."—*Bleak House.*

Dor, Madam.—A Swiss woman, Mr. Obenreizer's housekeeper.—" She was a true Swiss impersonation of another kind; from the breadth of her cushion-like back, and the ponderosity of her respectable legs (if the word be admissible), to the black velvet band tied tightly round her throat, for the repression of a rising tendency to goitre; or higher still to her great copper-coloured gold ear-rings; or higher still to her head-dress of black gauze, stretched on wire." —No Thoroughfare (*Christmas Stories*).

Dorker.—A pupil at Dotheboys Hall, who died there. —*Nicholas Nickleby.*

Dornton, Sergeant.—A London police officer.—" Sergeant Dornton, about fifty years of age, with a ruddy face and a high sunburnt forehead, has the air of one who has been a Sergeant in the army; he might have sat to Wilkie for the soldier in 'The Reading of the Will.' "—*The Detective Police* (Reprinted Pieces).

Dorrit, Amy (Little Dorrit).—A seamstress; daughter of Mr. Dorrit, the father of the Marshalsea Prison; afterwards married Arthur Clennam.—" It was not easy to make out Little Dorrit's face; she was so retiring; plied her needle in such removed corners; and started away so scared if encountered on the stairs; but it seemed to be a pale transparent face, quiet in expression, though not beautiful in feature; its soft hazel eyes excepted. A delicately bent head, a tiny form, a quiet little pair of busy hands, and a shabby dress—it must needs have been very shabby to look at all so, being so neat,—were Little Dorrit as she sat at work."—*Little Dorrit.*

Dorrit, Edward, Jr. (Tip).—Brother of Little Dorrit.—" Tip began to supersede Mrs. Bangham, and to execute commissions in a knowing manner; and to be of the prison prisonous, and of the streets streety."—(*See* **Tip.**)—*Little Dorrit.*

Dorrit, Fanny.—Sister of Little Dorrit; a theatre dancer; married Edmund Sparkler.—*Little Dorrit.*

Dorrit, Frederick.—Brother of William Dorrit.—" There was a ruined uncle in the family group; ruined by his brother, the Father of the Marshalsea, and knowing no more how than his ruiner did, but accepting the fact as an inevitable certainty. . . . Naturally a retired and simple man, he had shown no particular sense of being ruined at the time when that calamity fell upon him, further than that he left off washing himself when the shock was announced, and never took to that luxury any more. He had been a very indifferent musical amateur in his better days, and, when he fell with his brother, resorted for support to playing a clarionet, as dirty as himself, in a small theatre orchestra."—*Little Dorrit.*

Dorrit, Mrs. William.—Mother of Little Dorrit.—" When his youngest child was eight years old, his wife who had long been languishing away—of her own inherent weakness, not that she retained any greater sensitiveness as to her place of abode than he did—went upon a visit to a poor friend and old nurse in the country, and died there."—*Little Dorrit.*

Dorrit, William.—Father of Little Dorrit, for twenty-five years an inmate of a debtor's prison.—" He was a shy, retiring man; well looking, though in an effeminate style, with a mild voice, curling hair, and irresolute hands—rings upon the fingers in those days—which nervously wandered to his trembling lip a hundred times in the first half-hour of his acquaintance with the jail. Crushed at first with his imprisonment, he had soon found a dull relief in it; he was under lock and key; but the lock and key which kept him in, kept numbers of his troubles out. If he had been a man with strength of purpose to face those troubles, and fight them, he might have broken the net which held him—or broken his heart; but, being what he was, he languidly slipped into his smooth descent, and never more took one step upward. Tradition afterwards handed down from generation to generation—a Marshalsea generation might be calculated as about three months—that the shabby old debtor with the soft manner and the white hair was the Father of Marshalsea."—*Little Dorrit.*

Dot.—The pet name of Mrs. Peerybingle.—" I wish you wouldn't call me Dot, John. I don't like it, said Mrs. Peerybingle; pouting in a way that clearly showed she *did* like it very much."—*The Cricket on the Hearth.*

Dotheboys Hall.—Mr. Squeers' school.—" Youth are boarded, clothed, booked, furnished with pocket money, provided with all necessaries, instructed in all languages living and dead, mathematics, orthography, geometry, astromony, trigonometry, the use of the globes, algebra, single stick (if required), writing, arithmetic, fortification, and every other branch of classical literature; terms Twenty guineas per annum; no extras; no vacations; and diet unparalleled."—*Nicholas Nickleby.*

Doubledick, Richard.—The hero of a tale told at the Christmas Dinner at Watt's Charity for Poor Travellers.—"He came down to Chatham, to enlist in a cavalry regiment, if a cavalry regiment would have him; if not, to take King George's shilling from any Corporal or Sergeant who would put a band of ribbon in his hat; his object was to get shot; but he thought he might as well ride to death as be at the trouble of walking."—(*See* **Marshall, Mary.**)—The Seven Poor Travellers (*Christmas Stories*).

Dounce, John.—One of the steady old boys.—"The steady old boys are certain stout old gentlemen, of clean appearance, who are always to be seen in the same taverns, at the same hours every evening, smoking and drinking in the same company. Mr. John Dounce was an old boy of the latter class (we don't mean immortal but steady)—a retired glove and braces maker, a widower resident with three daughters—all grown up and all unmarried—in Cursitor Street, Chancery Lane. He was a short, round, large-faced, tubbish sort of man, with a broad-brimmed hat and a square coat, and had that grave but confident kind of roll peculiar to old boys in general."—*Sketches by Boz* (The Misplaced Attachment of Mr. John Dounce).

Dowdle, Misses.—Principals of a school in Devonshire where Kate Nickleby was educated.—"When she was at school in Devonshire, said Mrs. Nickleby, she was universally allowed to be beyond all exception the very cleverest girl there, and there were a great many clever ones too, and that's the truth; twenty-five young ladies; fifty guineas a year, without the et ceteras; both the Miss Dowdles the most accomplished, elegant, fascinating creatures."—*Nicholas Nickleby.*

Dowler, Mr.—A fellow-traveller to Bath with the Pickwickians.—"A stern-eyed man of about five-and-forty, who had a bald and glossy forehead, with a good deal of black hair at the sides and back of his head, and large black whiskers. He looked up from his breakfast, as Mr.

Pickwick entered, with a fierce and peremptory air which was very dignified; and having scrutinized that gentleman and his companions to his entire satisfaction, hummed a tune, in a manner which seemed to say that he rather suspected somebody wanted to take advantage of him, but it wouldn't do."—*Pickwick Papers.*

Dowler, Mrs.—Wife of Mr. Dowler.—" The fierce gentleman immediately proceeded to inform the friends, in the same short abrupt jerking sentences, that his name was Dowler; that he was going to Bath on pleasure; that he was formerly in the Army; that he had now set up in business as a gentleman; that he lived upon the profits; and that the individual for whom the second place was taken was a personage no less illustrious than Mrs. Dowler, his lady wife."—*Pickwick Papers.*

Doyce, Daniel.—A mechanical inventor.—" He was not much to look at, either in point of size, or in point of dress; being merely a short, square, practical-looking man, whose hair had turned grey, and in whose face and forehead there were deep lines of cogitation, which locked as though they were carved in hard wood. He was dressed in decent black, a little rusty, and had the appearance of a sagacious master in some handicraft. He had a spectacle case in his hand, which he turned over and over, with a certain free use of the thumb, that is never seen but in a hand accustomed to tools."—*Little Dorrit.*

Doze, Professor.—A Vice-President of the Zoology and Botany Section of the Mudfog Association.—*The Mudfog Sketches.*

Drawley, Mr.—A Vice-President of the Zoology and Botany Section of the Mudfog Association.—*The Mudfog Sketches.*

Dringworth Brothers.—The employers of Laurence Clissold who borrowed money from Mr. Tregarthen.—" He had borrowed it on the written statement that it was to be laid out in furtherance of a speculation, which he expected would raise him to independence; he being, at the time of writing that letter, no more than a clerk in the House of Dringworth Brothers, America Square, London."—A Message from the Sea (*Christmas Stories*).

Drooce.—A sergeant of marines on board the ship

Christopher Columbus.—" The Sergeant's name was Drooce. He was the most tyrannical non-commissioned officer in Her Majesty's Service."—The Perils of Certain English Travellers (*Christmas Stories*).

Drood, Edwin.—Nephew of John Jasper; mysteriously disappeared.—*Edwin Drood.*

Drowvey, Miss.—Partner with Miss Grimmer in girls' school.—" Drowvey and Grimmer is the partnership; and opinion is divided which is the greatest beast."—*Holiday Romance.*

Drummle, Bentley.—Pip's fellow-student at Matthew Pocket's.—" Bentley Drummle was so sulky a fellow that he even took up a book as if its writer had done him an injury, and did not take up an acquaintance in a more agreeable spirit. Heavy in figure, movement, and comprehension, in the sluggish complexion of his face, and in the large awkward tongue that seemed to loll about in his mouth, as he himself lolled about in a room—he was idle, forward, niggardly, reserved, and suspicious. He came of rich people down in Somersetshire, who had nursed this combination of qualities, until they made the discovery that it was just of age and a blockhead. Thus Bentley Drummle had come to Mr. Pocket when he was a head taller than that gentleman, and half a dozen heads thicker than most gentlemen."—*Great Expectations.*

Dubbley.—A constable at Ipswich.—" A dirty-faced man, something over six feet high, and stout in proportion. Mr. Dubbley was a man of few wants."—*Pickwick Papers.*

Duchess, The.—Alicia's doll.—" The Princess Alicia hurried upstairs to tell a most particular secret, to a most particular confidential friend of hers, who was a Duchess; people did suppose her to be a doll; but she was really a Duchess, although nobody knew it except the Princess."—*Holiday Romance.*

Duff.—One of the Bow Street officers who called at Mrs. Maylie's to investigate the burglary.—" A red-headed bony man, in top boots, with a rather ill-favoured countenance, and a turned-up sinister-looking nose."—*Oliver Twist.*

Dull, Mr.—A member of the Mudfog Association.—*The Mudfog Sketches.*

Dullborough.—The town where the Uncommercial Traveller spent his youth.—" I call my boyhood's home (and I feel like a Tenor in an English Opera when I mention it) Dullborough. Most of us come from Dullborough who come from a country town."—*The Uncommercial Traveller* (Dullborough Town).

Dumbledon.—A pupil at our school.—" We remember an idiotic goggle-eyed boy, with a big head and half-crowns without end, who suddenly appeared as a parlour boarder, and was rumoured to have come by sea from some mysterious part of the earth, where his parents rolled in gold."—*Our School* (Reprinted Pieces).

Dumkins, Mr.—A member of the All Muggleton Cricket Club.—*Pickwick Papers.*

Dummy, Mr.—A member of the Mudfog Association. —*The Mudfog Sketches.*

Dumps, Nicodemus.—Bachelor-uncle of Mr. Charles Kitterbell, and godfather to his child.—" Mr. Nicodemus Dumps, or as his acquaintance called him ' Long Dumps,' was a bachelor; six feet high, and fifty years old; cross, cadaverous, odd, and ill-natured. He was never happy but when he was miserable; and always miserable when he had the best reason to be happy."—*Sketches by Boz* (The Bloomsbury Christening).

Dundey, Doctor.—" There was a Bank in Ireland robbed of seven thousand pounds, by a person of the name of Doctor Dundey, who escaped to America."—*The Detective Police* (Reprinted Pieces).

Dunkle, Doctor Ginnery.—One of the interviewers of Elijah Pogram.—*Martin Chuzzlewit.*

Dunstable.—The village butcher with whom the pompous Pumblechook terrified Pip when a child, by supposing him to have been born a pig.—" And what would have been your destination? You would have been disposed of for so many shillings, according to the market price of the article, and Dunstable, the butcher, would have come to you as you lay in your straw, and he would have whipped you under his left arm, and with his right he would have tucked up his frock to get a penknife out of his waistcoat pocket, and he would have shed your blood, and had your life. No bringing up by hand, then,—not a bit of it."—*Great Expectations.*

Durdles.—A stonemason at Cloisterham.—" Durdles is a stonemason, chiefly in the gravestone tomb and monument way, and wholly of their colour from head to foot. In a suit of coarse flannel, with horn buttons, a yellow neckerchief, with draggled ends, an old hat more russet coloured than black, and laced boots of the hue of his stony calling, Durdles leads a lazy gipsy sort of life; carrying his dinner about with him in a small bundle, and sitting on all manner of tombstones to dine."—*Edwin Drood.*

Eatanswill.—The borough where Mr. Pickwick witnessed an election.—" The Eatanswill people, like the people of many other small towns, considered themselves of the utmost and most mighty importance; and every man in Eatanswill, conscious of the weight that attached to his example, felt himself bound to unite heart and soul with one of the two great parties that divided the town—the Blues and the Buffs."—*Pickwick Papers.*

" Eatanswill Gazette."—The political organ of the Blues. —" The *Gazette* warned the Electors of Eatanswill that the eyes, not only of England, but of the whole civilized world, were upon them."—*Pickwick Papers.*

" Eatanswill Independent."—The political organ of the Buffs.—" The *Independent* imperatively demanded to know whether the constituency of Eatanswill were the grand fellows they had always taken them for; or base and servile tools, undeserving alike of the name of Englishmen and the blessings of freedom."—*Pickwick Papers.*

Edkins, Mr.—One of the committee of the Steam Excursion.—" A pale young gentleman in a green stock, and spectacles of the same, a member of the honourable Society of the Inner Temple."—*Sketches by Boz* (The Steam Excursion).

Edmunds, John.—A convict whose story was related by the clergyman of Dingley Dell.—*Pickwick Papers.*

Edmunds, Mr.—Father of John. A drunkard.—" A morose, savage-hearted bad man, idle and dissolute in his habits; cruel and ferocious in his disposition."—*Pickwick Papers.*

Edmunds, Mrs.—Mother of John. Ill-used by her husband.—" The woman's increasing and unwearied exertions early and late, morning, noon and night kept them above actual want; these exertions were but ill repaid."—*Pickwick Papers.*

Edson, Jemmy.—Son of Mr. and Mrs. Edson, adopted by Mrs. Lirriper.—Mrs. Lirriper's Lodgings (*Christmas Stories*).

Edson, Mr.—A boarder at Mrs. Lirriper's who deserted his wife.—Mrs. Lirriper's Lodgings (*Christmas Stories*).

Edward.—The name of the donkey of the costermonger of whom Wegg inquired the way to Boffin's Bower.—" Why yer mean old Harmon's, do yer, said the hoarse gentleman who was driving his donkey in a truck, with a carrot for a whip, why didn't yer never say so. Eddard and me is going by him. Jump in."—*Our Mutual Friend.*

Edward.—One of two brothers wrecked in the ship *Polyphemus,* for whom his younger brother sacrificed himself.—*Dombey and Son.*

Edwards, Miss.—A pupil-teacher at Miss Monflathers' school.—" This young lady, being motherless and poor, was apprenticed at the school—taught for nothing—teaching others what she learned for nothing—boarded for nothing—lodged for nothing—and set down and rated as something immeasurably less than nothing by all the dwellers in the house."—*The Old Curiosity Shop.*

Edwin.—Charley's friend and supposed rival, whom he met at The Holly Tree Inn on his way to Gretna Green with Emmeline, cousin of Angela.—The Holly Tree (*Christmas Stories*).

Elizabeth, Miss.—The name given by Silas Wegg to one of the inmates of the house near which he set up his stall.—" He always spoke of it as our house . . . he knew so little about the inmates, that he gave them names of his own invention, as Miss Elizabeth; Master George; Aunt Jane; Uncle Parker; having no authority whatever for any such descriptions."—*Our Mutual Friend.*

Ellis, Mr.—One of the company at a City Road public-house.—" A sharp-nosed, light-haired man, in a brown surtout reaching nearly to his heels."—*Sketches by Boz* (The Parlour Orator).

Elwes, John.—A miser whose biography Mr. Boffin pretended to be interested in.—*Our Mutual Friend.*

Emile.—A private soldier billeted in a French town.—"Was there not Emile, billeted at the clockmaker's, perpetually turning to of an evening, with his coat off, winding up the stock."—Somebody's Luggage (*Christmas Stories*).

Emilia.—Mrs. Orange's baby.—*Holiday Romance.*

Emily.—The elder of two sisters removed in a prison van.—(*See* **Bella.**)—*Sketches by Boz* (The Prisoner's Van).

Emily, Little.—Niece of Daniel Peggotty. Seamstress at Omer and Joram's. Affianced to her cousin Ham, but eloped on the eve of the marriage day with Steerforth. Afterwards found by her uncle and taken to Australia.—*David Copperfield.*

Emma.—Waitress at an English Anglers' Inn.—"The peerless Emma, with the bright eyes and the pretty smile; who waited, bless her, with a natural grace, that would have converted a Blue Beard."—The Holly Tree (*Christmas Stories*).

Emma.—A maidservant at Manor Farm.—*Pickwick Papers.*

Emmeline.—Cousin of Angela Leath. Eloped with Charley's friend Edwin.—"Emmeline was Angela's cousin; lived with her; had been brought up with her; was her father's ward; had property. . . . She was wrapped in soft white fur, like the snowy landscape, but was warm, and young, and lovely."—The Holly Tree (*Christmas Stories*).

Endell, Martha.—A schoolmate of Little Emily, whom Emily befriended when Martha went astray; and who afterwards assisted Mr. Peggotty in his search for Little Emily, and ultimately emigrated with her.—*David Copperfield.*

Estella.—The adopted daughter of Miss Havisham, who was trained by her to heartless treatment of mankind. Ultimately married Pip.—*Great Expectations.*

Eugene.—A private soldier billeted in a French town. —" Was there not Eugene, billeted at the Tinman's, cultivating, pipe in mouth, a garden four feet square, for the Tinman, in the little Court behind the shop, and extorting the fruits of the earth from the same, on his knees, with the sweat of his brow."—Somebody's Luggage (*Christmas Stories*).

Evans, Miss Jemima.—Affianced to Mr. Samuel Wilkins.—" Down came Jemima herself soon afterwards, in a white muslin gown carefully hooked and eyed; a little red shawl plentifully pinned; a white straw bonnet, trimmed with red ribbons; a small necklace; a large pair of bracelets; Denmark satin shoes; and openwork stockings; white cotton gloves on her fingers; and a cambric pocket handkerchief, carefully folded up, in her hand—all quite genteel and ladylike."—*Sketches by Boz* (Miss Evans and the Eagle).

Evans, Miss Tilly.—Sister of Jemima Evans.—" I wos thinking, said Mr. Samuel Evans, during a pause in the conversation,—I wos thinking of taking J'mima to the Eagle to-night—Oh my! exclaimed Mrs. Evans. Lor how nice, said the youngest Miss Evans; well I declare, added the youngest Miss Evans but one; tell Jemima to put on her white muslin, Tilly, screamed Mrs. Evans, with motherly anxiety."—*Sketches by Boz* (Miss Evans and the Eagle).

Evans, Mr.—One of the players at the private theatricals at Rose Villa.—" A tall, thin, pale young gentleman, with extensive whiskers."—*Sketches by Boz* (Mrs. Joseph Porter).

Evans, Mrs.—Mother of Jemima.—" Miss Evans (or Ivins, to adopt the pronunciation most in vogue with her circle of acquaintance) had adopted in early life the useful pursuit of shoe binding; to which she afterwards super-added the occupation of a straw-bonnet maker. Herself, her maternal parent, and two sisters, formed an harmonious quartette in the most secluded portion of Camden Town."—*Sketches by Boz* (Miss Evans and the Eagle).

Evans, Richard.—A pupil at Mr. Marton's school.— " An amazing boy to learn; blessed with a good memory; with a good voice and ear for psalm-singing."—*The Old Curiosity Shop*.

Evans, Superintendent.—A Thames police officer.—*Down with the Tide* (Reprinted Pieces).

Evenson, John.—A boarder at Mrs. Tibbs'.—" Mr. John Evenson was in the receipt of an independent income, arising chiefly from various houses he owned in the different suburbs. He was very morose and discontented. He was a thorough radical, and used to attend a great variety of public meetings, for the express purpose of finding fault with everything that was proposed."—*Sketches by Boz* (The Boarding House).

Exchange or Barter.—The nickname of a pupil at Salem House.—" I heard that one boy, who was a coal merchant's son, came as a set off against the coal bill, and was called on that account Exchange or Barter, a name selected from the arithmetic book as expressing this arrangement."—*David Copperfield.*

Ezekiel.—The boy at Mugby Junction Refreshment Room.—" I am the boy at what is called the refreshment room at Mugby Junction, whose proudest boast is that it never yet refreshed a mortal being."—Mugby Junction (*Christmas Stories*).

Face Maker, The.—A performer at a fair in a Flemish town.—" A corpulent little man, in a large white waistcoat, with a comic countenance, and with a wig in his hand."—*The Uncommercial Traveller* (In the French Flemish Country).

Fagin.—Keeper of a thieves' den in London.—" A very old shrivelled Jew, whose villainous-looking and repulsive face was obscured by a quantity of matted red hair."—*Oliver Twist.*

Fairfax, Mr.—The censorious young gentleman.—" Has a reputation among his familiars of a remarkably clever person."—*Sketches of Young Gentlemen.*

Family Pet.—The name of a housebreaker whom Duff, the Bow Street officer, suspected of the burglary at Mrs. Maylie's.—" Blathers and Duff, being rewarded with a couple of guineas, returned to town, with divided opinions on the subject of their expedition; the latter gentleman, on mature consideration of all the circumstances, inclining to the belief that the burglarious attempt had originated with the Family Pet."—*Oliver Twist.*

Fan.—A little sister of Scrooge, whom the Ghost of Christmas Past showed him.—" Always a delicate creature, whom a breath might have withered, said the Ghost, but she had a large heart. So she had, cried Scrooge, you're right."—*A Christmas Carol.*

Fanchette.—Daughter of a Swiss innkeeper.—*Our Bore* (Reprinted Pieces).

Fang, Mr.—The magistrate before whom Oliver was charged with theft.—" Mr. Fang was a lean, long-backed, stiff-necked, middle-sized man, with no great quantity of hair, and what he had growing on the back and sides of his head. His face was stern, and much flushed. If he were really not in the habit of drinking rather more than was exactly good for him, he might have brought an action against his countenance for libel, and have recovered heavy damages."—*Oliver Twist.*

Fanny.—A pretty child.—" Presently they came to one of the prettiest girls that ever was seen,—just like Fanny in the corner there."—*The Child's Story* (Reprinted Pieces).

Fareway, Adelina.—Sister of Mr. Fareway.—" Everything in mental acquisition that her brother might have been if he would; and everything, in all gracious charms and admirable qualities, that no one but herself could be—this was Adelina."—*George Silverman's Explanation.*

Fareway, Lady.—Mother of Mr. Fareway.—" I saw in my Lady Fareway a handsome well-preserved lady, of somewhat large stature, with a steady glare in her great round dark eyes that embarrassed me."—*George Silverman's Explanation.*

Fareway, Mr.—A pupil of George Silverman's.—" This young gentleman's abilities were much above the average; but he came of a rich family, and was idle and luxurious. He presented himself to me too late; and afterwards came to me too irregularly, to admit of my being of much service to him."—*George Silverman's Explanation.*

Fareway, Sir George.—The deceased husband of Lady Fareway.—*George Silverman's Explanation.*

Fee, Doctor W. R.—A member of the Medical Section of the Mudfog Association.—*The Mudfog Sketches.*

Feeder, Mr.—Dr. Blimber's assistant, and ultimately his successor; married Cornelia Blimber.—"As to Mr. Feeder, B.A., Dr. Blimber's Assistant, he was a kind of human barrel-organ, with a little list of tunes, at which he was continually working over and over again, without any variation."—*Dombey and Son.*

Feeder, Rev. Alfred.—Brother of Mr. Feeder, who officiated at his marriage to Cornelia Blimber.—*Dombey and Son.*

Feenix, Lord.—Cousin of the second Mrs. Dombey.——"Cousin Feenix has come over from abroad expressly to attend the marriage. Cousin Feenix was a man about town, forty years ago; but he is still so juvenile in figure, and in manner, and so well got up, that strangers are amazed when they discover latent wrinkles in his Lordship's face, and crows' feet in his eyes, and first observe him not exactly certain, when he walks across a room, of going quite straight to where he wants to go."—*Dombey and Son.*

Fendall, Sergeant.—A London police officer.—"A light-haired, well-spoken polite person."—*The Detective Police* (Reprinted Pieces).

Ferdinand, Miss.—A lively pupil at Nuns' House.—"The daring Miss Ferdinand had even surprised the company with a sprightly solo on the comb-and-curlpaper, until suffocated in her own pillow by two flowing-haired executioners."—*Edwin Drood.*

Fern, Will.—A poor man whom Alderman Cute determined to put down.—"He came up to London it seems to look for employment, and being found at night asleep in a shed was taken into custody and carried next morning before the Alderman. The Alderman observes (very properly) that he is determined to put this sort of thing down."—*The Chimes.*

Feroce, M.—Owner of a bathing machine.—"How he ever came by his name we cannot imagine; he is as gentle and polite a man as M. Loyal Devasseur himself; immensely stout withal, and of a beaming aspect."—*Our French Watering Place* (Reprinted Pieces).

Fezziwig.—The merchant with whom Scrooge served

his apprenticeship.—" An old gentleman in a Welsh wig, sitting behind such a high desk, that, if he had been two inches taller, he must have knocked his head against the ceiling."—*A Christmas Carol.*

Fezziwig, Mrs.—Wife of Scrooge's apprentice master. —" In came Mrs. Fezziwig, one vast substantial smile."—*A Christmas Carol.*

Fezziwigs, The Three Miss.—Daughters of Scrooge's apprentice master.—" In came the three Miss Fezziwigs, beaming and lovable."—*A Christmas Carol.*

Fibbitson, Mrs.—An old lady who resided at an almshouse along with Mrs. Mell.—" How's Mrs. Fibbitson to-day, said the master, looking at another old woman in a large chair by the fire, who was such a bundle of clothes that I feel grateful to this hour for not having sat upon her by mistake."—*David Copperfield.*

Field, Inspector.—A London police officer.—*On Duty with Inspector Field* (Reprinted Pieces).

Field Lane.—The haunt of the trader in secondhand goods.—" Confined as the limits of Field Lane are, it has its barber, its coffee shop, its beer shop, and its fried fish warehouse. It is a commercial colony of itself; the emporium of petty larceny; visited at early morning, and setting in of dusk, by silent merchants, who traffic in dark back parlours, and who go as strangely as they come."—*Oliver Twist.*

Fielding, May.—A friend of Mrs. Peerybingle's who was being forced into a marriage with Tackleton, when Edward Plummer her old lover opportunely came home from South America and married her.—*The Cricket on the Hearth.*

Fielding, Mrs.—Mother of May.—" A little querulous chip of an old lady with a peevish face . . . who was very genteel and patronising indeed."—*The Cricket on the Hearth.*

Fielding, Sir John.—The magistrate at Bow Street before whom the captured rioters were taken.—" Sir John Fielding had the reputation of being a bold and active magistrate."—*Barnaby Rudge.*

Fikey.—A forger.—*The Detective Police* (Reprinted Pieces).

Filer, Mr.—A friend of Alderman Cute.—" A low-spirited gentleman of middle age, of a meagre habit, and a disconsolate face, who kept his hands continually in the pockets of his scanty pepper-and-salt trousers, very large and dog's-eared from that custom, and was not particularly well brushed or washed."—*The Chimes.*

Filletoville, Marquis of.—Father of the youth who abducted the lady rescued by the Bagman's uncle.—*Pickwick Papers.*

Finchbury, Lady Jane.—" There's an uncommon good church in the village, says Cousin Feenix thoughtfully,—pure specimen of the Anglo-Norman style, and admirably well sketched too by Lady Jane Finchbury—woman with tight stays—but they've spoilt it with whitewash I understand."—*Dombey and Son.*

Finches of the Grove.—A club of which Pip and Herbert Pocket became members.—" At Sartop's suggestion we put ourselves down for election with a Club called The Finches of the Grove; the object of which institution I have never divined, if it were not that the members shall dine expensively once a fortnight, to quarrel amongst themselves as much as possible after dinner, and to cause six waiters to get drunk on the stairs. I know that these gratifying social ends were so invariably accomplished, that Herbert and I understood nothing else to be referred to in the first standing toast of the Society, which ran,—Gentlemen, may the present promotion of good feeling ever reign predominant among the Finches of the Grove."—*Great Expectations.*

Finching, Mr.—The deceased husband of Flora Casby.—*Little Dorrit.*

Finching, Mrs.—Widow of Mr. Finching; daughter of Mr. Casby.—(*See* **Casby, Flora.**)—*Little Dorrit.*

Fips, Mr., of Austin Friars.—The solicitor of old Martin Chuzzlewit.—" Mr. Fips was small and spare, and looked peaceable, and wore black shorts and powder."—*Martin Chuzzlewit.*

Fish, Mr.—Secretary to Sir Joseph Bowley.—" A not very stately gentleman in black."—*The Chimes.*

Fisher, Mr.—Husband of Fanny Venning; one of the defenders of the Fort at Silver Store Colony.—The Perils of Certain English Travellers (*Christmas Stories*).

Fisher, Mrs. Fanny.—The married daughter of Mrs. Venning, a resident at Silver Store Colony.—"Her married daughter, a fair slight thing, was pointed out to me by the name of Fanny Fisher; quite a child she looked, with a little copy of herself holding to her dress, and her husband, just come back from the mine, exceeding proud of her."—The Perils of Certain English Travellers (*Christmas Stories*).

Fitz-Binkle, Lord.—Chairman at the Annual Dinner of the Indigent Orphans' Friends Benevolent Institution.—"A little man, with a long and rather inflamed face, and grey hair, brushed bolt upright in front; he wears a wisp of black silk round his neck, without any stiffener, as an apology for a neckerchief, and is addressed by his companions by the familiar appellation of Fitz, or some such monosyllable."—*Sketches by Boz* (Public Dinners).

Fitzmarshall, Mr. Charles.—The name assumed by Jingle at Mrs. Leo Hunter's garden-party.—*Pickwick Papers.*

Fixem.—A broker, in whose employment Bung was before being elected Beadle.—*Sketches by Boz* (Our Parish).

Fizkin, Horatio.—The defeated candidate at the Eatanswill Election.—"Horatio Fizkin, Esq., of Fizkin Lodge, near Eatanswill, had been prevailed upon by his friends to stand forward in the Buff interest."—*Pickwick Papers.*

Fladdock, General.—A fellow-passenger of Martin's on his voyage to America.—"An American gentleman in the after-cabin, who had been wrapped up in fur and oil-skin the whole passage, unexpectedly appeared in a very shiny tall black hat, and constantly overhauled a very little valise of pale leather, which contained his clothes, linen, brushes, shaving apparatus, books, trinkets, and other baggage."—*Martin Chuzzlewit.*

Flair, The Honourable Augustus.—A friend of Lord Peter.—*Sketches by Boz* (The Great Winglebury Duel).

Flamstead, Galileo Isaac Newton.—Son of Mr. Flamstead.—*The Lamplighter* (Reprinted Pieces).

Flamstead, Miss.—Daughter of Mr. Flamstead.—*The Lamplighter* (Reprinted Pieces).

Flamstead, Mr.—A scientific old gentleman.—" He was one of the strangest and most mysterious-looking files that ever Tom clapped his eyes on. He was dressed all slovenly and untidy, in a great gown, of a kind of bed furniture pattern, with a cap of the same on his head, and a long flapped waistcoat; with no braces, no strings, very few buttons—in short with hardly any of those artificial contrivances that hold Society together; Tom knew by these signs, and by his not being shaved, and by his not being over clean, and by a sort of wisdom not quite awake in his face, that he was a scientific old gentleman."—*The Lamplighter* (Reprinted Pieces).

Flamwell, Mr.—A guest asked to meet Horatio Sparkins at dinner at Oak Lodge.—" Mr. Flamwell was one of those gentlemen of remarkably extensive information, whom one occasionally meets in society, who pretend to know everybody, but in reality know nobody. He had rather a singular way of telling his greatest lies in parenthesis, and with an air of self-denial, as if he feared being thought egotistical."—*Sketches by Boz* (Horatio Sparkins).

Flanders, Sally.—Nurse in childhood to the Uncommercial Traveller.—" My first funeral, a fair representative funeral after its kind, was that of the husband of a married servant, once my nurse. She married for money. Sally Flanders, after a year or two of matrimony, became the relict of Flanders, a small master builder; and either she or Flanders had done me the honour to express a desire that I should follow. I may have been seven or eight years old—young enough certainly to feel rather alarmed by the expression, as not knowing where the invitation was held to terminate, and how far I was expected to follow the deceased Flanders."—*The Uncommercial Traveller* (Medicine Men of Civilization).

Flasher, Mr. Wilkins.—A London stockbroker employed by Mr. Weller.—" A day was fixed for selling out and transferring the stock; and waiting, with that view, upon Wilkins Flasher, Esq., Stockbroker, of somewhere near the Bank, who had been recommended by Mr. Solomon Pell for the purpose."—*Pickwick Papers.*

Fledgeby.—A moneylender who carried on business under the name of Pubsey and Co.—" In facetious homage to the smallness of his talk, and the jerky nature of his manners, Fledgeby's familiars had agreed to confer upon him (behind his back) the honorary title of Fascination Fledgeby. He was the meanest cur existing with a single pair of legs. Young Fledgeby had a peachy cheek, or a cheek compounded of the peach and the red red wall on which it grows, and was an awkward sandy-haired, small-eyed youth, exceeding slim (his enemies would have said lanky). . . . Whether this young gentleman (for he was but three-and-twenty) combined with the miserly vice of an old man, any of the open-handed vices of a young one was a moot point, so very honourably did he keep his own counsel. He was sensible of the value of appearances as an investment, and liked to dress well; but he drove a bargain for every movable about him, from the coat on his back to the china on his breakfast-table; and every bargain, by representing somebody's ruin, or somebody's loss, acquired a peculiar charm for him. Fascination Fledgeby feigned to be a young gentleman living on his means; but was known secretly to be a kind of outlaw in the bill broking line, and to put money out at high interest in various ways."—*Our Mutual Friend.*

Fledgeby, Mr., Senior.—The deceased father of Fascination Fledgeby.—" The father of this young gentleman had been a moneylender, who had transacted professional business with the mother of this young gentleman. The lady, a widow, being unable to pay the moneylender, married him."—*Our Mutual Friend.*

Fledgeby, Mrs.—The mother of Fascination Fledgeby. —" Fledgeby's mother offended her family by marrying Fledgeby's father. It is one of the easiest achievements in life to offend your family, when your family want to get rid of you. Fledgeby's mother's family had been very much offended with her for being poor; and broke with her for becoming comparatively rich. Fledgeby's mother's family was the Snigsworth family. She had even the high honour to be a cousin to Lord Snigsworth,—so many times removed that the noble Earl would have had no compunction in removing her one time more, and dropping her clean outside the cousinly pale; but cousin for all that."—*Our Mutual Friend.*

Fleetwood, Master.—A boy guest at the Steam Excursion. Son of Mr. and Mrs. Fleetwood.—" He was attired for the occasion in a nankeen frock, between the bottom of which, and the top of his plaid socks, a considerable portion of two small mottled legs was discernible. He had a light-blue cap, with a gold band and tassel, on his head, and a damp piece of gingerbread in his hand, with which he had slightly embossed his countenance."—*Sketches by Boz* (The Steam Excursion).

Fleetwood, Mr. and Mrs.—Guests at the Steam Excursion.—*Sketches by Boz* (The Steam Excursion).

Fleming, Agnes.—The mother of Oliver Twist, who had been betrayed by Edwin Leeford.—" Within the altar of the old village church, there stands a white marble tablet, which bears as yet but one word—Agnes. If the Spirits of the dead ever come back to earth, to visit spots hallowed by the love—the love beyond the grave—of those whom they knew in life, I believe that the shade of Agnes sometimes hovers round that solemn nook. I believe it none the less, because that nook is in a church, and she was weak and erring."—*Oliver Twist.*

Flintwich, Ephraim.—Brother of Jeremiah.—*Little Dorrit.*

Flintwich, Jeremiah.—Confidential clerk, and afterwards partner, in business of Clennam and Co.—" He was a short, bald old man, in a high-shouldered black coat and waistcoat, drab breeches, and long drab gaiters; he might, from his dress, have been either clerk or servant, and in fact had long been both; his head was awry, and he had a one-sided crab-like way with him, as if his foundations had yielded at about the same time as those of the house, and he ought to have been propped up in a similar manner."—*Little Dorrit.*

Flintwich, Mrs. Affery.—Wife of Jeremiah Flintwich. —(*See* **Affery.**)—*Little Dorrit.*

Flipfield.—A friend of the Uncommercial Traveller. " I have an illustrative birthday in my eye; a birthday of my friend Flipfield, whose birthdays had long been remarkable as social successes. There had been nothing set or formal about them, Flipfield having been accustomed merely to say, two or three days before,—don't forget to come and dine, old boy, according to custom. I don't know what he said to the ladies he invited; but I may safely assume it *not* to have been old girl."—*The Uncommercial Traveller* (Birthday Celebrations).

Flipfield, Miss.—Sister of Flipfield.—" She was accompanied by Miss Flipfield, the eldest of her numerous family, who held her pocket-handkerchief to her bosom in a majestic manner, and spoke to all of us (none of us had ever seen her before) in pious and condoning tones, of all the quarrels that had taken place in the family from her infancy—which must have been a long time ago—down to that hour."—*The Uncommercial Traveller* (Birthday Celebrations).

Flipfield, Mrs.—Mother of Flipfield.—" Mrs. Flipfield, Senior, formed an interesting feature in the group, with a blue-veined miniature of the late Mr. Flipfield round her neck, in an oval resembling a tart from a pastry-cook's."—*The Uncommercial Traveller* (Birthday Celebrations).

Flipfield, Tom.—Brother of Flipfield.—" A long lost brother of Flipfield's came to light in foreign parts. Where he had been hidden, or what he had been doing, I don't know; for Flipfield vaguely informed me that he had turned up on the banks of the Ganges,—speaking of him as if he had been washed ashore."—*The Uncommercial Traveller* (Birthday Celebrations).

Flitte, Miss.—An old lady whose head had been turned by a Chancery suit.—" A curious little old woman, in a squeezed bonnet, and carrying a reticule, came curtseying and smiling up to us."—*Bleak House.*

Flopsom.—One of the two nurses who relieved Mrs. Matthew Pocket of the care of her young children, Mrs. Pocket being so engrossed in the study of the Peerage as to have no time to devote to her family.—*Great Expectations.*

Flowers.—Mrs. Skewton's maid.—*Dombey and Son.*

Fluggers, Mr.—An actor in Mr. Crummles' company, who did the heavy business.—*Nicholas Nickleby.*

Flummery, Mr.—A member of the Mudfog Association.—*The Mudfog Sketches.*

Foderé and Mere.—French writers on spontaneous combustion.—*Bleak House.*

Fogg, Mr.—Partner of the firm of Dodson and Fogg, Solicitors.—" An elderly, pimply-faced, vegetable-diet sort of man, in a black coat, dark mixture trousers, and small black gaiters; a kind of being who seemed to be an essential part of the desk at which he was writing, and to have as much thought or sentiment."—*Pickwick Papers.*

Fogo.—A pugilist.—" An eminent public character, once known to fame as Frosty-faced Fogo, who in days of yore superintended the formation of the magic circle with the ropes and stakes."—*Edwin Drood.*

Folair, Mr.—The pantomimist in Mr. Crummles' company, who played the part of the Indian Savage.—" I can come it pretty well; nobody better, perhaps, in my own line."—*Nicholas Nickleby.*

Foley.—(*See* **Johnson, Tom.**)

Foulon.—A French aristocrat who had told the people they might eat grass, and who, being taken by the mob, was hanged upon a lamp-post.—*A Tale of Two Cities.*

Foxey.—Father of Sampson and Sally Brass.—" You will not have forgotten (said Brass) that it was a maxim with Foxey—our revered father, gentlemen—always suspect everybody; that's the maxim to go through life with." —*The Old Curiosity Shop.*

François, M.—A dealer at Poissy Cattle-Market.—" Monsieur François goes his way leisurely, and keeps a wary eye upon the stock; no other butcher jostles Monsieur François; Monsieur François jostles no other butcher."—*A Monument of French Folly* (Reprinted Pieces).

Frank.—A companion of Michael the Poor Relation. —" He is a diffident boy by nature, and in a crowd he is soon run over, as I may say, and forgotten. We talk but little, still we understand each other; we walk about hand in hand, and without much speaking he knows what I mean, and I know what he means."—*The Poor Relation's Story* (Reprinted Pieces).

French Officer, The.—Commander of a French force at Badajos, opposed to the English force under Major Taunton.—" There was an officer at their head encouraging his men, a courageous, handsome, gallant officer of five-and-thirty whom Doubledick saw hurriedly, almost momentarily, but saw well. He particularly noticed this officer waving his sword and rallying his men with an eager and excited cry when they fired in obedience to his gesture and Major Taunton dropped."—The Seven Poor Travellers (*Christmas Stories*).

Frost, Miss.—A school-mistress.—" Why a something in mourning, called Miss Frost, should still connect itself with our preparatory school, we are unable to say."—*Our School* (Reprinted Pieces).

Gabbleton, Lord.—Mentioned by Mr. Flamwell at the dinner to Horatio Sparkins at Oak Lodge.—*Sketches by Boz* (Horatio Sparkins).

Gabelle.—A retainer of the Marquis St. Evremonde.—" Monsieur Gabelle was the Postmaster, and some other taxing functionary, united."—*A Tale of Two Cities.*

Gallanbile, Mrs.—A client of The General Agency, in quest of a cook.—" Here's another, remarked Tom, turning over the leaves—Family of Mr. Gallanbile, M.P., fifteen guineas, tea and sugar, and servants allowed to see male cousins if godly. Note.—Cold dinner in the kitchen on the Sabbath, Mr. Gallanbile being devoted to the observance question; no victuals whatever cooked on the Lord's Day, with the exception of dinner for Mr. and Mrs. Gallanbile, which, being a work of piety and necessity, is exempted. Mr. Gallanbile dines late on the day of rest, in order to prevent the sinfulness of the cook's dressing herself."—*Nicholas Nickleby.*

Game Chicken, The.—A pugilist friend of Mr. Toots. —" A stoical gentleman, in a shaggy white great coat, and a flat-brimmed hat, with very short hair, a broken nose, and a considerable tract of bare and sterile country behind each ear. . . . Captain Cuttle proffered a glass of rum, which the Chicken, throwing back his head, emptied into himself as into a cask, after proposing the brief sentiment —Towards us."—*Dombey and Son.*

Gamfield.—A chimney-sweep who was willing to take

Oliver as an apprentice, but the magistrates refused to sanction the indenture.—" His villainous countenance was a stamped receipt for cruelty."—*Oliver Twist.*

Gamp, Mrs. Sarah.—A nurse.—" She was a fat old woman, this Mrs. Gamp, with a husky voice and a moist eye. She wore a very rusty black gown, rather the worse for snuff, and a shawl and bonnet to correspond. The face of Mrs. Gamp—the nose in particular—was somewhat red and swollen, and it was difficult to enjoy her society without becoming conscious of a smell of spirits."—*Martin Chuzzlewit.*

Gander, Mr.—A boarder at Todgers'.—" Mr. Gander was of a witty turn."—*Martin Chuzzlewit.*

Ganz, Doctor.—A medical man of Neuchâtel who granted a certificate proving the identity of Vendal with Wilding.—No Thoroughfare (*Christmas Stories*).

Gargery, Joe.—The brawny blacksmith who married Pip's sister, and was Pip's devoted friend.—" Joe was a fair man with curls of flaxen hair on each side of his smooth face, and with eyes of such a very undecided blue, that they seemed to have somehow got mixed with their own whites. He was a mild, good-natured, sweet-tempered, easy-going, foolish, dear fellow—a sort of Hercules in strength and also in weakness."—*Great Expectations.*

Gargery, Mrs.—Pip's sister, the strong-minded and sharp-tongued wife of the blacksmith, Joe Gargery.—" She had established a great reputation with herself and the neighbours because she had brought me up by hand. She was not a good-looking woman my sister, and I had a general impression that she must have made Joe Gargery marry her by hand. My sister Mrs. Joe, with black hair and eyes, had such a prevailing redness of skin that I sometimes used to wonder whether it was possible she washed herself with a nutmeg-grater instead of soap."—*Great Expectations.*

Garland, Abel.—Son of Mr. and Mrs. Garland. Articled clerk to Mr. Witherden.—" Mr. Abel, who had a quaint old-fashioned air about him, looked nearly of the same age as his father, and bore a wonderful resemblance to him in face and figure, though wanting something of his full round cheerfulness, and substituting in its place a timid reserve."—*The Old Curiosity Shop*.

Garland, Mr.—Kit's benefactor.—" A little, fat, placid old gentleman."—*The Old Curiosity Shop*.

Garland, Mrs.—Wife of Mr. Garland.—" A little old lady, plump and placid like himself."—*The Old Curiosity Shop*.

Gashford.—Secretary to Lord George Gordon—a recreant Roman Catholic who professed great interest in Lord George Gordon's mission, but was a self-seeking hypocrite.—" Gashford, the Secretary, was taller, angularly made, high-shouldered, bony and ungraceful. His dress, in imitation of his superior, was demure and staid in the extreme; his manner formal and constrained . . . his manner was smooth and humble, but very sly and shirking. He wore the aspect of a man who was always lying in wait for something that *wouldn't* come to pass; but he looked patient, very patient, and fawned like a spaniel dog."—*Barnaby Rudge*.

Gaspard.—One of a crowd in a Paris street, whose child was run down and killed by the Marquis St. Evremonde, whom, in revenge, Gaspard killed, and was hanged for it.—*A Tale of Two Cities*.

Gattleton Family.—" The whole family was infected with the mania for private theatricals; the house, usually so clean and tidy, was, to use Mr. Gattleton's expressive description, regularly turned out o' windows; the large dining-room, dismantled of its furniture and ornaments, presented a strange jumble of flats, flies, wings, lamps, bridges, clouds, thunder and lightning, festoons and flowers, daggers and foils, and various other messes in theatrical slang included under the comprehensive name of properties."—*Sketches by Boz* (Mrs. Joseph Porter).

Gattleton, Miss Caroline.—Daughter of Mr. Gattleton who played " Fenella " in the private theatricals at Rose Villa.—*Sketches by Boz* (Mrs. Joseph Porter).

Gattleton, Miss Lucina.—Daughter of Mr. Gattleton, played " Desdemona " in the private theatricals.—" Every sofa in the house was more or less damaged, by the perseverance and spirit with which Mr. Sempronius Gattleton and Miss Lucina rehearsed the smothering scene in Othello."—*Sketches by Boz* (Mrs. Joseph Porter).

Gattleton, Mr.—A stockbroker, who resided at Rose Villa, Clapham Rise.—*Sketches by Boz* (Mrs. Joseph Porter).

Gattleton, Mrs.—Wife of Mr. Gattleton of Rose Villa. —"Mrs. Gattleton was a kind, good-tempered, vulgar soul; exceedingly fond of her husband and children; and entertaining only three dislikes; in the first place she had a natural antipathy to anybody else's unmarried daughters; in the second, she was in bodily fear of anything in the shape of ridicule; lastly—almost a necessary consequence of this feeling—she regarded with feelings of the utmost horror one Mrs. Joseph Porter over the way."—*Sketches by Boz* (Mrs. Joseph Porter).

Gattleton, Sempronius.—Son of Mr. Gattleton.—"In consideration of his sustaining the trifling inconvenience of bearing all the expenses of the play, Mr. Sempronius had been, in the most handsome manner, unanimously elected stage manager."—*Sketches by Boz* (Mrs. Joseph Porter).

Gay, Walter.—Nephew of Solomon Gills, clerk in Dombey and Son's counting-house, shipped to Barbadoes and wrecked, but saved and returned, and ultimately married Florence Dombey.—"A cheerful-looking merry boy . . . fair faced, bright eyed, and curly haired."—*Dombey and Son.*

Gazingi, Miss.—An actress in Mr. Crummles' company.—"There was Miss Gazingi, with an imitation ermine boa, tied in a loose knot round her neck, flogging Mr. Crummles junior with both ends in fun."—*Nicholas Nickleby.*

General, Mrs.—Companion of the Misses Dorrit.—"An elderly lady who was a model of accurate dressing, and whose manner was perfect, considered as a piece of machinery. In person Mrs. General, including her skirts, which had much to do with it, was of a dignified and imposing appearance; ample, rustling, gravely voluminous; always upright behind the proprieties. If her countenance and hair had rather a floury appearance, as though from living in some transcendently genteel mill, it was rather because she was a chalky creation altogether, than because she mended her complexion with violet powder, or had turned grey; if her eyes had no expression it was probably because they had nothing to express; if she had few wrinkles it was because her mind had never traced its name, or any other inscription, on her face; a cool, waxy, blown-out woman, who had never lighted well."—*Little Dorrit.*

George.—An insolvent coachman whom Mr. Weller visited at the Insolvent Court.—"The insolvent gentleman, who had contracted a speculative but imprudent passion for horsing long stages, which had led to his present embarrassments, looked extremely well, and was soothing the excitement of his feelings with shrimps and porter."—*Pickwick Papers.*

George.—The guard of the coach by which David travelled on his way to Salem House.—*David Copperfield.*

George.—The driver of Mrs. Jarley's touring-van; afterwards her husband.—"She sat down upon the steps, and called George; whereupon a man in a carter's frock, who had been so shrouded in a hedge up to this time as to see everything that passed without being seen himself, parted the twigs that concealed him, and appeared in a sitting attitude, supporting on his legs a baking dish, and a half-gallon stone bottle, and bearing in his right hand a knife, and in his left a fork."—*The Old Curiosity Shop.*

George.—Clerk to Mr. Buffles, the tax-collector.—Mrs. Lirriper's Legacy (*Christmas Stories*).

George.—Guard of the coach by which Charley travelled to the Holly Tree Inn.—"Now the landlord, and the landlady, and the ostler, and the postboy, and all the stable authorities, had already asked the coachman if he meant to go on; the coachman had already replied yes, he'd take her through it—meaning by her the coach—if so be as George would stand by him. George was the guard, and he had already sworn that he would stand by him—so the helpers were already getting the horses out."—The Holly Tree (*Christmas Stories*).

George.—Second assistant to Christopher the head waiter.—"When he said orange brandy, I said so too, in a lower tone, to George my second Lieutenant (my first was absent on leave) who acts between me and the bar." —Somebody's Luggage (*Christmas Stories*).

George.—A friend of Mr. Kenwigs present at his supper-party.—"A young man who had known Mr. Kenwigs when he was a bachelor, and was much esteemed by the ladies, as bearing the reputation of a rake."—*Nicholas Nickleby*.

George.—Eldest son in a family party at Astley's Circus.—"Then came Pa and Ma; and then the eldest son, a boy of fourteen years old, who was evidently trying to look as if he did not belong to the family. Two of the little boys who had been discussing the point whether Astley's was more than twice as large as Drury Lane, agreed to refer it to George for his decision, at which George, who was no other then the young gentleman before noticed, waxed indignant.—One of the little boys wound up by expressing his opinion that George began to think himself quite a man now; whereupon both Pa and Ma laughed too; and George (who carried a dress cane and was cultivating whiskers) muttered that William was always encouraged in his impertinence; and assumed a look of profound contempt which lasted the whole evening."—*Sketches by Boz* (Astley's).

George, Master.—(*See* **Elizabeth, Miss.**)—*Our Mutual Friend*.

George, Mrs.—A guest at Mrs. Quilp's tea-party.—"Before I'd let a man order me about as Quilp orders her, said Mrs. George, before I'd consent to stand in awe of a man as she does of him; I'd—I'd kill myself, and write a letter first to say he did it."—*The Old Curiosity Shop*.

George, Uncle.—The host of the Christmas Family Dinner.—"The Christmas Family Party that we mean is not a mere assemblage of relations, got up at a week or two's notice, originating this year, having no family precedent in the last, and not likely to be repeated in the next. No. It is an annual gathering of all the accessible members of the family, young or old, rich or poor, and all the children look forward to it for two months beforehand, in a fever of anticipation. Formerly it was held at Grandpapa's, but Grandpapa getting old, and Grandmamma getting old too, and rather infirm, they have given up housekeeping and domesticated themselves with Uncle George, so the party always takes place at Uncle George's house."—*Sketches by Boz* (A Christmas Dinner).

Gibbs, William.—A hairdresser whose story Sam Weller told to his father.—*Master Humphrey's Clock.*

Giggles, Miss.—A pupil at Nuns' House.—" On charges of inviolable secrecy, confidences were interchanged respecting golden youth of England, expected to call at home on the first opportunity. Miss Giggles (deficient in sentiment) did indeed profess that she for her part acknowledged such homage by making faces at the golden youth; but this young lady was outvoted by an immense majority."—*Edwin Drood.*

Giles, Jeremie and Giles.—London bankers to whom Mrs. Miller referred Trustees of Foundling Hospital relative to the adoption of Walter Wilding.—No Thoroughfare (*Christmas Stories*).

Giles, Mr.—The butler at the house at Chertsey who shot Oliver.—" Mr. Giles acted in the double capacity of butler and steward to the old lady of the mansion."—*Oliver Twist.*

Gill, Mrs.—A client of Sarah Gamp's.—*Martin Chuzzlewit.*

Gill, Mr.—Her husband.—*Martin Chuzzlewit.*

Gills, Solomon.—A nautical instrument maker, uncle of Walter Gay.—" Solomon Gills himself (more generally called old Sol) was far from having a maritime appearance. . . . He was a slow, quiet spoken, thoughtful old fellow, with eyes as red as if they had been small suns looking at you through a fog, and a newly awakened manner, such as he might have acquired by having stared for three or four days successively through every optical instrument in his shop, and suddenly come back to the world again to find it green."—*Dombey and Son.*

Gimblet.—One of a narrow sectarian congregation.—" Brother Hawkyard was the popular expounder in this assembly. He was by trade a drysalter. Brother

Gimblet, an elderly man with a crabbed face, a large dog's-eared collar, and a spotted blue neckerchief, reaching up behind to the crown of his head, was also a drysalter, and an expounder."—*George Silverman's Explanation.*

Glamour, Bob.—A customer at the Fellowship Porters.—(*See* **Williams.**)—*Our Mutual Friend.*

Glavormelly, Mr.—Of the Coburg Theatre. A deceased actor friend of Mr. Snevellicci.—*Nicholas Nickleby.*

Glibbery, Bob.—The pot boy at the Fellowship Porters.—" In such an establishment, the white-aproned pot boy, with his shirt sleeves arranged in a tight roll on each bare shoulder, was a mere hint of the possibility of physical force, thrown out as a matter of state and form."—*Our Mutual Friend.*

Globson.—A boy who bullied the Uncommercial Traveller at school.—" He was a big fat boy, with a big fat head, and a big fat fist, and, at the beginning of that Half, had raised such a bump on my forehead that I couldn't get my hat of state on to go to church."—The Uncommercial Traveller (*Birthday Celebrations*).

Glubb.—An old man at Brighton who wheeled Paul's chair on the parade.—" He's a very nice old man, ma'am, he said, he used to draw my couch. He knows all about the deep sea, and the fish that are in it, and the great monsters that come and lie on the rocks in the sun, and dive into the water again when they're startled, blowing and splashing so that they can be heard for miles."—*Dombey and Son.*

Glumper, Sir Thomas.—One of the audience at the private theatricals at Rose Villa.—" Seven o'clock came; and so did the audience; all the rank and fashion of Clapham and its vicinity was fast filling the theatre. There were the Smiths; the Gubbinses; the Nixons; the Dixons; the Hicksons; people with all sorts of names; two aldermen; a sheriff in perspective; Sir Thomas Glumper (who had been knighted in the last reign for carrying up an address on somebody's escaping from nothing); and, last not least, there were Mrs. Joseph Porter and Uncle Tom, seated in the centre of the third row from the stage, Mrs. P. amusing Uncle Tom with all sorts of stories, and Uncle Tom amusing every one else by laughing most immoderately."—*Sketches by Boz* (Mrs. Joseph Porter).

Gobbler, Mr.—A boarder at Mrs. Tibbs', who married Mrs. Bloss.—" He was tall, thin, and pale; he always fancied he had a severe pain somewhere or other, and his face invariably wore a pinched screwed-up expression; he looked indeed like a man who had got his feet in a tub of exceedingly hot water, against his will."—*Sketches by Boz* (The Boarding House).

Gog.—One of the Guildhall giants of whom Joe Toddyhigh dreamt that they came to life.—" The statues of the two giants Gog and Magog were endowed with life and motion. These guardian genii of the city had quitted their pedestals, and reclined in easy attitudes in the great stained glass window. Between them was an ancient cask which seems to be full of wine."—*Master Humphrey's Clock.*

" Golden Mary."—The name of the ship commanded by William George Ravender which collided with an iceberg and was wrecked.—" Our ship was a barque of three hundred tons, carrying a crew of eighteen men, a second mate in addition to John, a carpenter, an armourer or smith, and two apprentices (one a Scotch boy, poor little fellow)."—The Wreck of the *Golden Mary* (*Christmas Stories*).

Golding, Mary.—Recognized by Captain and Mrs. Waters amongst the bathers at Ramsgate.—" There's Mary Golding, said the Captain, pointing to one of the young ladies before noticed, who, in her bathing costume, looked as if she were enveloped in a patent mackintosh of scanty dimensions."—*Sketches by Boz* (The Tuggses at Ramsgate).

Goldstraw, Dick.—Husband of Sally, the Foundling Hospital Nurse.—No Thoroughfare (*Christmas Stories*).

Goldstraw, Mrs.—The housekeeper at Cripple Corner. —" A woman, perhaps fifty, but looking younger, with a face remarkable for its quiet expression of equability of temper."—No Thoroughfare (*Christmas Stories*).

Goodchild, Francis.—One of the two lazy apprentices.

I

—"Goodchild was laboriously idle, and would take upon himself any amount of pains and labour to assure himself that he was idle; in short, had no better idea of idleness than that it was a useless industry."—The Lazy Tour of Two Idle Apprentices (*Christmas Stories*).

Goodwin.—Mrs. Pott's maid.—"Attached to Mrs. Pott's person, was a bodyguard of one; a young lady, whose ostensible employment was to preside over her toilet, but who rendered herself useful in a variety of ways, and in none more so than in the particular department of constantly aiding and abetting her mistress in every wish and inclination opposed to the desires of the unhappy Pott."—*Pickwick Papers*.

Goody, Mrs.—The grandmother of a boy suggested by Mr. Milvey for adoption by Mr. and Mrs. Boffin, but whom Mrs. Milvey discarded.—"She is an inconvenient woman. I hope it's not uncharitable to remember that last Christmas Eve she drank eleven cups of tea, and grumbled all the time; and she is not a grateful woman, Frank; you recollect her addressing a crowd outside this house, about her wrongs, when one night, after we had gone to bed, she brought back the petticoat of new flannel that had been given her, because it was too short."—*Our Mutual Friend*.

Gordon, Colonel.—A member of Parliament who, with General Conway, faced the rioters at Westminster.—"And my Lord George, said the other gentleman, addressing him in like manner, I desire them to hear this from me, Colonel Gordon, your near relation, if a man among this crowd whose uproar strikes us deaf, crosses the threshold of the House of Commons, I swear to run my sword that moment—not into his—but into your body."—*Barnaby Rudge*.

Gordon, Emma.—One of Sleary's Circus troupe, who comforted Sissy Jupe when her father disappeared.—*Hard Times*.

Gordon, Lord George.—The president of the great Protestant Association, who died in prison at the early age of forty-three.—"About the middle height, of a slender make and sallow complexion; with an acquiline nose, and long hair of a reddish-brown, combed perfectly straight and smooth about his ears, and slightly powdered, but without the slightest vestige of a curl . . . it was striking to observe his very bright large eye, which betrayed a restlessness of thought and purpose singularly at variance with the studied composure and sobriety of his mien, and with his quaint and sad apparel. It had nothing harsh or cruel in its expression; neither had his face, which was thin and mild, and wore an air of melancholy; but it was suggestive of an air of indefinable uneasiness, which infected those who looked upon him, and filled them with a kind of pity for the man."—*Barnaby Rudge.*

Goswell Street.—Mr. Pickwick's place of residence.—"Mr. Pickwick's apartments in Goswell Street, although on a limited scale, were not only of a very neat and comfortable description, but peculiarly adapted for the residence of a man of his genius and observation. His sitting-room was the first floor front, his bed-room the second floor front; and thus, whether he were sitting at his desk in his parlour, or standing before the dressing-glass in his dormitory, he had an equal opportunity of contemplating human nature, in all the numerous phases it exhibits in that not more populous than popular thoroughfare."—*Pickwick Papers.*

Governor, Jack.—One of the guests at The Haunted House.—"My old friend Jack Governor slung his hammock, as he called it, in the corner room; a portly, cheery, well-built figure of a broad-shouldered man, with a frank smile, a brilliant dark eye, and a rich dark eyebrow . . . and so unmistakably a naval officer, that if you were to meet him coming out of an Esquimaux snow-hut, in seals' skin, you could be vaguely persuaded he was in full naval uniform."—The Haunted House (*Christmas Stories*).

Gowan, Henry.—An artist, who married Minnie Meagles.—"He was well dressed, of a sprightly and gay appearance, a well-knit figure, and a rich dark complexion. Mr. Henry Gowan, inheriting from his father that very questionable help in life a small independence, had been difficult to settle; the rather as public appointments chanced to be scarce, and his genius during his earlier manhood was of that exclusively argricultural character, which applies itself to the cultivation of wild oats. At last he had declared that he would become a Painter."—*Little Dorrit.*

Gowan, Mr.—The father of Henry Gowan.—"The paternal Gowan, originally attached to a legation abroad, had been pensioned off as a Commissioner of nothing particular, somewhere or other, and had died at his post, with his drawn salary in his hand, nobly defending it to the last extremity."—*Little Dorrit.*

Gowan, Mrs.—Mother of Henry Gowan.—"A courtly old lady, formerly a beauty, and still sufficiently well-favoured to have dispensed with the powder on her nose, and a certain impossible bloom under each eye."—*Little Dorrit.*

Gradgrind, Thomas.—A retired merchant.—"A kind of cannon loaded to the muzzle with facts. . . . Thomas Gradgrind, sir, a man of realities—a man of facts and calculations—a man who proceeds upon the principle that two and two are four, and nothing over, and who is not to be talked into allowing for anything over. In such terms Mr. Gradgrind always mentally introduced himself, whether to his private circle of acquaintance, or to the public in general."—*Hard Times.*

Gradgrind, Mrs.—The invalid wife of Thomas Gradgrind.—"A little, thin, white, pink-eyed bundle of shawls, of surpassing feebleness mentally and bodily; who was always taking physic without any effect; and who, whenever she showed a symptom of coming to life, was invariably stunned by some weighty piece of fact tumbling on her."—*Hard Times.*

Gradgrind, Louisa.—Elder daughter of Thomas Gradgrind, afterwards married Bounderby.—"She was a child now, of fifteen or sixteen, but at no distant day would seem to become a woman all at once. Her father thought so as he looked at her. She was pretty; would have been self-willed (he thought in his eminently practical way) but for her bringing up."—*Hard Times.*

Gradgrind, Tom (The Whelp).—The cowed and mean-spirited son of Mr. Gradgrind. Robbed Bounderby's Bank.—"As to me, said Tom, tumbling his hair all manner of ways, with his sulky hands, I am a donkey—that's what I am. I am as obstinate as one; I am more stupid than one; I get as much pleasure as one; and I should like to kick like one."—*Hard Times.*

Gradgrind, Jane.—Younger daughter of Thomas Gradgrind.—"Little Jane, after manufacturing a good deal of moist pipe-clay on her face with slate pencil and tears, had fallen asleep over vulgar fractions."—*Hard Times.*

Gradgrind, Adam Smith.—One of the younger sons of Thomas Gradgrind.—"Adam Smith and Malthus, two younger Gradgrinds, were out at lecture in custody." —*Hard Times.*

Gradgrind, Malthus.—One of the younger sons of Thomas Gradgrind.—*Hard Times.*

Graham, Mary.—Companion of old Martin Chuzzlewit; ultimately married Martin the younger.—"She was very young, apparently no more than seventeen, timid and shrinking in her manner, and yet with a greater share of self-possession and control over her emotions than usually belongs to a far more advanced period of female life."—*Martin Chuzzlewit.*

Graham, Hugh.—A London apprentice.—"In the sixteenth century, and in the reign of Queen Elizabeth of glorious memory (albeit her golden days are sadly rusted with blood), there lived in the City of London a bold young 'prentice who loved his master's daughter; there were no doubt within the walls a great many 'prentices in this conditon, but I speak of only one, and his name was Hugh Graham."—*Master Humphrey's Clock.*

Grainger.—One of Steerforth's friends who dined with David at his chambers at the Adelphi.—*David Copperfield.*

Grainger, Mrs. Edith.—Daughter of Mrs. Skewton; widow of an army officer; a hard-natured, cold, proud woman who became the second Mrs. Dombey.—"Carrying her gossamer parasol with a proud and weary air, as if so great an effort must soon be abandoned, and the parasol dropped, sauntered a very much younger lady, very handsome, very haughty, very wilful, who tossed her head and dropped her eyelids."—*Dombey and Son.*

Grainger, Col. (deceased).—The first husband of Edith Skewton.

Grandmarina.—A fairy.—"Just then the old lady came

trotting up. She was dressed in shot silk, of the richest quality, smelling of dried lavender."—*Holiday Romance.*

Grannett, Mr.—The overseer of the parish where Oliver Twist was born.—*Oliver Twist.*

Graymarsh, Master.—A pupil at Dotheboys Hall.—*Nicholas Nickleby.*

Grayper, Mr.—A neighbour of Mrs. Copperfield's, at whose house she first met Mr. Murdstone.—*David Copperfield.*

Grayper, Mrs.—Wife of Mr. Grayper.—*David Copperfield.*

Grazinglands, Mr. and Mrs.—Visitors to London.—"Mr. Grazinglands of the Midland Counties came to London by railroad one morning last week, accompanied by the amiable and fascinating Mrs. Grazinglands. Mr. G. is a gentleman of comfortable property, and had a little business to transact at the Bank of England, which required the concurrence and signature of Mrs. G."—*The Uncommercial Traveller* (Refreshments for Travellers).

Great White Horse.—The inn at Ipswich where Mr. Pickwick mistook his room number.—"Never were such labyrinths of uncarpeted passages; such clusters of mouldy ill-lighted rooms; such huge numbers of small dens for eating or sleeping in; beneath any one roof, as are collected together between the four walls of the Great White Horse at Ipswich."—*Pickwick Papers.*

Greedy.—One of Mrs. Lemon's pupils.—*Holiday Romance.*

Green, Lucy.—A companion of the Uncommercial Traveller's boyhood at Dullborough, who afterwards became the wife of Dr. Specks.—"So I saw her, and she was fat, and if all the hay in the world had been heaped upon her, it could scarcely have altered her face more than Time had altered it from my remembrance; . . . but when her youngest child came in after dinner, I saw again in that little daughter the little face of the hayfield unchanged, and it quite touched my foolish heart."—*The Uncommercial Traveller* (Dullborough Town).

Green, Mrs.—A friend of Mrs. Nubbles.—"Kit's

mother dropped a curtsey, and became consoled; then the good woman entered into a long and minute account of Kit's life and history . . . for proof of which statements reference was made to Mrs. Green, lodger at the Cheese-monger's round the corner."—*The Old Curiosity Shop*.

Green, Tom.—The name young Willet assumed when he returned from the wars.—" He was a gallant, manly, handsome fellow, but he had lost his left arm."—*Barnaby Rudge*.

Green, Miss.—A dressmaker; a neighbour of the Kenwigs, and a guest at their supper-party.—" Then there was a young lady who had made Mrs. Kenwigs' dress, and who—it was the most convenient thing in the world—living in the two pair back—gave up her bed to the baby and got a little girl to watch it."—*Nicholas Nickleby*.

Green.—A London constable.—*On Duty with Inspector Field* (Reprinted Pieces).

Green, Messrs.—Balloonists at Vauxhall Gardens.—" Then Mr. Green, Senr., and his noble companion entered one car; and Mr. Green, Junr., and his companion the other; and then the balloons went up, and the aerial travellers stood up, and the crowd outside roared with delight."—*Sketches by Boz* (Vauxhall Gardens by Day).

Greenacre, Mr.—The deceased gentleman whose skull Professor Ketch exhibited at the meeting of the Mudfog Association.—*The Mudfog Sketches*.

Greenleaf.—The name of the house where the Misses Donny kept a boarding-school for girls.—" Nothing could be more precise, exact and orderly than Greenleaf; there was a time for everything, all round the dial of the clock, and everything was done at its appointed moment."—*Bleak House*.

Greenwood.—One of the persons mentioned by Ikey as having seen the ghost at the Haunted House.—" Also that a personage—dimly described as a bold chap, a sort of one-eyed tramp, answering to the name of Joby, unless you challenged him as Greenwood, and then he said why not, and even if so mind your own business—had encountered the hooded woman a matter of five or six times."—The Haunted House (*Christmas Stories*).

Gregory.—The foreman packer at Murdstone and Grinby's.—"A certain man named Gregory, who was foreman of the packers, and another named Tipp who was the carman and wore a red jacket, used to address me sometimes as David."—*David Copperfield.*

Gregsbury, Mr., M.P.—The gentleman whose secretaryship Nicholas declined.—"He was a tough, burly, thick-headed gentleman with a loud voice, a pompous manner, a tolerable command of sentences with no meaning in them, and in short every requisite for a very good member indeed. . . . There are other duties, Mr. Nickleby, which a Secretary to a Parliamentary gentleman must never lose sight of. I shall require to be crammed. My meaning, sir, is perfectly plain, replied Mr. Gregsbury, with a solemn aspect,—My secretary would have to make himself master of the foreign policy of the world, as it is mirrored in the newspapers; to run his eye over all accounts of public meetings; all leading articles; and accounts of the proceedings of the public bodies; and to make notes of anything which it appeared to him might be made a point of in any little speech, and now and then, during great debates, sitting in the front row of the gallery, and saying to the people about: You see that gentleman with his hand to his face and his arm twisted round the pillar, that's Mr. Gregsbury, the celebrated Mr. Gregsbury, with any other eulogium that might strike you at the moment; and for salary I don't mind saying at once in round numbers, to prevent any dissatisfaction, although it's more than I've been accustomed to give, fifteen shillings a week and find yourself."—*Nicholas Nickleby.*

Grewgious, Hiram.—A lawyer of Staple Inn; guardian of Rosa Bud.—"He was an arid sandy man; who, if he had been put into a grinding mill, looked as if he would have ground immediately into high-dried snuff. He had a scanty, flat crop of hair, in colour and consistency like some very mangy yellow fur tippet; it was so unlike hair, that it must have been a wig, but for the stupendous improbability of anybody's voluntarily sporting such a head. With too great length of throat at his upper end, and too much ankle-bone and heel at his lower; with an awkward and hesitating manner; with a shambling walk; and with what is called near sight—which perhaps prevented his observing how much white cotton stocking he displayed to the public eye in contrast with his black suit, Mr. Grewgious still had some strange capacity in him of making on the whole an agreeable impression."—*Edwin Drood.*

Gride, Arthur.—A miserly old moneylender.—" A little old man of about seventy or seventy-five years of age, of a very lean figure, much bent and slightly twisted. He wore a grey coat, with a very narrow collar; an old-fashioned waistcoat of ribbed black silk; and such scanty trousers as displayed his shrunken spindle shanks in their full ugliness. The whole air and attitude of the form was one of stealthy, cat-like obsequiousness; the whole expression of the face was concentrated in a wrinkled leer, compounded of cunning, lecherousness, slyness and avarice . . . in an old house, dismal, dark, and dusty, which seemed to have withered like himself, and to have grown yellow and shrivelled in hoarding him from the light of day, as he had in hoarding his money, lived Arthur Gride."—*Nicholas Nickleby.*

Gridley, Mr.—A man from Shropshire, a party in the Jarndyce Chancery suit which ruined him.—" Another ruined suitor, who periodically appears from Shropshire, and breaks out into efforts to address the Chancellor at the close of the day's business; and who can by no means be made to understand that the Chancellor is legally ignorant of his existence. . . . A tall, sallow man, with a careworn head, on which but little hair remained, a deeply lined face, and prominent eyes."—*Bleak House.*

Griffin, Miss.—The principal of a school which the ghost of Master B. called a Seraglio.—" Miss Griffin was a model of propriety."—The Haunted House (*Christmas Stories*).

Grigg, Tom.—A lamplighter.—" Tom Grigg, gentlemen, was, as I have said, one of us; and I may go further and say he was an ornament to us, and such a one as only the good old times of oil and cotton could have produced; Tom's family, gentlemen, were all Lamplighters."—*The Lamplighter* (Reprinted Pieces).

Griggins, Mr.—The funny young gentleman.—" We have offered no description of the funny young gentleman's personal appearance, believing that almost every society has a Griggins of its own."—*Sketches of Young Gentlemen.*

Griggs, The.—A family at Ipswich in the social circle of Mr. Nupkin.—*Pickwick Papers.*

Grime, Professor.—A member of the Mechanical Science Section of the Mudfog Association.—*The Mudfog Sketches.*

Grimmer, Miss.—One of the principals of the ladies' school where Nettie Ashford was a pupil.—" My peerless bride was, at the period of which we now treat, in captivity at Miss Grimmer's."—*Holiday Romance.*

Grimwig, Mr.—A friend of Mr. Brownlow. A short-tempered old gentleman, who backed all his assertions by an offer to eat his head if wrong.—" At this moment there walked into the room, supporting himself by a thick stick, a stout old gentleman, rather lame in one leg. . . . He had a manner of screwing his head on one side when he spoke, and of looking out of the corners of his eyes at the same time, which irresistibly reminded the beholder of a parrot."—*Oliver Twist.*

Grimwood, Eliza.—A woman whose murder was investigated by Inspector Field.—" She was commonly called the Countess, because of her handsome appearance, and her proud way of carrying herself."—*Three Detective Anecdotes* (Reprinted Pieces).

Grinder, Mr.—Proprietor of a travelling show company.—" Mr. Grinder's company, familiarly termed a lot, consisted of a young gentleman and a young lady on stilts, and Mr. Grinder himself, who used his natural legs for pedestrian purposes, and carried at his back a drum."—*The Old Curiosity Shop.*

Grinder, Rob., The.—The name applied to Robin Toodles, in consequence of his having been nominated by Mr. Dombey as a scholar on the foundation of The Charitable Grinders.—*Dombey and Son.*

Grinders, The Charitable.—A city corporation to whose school Mr. Dombey nominated Robin Toodle.—*Dombey and Son.*

Grip.—A raven, Barnaby's companion.—" Halloa, a hoarse voice in his ear. . . . The speaker, who made the locksmith start as if he had seen some supernatural agent, was a large raven, who had perched upon the top of the easy chair, unseen by him and Edward, and listened with a polite attention, and a most extraordinary appearance of comprehending every word, to all they had said up to this point; turning his head from one to the other, as if his office were to judge between them, and it were of the very last importance that he should not lose a word."—*Barnaby Rudge.*

Groffin, Mr. Thomas.—A juror in the Bardell and Pickwick trial.—*Pickwick Papers.*

Grompus, Mr.—A partner presented to Miss Podsnap at her birthday party.—" The ogre advanced, under the pilotage of Ma; and Ma said Georgiana—Mr. Grompus—and the ogre clutched his victim, and bore her off to his castle in the top couple."—*Our Mutual Friend.*

Groper, Colonel.—One of the interviewers of Elijah Pogram.—*Martin Chuzzlewit.*

Groves, Jem.—Landlord of the Valiant Soldier public-house.—" This is the 'Valiant Soldier' by Jem Groves—honest Jem Groves—as is a man of unblemished moral character, and has a good dry skittle ground. . . . With these words the speaker tapped himself on the waistcoat, to intimate that he was the Jem Groves so highly eulogized." —*The Old Curiosity Shop.*

Growlery, The.—The private room of Mr. Jarndyce at Bleak House.—" A small room next his bed-chamber, which I found to be in part a little library of books and papers, and in part quite a little museum of his boots and shoes and hatboxes."—*Bleak House.*

Grub, Gabriel.—A sexton, of whom Mr. Wardle told a tale.—" Gabriel Grub was an ill-conditioned cross-grained surly fellow—a morose and lonely man, who consorted with nobody but himself and an old wicker bottle, which fitted into his large deep waistcoat pocket."—*Pickwick Papers.*

Grub, Mr.—A member of the Mudfog Association.—*The Mudfog Sketches.*

Grubble.—Landlord of the Dedlock Arms inn.—" A pleasant-looking, stoutish, middle-aged man, who never seemed to consider himself cosily dressed for his own fireside without his hat and top boots, but who never wore a coat except at Church."—*Bleak House.*

Grudden, Mrs.—A member of Mr. Crummles' company. —" There was Mrs. Grudden, in a brown cloth pelisse, and a beaver bonnet; who assisted Mrs. Crummles in her domestic affairs; and took money at the doors; and dressed the ladies; and swept the house; and held the prompt book when everybody else was on for the last scene; and acted any kind of part on any emergency, without ever learning it, and was put down in the bills under any name or names whatever that occurred to Mr. Crummles as looking well in print."—*Nicholas Nickleby.*

Grueby, John.—Servant to Lord George Gordon.—" A square-built, strong-made, bull-necked fellow of the true English breed . . . one of these self-possessed, hard-headed, imperturbable fellows, who if they are ever beaten at fisticuffs, or other kind of warfare, never know it, and go coolly on till they win."—*Barnaby Rudge.*

Gruff and Glum.—A Greenwich pensioner present at Bella Wilfer's marriage to John Rokesmith.—*Our Mutual Friend.*

Grummer.—Officer to Mr. Nupkins, the Ipswich magistrate.—" An elderly gentleman in top boots, who had been a peace officer, man and boy, for half a century at least,—who was chiefly remarkable for a bottle nose; a hoarse voice; a snuff-coloured surtout; and a wandering eye."—*Pickwick Papers.*

Grummidge, Doctor.—A member of the Medical Section of the Mudfog Association.—*The Mudfog Sketches.*

Grundy, Mr.—One of the company of law clerks whom Mr. Pickwick met at the Magpie and Stump tavern.—*Pickwick Papers.*

Gubbinses, The.—In the audience at the private theatricals at Rose Villa.—(*See* **Glumper.**)—*Sketches by Boz* (Mrs. Joseph Porter).

Gulpidge, Mr. and Mrs.—Guests at Mr. Waterbrook's

dinner-party.—" A Mr. and Mrs. Gulpidge were of the party, who had something to do at second hand (at least Mr. Gulpidge had) with the law business of the Bank."—*David Copperfield.*

Gummidge, Mrs.—Housekeeper of Daniel Peggotty; widow of a fisherman who had been Daniel Peggotty's partner. A lady of a melancholy turn of mind who said of herself " that she was a lone lorn creetur and everythink went contrairy with her," but whose moody behaviour Daniel Peggotty excused on the ground that " She's been thinking of the old 'un."—*David Copperfield.*

Gunter, Mr.—A friend of Bob Sawyer.—" A gentleman in a shirt emblazoned with pink anchors."—*Pickwick Papers.*

Guppy, Mr.—Clerk to Kenge and Carboy, who was sent to meet Esther Summerson.—" A young gentleman, who had linked himself by accident, addressed me from the pavement and said, I am from Kenge and Carboy's, Miss, of Lincoln's Inn."—*Bleak House.*

Guppy, Mrs.—Mother of Mr. William Guppy.—" My mother has a little property, which takes the form of a small life annuity, upon which she lives in an independent though unassuming manner in the Old Street Road. She has her failings—as who has not—but I never knew her do it when company was present, at which time you may freely trust her with wines, spirits, or malt liquors."—*Bleak House.*

Gusher, Mr.—A philanthropist orator.—" A flabby gentleman, with a moist surface, and eyes so much too small for his moon of a face, that they seemed to have been originally made for somebody else."—*Bleak House.*

Guster.—Mrs. Snagsby's maid.—" This proper name is the possession, and the only possession, except fifty shillings per annum and a very small box indifferently filled with clothing, of a lean young woman from a workhouse (by some supposed to have been christened Augusta) who, although she was farmed or contracted for during her growing time by an amiable benefactor of his species resident in Tooting, and cannot fail to have been developed under the most favourable circumstances, has fits, which the parish cannot account for. Guster, really aged three or four-and-twenty, but looking a round ten years older, goes cheap with this unaccountable drawback of fits."—*Bleak House.*

Gwynn, Miss.—A governess at the Bury St. Edmunds girls' school.—*Pickwick Papers.*

Haggage, Doctor.—A prisoner in the Marshalsea who attended at Little Dorrit's birth.—" The doctor was amazingly shabby, in a torn and darned rough-weather sea-jacket, out at elbows and eminently short of buttons (he had been in his time the experienced surgeon carried by a passenger ship); the dirtiest white trousers conceivable by mortal man; carpet slippers; and no visible linen."—*Little Dorrit.*

Hancock and Floby, Messrs.—Proprietors of the dry goods store where Putnam Smif was a clerk.—*Martin Chuzzlewit.*

Handford, Julius.—The name John Harmon gave the police inspector when he viewed the body found in the river and supposed to be his.—*Our Mutual Friend.*

Hannah.—Housemaid at Miss La Creevy's.—" A servant-girl with an uncommonly dirty face."—*Nicholas Nickleby.*

Hardy, Mr.—One of the party on the Steam Excursion.—" How are you, said a stout gentleman of about forty, pausing at the door in the attitude of an awkward harlequin. This was Mr. Hardy, whom we have before described, on the authority of Mrs. Stubbs, as the funny gentleman. He was an Astley-Cooperish Joe Miller—a practical joker; immensely popular with married ladies; and a general favourite with young men."—*Sketches by Boz* (The Steam Excursion).

Haredale, Geoffrey of " The Warren."—A Roman Catholic gentleman, whose house the Gordon Rioters burnt. A man whose life was embittered by an unjust suspicion attaching to him regarding the murder of his brother Reuben, and who spent his life trying to unravel the mystery, and ultimately traced the murder to Rudge.—" A burly, square-built man, negligently dressed, rough and abrupt in manner, stern and forbidding both in look and speech."—*Barnaby Rudge.*

Haredale, Miss Emma.—Niece of Mr. Geoffrey Haredale, in love with, and ultimately married, Edward Chester, son of Sir John Chester.—*Barnaby Rudge.*

Haredale, Reuben.—Brother of Geoffrey Haredale. Father of Emma, who was a child when her father was found murdered at The Warren, and was brought up by her uncle Geoffrey.—*Barnaby Rudge.*

Harker, Mr.—The officer in charge of the jury.—"He was intelligent, highly polite, and obliging; and (I was glad to hear) much respected in the city. He had an agreeable presence, good eyes, enviable black whiskers, and a fine sonorous voice; his name was Mr. Harker."—The Trial for Murder (*Christmas Stories*).

Harker, Rev. John.—One of the references given by Mrs. Miller to the Foundling Hospital on the adoption of Walter Wilding.—No Thoroughfare (*Christmas Stories*).

Harleigh, Mr.—A musical man, who took part in the private theatricals at Rose Villa.—"Mr. Harleigh smiled, and looked foolish—not an unusual thing with him."—*Sketches by Boz* (Mrs. Joseph Porter).

Harmon, Deceased.—A dust contractor who amassed a fortune which he bequeathed to his son John conditional upon his marrying Bella Wilfer, and failing him to his old servant Boffin.—*Our Mutual Friend.*

Harmon, John.—The son and heir of old Harmon. Arrives from abroad, but is attacked at the London Docks. Supposed to have been drowned. He conceals his identity, and under the name of John Rokesmith, and as a supposed poor man, woos and wins Bella Wilfer as his wife, to whom a year later he discloses that he is the wealthy John Harmon.—*Our Mutual Friend.*

Haroun, Alraschid.—The Sultan in the Seraglio at Miss Griffin's school.—"Every day after dinner for an hour we were all together, and then the Favourite and the rest of the Royal Harem competed who should most beguile the leisure of the Serene Haroun, reposing from the cares of State—which were generally, as in most affairs of State, of an arithmetical character, the Commander of the Faithful being a fearful boggler at a sum."—The Haunted House (*Christmas Stories*).

Harris, Mr.—A Bath greengrocer, who purveyed for the select company of Footmen.—" Crossing the Greengrocer's shop, and putting their hats on the stairs in the little passage behind it, they walked into a small parlour; and here the full splendour of the scene burst upon Mr. Weller's view. A couple of tables were put together in the middle of the parlour, covered with three or four cloths, of different ages and dates of washing, arranged to look as much like one as the circumstances of the case would allow. Upon these were laid knives and forks for six or eight people; some of the knife handles were green, others red, and a few yellow, and as all the forks were black, the combination of colours was exceedingly striking. Plates for a corresponding number of guests were warming behind the fender; and the guests themselves were warming before it."—*Pickwick Papers.*

Harris, Mr.—A law stationer—one of the steady old boys and a friend of Mr. Dounce.—(*See* **Dounce, John.**) —*Sketches by Boz* (The Misplaced Attachment of Mr. John Dounce).

Harris, Mr.—The family name of Short, the Showman.—(*See* **Short.**)—*The Old Curiosity Shop.*

Harris, Mrs.—An imaginary friend of Mrs. Gamp.—" A fearful mystery surrounded this lady of the name of Harris; whom no one in the circle of Mrs. Gamp's acquaintance had ever seen; neither did any human being know her place of residence; though Mrs. Gamp appeared, on her own showing, to be in constant communication with her. There were conflicting rumours on the subject; but the prevalent opinion was that she was a phantom of Mrs. Gamp's brain—as Messrs. Doe and Roe and fictions of the law—created for the express purpose of holding visionary dialogues with her, on all manner of subjects, and invariably winding up with a compliment to the excellence of her nature."—*Martin Chuzzlewit.*

Harris, Tommy.—An imaginary child of Mrs. Harris. —*Martin Chuzzlewit.*

Harrison.—A boy suggested by Mr. Milvey for adoption by Mr. and Mrs. Boffin.—" Oh Frank, remonstrated his emphatic wife, I don't think Mrs. Boffin would like an orphan who squints so much."—*Our Mutual Friend.*

Harry.—The favourite pupil of Mr. Marton, the village school-master.—" He was a very young boy—quite a little child; his hair still hung in curls about his face; and his eyes were very bright; but their light was of heaven not of earth."—*The Old Curiosity Shop.*

Harry.—A pedlar who sold a composition for removing stains, and who met Bill Sikes at a public-house after he had killed Nancy, and alarmed the burglar by noticing and offering to remove a spot of blood on his hat.—" This was an antic fellow, half pedlar and half mountebank, who travelled about the country on foot, to vend hones, strops, razors, washballs, harness-paste, medicine for dogs and horses, cheap perfumery, cosmetics, and such like wares, which he carried in a case slung to his back."—*Oliver Twist.*

Harry.—A debtor detained in Solomon Jacobs' Sponging House. Husband of Kate.—*Sketches by Boz* (A Passage in the Life of Mr. Watkins Tottle).

Hart, Mr.—An assistant master at Boston Asylum for the Blind.—*American Notes.*

Harthouse, James.—A man of the world, put up by Bounderby as a Parliamentary candidate for Coketown.—" Who had tried life as a Cornet of Dragoons and found it a bore; and had afterwards tried it in the train of an English Minister abroad and found it a bore; and had then strolled to Jerusalem and got bored there; and had then gone yachting about the world and got bored everywhere. He coached himself up with a blue-book or two; and his brother put it about among the hard-fact fellows and said—If you want to bring in for any place a handsome dog who can make you a devilish good speech, look after my brother Jem."—*Hard Times.*

Harvey, Mr. and Mrs.—The Young Couple.—" There is to be a wedding this morning at the corner house in the Terrace—Miss Emma Fielding is going to be married to young Mr. Harvey."—*Sketches of Young Couples.*

Havisham, Miss.—Had in her youth been engaged to Compeyson, but on the wedding day he failed to appear, and Miss Havisham retired from the world but always wore her wedding dress, and kept the house exactly in the condition in which it had been prepared for the wedding feast, and when she had, whilst putting on her wedding dress, received a letter from Compeyson breaking off the match. In revenge upon mankind she adopted Estella, and trained her to be a heartless flirt.—" Everybody for miles round had heard of Miss Havisham up town, as an immensely rich and grim lady, who lived in a large and dismal house, barricaded against robbers, and who led a life of seclusion."—*Great Expectations.*

Havisham, Arthur.—The brother of Miss Havisham who had been led into criminal courses by Compeyson, the scoundrel who had professed to be Miss Havisham's lover. —*Great Expectations.*

Hawdon, Captain.—The father of Esther Summerson, who in poverty assumed the name of Mr. Nemo.—*Bleak House.*

Hawk, Sir Mulberry.—A tool of Ralph Nickleby. A selfish man of the world, who preyed upon Lord Verisopht. —" Sir Mulberry Hawk was remarkable for his tact in ruining, by himself and his creatures, young gentlemen of fortune—a genteel and elegant profession, of which he undoubtedly gained the head."—*Nicholas Nickleby.*

Hawkins, Mr.—A baker of Pentonville, sued by Miss Rugg for damages for breach of promise.—*Little Dorrit.*

Hawkins, Mr.—The political young gentleman.— " His great topic is the Constitution, upon which he will declaim, by the hour together, with much heat and fury." —*Sketches of Young Gentlemen.*

Hawkinson, Mrs.—Aunt of Georgiana Podsnap, who had presented her with the only trinket she possessed, and which she offered to Mrs. Lammle to sell when Mrs. Lammle was in monetary difficulties.—*Our Mutual Friend.*

Hawkyard, Mr. Verity.—Trustee for George Silverman.—" A yellow-faced, peak-nosed gentleman, clad all in iron grey, to his gaiters."—*George Silverman's Explanation.*

Haynes, Inspector.—A London police officer.— " Strapped, and great-coated, and waiting in dim Borough doorway by appointment."—*On Duty with Inspector Field* (Reprinted Pieces).

Headstone, Bradley.—A school teacher who befriended and trained Charley Hexam; fell in love with Lizzie Hexam; in a fit of jealous rage attacked Eugene Wrayburn; and ultimately was drowned in a struggle with Rogue Riderhood.—"Bradley Headstone, in his decent black coat and waistcoat, and decent white shirt, and decent formal black tie, and decent pantaloons of pepper and salt, with his decent silver watch in his pocket, and his decent hair guard round his neck, looked a thoroughly decent young man of six-and-twenty. There was a kind of settled trouble in the face. It was the face belonging to a naturally slow or inattentive intellect; that had toiled hard to get what it had won; and that had to hold it now that it was gotten. He always seemed to be uneasy, lest anything should be missing from his mental warehouse, and taking stock to assure himself."—*Our Mutual Friend.*

Heathfield, Alfred.—Ward of Dr. Jeddler, who after his travels settled down as a country doctor and married Grace Jeddler.—"He had not become a great man; he had not grown rich; he had not forgotten the scenes and friends of his youth; he had not fulfilled any one of the Doctor's old predictions. But in his useful, patient, unknown, visiting of poor men's homes; and in his watching of sick beds, and in his daily knowledge of the gentleness and goodness flowering the by-paths of this world, not to be trodden down beneath the heavy foot of poverty, but springing up elastic in its track, and making its way beautiful; he had better learned and proved in each succeeding year the truth of his old faith. The manner of his life, though quiet and remote, had shown him how often men still entertained angels unawares, as in the olden time; and how the most unlikely forms—even some that were mean and ugly to the view and poorly clad—became irradiated by the couch of sorrow, want and pain; and changed to ministering spirits with a glory round their heads."—*The Battle of Life.*

Heathfield, Marion.—Daughter of Dr. and Mrs. Grace Heathfield.—*The Battle of Life.*

Heep, Uriah.—A hypocritical plotter, who aped humility. Was Mr. Wickfield's clerk, and afterwards became his partner. A swindler and forger, who was ultimately exposed by Micawber.—"I saw a cadaverous face appear at a small window. . . . The low orchard door then opened, and the face came out. It was quite as cadaverous as it had looked in the window, though in the grain of it there was that tinge of red which is sometimes to be observed in the skins of red-haired people. It belonged to a red-haired person—a youth of fifteen as I take it now, but looking much older—whose hair was cropped as close as the closest stubble, who had hardly any eyebrows, and no eyelashes, and eyes of a red brown, so unsheltered and unshaded that I remember wondering how he went to sleep."—*David Copperfield.*

Heep, Mrs.—Mother of Uriah.—" We entered a low old-fashioned room, walked straight into from the street, and found there Mrs. Heep, who was the dead image of Uriah, only short. She received me with the utmost humility, and apologised to me for giving her son a kiss, observing that lowly as they were they had their natural affections. . . . It was perhaps a part of Mrs. Heep's humility that she still wore weeds. Notwithstanding the lapse of time that had occurred since Mr. Heep's decease, she still wore weeds. I think there was some compromise in the cap; but otherwise she was as weedy as in the early days of her mourning."—*David Copperfield.*

Heep, Mr.—The father of Uriah.—" Father got made a sexton by being 'umble. He had the character amongst the gentlefolks of being such a well-behaved man that they were determined to bring him in. Be 'umble, Uriah, says father to me, and you'll get on."—*David Copperfield.*

Helves, Captain.—A guest at the Steam Excursion.—" Captain Helves gave slight descriptions of battles and duels, with a most bloodthirsty air, which made him the admiration of the women, and the envy of the men."—*Sketches by Boz* (The Steam Excursion).

Henri.—The man who was murdered by Louis at a Swiss inn.—(*See* **Louis.**)—The Holly Tree (*Christmas Stories*).

Henrietta.—A young lady to whom Tom the Artist paid court.—" To say that Henrietta was volatile, is but to say she was a woman; to say that she was in the bonnet trimming, is feebly to express the taste which reigned predominant in her own. She consented to walk with me. Let me do her the justice to say that she did so upon trial. I am not, said Henrietta, as yet prepared to regard you,

Thomas, in any other light than as a friend, but as a friend I am willing to walk with you, on the understanding that softer sentiments may follow—we walked."—Somebody's Luggage (*Christmas Stories*).

Henry.—Cousin of Maria Lobbs.—"The only eyesore of the whole place was another cousin of Maria Lobbs, and a brother of Kate, whom Maria Lobbs called Henry, and who seemed to keep Maria Lobbs all to himself."—*Pickwick Papers.*

Henry, Mr.—A pawnbroker's assistant.—"The gentleman behind the counter, with the curly black hair, diamond ring, and double silver watch guard."—*Sketches by Boz* (The Pawnbroker's Shop).

Herbert, Mr.—A Member of Parliament.—"While the question was under debate, Mr. Herbert, one of the members present, indignantly rose and called upon the House to observe that Lord George Gordon was there sitting under the Gallery with the blue cockade, the signal of rebellion, in his hat."—*Barnaby Rudge.*

Herschel, Mr. and Mrs.—Two of the guests at the Haunted House.—"Next there was our first cousin John Herschel, so called after the great astronomer, than whom I suppose at a telescope a better man does not breathe; with him was his wife, a charming creature to whom he had been married in the previous spring."—The Haunted House (*Christmas Stories*).

Hexam (Gaffer), Jesse.—A riverside body searcher.—"A strong man with rugged, grizzled hair, and a sunbrowned face. He had no net, hook, or line, and he could not be a fisherman; his boat had no cushion for a sitter, no paint, no inscription, no appliance beyond a rusty boat hook and a coil of rope; and he could not be a waterman; his boat was too crazy and too small to take in a cargo for delivery, and he could not be a lighterman or river carrier; there was no clue to what he looked for, but he looked for something with a most intent and searching gaze."—*Our Mutual Friend.*

Hexam, Lizzie.—Daughter of Gaffer Hexam. Assisted him on the river. After his death became a factory worker. Pursued by Bradley Headstone, who, being rejected, in mad jealousy of Eugene Wrayburn attacked him and flung him into the river, whence he was rescued by Lizzie, whom he ultimately married.—*Our Mutual Friend.*

Hexam, Charley.—Son of Gaffer Hexam, a selfish and ambitious youth, who raised himself to be a schoolmaster, but failed to appreciate his sister's devotion to him.—*Our Mutual Friend.*

Heyling, George.—The queer client whose tale Jack Bamber told to Mr. Pickwick.—*Pickwick Papers.*

Heyling, Mrs. Mary.—Wife of George Heyling.—*Pickwick Papers.*

Hicks, Mr. Septimus.—A boarder at Mrs. Tibbs', married Matilda Maplestone.—"A tallish, white-faced young man, with spectacles, and a black ribbon round his neck instead of a neckerchief; a most interesting person; a poetical walker of the hospitals. He was fond of lugging into conversation all sorts of quotations from *Don Juan,* without fettering himself by the propriety of their application, in which particular he was remarkably independent." —*Sketches by Boz* (The Boarding House).

Hicksons, The.—In the audience at the private theatricals at Rose Villa.—(*See* **Glumper.**)—*Sketches by Boz* (Mrs. Joseph Porter).

Higden, Mrs. Betty.—The great grandmother of Johnny, the orphan Mr. and Mrs. Boffin decided to adopt. A poor woman who kept a mangle, and cared for parish children, and whose great fear was that she should come on the parish.—"She was one of those old women, was Mrs. Betty Higden, who by dint of an indomitable purpose, and a strong constitution, fight out many years, though each year has come with its new knock-down blows, fresh to the fight against her; wearied by it, an active old woman, with a bright dark eye, and a resolute face, yet quite a tender creature too, not a logically reasoning woman, but God is good, and hearts may count in Heaven as high as heads." —*Our Mutual Friend.*

Hilton, Mr.—The master of ceremonies at the school ball at Minerva House.—"The popular Mr. Hilton was the next arrival; and he having, at the request of the Miss Cruptons, undertaken the office of Master of Ceremonies, the quadrilles commenced with considerable spirit."—*Sketches by Boz* (Sentiment).

Hooded Woman, The.—A supposed ghost at the Haunted House.—The Haunted House (*Christmas Stories*).

Holliday, Arthur.—Only son of a rich manufacturer.—" He was one of those reckless, rattle-pated, open-hearted, and open-mouthed young gentlemen, who possess the gift of familiarity in its highest perfection, and who scramble carelessly along the journey of life, making friends, as the phrase is, wherever they go."—The Lazy Tour of Two Idle Apprentices (*Christmas Stories*).

Holliday, Mrs. Arthur.—Wife of Arthur Holliday.—The Lazy Tour of Two Idle Apprentices (*Christmas Stories*).

Holly Tree Inn, The.—Name of a Yorkshire inn where Charley was snowed up for a week.—The Holly Tree (*Christmas Stories*).

Holms, Captain.—The heir of the miser Daniel Dancer.—*Our Mutual Friend.*

Hominy, Mrs.—An American authoress who interviewed Martin.—" Mrs. Hominy was a philosopher, and an authoress. She certainly could not be considered young —that was matter of fact; and probably could not be considered handsome—but that was matter of opinion. She was very straight, very tall, and not at all flexible in face or figure. On her head she wore a great straw bonnet, with trimmings of the same, in which she looked as if she had been thatched by an unskilful labourer."—*Martin Chuzzlewit.*

Hominy, Major.—Husband of Mrs. Hominy.—*Martin Chuzzlewit.*

Honeythunder, Luke.—Chairman of the Haven of Philanthropy.—" His philanthropy was of that gunpowderous sort that the difference between it and animosity was hard to determine; you were to have universal concord, and were to get it by eliminating all the people who wouldn't or conscientiously couldn't, be concordant; you were to love your brother as yourself, but after an indefinite interval of maligning him (very much as if you hated him) and calling him all manner of names; above all things you were to do nothing in private, or on your own account; you were to go to the offices of the Haven of Philanthropy, and put your name down as a member, and a Professing Philanthropist."—*Edwin Drood.*

Hopkins.—A candidate for the office of beadle—resigned in favour of Spruggins.—*Sketches by Boz* (Our Parish).

Hopkins.—A witch-finder who investigated Will Marks' witch story.—" The story gained such universal applause, that it soon afterwards brought down express from London the great witch-finder of the age, the Heaven-born Hopkins."—*Master Humphrey's Clock.*

Hopkins Captain.—A fellow-prisoner with Mr. Micawber in the debtors' prison.—" The Captain himself was in the last extremity of shabbiness, with large whiskers, and an old brown greatcoat, with no other coat below it."—*David Copperfield.*

Hopkins, Mr.—The bashful young gentleman.—" A fresh-coloured young gentleman with as good a promise of light whiskers as one might wish to see, and possessed of a very velvet-like soft-looking countenance. . . . His whole face was suffused with a crimson blush and bore that down-cast timid retiring look which betokens a man ill at ease with himself."—*Sketches of Young Gentlemen.*

Hopkins, Harriet.—Sister of the bashful young gentleman.—*Sketches of Young Gentlemen.*

Hopkins, Jack.—A friend of Bob Sawyer.—" A heavy footstep was heard upon the stairs, and Jack Hopkins presented himself. He wore a black velvet waistcoat, with thunder-and-lightning buttons, and a blue striped shirt with a white false collar."—*Pickwick Papers.*

Hopkins, The Misses.—Daughters of Captain Hopkins. —" There was a very dirty lady in his little room, and two wan girls, his daughters, with shock heads of hair."—*David Copperfield.*

Hopkins, Vulture.—A miser whose biography Mr. Boffin pretended to be interested in.—*Our Mutual Friend.*

Hortense.—Lady Dedlock's French maid.—" My Lady's maid is a Frenchwoman of two-and-thirty, from somewhere in the Southern country about Avignon and Marseilles; a large-eyed, brown woman with black hair, who would be handsome but for a certain feline mouth, and general uncomfortable tightness of face, rendering the jaws too eager, and the skull too prominent. Through all the good taste of her dress and little adornments these objections so express themselves, that she seems to go about like a very neat shewolf, imperfectly tamed."—*Bleak House.*

Howe, Dr.—A Boston medical man.—*American Notes.*

Howler, Rev. Melchisedech.—A ranter, whose ministrations Mrs. MacStinger attended.—" Mrs. MacStinger resorted to a great distance, every Sunday morning, to attend the ministry of the Reverend Melchisedech Howler, who, having been one day discharged from the West India Docks, on a false suspicion (got up expressly against him by the general enemy) of screwing gimlets into puncheons, and applying his lips to the orifice, had announced the destruction of the world for that day two years at ten in the morning, and opened a front parlour for the reception of ladies and gentlemen of the Ranting persuasion."—*Dombey and Son.*

Hubble.—A wheelwright, one of the Gargerys' social circle.—" I remember Mr. Hubble as a tough high-shouldered stooping old man, of a sawdusty fragrance, with his legs extraordinarily wide apart, so that, in my short days, I always saw some miles of open country between them, when I met him coming up the lane."—*Great Expectations.*

Hubble, Mrs.—The wheelwright's wife.—" I remember Mrs. Hubble, as a little, curly, sharp-edged person, in sky blue, who held a conventionally juvenile position, because she had married Mr. Hubble,—I don't know at what remote period,—when she was so much younger than he." —*Great Expectations.*

Hugh.—A lawless man, and a drunkard, son of a gipsy woman, who afterwards discovered that his father was Sir John Chester; at first ostler at the Maypole inn, afterwards a leader amongst the Gordon rioters, taken and hanged.—" A young man of a hale athletic figure, and a giant's strength, whose sunburnt face and swarthy throat, overgrown with jet black hair, might have served a painter for a model."—*Barnaby Rudge.*

Hughes, Rev. Stephen.—The clergyman of Llanallgo. —" I had heard of that clergyman, as having buried many scores of the shipwrecked people; of his having opened his house and heart to their agonized friends; of his having used a most sweet and patient diligence, for weeks and weeks, in the performance of the forlornest offices that man can render to his kind; of his having most tenderly and thoroughly devoted himself to the dead, and to those who were sorrowing for the dead. I had said to myself—In the Christmas season of the year I should like to see that man."—*The Uncommercial Traveller* (The Shipwreck).

Hughes, Rev. Hugh.—Brother of Rev. Stephen Hughes and clergyman of Penrhos, a neighbouring parish, who assisted Stephen in burying the drowned of the ship *Royal Charter.*—" He was there with his neatly arranged papers, and made no more account of his trouble than anybody else did."—*The Uncommercial Traveller* (The Shipwreck).

Humm, Anthony.—President of the Brick Lane Branch of the United Grand Junction Ebenezer Temperance Association.—" The President was the straight-walking Mr. Anthony Humm, a converted fireman, now a schoolmaster, and occasionally an itinerant preacher; . . . a sleek, white-faced man in a perpetual perspiration."—*Pickwick Papers.*

Humphrey, Master.—Owner of the clock.—" I have all my life been attached to the inanimate objects that people my chamber; and I have come to look upon them rather in the light of old and constant friends, than as mere chairs and tables, which a little money could replace at will. Chief and first among all these is my clock—my old, cheerful, companionable clock."—*Master Humphrey's Clock.*

Hunt.—Head gardener to Captain Boldwig.—*Pickwick Papers.*

Hunt and Roskell.—London jewellers in the holiday season.—" From Messrs. Hunt and Roskell's, the Jewellers, all things are absent but the precious stones, and the gold and silver, and the soldierly pensioner at the door with his decorated breast."—*The Uncommercial Traveller* (Arcadian London).

Hunter, Horace.—The successful rival of Mr. Trott

for the hand of Emily Brown.—*Sketches by Boz* (The Great Winglebury Duel).

Hunter, Mrs. Leo.—A lady to whom the Pickwickians were introduced at Eatanswill.—" His faithful valet put into his hand a card on which was engraved the following inscription : Mrs. Leo Hunter, The Den, Eatanswill."—*Pickwick Papers.*

Hunter, Mr. Leo.—Husband of Mrs. Leo Hunter.—" A grave man."—*Pickwick Papers.*

Hutley, Mr.—The name of the player known as Dismal Jemmy.—(*See* **Dismal Jemmy.**)—*Pickwick Papers.*

Hyppolite, Private.—A soldier billeted in a French town.—" Was there not Private Hyppolite billeted at the Perfumer's, who, when not on duty, volunteered to keep shop, while the fair Perfumeress stepped out to speak to a neighbour or so, and laughingly sold soap with his war sword girded on him."—Somebody's Luggage (*Christmas Stories*).

Idle, Thomas.—One of the two lazy apprentices.—" An idler of the unmixed Irish or Neapolitan type; a passive idler; a born and bred idler; a consistent idler, who practised what he would have preached if he had not been too idle to preach; a one entire and perfect chrysolite of idleness."—The Lazy Tour of Two Idle Apprentices (*Christmas Stories*).

Ikey.—A bailiff's assistant.—" A man in a coarse Petersham greatcoat; whitey-brown neckerchief; faded black suit; gamboge-coloured top-boots; and one of those large-crowned hats, formerly seldom met with, but now very generally patronized by gentlemen and costermongers."—*Sketches by Boz* (A Passage in the Life of Mr. Watkins Tottle).

Ikey.—Stable-boy at the village inn near the Haunted House.—" A high-shouldered young fellow, with a round red face, a short crop of sandy hair, a very broad, humorous mouth, a turned-up nose, and a great sleeved waistcoat of purple bars, with mother-of-pearl buttons that seemed to be growing upon him, and to be in a fair way—if it were not pruned—of covering his head and over-running his boots."—The Haunted House (*Christmas Stories*).

Infant Phenomenon.—Stage name of Miss Ninetta Crummles.—" The infant phenomenon, though of short stature had a comparatively aged countenance, and had moreover been precisely the same age,—not perhaps to the full extent of the memory of the oldest inhabitant, but certainly for five good years; but she had been kept up late every night, and put upon an unlimited allowance of gin-and-water from infancy, to prevent her growing tall, and perhaps this system of training had produced in the infant phenomenon these additional phenomena."—*Nicholas Nickleby*.

Isaac.—The officer who conveyed Mrs. Bardell to the Fleet Prison.—*Pickwick Papers*.

Issard, Mr.—One of the interviewers of Elijah Pogram.—*Martin Chuzzlewit*.

Jack.—The type of sailor whom the Uncommercial Traveller met at the Harmony public-house.—" There was British Jack, a little maudlin and sleepy, lolling over his empty glass, as if he were trying to read his fortune at the bottom; there was Loafing Jack of the Stars and Stripes, rather an unpromising customer, with his long nose, lank cheek, high cheek-bones, and nothing soft about him but his cabbage leaf hat; there was Spanish Jack, with curls of black hair, rings in his ears, and a knife not far from his hand if you got into trouble with him; there were Maltese Jack, and Jack of Sweden, and Jack the Finn, looming through the smoke of their pipes and turning faces, that looked as if they were carved out of dark wood, towards the young lady dancing the hornpipe; . . . there were Dark Jack and Dark Jack's delight, his white unlovely Nan."—*The Uncommercial Traveller* (Poor Mercantile Jack).

Jack.—The driver of the mail coach on which Tom Pinch went to London, when he left Pecksniff.—*Martin Chuzzlewit*.

Jack.—A hanger-on at the public-house by the river-side where Pip and his friends spent the night, when endeavouring to smuggle Magwitch out of the country.—" No other company was in the house than the landlord, his wife, and a frizzled male creature, the Jack of the little causeway, who was as slimy and smeary as if he had been low water mark too."—*Great Expectations*.

Jack.—A man who was taken to the hospital for identification by a woman he was charged with assaulting.—*Sketches by Boz* (The Hospital Patient).

Jackman, Major.—A boarder at Mrs. Lirriper's.—"Madam, my name is Jackman. Should you require any other reference than what I have already said, I name the Bank of England—perhaps you know it; such was the beginning of the Major's occupying the parlours, and from that hour to this the same, and a most obliging lodger, and punctual in all respects except one irregular which I need not particularly specify."—Mrs. Lirriper's Lodgings (*Christmas Stories*).

Jackson.—A former turnkey at the Marshalsea.—*Little Dorrit.*

Jackson.—An acquaintance of Lord Feenix.—"Kept boxing rooms in Bond Street—a man of very superior qualifications."—*Dombey and Son.*

Jackson.—The passenger who alighted at Mugby Junction.—"A man within five years of fifty either way, who had turned grey too soon, like a neglected fire; a man of pondering habit, brooding carriage of the head and suppressed internal voice; a man with many indications on him of having been much alone."—Mugby Junction (*Christmas Stories*).

Jackson, Mr.—Clerk to Dodson and Fogg.—"Come in, can't you, cried a voice from behind the partition, in reply to Mr. Pickwick's gentle tap at the door. The head to which the voice belonged, with a pen behind its ear, looked over the partition, and at Mr. Pickwick. It was a rugged head, the sandy hair of which, scrupulously parted on one side, and flattened down with pomatum, was twisted into little semicircular tails, round a flat face ornamented with a pair of small eyes, and garnished with a very dirty shirt collar, and a rusty black stock."—*Pickwick Papers.*

Jackson, Michael.—An imaginary informant of Detective Bucket.—"And who told you as there was anybody here, inquired Jenny's husband. A person of the name of Michael Jackson, with a blue velveteen waistcoat, with a double row of mother-of-pearl buttons, Mr. Bucket immediately answered."—*Bleak House.*

Jacksonini, Signor.—Clown at Cloisterham Theatre.—" A new grand comic Christmas pantomime is to be produced at the theatre; the latter heralded by the portrait of Signor Jacksonini the clown; saying How-do-you-do-to-morrow; quite as large as life and almost as miserable."—*Edwin Drood.*

Jacobs, Solomon.—A bailiff who arrested Mr. Watkins Tottle for debt.—*Sketches by Boz* (A Passage in the Life of Mr. Watkins Tottle).

Jacques.—The name assumed by the five members of the Patriots' Committee which met at Defarge's wine-shop.—*A Tale of Two Cities.*

Jaggers, Mr.—A lawyer in large practice at the Old Bailey, and greatly esteemed as well as feared by his clients of the criminal classes. Also the family solicitor and adviser of Miss Havisham, and the confidential solicitor of Magwitch, Pip's benefactor.—" He was a burly man of an exceedingly dark complexion, with an exceedingly large head, and a corresponding large hand. He took my chin in his large hand, and turned up my face to have a look at me. He was prematurely bald on the top of his head, and had bushy black eyebrows, that wouldn't lie down, but stood up bristling. His eyes were set very deep in his head, and were disagreeably sharp and suspicious. He had a large watch chain, and shiny black dots where his beard and whiskers would have been if he had let them."—*Great Expectations.*

Jairings.—A London hotel.—" Jairings being an hotel for families and gentlemen, in high repute among the Midland Counties. Mr. Grazinglands plucked up a great spirit when he told Mrs. Grazinglands she should have a chop there. That lady otherwise felt that she was going to see life."—*The Uncommercial Traveller* (Refreshments for Travellers).

James.—Mr. Bayham Badger's butler.—*Bleak House.*

James.—Son of Old John, the inventor.—" One of my sons (James) went wild and for a soldier, where he was shot in India, living six weeks in hospital with a musket ball lodged in his shoulder-blade, which he wrote with his own hand."—*A Poor Man's Tale of a Patent* (Reprinted Pieces).

James and John.—Twin brothers in business at Goodman's Fields.—*To be Read at Dusk* (Reprinted Pieces).

James, Henry.—The captain of the barque *Defiance* who sighted and reported the wreck of Dombey and Son's ship *The Son and Heir*, in which Walter Gay had sailed for the West Indies.—*Dombey and Son.*

Jane.—Maidservant to Mrs. Potts at Eatanswill.—*Pickwick Papers.*

Jane.—A maidservant at Manor Farm.—*Pickwick Papers.*

Jane.—Maidservant at Mr. Pecksniff's.—*Martin Chuzzlewit.*

Jane.—Sister of the lively young lady, a client of Madame Mantalini, who insisted on being attended by Kate Nickleby.—*Nicholas Nickleby.*

Jane.—A young lady visitor at Ramsgate.—"The eldest daughter of a stout lady with four girls."—*Sketches by Boz* (The Tuggses at Ramsgate).

Jane.—Mrs. Kitterbell's maid.—"Jane, tell Nurse to bring down baby, said Mrs. Kitterbell, addressing the servant."—*Sketches by Boz* (The Bloomsbury Christening).

Jane.—A waitress at Bellamy's.—"That female in black is Jane, the Hebe of Bellamy's. Jane is as great a character as Nicholas in her way. Her leading features are a thorough contempt for the great majority of her visitors, her predominant quality love of admiration. Jane is no bad hand at repartees, and showers them about with a degree of liberality, and total absence of reserve or constraint, which occasionally excites no small amazement in the minds of strangers."—*Sketches by Boz* (A Parliamentary Sketch).

Jane, Aunt.—One of the guests at the Christmas family party.—"Suddenly a hackney-coach is heard to stop, and Uncle George, who has been looking out of the window, exclaims Here's Jane; on which the children rush to the door, and helter skelter downstairs, and Uncle Robert and Aunt Jane, and the dear little baby, and the nurse, and the whole party, are ushered upstairs, amidst tumultuous shouts of Oh my! from the children, and frequently repeated warnings not to hurt the baby from the nurse."—*Sketches by Boz* (A Christmas Dinner).

Jane, Aunt.—(*See* **Elizabeth, Miss.**)—*Our Mutual Friend.*

Janet.—Miss Betsy Trotwood's servant.—" Janet was a pretty blooming girl of about nineteen or twenty, and a perfect picture of neatness. . . . She was one of a series of protegées whom my aunt had taken into her service, expressly to educate in a renouncement of mankind, and who had generally completed their abjuration by marrying the baker."—*David Copperfield.*

Jarber.—The man who read to Trottle the story of the House to Let.—Going into Society (*Christmas Stories*).

Jardine, The Brothers.—Misers whose biography Mr. Boffin pretended to be interested in.—*Our Mutual Friend.*

Jarley's Wax-works.—" It isn't funny at all, repeated Mrs. Jarley. It's calm and—what's that word again—critical—no classical, that's it—it's calm and classical; no low beatings and knockings about; no jokings and squeakings like your precious Punches; but always the same, with a constantly unchanging air of coldness and gentility; and so like life that, if wax-work only spoke and walked about, you'd hardly know the difference. I won't go so far as to say that, as it is, I've seen wax-work quite like life; but I've certainly seen some life that was exactly like wax-work."—*The Old Curiosity Shop.*

Jarley, Mrs.—Proprietrix of a travelling wax-work show, who befriended Little Nell.—" At the open door sat a Christian lady, stout and comfortable to look upon, who wore a large bonnet trembling with bows."—*The Old Curiosity Shop.*

Jarndyce and Jarndyce.—A Chancery suit of long standing, regarding a fund which is ultimately eaten up in costs.—" It was about a will. A certain Jarndyce in an evil hour made a great fortune, and made a great will. In the question how the trusts under that will are to be administered, the fortune left by the will is squandered away. This scarecrow of a suit has in course of time become so complicated that no man alive knows what it means."—*Bleak House.*

Jarndyce, John.—The owner of Bleak House, guardian of Ada Clare and Richard Carstone.—"I glanced (I need not say with how much interest) at his face. It was a handsome, lively, quick face; full of change and motion; and his hair was a silvered iron-grey. I took him to be nearer sixty than fifty, but he was upright, hearty and robust."—*Bleak House.*

Jarndyce, Tom.—Great uncle of John Jarndyce and originator of the Chancery suit.—"Old Tom Jarndyce in despair blew his brains out at a Coffee House in Chancery Lane."—*Bleak House.*

Jarrel, Dick.—A miser whose biography Mr. Boffin pretended to be interested in.—*Our Mutual Friend.*

Jarvis.—Clerk to Wilding and Co., Wine Merchants.—No Thoroughfare (*Christmas Stories*).

Jasper, John.—Lay Precentor at Cloisterham Cathedral.—"Mr. Jasper is a dark man, of some six-and-twenty, with thick, lustrous, well-arranged black hair and whiskers. He looks older than he is, as dark men often do. His voice is deep and good, his face and figure are good, his manner is a little sombre."—*Edwin Drood.*

Jeddler, Doctor.—A retired medical man, father of Grace and Marion.—"Doctor Jeddler was, as I have said, a good philosopher and the heart and mystery of his philosophy was to look upon the world as a gigantic practical joke; as something too absurd to be considered seriously by any rational man."—*The Battle of Life.*

Jeddler, Grace.—The elder daughter of Doctor Jeddler, sister of Marion.—"The difference between them, in respect of age, could not exceed four years at most, but Grace, as often happens in such cases when no mother watches over both (the Doctor's wife was dead), seemed, in her gentle care of her young sister, and in the steadiness of her devotion to her, older than she was; and more removed in the course of nature from all competition with her, or participation, otherwise than through her sympathy and true affection, in her wayward fancies, than their ages seemed to warrant; great character of mother, that, even in this shadow and faint reflection of it, purifies the heart, and raises the exalted nature nearer to the angels."—*The Battle of Life.*

Jeddler, Marion.—Younger daughter of Dr. Jeddler. Affianced to Alfred Heathfield, but knowing her sister Grace to be also in love with him, left on the eve of her marriage and allowed herself to be supposed to have eloped with Michael Warden.—*The Battle of Life.*

Jeddler, Martha.—Sister of Dr. Jeddler, who received her niece Marion when she ran away from home.—" My good spinster sister Martha Jeddler, who had what she calls her domestic trials ages ago, and has led a sympathising life with all sorts of people ever since."—*Battle of Life.*

Jellyby, Mrs.—A lady who devoted herself to African mission work, and neglected her own household.—" She was a pretty, very diminutive, plump woman of from forty to fifty, with handsome eyes, though they had a curious habit of seeming to look a long way off, as if they could see nothing nearer than Africa. Mrs. Jellyby had very good hair, but was too much occupied with her African duties to brush it; the shawl in which she had been loosely muffled dropped on to her chair when she advanced to us, and as she turned to resume her seat we could not help noticing that her dress didn't nearly meet up the back, and that the open space was railed across with a lattice-work of stay-lace—like a summer-house."—*Bleak House.*

Jellyby, Mr.—The meek husband of Mrs. Jellyby.—" He was a Custom House and General Agent, and the only thing I ever understood about that business was that, when he wanted money more than usual, he went to the Docks to look for it, and hardly ever found it."—*Bleak House.*

Jellyby, Caroline (Caddy).—Daughter of, and amanuensis to, Mrs. Jellyby.—" What principally struck us was a jaded and unhealthy-looking, though by no means plain, girl at the writing-table, who sat biting the feather of her pen and staring at us. I suppose nobody ever was in such a state of ink, and from her tumbled hair to her pretty feet, which were disfigured with frayed and broken satin slippers trodden down at heel, she really seemed to have no article of dress upon her, from a pin upwards, that was in its proper condition or its right place."—*Bleak House.*

Jem.—One of Mr. Wardle's farm servants.—*Pickwick Papers.*

Jemima.—Sister of Mrs. Polly Toodles, who took charge of her family whilst she was nursing Paul Dombey.—*Dombey and Son.*

Jenkins.—Sir Mulberry Hawk's manservant.—*Nicholas Nickleby.*

Jenkins, Miss.—One of the orchestra at the private theatricals.—" A self-taught, deaf gentleman, who had kindly offered to bring his flute, would be a most valuable addition to the orchestra. Miss Jenkins' talent for the piano was too well known to be doubted for an instant; Mr. Cape had practised the violin accompaniment with her frequently; and Mr. Brown, who had kindly undertaken at a few hours' notice, to bring the violoncello, would no doubt manage extremely well."—*Sketches by Boz* (Mrs. Joseph Porter).

Jenkinson.—A messenger at the Circumlocution Office.—*Little Dorrit.*

Jennings, Mr.—A robe-maker, one of the steady old boys, friend of Mr. Dounce.—(*See* **Dounce, John.**)—*Sketches by Boz* (The Misplaced Attachment of Mr. John Dounce).

Jennings, Mr.—Secretary to Mr. Tulrumble, the Mayor of Mudfog.—*The Mudfog Sketches.*

Jennings, Miss.—A pupil at Nuns' House.—*Edwin Drood.*

Jenny.—Wife of a brickmaker, visited by Mrs. Pardiggle.—" A woman with a black eye, nursing a poor little gasping boy."—*Bleak House.*

Jerry.—Proprietor of a troupe of performing dogs.—" Jerry, the manager of these dancing dogs, was a tall, black-whiskered man, in a velveteen coat."—*The Old Curiosity Shop.*

Jilkins.—A medical man consulted by Our Bore.—" At that period in a very small practice, and living in the upper part of a house in Great Portland Street. . . . His words were these—you have been humbugged; this is a case of indigestion, occasioned by a deficiency of power in the stomach; take a mutton chop in half-an-hour, with a glass of the finest old Sherry that can be got for money;

take two mutton chops to-morrow, and two glasses of the finest old Sherry; next day I'll come again. In a week Our Bore was on his legs, and Jilkins' success dates from that period."—*Our Bore* (Reprinted Pieces).

Jingle, Alfred ("of No Hall, Nowhere").—An adventurer.—"He was about the middle height; but the thinness of his body and the length of his legs gave him the appearance of being much taller. The green coat had been a smart dress garment in the days of swallow-tails, but had evidently in those times adorned a much shorter man, for the soiled and faded sleeves scarcely reached to his wrists. It was buttoned closely up to his chin, at the imminent hazard of splitting the back; and an old stock, without a vestige of collar, ornamented his neck. His scanty black trousers displayed here and there those shiny patches which bespeak long service, and were strapped very tightly over a pair of patched and mended shoes, as if to conceal the dirty white stockings, which were, nevertheless, distinctly visible. His long black hair escaped in negligent waves from beneath each side of his old pinched-up hat; and glimpses of his bare wrists might be observed between the tops of his gloves and the cuffs of his coat sleeves. His face was thin and haggard, but an indescribable air of jaunty impudence and perfect self-possession pervaded the whole man."—*Pickwick Papers.*

Jiniwin, Mrs.—Mother of Mrs. Quilp.—"Mrs. Quilp's parent was known to be laudably shrewish in her disposition, and inclined to resist male authority."—*The Old Curiosity Shop.*

Jinkins.—A pawnbroker's customer.—"An unshaven, dirty, sottish-looking fellow; whose tarnished paper cap, stuck negligently over one eye, communicates an additionally repulsive expression to his very uninviting countenance."—*Sketches by Boz* (The Pawnbroker's Shop).

Jinkins, Mr.—The senior boarder at Todgers'.—"Mr. Jinkins was of a fashionable turn, being a regular frequenter of the Parks on Sundays, and knowing a great many carriages by sight. Mr. Jinkins, it may be added, was much the oldest of the party, being a fish salesman's book-keeper aged forty. He was the oldest boarder also, and, in right of his double seniority, took the lead in the house."—*Martin Chuzzlewit.*

Jinkins, Mr.—An admirer of the landlady of the inn at Marlborough Downs patronized by Tom Smart.—" A tall man—a very tall man—in a brown coat and bright basket buttons; and black whiskers and wavy hair; who was seated at tea with the widow, and who, it required no great penetration to discover, was in a fair way of persuading her to be a widow no longer."—*Pickwick Papers* (The Bagman's Story).

Jinkinson.—A barber friend of Mr. Weller.—*Master Humphrey's Clock.*

Jinks.—Clerk to Mr. Nupkins, the Ipswich magistrate. —" A pale sharp-nosed, half-fed, shabbily-clad clerk of middle age."—*Pickwick Papers.*

Jip.—Dora Spenlow's pet dog.—" On my way through the hall I encountered her little dog, who was called Jip—short for Gipsy. I approached him tenderly, for I loved even him; but he showed his whole set of teeth, got under a chair expressly to snarl and wouldn't hear of the least familiarity."—*David Copperfield.*

Jo.—A crossing-sweeper.—" Jo sweeps his crossing all day long. He sums up his mental condition, when asked a question, by replying that he don't know nothink; he knows that it is hard to keep the mud off the crossing in dirty weather, and harder still to live by doing it; nobody taught him even that much; he found it out."—*Bleak House.*

Jobba, Mr.—A member of the Mechanical Science Section of the Mudfog Association.—" Mr. Jobba produced a forcing machine, on a novel plan, for bringing joint stock railway shares prematurely to a premium."—*The Mudfog Sketches.*

Jobbling, Anthony.—A friend of Mr. Guppy.—" Mr. Jobbling is buttoned up closer than mere adornment might require; his hat presents at the rims a peculiar appearance of a glistening nature, as if it had been a favourite snail promenade; the same phenomenon is visible on some parts of his coat, and particularly at the seams; he has the faded appearance of a gentleman in embarrassed circumstances;

even his light whiskers droop with something of a shabby air."—*Bleak House.*

Jobling, Doctor.—The medical officer of the Anglo-Bengalee Insurance Company.—" He had a portentously sagacious chin; and a pompous voice, with a rich huskiness in some of its tones, that went directly to the heart . . . perhaps he could shake his head, rub his hands, or warm himself before a fire, better than any man alive; and he had a peculiar way of smacking his lips and saying Ah, at intervals, whilst patients detailed their symptoms, which inspired great confidence."—*Martin Chuzzlewit.*

Jobson Family.—Emigrants on board the *Amazon*, bound for Salt Lake City.—" This group is composed of an old grandfather and grandmother; their married son and his wife, and *their* family of children. Orson Jobson is a little child, asleep in his mother's arms. The Doctor, with a kind word or so, lifts up the corner of the mother's shawl, looks at the child's face, and touches the little clenched hand. If we were all as well as Orson Jobson, doctoring would be a poor profession."—*The Uncommercial Traveller* (Bound for the Great Salt Lake).

Jobson, Brigham.—One of the Jobson children, on board the *Amazon*, kissed by Anastasia Weedle.—" Away she goes, and joins the Jobsons, who are waiting for her, and stoops and kisses Brigham Jobson—who appears to be considered too young for the purpose, by several Mormons rising twenty, who are looking on."—*The Uncommercial Traveller* (Bound for the Great Salt Lake).

Jodd, Mr.—One of the interviewers of Elijah Pogram. —*Martin Chuzzlewit.*

Joey, Captain.—A customer at the Fellowship Porters Tavern.—" A bottle-nosed person in a glazed hat."—*Our Mutual Friend.*

Joe.—Mr. Wardle's page-boy.—" On the box sat a fat and red-faced boy in a state of somnolency."—*Pickwick Papers.*

Joe.—The guard of the Dover mail.—*A Tale of Two Cities.*

Joe.—The hotel porter who took Nancy's message to Rose Maylie.—*Oliver Twist.*

Joe.—A dock labourer who called Walter Gay to take charge of Florence Dombey when she got lost at the docks.—*Dombey and Son.*

Joe.—Keeper of a rag store and receiver of stolen property.—" Sitting among the wares he dealt in, by a clear coal stove made of old bricks, was a grey-haired rascal nearly seventy years of age, who had screened himself from the cold air without by a frowsy curtaining of miscellaneous tatters, hung upon a line, and smoked his pipe in all the luxury of calm retirement."—*A Christmas Carol.*

Joe.—The driver of the Cloisterham omnibus.—*Edwin Drood.*

Jogg, Miss.—An artist's model.—*Bleak House.*

John.—A clown visited by Dismal Jemmy in sickness. —" A low pantomime actor, and like many people of his class an habitual drunkard."—*Pickwick Papers.*

John.—A riverside labourer.—*Dombey and Son.*

John.—The tenant of the Haunted House.—" My health required a temporary residence in the country, and a friend of mine who knew that, and who had happened to drive past the house, had written to me to suggest it as a likely place."—The Haunted House (*Christmas Stories*).

John.—The carpenter of the *Golden Mary.*—The Wreck of the *Golden Mary* (*Christmas Stories*).

John, Old.—A mechanical inventor.—" My name is John; I have been called Old John ever since I was nineteen years of age on account of not having much hair."—*A Poor Man's Tale of a Patent* (Reprinted Pieces).

Johnny.—Great grandchild of Betty Higden. A boy whom Mr. and Mrs. Boffin proposed to adopt, but he died before being transferred to their home.—" Yes, ma'am, he's a pretty boy; he's a dear darling boy; he's the child of my own last left daughter's daughter; but she's gone the way of all the rest. . . . With his chin tucked down, in his shy childish manner, he was looking furtively at Mrs. Boffin out of his blue eyes."—*Our Mutual Friend.*

Johnson.—A pupil at Dr. Blimber's.—*Dombey and Son.*

Johnson, Mr.—The name assumed by Nicholas when he became tutor to the Kenwigs' children, and also when in Mr. Crummles' company on the stage.—"Mrs. Kenwigs returned to propose that Mr. Johnson should instruct the four Miss Kenwigs in the French language, as spoken by natives, at the weekly stipend of five shillings, current coin of the realm, being at the rate of one shilling per week for each Miss Kenwigs, and one shilling over, until such time as the baby might be able to take it out in grammar." —*Nicholas Nickleby.*

Johnson, Tom.—One of the acquaintances whom Lord Feenix pointed out to Mr. Dombey at Brighton at Mrs. Skewton's funeral.—"Cousin Feenix, sitting in the mourning coach, recognizes innumerable acquaintances on the road, but takes no other notice of them in decorum than checking them off aloud as they go by, for Mr. Dombey's information,—as Tom Johnson—man with cork leg from White's—what—are you here, Tommy—Foley on a blood mare, the Smalder girls, and so forth."—*Dombey and Son.*

Jollson, Mrs.—Tenant of No. 9, Brig Place, prior to MacStinger.—"There was a Mrs. Jollson lived at Number Nine before me, and perhaps you're mistaking me for her." —*Dombey and Son.*

Jolly Sandboys, The.—The inn where Little Nell and her grandfather stayed with Codlin and Short.—"The 'Jolly Sandboys' was a small roadside inn, of pretty ancient date, with a sign representing three sandboys, increasing their jollity with as many jugs of ale and bags of gold, creaking and swinging on its post on the opposite side of the road."—*The Old Curiosity Shop.*

Joltered, Sir William.—President of the Zoology and Botany Section of the Mudfog Association.—*The Mudfog Sketches.*

Jonathan.—A customer at the Fellowship Porters.—(*See* **Williams.**)—*Our Mutual Friend.*

Jones.—A shopman with Blaze and Sparkle, Jewellers.

—" Our people, Mr. Jones, said Blaze and Sparkle to the hand in question on engaging him, our people, sir, are sheep—mere sheep; where two or three marked ones go, all the rest follow; keep these two or three in your eye, Mr. Jones, and you have the flock."—*Bleak House.*

Jones.—A barrister's clerk; one of the steady old boys; a friend of Mr. Dounce.—(*See* **Dounce, John.**)—*Sketches by Boz* (The Misplaced Attachment of Mr. Dounce).

Jones, George.—A customer at the Fellowship Porters Tavern.—" On the clock's striking ten, and Miss Abbey's appearing at the door, and addressing a certain person in a faded scarlet jacket with—George Jones, your time's up; I told your wife you should be punctual; Jones submissively rose, gave the company good night, and retired."—*Our Mutual Friend.*

Jones, Master.—A Canterbury school-boy. An admirer of Miss Shepherd, and rival of David's.—" Whispers reach me of Miss Shepherd having said she wished I wouldn't stare so, and having avowed a preference for Master Jones—for Jones, a boy of no merit whatever." —*David Copperfield.*

Jones, Mr.—A guest at the dinner given by Mr. Buddon to his cousin Mr. Minns.—" A little smirking man with red whiskers."—*Sketches by Boz* (Mr. Minns and His Cousin).

Jones, Rev. Mr. (of Blewbury).—A miser whose biography Mr. Boffin pretended to be interested in.—*Our Mutual Friend.*

Jones, Spruggins and Smith.—A cheap shop where Mrs. Malderton and her daughters went shopping, and discovered Horatio Sparkins to be Smith the junior partner.—" The vehicle stopped before a dirty-looking ticketed linen-draper's shop, with goods of all kinds, and labels of all sorts and sizes, in the window; there were dropsical figures of seven, with a little three farthings in the corner, perfectly invisible to the naked eye; three hundred and fifty thousand ladies' boas *from* one shilling and a penny halfpenny; real French kid shoes at two and ninepence per pair; green parasols at an equally cheap rate; and every description of goods, as the proprietors said—and they must know best—fifty per cent. under cost price."—*Sketches by Boz* (Horatio Sparkins).

Joper.—A club acquaintance of Lord Feenix.—"In point of fact I said so to a man at Brooks'—little Billy Joper—you know him no doubt—man with a glass in his eye."—*Dombey and Son.*

Joram.—Assistant to Mr. Omer, the funeral undertaker; afterwards partner in the firm of Omer and Joram. Married Minnie Omer.—*David Copperfield.*

Joram, Joe.—Child of Mrs. Joram (Minnie Omer).—*David Copperfield.*

Jorgan, Captain Silas.—Who found Hugh Raybrock's message on a lonely island.—"He had seen many things and places, and had stowed them all away in a shrewd intellect and a vigorous memory. He was an American born was Captain Jorgan—a New Englander—but he was a citizen of the world, and a combination of most of the best qualities of most of its best countries."—A Message from the Sea (*Christmas Stories*).

Jorkins, Mr.—Junior partner of Spenlow and Jorkins.—"I was quite dismayed by the idea of this terrible Jorkins, but I found out afterwards that he was a mild man of a heavy temperament, whose place in the business was to keep himself in the background, and be constantly exhibited as the most obdurate and ruthless of men. If a clerk wanted his salary raised, Mr. Jorkins wouldn't listen to such a proposition; if a client were slow to settle his bill of costs, Mr. Jorkins was resolved to have it paid, and however painful these things might be (and always were) to the feelings of Mr. Spenlow, Mr. Jorkins would have his bond. The heart and hand of the good angel Spenlow would have always been open but for the restraining demon Jorkins. As I have grown older, I think I have had experience of some other houses doing business on the principle of Spenlow and Jorkins."—*David Copperfield.*

Joseph.—"Much respected Head Waiter at the Slamjam Coffee House, London, E.C., than which a individual more eminently deserving of the name of man, or a more amenable honour to his own head and heart, whether considered in the light of a waiter, or regarded as a human being, do not exist."—Somebody's Luggage (*Christmas Stories*).

Joseph and Cecilia.—Two charity children whom the Uncommercial Traveller met in a city church.—"In another city churchyard, of similar cramful dimensions, I saw, that self-same summer, two comfortable charity children. They were making love—tremendous proof of the vigour of that immortal article—for they were in the graceful uniform under which English charity delights to hide herself; and they were overgrown; and their legs (his legs at least, for I am modestly incompetent to speak of hers) were as much in the wrong as mere passive weakness of character can render legs."—*The Uncommercial Traveller* (The City of the Absent).

Jowl, Joe.—A gambler whom Mr. Trent met at The Valiant Soldier public-house.—"A burly fellow, of middle age; with large black whiskers, broad cheeks, a coarse wide mouth, and bull neck, which was pretty freely displayed, as his shirt collar was only confined by a loose red neckerchief."—*The Old Curiosity Shop*.

Joy, Thomas.—A friend of Old John, the inventor.—"T. J. is a carpenter six foot four in height and plays quoits well."—*A Poor Man's Tale of a Patent* (Reprinted Pieces).

Julia.—The Temple bachelor's sweetheart.—"I am a bachelor, residing in a rather dreary set of chambers in the Temple. I need scarcely add perhaps that I am in love, and that the father of my charming Julia objects to our union."—*The Ghost of Art* (Reprinted Pieces).

Jupe.—A clown in Sleary's Circus.—"Signor Jupe was to enliven the varied performances, at frequent intervals, with his chaste Shakesperian quips and retorts. Lastly he was to wind them up by appearing in his favourite character of Mr. William Burton of Tooley Street, in the highly novel and laughable hippo-comedietta of The Tailor's Journey to Brentford."—*Hard Times*.

Jupe, Sissy.—Daughter of a circus clown. Scholar at Mr. Gradgrind's school; afterwards servant in his family.

—" Girl number twenty, said Mr. Gradgrind, squarely pointing with his square forefinger,—I don't know that girl—who is that girl. Sissy Jupe, sir, explained number twenty, blushing, standing up and curtseying. Sissy is not a name, said Mr. Gradgrind, don't call yourself Sissy, call yourself Cecilia."—*Hard Times*.

Kags.—A convict.—" There were assembled three men who, regarding each other every now and then with looks expressive of perplexity and expectation, sat for some time in profound and gloomy silence. One of these was Toby Crackit, another Mr. Chitling, and the third a robber of fifty years, whose nose had been almost beaten in in some old scuffle, and whose face bore a frightful scar which might probably be traced to the same occasion. This man was a returned transport, and his name was Kags."—*Oliver Twist*.

Kate.—A young lady visiting at Sir Barnet Skettles' country house when Florence Dombey was there.—*Dombey and Son*.

Kate.—Wife of Harry, a debtor detained in Solomon Jacobs' sponging house.—*Sketches by Boz* (A Passage in the Life of Mr. Watkins Tottle).

Kate.—Cousin of Maria Lobbs.—" An arch, impudent-looking, bewitching little person."—*Pickwick Papers*.

Kedgick, Captain.—Landlord of the National Hotel, where Martin stayed en route to Eden.—*Martin Chuzzlewit*.

Kenge, Mr.—A London solicitor, of the firm of Kenge and Carboy.—" A portly, important-looking gentleman, dressed all in black, with a white cravat, large gold watch seals, a pair of gold eyeglasses, and a large seal ring upon his little finger. He appeared to enjoy beyond everything the sound of his own voice. I was very much impressed by him, even then, before I knew that he formed himself on the model of a great lord who was his client, and that he was generally called Conversation Kenge."—*Bleak House*.

Kenwigs, Mr.—The tenant of the first floor of the building in which Mr. Crowel and Mr. Newman Noggs occupied garrets.—" Mr. Kenwigs, a turner in ivory, was looked upon as a person of some consideration on the premises, inasmuch as he occupied the whole of the first floor, comprising a suite of two rooms."—*Nicholas Nickleby*.

Kenwigs, Mrs. Susan.—Wife of Mr. Kenwigs.—"Mrs. Kenwigs was quite a lady in her manners, and of a very genteel family, having an uncle who collected a water rate; besides which distinction, the two eldest of her little girls went twice a week to a dancing school in the neighbourhood, and had flaxen hair tied with blue ribands hanging in luxuriant pig-tails down their backs, and wore little white trousers with frills round the ankles; for all which reasons, and many more equally valid but too numerous to mention, Mrs. Kenwigs was considered a very desirable person to know, and was the constant theme of all the gossips in the street, and even three or four doors round the corner at both ends."—*Nicholas Nickleby*.

Kenwigs, Miss Morlena.—Eldest child of Mr. and Mrs. Kenwigs.—"Regarding whose uncommon Christian name, it may be here remarked that it had been invented and composed by Mrs. Kenwigs, previous to her first lying-in, for the special distinction of her eldest child, in case it should prove a daughter."—*Nicholas Nickleby*.

Kenwigs, Lillyvick.—The baby of Mr. and Mrs. Kenwigs, named after Mrs. Kenwigs' uncle, the tax-collector.—*Nicholas Nickleby*.

Ketch, Professor.—A member of the Mudfog Association.—*The Mudfog Sketches*.

Kettle, Mr. la Fayette.—Editor of the *Watertouch Gazette*, whom Martin met in a train.—"He was as languid and listless in his looks as most of the gentlemen they had seen; his cheeks were so hollow, that he seemed to be always sucking them in; and the sun had burnt him, not a wholesome red or brown, but a dirty yellow; he had bright dark eyes, which he kept half closed, only peeping out of the corners, and even then with a glance that seemed to say—now you won't overreach me; you want to, but you won't."—*Martin Chuzzlewit*.

Kibble, Jacob.—A fellow-passenger with John Harmon on his homeward voyage, and a witness at the inquest upon the body supposed to be Harmon's found in the river by Gaffer Hexam.—"And Mr. Kibble. Ain't he a passenger all over,—there's that mercantile cut upon him which would make you happy to give him credit for five hundred pounds."—*Our Mutual Friend.*

Kidgerbury, Mrs.—A person employed as temporary servant of David and Dora.—"After an interval of Mrs. Kidgerbury—the oldest inhabitant of Kentish Town I believe—who went out charing, but was too feeble to execute her conceptions of that art, we found another treasure."—*David Copperfield.*

Kimmeens, Kitty.—A pupil at Miss Pupford's school. —"The holidays began. Five of the six pupils kissed little Kitty Kimmeens twenty times over (round total one hundred times, for she was very popular) and so went home. Miss Kitty Kimmeens remained behind, for her relations and friends were all in India far away. A self-helpful, steady little child is Miss Kitty Kimmeens, a dimpled child too, and a loving."—Tom Tiddler's Ground (*Christmas Stories*).

Kinch, Horace.—A man who had gone down-hill.—"A very curious disease the dry rot in men, and difficult to detect the beginning of. It had carried Horace Kinch inside the wall of the old King's Bench prison, and it carried him out with his feet foremost . . . like some fair-looking houses or fair-looking ships, he took the dry rot . . . a certain slovenliness and deterioration, which is not poverty, nor dirt, nor intoxication, nor ill-health, but simply dry rot. To this succeeds a smell as of strong waters in the morning; to that a looseness respecting money; to that a stronger smell as of strong waters at all times; to that a looseness respecting everything; to that a trembling of the limbs, somnolency, misery, and crumbling to pieces."—*The Uncommercial Traveller* (Night Walks).

Kindheart, Mr.—An Englishman whom the Uncommercial Traveller met abroad.—"Once I dwelt in an Italian city, where there dwelt with me for a while an Englishman, of an amiable nature, great enthusiasm, and no discretion."—*The Uncommercial Traveller* (Medicine Men of Civilization).

King, Christian George.—A negro traitor who betrayed the Silver Store Colony to the pirates.—" If I had been Captain of the *Christopher Columbus,* instead of a private in the Royal Marines, I should have kicked Christian George King—who was no more a Christian than he was a King or a George—over the side, without exactly knowing why, except that it was the right thing to do." —The Perils of Certain English Travellers (*Christmas Stories*).

Kit.—The shop-boy at the Old Curiosity Shop.—" Kit was a shock-headed, shambling, awkward lad, with an uncommonly wide mouth, very red cheeks, a turned-up nose, and certainly the most comical expression of face I ever saw."—*The Old Curiosity Shop.*

Kitten, Mr.—Deputy-commissioner at Silver Store Colony.—" Mr. Kitten, a small, youngish, bald, botanical and mineralogical gentleman, also connected with the mine —but everybody there was that more or less—was sometimes called by Mr. Commissioner Pordage his Vice-Commissioner; and sometimes his Deputy Consul; or sometimes he spoke of Mr. Kitten merely as being ' under Government.' "—The Perils of Certain English Travellers (*Christmas Stories*).

Kitterbell, Charles.—Nephew of Nicodemus Dumps.— " Mr. Charles Kitterbell was a small, sharp, spare man with a very large head, and a broad good-humoured countenance. He looked like a faded giant, with the head and face partially restored, and he had a cast in his eye, which rendered it quite impossible for any one with whom he conversed to know where he was looking."—*Sketches by Boz* (The Bloomsbury Christening).

Kitterbell, Mrs. Jemima.—Wife of Charles Kitterbell. —" Mrs. Kitterbell was a tall thin young lady, with very light hair, and a particularly white face; one of those young women who almost invariably, though one hardly knows why, recall to one's mind the idea of a cold fillet of veal."—*Sketches by Boz* (The Bloomsbury Christening).

Kitterbell, Frederick Charles William.—Son of Mr. and Mrs. Kitterbell, to whom Mr. Dumps acted as godfather.—" Suffice it to say that the single ladies unanimously voted him an angel; and that the married ones *nem. con.* agreed that he was decidedly the finest baby they had ever beheld—except their own."—*Sketches by Boz* (The Bloomsbury Christening).

Klem, Mrs.—A summer caretaker.—"My landlord having taken his whole establishment to be salted down, I am waited on by an elderly woman, labouring under a chronic sniff, who, at the shadowy hour of half-past nine o'clock of every evening, gives admittance at the street door to a meagre and mouldy old man, whom I have never yet seen detached from a flat pint of beer in a pewter pot. The meagre and mouldy old man is her husband, and the pair have a dejected consciousness that they are not justified in appearing on the surface of the earth. They come out of some hole when London empties itself, and go in again when it fills."—*The Uncommercial Traveller* (Arcadian London).

Klem, Mr.—Husband of Mrs. Klem.—"What becomes of Mr. Klem all day, or when he goes out, or why, is a mystery I cannot penetrate; but at half-past nine he never fails to turn up on the doorstep with the flat pint of beer; and the pint of beer, flat as it is, is so much more important than himself, that it always seems to my fancy as if it had found him drivelling in the street, and had humanely brought him home."—*The Uncommercial Traveller* (Arcadian London).

Klem, Miss.—Daughter of Mr. and Mrs. Klem.—"The most extraordinary circumstance I have traced in connection with this aged couple is that there is a Miss Klem, their daughter,—apparently ten years older than either of them."—*The Uncommercial Traveller* (Arcadian London).

Knag, Miss.—The chief assistant at Madame Mantalini's.—"A short, bustling, over-dressed female, full of importance. It may be further remarked that Miss Knag still aimed at youth, although she had shot beyond it years ago; that she was weak and vain, and one of those people who are best described by the axiom that you may trust them as far as you can see them, and no farther."—*Nicholas Nickleby*.

Knag, Mortimer.—Brother of Miss Knag.—"An ornamental stationer, and small circulating library keeper, in a by-street off Tottenham Court Road. Mr. Knag was a tall lank gentleman of solemn features, wearing spectacles, and garnished with much less hair than a gentleman bordering on forty or thereabouts usually boasts."—*Nicholas Nickleby.*

Knitt, Miss.—One of the guests at a picnic party on Dora Spenlow's birthday.—"A young creature in pink, with little eyes."—*David Copperfield.*

Koëldwethout, The Baron Von, of Grogzwig.—The hero of a tale told by the merry-faced gentleman at the inn where Squeers and Nicholas and other passengers by the capsized coach spent the night.—"The Baron Von Koëldwethout of Grogzwig in Germany was as likely a young baron as you would wish to see. I needn't say that he lived in a castle, for that's of course. Neither need I say that he lived in an old castle, for what German baron ever lived in a new one. He was a fine swarthy fellow with dark hair and large moustachios who rode a hunting in clothes of Lincoln Green, with russet boots on his feet, and a bugle slung over his shoulder, like the guard of a long stage."—*Nicholas Nickleby.*

Koëldwethout, Baroness Von.—Wife of the Baron.—*Nicholas Nickleby.*

Krook.—Keeper of a marine-store.—"An old man in spectacles and a hairy cap. He was short, cadaverous, and withered; with his head sunk edgeways between his shoulders, and the breath issuing in visible smoke from his mouth, as if he were on fire within. His throat, chin, and eyebrows were so frosted with white hairs, and so gnarled with veins and puckered skin, that he looked, from his breast upward, like some old root in a fall of snow."—*Bleak House.*

Kutankumagen, Doctor.—A member of the Medical Section of the Mudfog Association.—"Doctor Kutankumagen of Moscow read to the Section a report of a case which had occurred within his own practice strikingly illustrative of the power of medicine."—*The Mudfog Sketches.*

Kwakley, Mr.—A member of the Statistical Section of the Mudfog Association.—*The Mudfog Sketches.*

Ladle, Joey.—The head cellarman of Wilding and Co., wine merchants.—"A slow and ponderous man, of the drayman order of human architecture, dressed in a corrugated suit, and bibbed apron, apparently a composite of door-mat and rhinoceros-hide."—No Thoroughfare (*Christmas Stories*).

Lady Jane.—The name of Krook's cat.—*Bleak House.*

Lagnier.—A name adopted by Rigaud to conceal his identity.—*Little Dorrit.*

Lambert, Miss.—The bashful young man's dance partner.—" Miss Lambert, let me introduce Mr. Hopkins for the next quadrille. Miss Lambert inclines her head graciously. Mr. Hopkins bows, and his fair conductress disappears, leaving Mr. Hopkins, as he too well knows, to make himself agreeable."—*Sketches of Young Gentlemen.*

Lammle, Alfred.—An impecunious adventurer who pretended to be a man of property and married Sophronia Akershem believing she had money, which she had not.—" A mature young gentleman with too much nose on his face, too much ginger in his whiskers, too much torso in his waistcoat, too much sparkle in his studs, his eyes, his buttons, his talk, and his teeth. The mature young gentleman is a gentleman of property. He invests his property. He goes, in a condescending amateurish way, into the City, attends meetings of Directors, and has to do with traffic in shares.—As is well known to the wise in their generation, traffic in shares is the one thing to have to do with in this world. Have no antecedents; no established character; no cultivation; no ideas; no manners; have shares."—*Our Mutual Friend.*

Lammle, Mrs.—Wife of Alfred Lammle.—(*See* **Akershem, Sophronia.**)

Lamplighter, The.—Chairman of the Lamplighters.—" If any of our readers have had the good fortune to behold a lamplighter's funeral, they will not be surprised to learn that lamplighters are a strange and primitive people. It is an article of their creed that the first faint glimmering of true civilization shone in the first street light maintained at the public expense."—*The Lamplighter* (Reprinted Pieces).

Lamps.—A railway porter at Mugby Junction.—" He

was a spare man, of about the Barbox Brothers' time of life, with his features whimsically drawn upward, as if they were attracted by the roots of his hair. He had a peculiarly shining transparent complexion, probably occasioned by constant oleaginous application; and his attractive hair, being cut short and being grizzled, and standing straight up on end, as if it in its turn were attracted by some invisible magnet above it, the top of his head was not very unlike a lamp wick."—Mugby Junction (*Christmas Stories*).

Landless, Neville and Helena.—Wards of Mr. Honeythunder.—"An unusually handsome, lithe young fellow, and an unusually lithe girl; much alike; both very dark and very rich in colour; she of almost the gipsy type; something untamed about them both; a certain air upon them of hunter and huntress; yet, withal, a certain air of being the objects of the chase, rather than the followers; slender, supple, quick of eye and limb; half shy, half defiant; fierce of look; an indefinable kind of pause coming and going on the whole expression, both of face and form, which might be equally likened to the pause before a crouch or a bound."—*Edwin Drood.*

Lane, Miss.—Governess at Mrs. Borum's at Portsmouth. —*Nicholas Nickleby.*

Langdale, Mr.—Of Holborn Hill. A vinter and distiller whose house was wrecked by the rioters.—"A portly old man, with a very red, or rather purple, face."—*Barnaby Rudge.*

Langley.—The tenant of the second floor at Madam Bouclet's.—"The Englishman, on taking his apartment —or as one might say on our side of the Channel his set of chambers—had given his name, correct to the letter,—Langley."—Somebody's Luggage (*Christmas Stories*).

Lant Street.—The residence of Bob Sawyer.—"There is a repose about Lant Street in the borough which sheds a gentle melancholy upon the soul. The majority of the inhabitants either direct their energies to the letting of furnished apartments or devote themselves to the healthful and invigorating pursuit of mangling. The chief features in the still life of the street are green shutters, lodging bills, brass door plates, and bell handles; the principal specimens of animated Nature the potboy, the muffin youth, and the baked potato man. The population is migratory, usually disappearing on the verge of quarter day, and generally by night; His Majesty's revenues are seldom collected in this happy valley; the rents are dubious; and the water communication is very frequently cut off."—*Pickwick Papers.*

Larkins, The Eldest Miss.—A lady of thirty with whom at the age of seventeen David fell in love.—"The eldest Miss Larkins is not a little girl. She is a tall, dark, black-eyed, fine figure of a woman. The eldest Miss Larkins is not a chicken, for the youngest Miss Larkins is not that, and the eldest must be three or four years older. Perhaps the eldest Miss Larkins may be about thirty."—*David Copperfield.*

Larkins, Mr.—The father of Miss Larkins.—"A gruff old gentleman with a double chin, and one of his eyes immovable in his head."—*David Copperfield.*

Larkins, Jem.—A member of an amateur dramatic company.—"That gentleman, in the white hat and checked shirt, brown coat, and brass buttons, lounging behind the stage box on the O.P. side, is Mr. Horatio St. Julien, *alias* Jem Larkins. His line is genteel comedy—his father's, coal and potato."—*Sketches by Boz* (Private Theatres).

Latin Grammar Master.—Capt. Boldheart's enemy.—"To do him justice he was no craven, though his white hat, his short grey trousers, and his long snuff-coloured coat (the self-same coat in which he had spited Boldheart) contrasted most unfavourably with the brilliant uniform of the latter."—*Holiday Romance.*

Lazarus, Abraham.—A Jew, arrested on suspicion of plate stealing, to prosecute whom Mr. Jaggers had been retained, and whose brother beseeched Mr. Jaggers, to his great indignation, to allow himself to be bought over for the defence.—*Great Expectations.*

Lazzarone, Capo.—An umpire at a Neapolitan Lottery Drawing.—"The man on the little stool behind the president is Capo Lazzarone, a kind of tribune of the people, appointed on their behalf to see that all is fairly conducted. . . . A ragged swarthy fellow he is, with long matted hair hanging down all over his face, and covered from head to foot with most unquestionably genuine dirt." —*Pictures from Italy*.

Leath, Angela.—Married Charley, who was "snowed up at The Holly Tree Inn.—(*See* **Charley.**)—The Holly Tree (*Christmas Stories*).

Leaver, Mr. and Mrs.—The loving couple.—" There cannot be a better practical illustration of the wise saw and ancient instance that there may be too much of a good thing, than is presented by a loving couple . . . there is a time for all things, and the couple who happen to be always in a loving state, before company, are well-nigh intolerable."—*Sketches of Young Couples*.

Leaver, Mr.—A vice-president of the Mechanical Science Section of the Mudfog Association.—*The Mudfog Sketches*.

Ledbram, Mr.—A vice-president of the Statistical Section of the Mudfog Association.—*The Mudfog Sketches*.

Ledrook, Miss.—An actress in Mr. Crummles' company.—*Nicholas Nickleby*.

Leeford, Edward.—Known as Monks. Half-brother of Oliver Twist.—(*See* **Monks.**)—*Oliver Twist*.

Lemon, Miss.—A friend of Mrs. Orange.—" A lady of the name of Mrs. Lemon, who kept a preparatory establishment."—*Holiday Romance*.

Lenville, Mr.—The tragedy actor in Mr. Crummles' company.—" A dark-complexioned man, inclining indeed to sallow, with long thick black hair, and very evident indications (although he was close shaved) of a stiff beard and whiskers of the same deep shade; his age did not appear to exceed thirty, though many at first sight would have considered him much older, and his face was very long, and very pale, from the constant application of stage paint."—*Nicholas Nickleby*.

Lenville, Mrs.—Wife of Mr. Lenville.—" There was Mrs. Lenville in a very limp bonnet and veil."—*Nicholas Nickleby*.

Lewsome, Doctor.—A young surgeon who supplied Jonas Chuzzlewit with drugs to poison his father.—*Martin Chuzzlewit.*

Licensed Victualler, Mr.—The landlord of a singing house frequented by sailors.—" A sharp and watchful man Mr. Licensed Victualler, the host, with tight lips and a complete edition of Cocker's arithmetic in each eye; attended to his business himself he said; always on the spot."—*The Uncommercial Traveller* (Poor Mercantile Jack).

Lightwood, Mortimer.—A London solicitor with little practice, most intimate friend of Eugene Wrayburn, a guest at Veneering's.—" A certain Mortimer—another of Veneering's oldest friends—who never was in the house before, and appears not to want to come again; who sits disconsolate on Mrs. Veneering's left, and who was inveigled by Lady Tippins (a friend of his boyhood) to come to these people's and talk, and who won't talk."—*Our Mutual Friend.*

Lillerton, Miss.—A friend of Mrs. Gabriel Parsons.—" On the sofa was seated a lady of very prim appearance, and remarkably inanimate. She was one of these persons at whose age it is impossible to make any reasonable guess; her features might have been remarkably pretty, when she was younger, and they might always have presented the same appearance. Her complexion—with a slight trace of powder here and there—was as clear as that of a well-made wax doll, and her face as expressive. She was handsomely dressed and was winding up a gold watch." —*Sketches by Boz* (A Passage in the Life of Mr. Watkins Tottle).

Lilliputian College.—A Ladies' Seminary.—" Miss Pupford's establishment for young Ladies of tender years is an establishment of a compact nature; an establishment in miniature; quite a pocket establishment. Miss Pupford; Miss Pupford's Assistant with the Parisian accent; Miss Pupford's cook; and Miss Pupford's housemaid; complete what Miss Pupford calls the educational and domestic staff of her Lilliputian College."—Tom Tiddler's Ground (*Christmas Stories*).

Lillyvick, Mr.—Uncle of Mrs. Kenwigs. A guest at their supper-party, where he met Miss Petowker, whom he ultimately married, to the chagrin of the Kenwigs family.—" A short old gentleman, in drabs and gaiters, with a face that might have been carved out of *lignum vitæ*, for anything that appeared to the contrary. Here was a collector of water rates without his book, without his pen and ink, without his double knock, without his intimidation; kissing—actually kissing—an agreeable female, and leaving taxes, summonses, notices that he had called, or announcements that he would never call again, for two quarters due, wholly out of the question. It was pleasant to see how the company looked on quite absorbed in the sight, and to behold the nods and winks with which they expressed their gratification at finding so much humanity in a tax-gatherer."—*Nicholas Nickleby.*

Lily.—Niece of Will Fern, whom Trotty Veck met wandering with her uncle in the London streets on New Year's Eve and took to his house.—*The Chimes.*

Limkins, Mr.—Chairman of the parochial board.—" Eight or ten fat gentlemen were sitting round a table. At the top of the table, seated in an arm-chair rather higher than the rest, was a particularly fat gentleman with a very round red face."—*Oliver Twist.*

Linderwood, Lieutenant.—The officer commanding the Royal Marines on board the ship *Christopher Columbus.* —" How I came to be aboard the armed sloop is easily told. Four-and-twenty marines, under command of a lieutenant—that officer's name was Linderwood—had been told off at Belize to proceed to Silver Store, in aid of boats and seamen stationed there, for the chase of the Pirates."—The Perils of Certain English Travellers (*Christmas Stories*).

Linkinwater, Tim.—Bookkeeper and confidential clerk at Cheeryble Brothers; married Miss la Creevy.—" Punctual as the Counting House Dial, which he maintained to be the best time-keeper in London, next after the clock of some old hidden unknown church hard by; (for Tim held the fabled goodness of that at the Horse Guards to be a pleasant fiction invented by jealous Westenders); the old clerk performed the minutest actions of the day, and arranged the minutest articles in the little room, in a precise and regular order, which could not have been exceeded if it had actually been a real glass case, fitted with the choicest curiosities."—*Nicholas Nickleby*.

Linkinwater, Miss.—Sister of Tim.—"There was the chubby old lady, Tim Linkinwater's sister."—*Nicholas Nickleby*.

Linseed, Duke of.—One of the correspondents who solicited subscriptions from Mr. Boffin.—"Nickodemus Boffin, Esquire. My dear Sir,—Having consented to preside at the forthcoming annual dinner of the Family Party Fund, and feeling deeply impressed with the immense usefulness of that noble Institution, and the great importance of its being supported by a List of Stewards, that shall prove to the public the interest taken in it by popular and distinguished men, I have undertaken to ask you to become a Steward on that occasion. Soliciting your favourable reply before the 14th inst. I am, My Dear Sir, Your faithful servant, Linseed. P.S.—The Steward's fee is limited to three guineas."—*Our Mutual Friend*.

Linx, Miss.—A pupil at Miss Pupford's school.—"A sharply observant pupil."—Tom Tiddler's Ground (*Christmas Stories*).

Lion.—Mr. Henry Gowan's dog.—*Little Dorrit*.

Lion, The.—Landlord of the Black Lion Tavern.—"This Lion, or Landlord, for he was called both man and beast, by reason of his having instructed the artist who painted his sign, to convey into the features of the lordly brute whose effigy it bore, as near a counterpart of his own face, as his skill could compass and devise,—was a gentleman almost as quick of apprehension, and of almost as subtle a wit as the mighty John himself; but the difference between them lay in this, that whereas Mr. Willet's extreme sagacity and acuteness were the efforts of unassisted nature, the Lion stood indebted in no small amount to beer, of which he swigged such copious draughts that most of his faculties were utterly drowned and washed away, except the one great faculty of sleep, which he retained in surprising perfection."—*Barnaby Rudge*.

Lirriper, Mrs. Emma.—A loquacious widow, keeper of a London boarding-house.—"It was about lodgings that I was intending to hold forth, and certainly I ought to know something of the business, having been in it so long, for it was early in the second year of my married life that I lost my poor Lirriper, and I set up at Islington directly afterwards, and afterwards came here, being two houses, and eight-and-thirty years, and some losses and a deal of experience."—Mrs. Lirriper's Lodgings (*Christmas Stories*).

Lirriper, Mr.—The deceased husband of Mrs. Lirriper. —" My poor Lirriper was a handsome figure of a man, with a beaming eye and a voice as mellow as a musical instrument made of honey and steel; but he had ever been a free liver, being in the commercial travelling line."—Mrs. Lirriper's Lodgings (*Christmas Stories*).

Lirriper, Joshua.—Brother-in-law of Mrs. Lirriper.—" Mentioning my poor Lirriper brings into my head his own youngest brother the Doctor, though Doctor of what I am sure it would be hard to say, unless liquor, for neither physic nor music nor yet law does Joshua Lirriper know a morsel of, except continually being summoned to the County Court."—Mrs. Lirriper's Legacy (*Christmas Stories*).

List, Isaac.—One of the gamblers whom Mr. Trent met at the Valiant Soldier public-house.—" The other man, whom his companion had called Isaac, was of a more slender figure—stooping and high in the shoulders—with a very ill-favoured face, and a most sinister and villainous squint."—*The Old Curiosity Shop*.

Littimer.—Steerforth's serving-man.—" I believe there never existed in his station a more respectable-looking man. He was taciturn, soft-footed, very quiet in his manner, deferential, observant, always at hand when wanted, and never near when not wanted. . . . Such a self-contained man I never saw."—*David Copperfield*.

Little, John.—A miser whose biography Mr. Boffin pretended to be interested in.—*Our Mutual Friend*.

Little Nell.—A sweet child, who lived with her grandfather, Mr. Trent, and took care of him in his wanderings.—*The Old Curiosity Shop*.

Lively, Mr.—A trader in Field Lane.—*Oliver Twist*.

Liz.—A bricklayer's wife, friend of Jenny.—*Bleak House.*

Lobbs, Mr.—A saddler.—"The fiery old Lobbs, the great saddler, who could have bought up the whole village at one stroke of his pen, and never felt the outlay." —*Pickwick Papers.*

Lobbs, Maria.—Daughter of Mr. Lobbs.—"A prettier foot, a gayer heart, a more dimpled face, or a smarter form, never bounded so lightly over the earth they graced, as did those of Maria Lobbs, the old saddler's daughter." —*Pickwick Papers.*

Lobley.—Boatman to Lieutenant Tartar.—"He was a jolly favoured man, with tawny hair and whiskers, and a big red face. He was the dead image of the sun in old woodcuts; his hair and whiskers answering for rays all round him."—*Edwin Drood.*

Lobskini, Signor.—A guest at the school ball at Minerva House.—"Repeated pulls at the bell—and arrivals too numerous to particularize; papas and mammas; and aunts and uncles; the owners and guardians of the different pupils; the singing master Signor Lobskini in a black wig; the pianoforte player and the violins; the harp in a state of intoxication; and some twenty young men, who stood near the door and talked to one another, occasionally bursting into a giggle."—*Sketches by Boz* (Sentiment).

Loggins, Mr.—One of the Committee invited to a meeting to arrange the Steam Excursion.—"Mr. Loggins, the solicitor of Boswell Court, sent an excuse; Mr. Briggs, the ditto of Furnival's Inn, sent his brother."—*Sketches by Boz* (The Steam Excursion).

Longford, Edward.—A student in the Institution under Mr. Redlaw.—(*See* **Denham.**)—*The Haunted Man.*

Longford, Mr.—Father of Edward Longford,—a bad man, who had wronged Mr. Redlaw in his early life, but was succoured by him when he had fallen into poverty and illness.—*The Haunted Man.*

Lord Peter.—A young gentleman who proposed to elope with Miss Julia Manners.—"Lord Peter not being considered very prudent or sagacious by his friends."—*Sketches by Boz* (The Great Winglebury Duel).

Lorn, Mr.—Assistant to Doctor Speedie.—" What was startling in him was his remarkable paleness; his large black eyes, his sunken cheeks, his long and heavy iron-grey hair, his wasted hands, and even the attenuation of his figure were at first forgotten in his extraordinary pallor; there was no vestige of colour in the man."—The Lazy Tour of Two Idle Apprentices (*Christmas Stories*).

Lorry, Mr. Jarvis.—The confidential representative of Tellson's Bank.—" A gentleman of sixty, formally dressed in a brown suit of clothes, pretty well worn, but very well kept; . . . a face, habitually suppressed and quieted, was still lighted up under the quaint wig by a pair of moist bright eyes, that it must have cost their owner in years gone by some pains to drill to the composed and reserved expression of Tellson's Bank."—*A Tale of Two Cities.*

Losberne, Doctor.—The medical man who attended Oliver at Mrs. Maylie's.—" Mr. Losberne, a surgeon in the neighbourhood known through a circuit of ten miles round as the doctor, had grown fat, more from good humour than from good living; and was as kind and hearty, and withal as eccentric, an old bachelor, as will be found in five times that space by any explorer alive."—*Oliver Twist.*

Louis.—The Uncommercial Traveller's cheerful servant, who went abroad with him.—" I must have fallen asleep after lunch, for, when a bright face looked in at the window, I started and said—Good God, Louis, I dreamed you were dead. My cheerful servant laughed, and answered Me! not at all, sir."—*The Uncommercial Traveller* (Refreshments for Travellers).

Louis.—A man who murdered Henri at the Swiss inn.—" I saw him once again, on the day of my departure from the Inn. In that canton, the headsman still does his office with a sword; and I came upon this murderer, sitting bound to a chair, with his eyes bandaged, on a little scaffold in the market-place."—The Holly Tree (*Christmas Stories*).

Lowten, Mr.—Clerk to Mr. Perker, solicitor.—" A puffy-faced young man."—*Pickwick Papers.*

Lucas, Solomon.—A fancy-dress costumier—at Eatanswill.—" His wardrobe was extensive—very extensive—not strictly classical perhaps, nor quite new, nor did it contain any one garment made precisely after the fashion of any age or time, but everything was more or less spangled, and what can be prettier than spangles."—*Pickwick Papers.*

Luffey, Mr.—A member of the Dingley Dell Cricket Club.—*Pickwick Papers.*

Lumbey, Doctor.—The medical attendant of Mrs. Kenwigs.—" He was a stout bluff-looking gentleman, with no shirt collar to speak of, and a beard that had been growing since yesterday morning; for Doctor Lumbey was popular, and the neighbourhood was prolific."—*Nicholas Nickleby.*

Lummey, Ned.—A musical friend of William Simmons, the musical coachman.—" Ah! said Bill, with a sigh, as he drew the back of his hand across his lips, and put the key bugle in his pocket, after screwing off the mouthpiece to drain it; Lummy Ned of the Light Salisbury he was the one for musical talents; he *was* a guard; what you may call a guard'an angel was Ned."—*Martin Chuzzlewit.*

Lupin, Mrs.—Landlady of the Blue Dragon inn.—" She was a widow, but years ago had passed through her state of weeds, and burst into flower again; and in full bloom she had continued ever since; and in full bloom she was now, with roses on her ample skirts, and roses on her bodice; roses in her cap, roses in her cheeks, ay, and roses worth the gathering, too, on her lips for that matter. She had still a bright black eye and jet black hair; was comely, dimpled, plump, and tight as a gooseberry, though she was not exactly what the world calls young."—*Martin Chuzzlewit.*

Macey, Mr.—The husband of Miss Maryon's sister—an officer at the Silver Store Mines.—The Perils of Certain English Travellers (*Christmas Stories*).

Macey, Mrs.—The married sister of Captain Maryon with whom Miss Maryon resided at Silver Store Colony.—

The Perils of Certain English Travellers (*Christmas Stories*).

Mackin, Mrs.—A pawnbroker's customer.—" A slip-shod woman with two flat irons in a little basket."—*Sketches by Boz* (The Pawnbroker's Shop).

Macklin, Mrs.—A suburban resident.—" In the suburbs, the Muffin Boy rings his way down the little street, much more slowly than he is wont, for Mrs. Macklin of No. 4 has no sooner opened her little street door, and screamed out Muffins with all her might, than Mrs. Walker at No. 5 puts her head out of the parlour window and screams Muffins too; and Mrs. Walker has scarcely got the words out of her lips, than Mrs. Peploe over the way lets loose Master Peploe, who darts down the street with a velocity which nothing but buttered muffins in prospect could possibly inspire. Mrs. Walker sees her husband coming down the street, and, as he must want his tea, poor man, after his dirty walk from the docks, she instantly runs across, muffins in hand; and Mrs. Macklin does the same; and after a few words to Mrs. Walker they all pop into their little houses, and slam their little street doors, which are not opened again for the remainder of the evening except to the nine o'clock beer."—*Sketches by Boz* (The Streets—Night).

Macmanus, Mr.—A midshipman on the *Haleswell* East Indiaman.—*The Long Voyage* (Reprinted Pieces).

MacStinger, Mrs. (of No. 9, Brig Place).—Captain Cuttle's landlady; a shrew of whom he stood in awe.—" A widow lady, with her sleeves rolled up to her shoulders, and her arms frothy with soap suds."—*Dombey and Son.*

MacStinger, Alexander.—Son of Mrs. MacStinger.—*Dombey and Son.*

MacStinger, Juliana.—Daughter of Mrs. MacStinger, " who was the picture of her mother."—*Dombey and Son.*

MacStinger, Charles.—One of Mrs. MacStinger's children.—" Charles MacStinger, popularly known about the scenes of his youthful sports as Chowley."—*Dombey and Son.*

Madgers, Winifred.—A maid of Mrs. Lirriper's.—" She was what is termed a Plymouth Sister, and the Plymouth Brother that made away with her was quite right; for a tidier young woman for a wife never came into a house, and afterwards called with the beautifullest Plymouth Twins."—Mrs. Lirriper's Legacy (*Christmas Stories*).

Magg, Mr.—A vestryman.—" One of our first orators, Mr. Magg of Little Winkling Street."—*Our Vestry* (Reprinted Pieces).

Maggy.—A woman of weak intellect befriended by Little Dorrit.—" She was about eight-and-twenty, with large bones, large features, large feet and hands, large eyes, and no hair . . . a great white cap, with a quantity of opaque frilling, that was always flapping about, apologized for Maggy's baldness, and made it so difficult for her old black bonnet to retain its place upon her head, that it held on round her neck like a gipsy's baby,—a commission of haberdashers could alone have reported what the rest of her poor dress was made of; but it had a strong general resemblance to seaweed, with here and there a gigantic tea-leaf. Her shawl looked particularly like a tea-leaf, after long infusion."—*Little Dorrit.*

Magnus, Peter.—A gentleman who travelled with Mr. Pickwick to Ipswich.—" A red-haired man, with an inquisitive nose and blue spectacles;—with a bird-like habit of giving his head a jerk every time he said anything."—*Pickwick Papers.*

Magog.—(*See* **Gog.**)—*Master Humphrey's Clock.*

Magpie and Stump.—The tavern where Mr. Lowten, Mr. Perker's clerk, introduced Mr. Pickwick to a convivial meeting of law clerks.—" This favoured Tavern, sacred to the evening orgies of Mr. Lowten and his companions, was what ordinary people would designate a public-house; the weather-beaten signboard bore the half-obliterated semblance of a magpie, intently eyeing a crooked streak of brown paint, which the neighbours had been taught from infancy to consider as the Stump."—*Pickwick Papers.*

Magsman, Toby.—The proprietor of a show called Magsman's Amusements.—" A grizzled personage in velveteen, with a face so cut up by varieties of weather, that he looked as if he had been tattooed, was found smoking a pipe at the door of a wooden house on wheels."—Going into Society (*Christmas Stories*).

Magwitch, Abel.—A convict who escaped from the hulks, and met Pip, as a small boy, at the church on the marshes. There he fought with his enemy Compeyson, another convict who had also escaped, and was retaken, but again escaped and went abroad, and made a fortune which he secretly devoted to making Pip a gentleman, but returning home, and being a prison-breaker he was caught and condemned to death, and his property forfeited, which dispelled Pip's "Great Expectations," and left him in poverty.—*Great Expectations.*

Malderton, Mr.—Of Oak Lodge, Camberwell.—"Mr. Malderton was a man whose whole scope of ideas was limited to Lloyds, the Exchange, the India House, and the Bank. A few successful speculations had raised him from a situation of obscurity and comparative poverty, to a state of affluence. As frequently happens in such cases, the ideas of himself and his family became elevated to an extraordinary pitch, as their means increased."—*Sketches by Boz* (Horatio Sparkins).

Malderton, Mrs.—Wife of Mr. Malderton.—"A little fat woman."—*Sketches by Boz* (Horatio Sparkins).

Malderton, Miss Teresa.—Elder daughter of Mr. Malderton.—"Miss Teresa Malderton was a very little girl, rather fat, with vermilion cheeks, but good-humoured, and still disengaged, although, to do her justice, the misfortune arose from no lack of perseverance on her part; in vain had she flirted for ten years."—*Sketches by Boz* (Horatio Sparkins).

Malderton, Miss Marianne.—Younger daughter of Mr. Malderton.—*Sketches by Boz* (Horatio Sparkins).

Malderton, Frederick.—Elder son of Mr. Malderton.—"Mr. Frederick Malderton, the eldest son, in full dress costume, was the very beau ideal of a smart waiter."—*Sketches by Boz* (Horatio Sparkins).

Malderton, Tom.—Younger son of Mr. Malderton.—"Mr. Thomas Malderton, the youngest, with his white dress-stock, blue coat, bright buttons, and red watch ribbon, strongly resembled the portrait of that interesting but rash young gentleman George Barnwell."—*Sketches by Boz* (Horatio Sparkins).

Maldon, Jack.—Cousin of Mrs. Strong, and in love with her.—" I see among it Mr. Jack Maldon from his Patent Place, sneering at the hand that gave it him, and speaking to me of the Doctor as so charmingly antique."—*David Copperfield.*

Mallard, Mr.—Clerk to Serjeant Snubbin.—" Upon the table were numerous little bundles of papers, tied with red tape; and behind it sat an elderly clerk whose sleek appearance and heavy gold watch-chain presented imposing indications of the extensive and lucrative practice of Mr. Serjeant Snubbin."—*Pickwick Papers.*

Mallett, Mr.—President of the Mechanical Science Section of the Mudfog Association.—*The Mudfog Sketches.*

Manette, Doctor.—Father of Lucie. Imprisoned in France for eighteen years, and lost his memory, but being released, and recalled to life, recovered himself and resided with Lucie till her marriage to Darnay and afterwards with her and her husband. Whilst in prison wrote a history of his life which incriminated the St. Evremonde family and led to the condemnation of Darnay.—*A Tale of Two Cities.*

Manette, Lucie.—Daughter of Dr. Manette, who had been brought up under the belief that her father was dead, but on his release from prison was restored to him, and nursed him back to life; ultimately married Charles Darnay.—" His eyes rested on a short, slight, pretty figure, a quantity of golden hair, a pair of blue eyes that met his own with an inquiring look, and a forehead with a singular capacity (remembering how young and smooth it was) of lifting and knitting itself into an expression that was not quite one of perplexity, or wonder, or alarm, or merely of a bright fixed attention, though it included all the four expressions."—*A Tale of Two Cities.*

Mann, Mrs.—The matron of the branch parish workhouse where Oliver lived till he was nine.—" The Parish

Authorities magnanimously resolved that Oliver should be farmed; or in other words that he should be despatched to a branch workhouse, some three miles off, where twenty or thirty other juvenile offenders against the poor laws rolled about the floor all day, without the inconvenience of too much food or too much clothing, under the parental superintendence of an elderly female, who received the culprits at and for the consideration of sevenpence half-penny per small head per week. . . . The elderly female was a woman of wisdom and experience. She knew what was good for children; and she had a very accurate perception of what was good for herself."—*Oliver Twist.*

Manners, Miss Julia.—A wealthy lady who married Mr. Alexander Trott.—" A buxom, richly dressed female of about forty."—*Sketches by Boz* (The Great Winglebury Duel).

Mansel, Miss.—A passenger on board the *Haleswell* East Indiaman.—*The Long Voyage* (Reprinted Pieces).

Mantalini, Madame.—A dressmaker in whose employment Kate Nickleby was.—" The dressmaker was a buxom person, handsomely dressed, and rather good-looking, but much older than the gentleman whom she had wedded some six months before. His name was originally Muntle, but it had been converted by an easy transition into Mantalini, the lady rightly considering that an English appellation would be of serious injury to the business."—*Nicholas Nickleby.*

Mantalini, Alfred.—Husband of Madame Mantalini. A selfish coxcomb who lived on his wife and ultimately ruined her by his extravagance.—" He had married on his whiskers, upon which property he had recently improved, after patient cultivation, by the addition of a moustache, which promised to secure him an easy independence; his share in the labours of the business being at present confined to spending the money."—*Nicholas Nickleby.*

Maplesone, Mrs.—A boarder at Mrs. Tibbs'.—" Mrs. Maplesone was an enterprising widow of about fifty; shrewd, scheming, and good-looking; she was amiably anxious on behalf of her daughters, in proof whereof she used to remark that she would have no objection to marry again, if it would benefit her dear girls,—she could have no other object."—*Sketches by Boz* (The Boarding House).

Maplesone, Miss Matilda.—A boarder at Mrs. Tibbs', elder of Mrs. Maplesone's two daughters.—" The dear girls themselves were not insensible to the merits of a good establishment; one of them was twenty-five, the other three years younger; they had been at different watering-places for four seasons; they had gambled at Libraries; read books in balconies; sold at fancy fairs; danced at assemblies; talked sentiment—in short they had done all that industrious girls could do—but as yet to no purpose."—*Sketches by Boz* (The Boarding House).

Maplesone, Miss Julia.—Boarder at Mrs. Tibbs', younger of Mrs. Maplesone's two daughters.—*Sketches by Boz* (The Boarding House).

Marchioness, The.—Sally Brass's servant-maid,—so called by Dick Swiveller, who ultimately married her.—*The Old Curiosity Shop.*

Margaret, Aunt.—One of the guests at the Christmas Family Party.—" Grandmamma draws herself up, rather stiff and stately, for Margaret married a poor man without her consent; and, poverty not being a sufficiently weighty punishment for her offence, has been discarded by her friends, and debarred the society of her dearest relatives. But Christmas has come round, and the unkind feelings, that have struggled against better dispositions during the year, have melted away before its genial influence, like half-formed ice beneath the morning sun."—*Sketches by Boz* (A Christmas Dinner).

Margaret.—Maidservant at Mr. Winkle's at Birmingham.—" The girl looked timidly at Mr. Bob Sawyer, who was expressing his admiration of her personal charms by a variety of wonderful grimaces; and, casting an eye at the hats and great coats which hung in the passage, called another girl to mind the door, while she went upstairs."—*Pickwick Papers.*

Margery, Little.—The heroine of a tale in a school book used at the night school where Charley Hexam taught.—" It was a school for all ages and for both sexes. The place was prevalent of a grimly ludicrous pretence that every pupil was childish and innocent. This pretence, much favoured by the lady visitors, led to the ghastliest absurdities. Young women, old in the vices of the commonest and worst life, were expected to profess themselves enthralled by the good child's book, the Adventures of Little Margery, who resided in the village cottage by the Mill; severely reproved and morally squashed the Miller when she was five and he was fifty, who plaited straw and delivered the dreariest orations to all comers at all sorts of unseasonable times."—*Our Mutual Friend.*

Marguarite.—A Swiss girl, niece of Mr. Obenreizer.—"The young lady wore an unusual quantity of fair bright hair, very prettily braided, about a rather rounder white forehead than the average English type; and so her face might have been a shade—or say a light—rounder than the average English face; and her figure slightly rounder than the figure of the average English girl at nineteen. Switzerland too, though the general fashion of her dress was English, peeped out of the fanciful bodice she wore, and lurked in the curious clocked red stocking, and in its little silver-buckled shoe."—No Thoroughfare (*Christmas Stories*).

Marigold, Doctor.—"I am a Cheap Jack. I was born on the Queen's Highway; but it was the King's at that time. A doctor was fetched to my own mother by my own father, when it took place on a common, and in consequence of his being a very kind gentleman, and accepting no fee but a tea tray, I was named Doctor, out of gratitude and compliment to him; there you have me; Doctor Marigold."—Doctor Marigold (*Christmas Stories*).

Marigold, Mrs.—Wife of Doctor Marigold.—"She wasn't a bad wife, but she had a temper; if she could have parted with that one article, at a sacrifice, I wouldn't have swopped her away in exchange for any other woman in England."—Doctor Marigold (*Christmas Stories*).

Marigold, Sophy.—Daughter of Doctor Marigold.—"She had a wonderful quantity of shining dark hair all curling natural about her."—Doctor Marigold (*Christmas Stories*).

Marigold, William.—Father of Doctor Marigold.—"My own father's name was William Marigold. It was in his lifetime supposed by some that his name was William; but my own father always consistently said No it was Willum."—Doctor Marigold (*Christmas Stories*).

Mark, Gilbert.—A lieutenant in the United Bulldogs, of which Simon Tappertit was the Captain.—*Barnaby Rudge.*

Markham.—A friend of Steerforth's who dined with David at his chambers at the Adelphi.—" Markham was youthful looking, and I should say not more than twenty. I observed that he always spoke of himself indefinitely as —a man—and seldom or never in the first person singular. A man might get on very well here, Mr. Copperfield, said Markham—meaning himself."—*David Copperfield.*

Marker, Mrs.—A client of the General Agency, in want of a cook.—" Mrs. Marker, said Tom reading, Russell Place, Russell Square, offers eighteen guineas, tea and sugar found; two in family and see very little company; five servants kept; no man; no followers."—*Nicholas Nickleby.*

Markleham, Mrs.—The mother of Mrs. Strong, and one of her poor relations.—" Mrs. Strong's mamma was a lady I took great delight in. Her name was Mrs. Markleham; but our boys used to call her The Old Soldier, on account of her generalship, and the skill with which she marshalled great forces of relations against the Doctor. She was a little sharp-eyed woman, who used to wear when she was dressed one unchangeable cap, ornamented with some artificial flowers, and two artificial butterflies supposed to be hovering over the flowers."—*David Copperfield.*

Marks, Will.—Nephew of John Podgers.—" A wild roving young fellow of twenty, who had been brought up in his uncle's house, and lived there still, that is to say when he was at home, which was not as often as it might have been."—*Master Humphrey's Clock.*

Marley, Jacob.—The deceased partner of Scrooge, whose ghost visited Scrooge on Christmas Eve.—" Marley was dead to begin with. There is no doubt whatever about that. The register of his burial was signed by the clergyman, the clerk, the undertaker, and the chief mourner. Scrooge signed it, and Scrooge's name was good upon 'Change for anything he chose to put his hand to. Old Marley was as dead as a door nail."—*A Christmas Carol.*

Maroon, Captain.—The creditor who imprisoned Tip for debt.—" A gentleman with tight drab legs, a rather old hat, a little hooked stick, and a blue neckerchief."—*Little Dorrit.*

Marquis of Granby.—The tavern at Dorking kept by Mrs. Weller.—" The 'Marquis of Granby' in Mrs. Weller's time was quite a model of a road-side public-house of the better class—just large enough to be convenient, and small enough to be snug."—*Pickwick Papers.*

Marshall, Mary.—Sweetheart of Richard Doubledick, who discarded him because of his conduct, and sent him to the wars, but in the end married him.—" He had gone wrong and run wild. His heart was in the right place, but it was sealed up. He had been betrothed to a good and beautiful girl, whom he had loved better than she—or perhaps even he—believed; but in an evil hour he had given her cause to say to him solemnly, Richard, I will never marry another man. I will live single for your sake, but Mary Marshall's lips—her name was Mary Marshall—never address another word to you on earth. So, Richard, Heaven forgive you. This finished him. This brought him down to Chatham. This made him Private Richard Doubledick with a determination to be shot."—(*See* **Doubledick, Richard.**)—The Seven Poor Travellers (*Christmas Stories*).

Martha.—Daughter of a riverside labourer with whom Florence Dombey became acquainted, when visiting at Sir Barnet Skettles' country house.—*Dombey and Son.*

Martha.—One of the two old pauper women who attended Agnes Fleming in the workhouse.—*Oliver Twist.*

Martha.—Tablemaid of Mrs. Gabriel Parsons.—*Sketches by Boz* (A Passage in the Life of Mr. Watkins Tottle).

Martin.—Coachman to Ben Allen's aunt.—" A surly-looking man, with his legs dressed like the legs of a groom, and his body attired in the coat of a coachman."—*Pickwick Papers.*

Martin.—Head gamekeeper to Sir Geoffrey Manning.—" The driver pulled up by a gate at the roadside, before which stood a tall raw-boned gamekeeper, and a half-booted leather-legginged boy; each bearing a bag of capacious dimensions, and accompanied by a brace of pointers."—*Pickwick Papers.*

Martin, Betsey.—A case mentioned in the Report upon Converts by the Committee of the Brick Lane Branch of the United Grand Junction Ebenezer Temperance Association.—"Betsey Martin; widow; one child and one eye; goes out charing by the day; never had more than one eye; but knows her mother drank bottled stout, and shouldn't wonder if that caused it (immense cheering); thinks it not impossible that, if she had always abstained from spirits, she might have had two eyes by this time (tremendous applause)."—*Pickwick Papers.*

Martin, Captain.—A prisoner at the Marshalsea.—*Little Dorrit.*

Martin, Jack.—The Bagman's uncle.—"My uncle, gentlemen, said the Bagman, was one of the merriest, pleasantest, cleverest fellows that ever lived; if any two of his numerous virtues predominated over the many that adorned his character, I should say they were his mixed punch, and his after supper song."—*Pickwick Papers.*

Martin, Miss.—An hotel clerkess.—"Miss Martin is the young lady at the bar as makes out our bills; and, though higher than I could wish considering her station, is perfectly well-behaved."—Somebody's Luggage (*Christmas Stories*).

Martin, Miss Amelia.—A milliner.—"Miss Amelia Martin was pale, tallish, thin, and thirty-two, what ill-natured people would call plain, and police reports interesting. She was a milliner and dressmaker, living on her business, and not above it."—*Sketches by Boz* (The Mistaken Milliner).

Martin, Tom.—A butcher imprisoned in The Fleet. —"A gentleman prematurely broad for his years, clothed in a professional blue jean frock, and top boots with circular toes."—*Pickwick Papers.*

Martin, Mr.—A village school-master who befriended Little Nell and her Grandfather.—"There was but one old man, in the little garden before his cottage, and him they were timid of approaching, for he was the Schoolmaster, and had 'School' written up over his window, in black letters on a white board. He was a pale, simple-looking man, of a spare and meagre habit, and sat among his flowers and beehives, smoking his pipe, in the little porch before his door."—*The Old Curiosity Shop.*

Marwood, Alice.—Daughter of the old woman who called herself Mrs. Brown. A handsome young woman who had been ruined and cast off by James Carker, and afterwards had been in prison.—*Dombey and Son.*

Mary.—Housemaid at Mr. Nupkins, Ipswich, afterwards married Sam Weller.—" Mary, said Mr. Muzzle, to the pretty servant girl,—this is Mr. Weller, a gentleman as master has sent down to be made as comfortable as possible. And your master's a knowin' hand, and has just sent me to the right place, said Mr. Weller, with a glance of admiration at Mary. If I was master o' this here house, I should always find the materials for comfort vere Mary wos. Lor, Mr. Weller, said Mary, blushing. . . . Sam Weller kept his word, and remained unmarried for two years. The old housekeeper dying at the end of that time, Mr. Pickwick promoted Mary to the situation, on condition of her marrying Mr. Weller at once, which she did without a murmur."—*Pickwick Papers.*

Mary.—A resident of Seven Dials, a champion of Sarah in her quarrel with Mrs. Sullivan.—" What do you mean by hussies, interrupts a champion of the other party, who has evinced a strong inclination throughout to get up a branch fight on her own account. Hooraar ejaculates a pot-boy in parenthesis,—Put the kye-bosk on her, Mary."—*Sketches by Boz* (The Streets—Night).

Mary.—Daughter of Old John, the inventor.—" One of my two daughters (Mary) is comfortable in her circumstances, but water on the chest."—*A Poor Man's Tale of a Patent* (Reprinted Pieces).

Mary.—A maid-of-all-work who walked out on Sunday with William.—*Sunday under Three Heads* (Reprinted Pieces).

Mary.—The barmaid at the Peacock inn at Eatanswill.—*Pickwick Papers.*

Mary.—A maidservant at Manor Farm.—*Pickwick Papers.*

Mary Ann.—One of the assistants at Ramsgate Concert Room.—" There were young ladies, in maroon-coloured gowns, and black velvet bracelets, dispensing fancy articles in the shop, and presiding over games of chance in the Concert Room."—*Sketches by Boz* (The Tuggses at Ramsgate).

Mary Anne.—The little maid who looked after the aged P. and the toy castle at Walworth during the day-time, when Wemmick was at Mr. Jaggers' office in the city.—*Great Expectations.*

Mary Anne.—Pupil and housemaid of Miss Peecher, the school-mistress.—" Miss Peecher's favourite pupil, who assisted her in her little household . . . sufficiently divined the state of Miss Peecher's affections, to feel it necessary that she herself should love young Charley Hexam. So there was a double palpitation among the double stocks and double wallflowers, when the master and the boy looked over the little gate."—*Our Mutual Friend.*

" **Mary Anne.**"—The name of the ship in which Fred Trent sailed for Demerara.—*The Old Curiosity Shop.*

Maryon, Captain.—The commander of the armed sloop *Christopher Columbus.*—The Perils of Certain English Travellers (*Christmas Stories*).

Maryon, Miss Marion.—A resident at Silver Store. Sister of Captain Maryon; afterwards married Captain Carton.—" She was the child of a military officer, and had come out there with her sister, who was married to one of the owners of the Silver Mine, and who had three children with her. It was easy to see that she was the life and spirit of the Island."—The Perils of Certain English Travellers (*Christmas Stories*).

Matinters, The Misses.—Visitors at Bath.—" The two Miss Matinters who, being single, and singular, paid great court to the Master of the Ceremonies, in the hope of getting a stray partner now and then."—*Pickwick Papers.*

Matthews.—Page to Mr. Gregsbury, M.P.—" A very pale shabby boy, who looked as if he had slept under-ground from his infancy, as very likely he had."—*Nicholas Nickleby.*

Maunders.—Proprietor of a variety show.—" I re-member the time when old Maunders had in his cottage in Spa Fields, in the winter time when the season was over, eight male and female dwarfs, sitting down to dinner every day; who was waited on by eight old giants, in green coats, red smalls, blue cotton stockings and high-lows; and there was one dwarf, as had grown elderly and wicious, who, whenever his giant wasn't quick enough to please him, used to stick pins in his legs, not being able to reach up any higher. I know that's a fact, for Maunders told it me himself."—*The Old Curiosity Shop.*

Mawls, Master.—A school-boy.—"An equally impersonal boy, whose name has long shaped itself unalterably into Master Mawls, is not to be dislodged from our brain." —*Our School* (Reprinted Pieces).

Maxby.—A day boarder at Our School.—*Our School* (Reprinted Pieces).

Maxey, Caroline.—A maid at Mrs. Lirriper's.—"And then there's temper, though such a temper as Caroline Maxey's I hope not often; a good-looking, black-eyed girl was Caroline; and a comely made girl, to your cost, when she did break out and laid about her."—Mrs. Lirriper's Lodgings (*Christmas Stories*).

Maxwell, Mrs.—A guest at the Kitterbell's Christening Party.—*Sketches by Boz* (The Bloomsbury Christening).

Maylie, Mrs.—The old lady whose house at Chertsey Sikes tried to rob.—"The high-backed oaken chair in which she sat was not more upright than she. Dressed with the utmost nicety and precision, in a quaint mixture of bygone costume, with some slight concessions to the prevailing taste, which rather served to point the old style pleasantly than to impair its effect, she sat in a stately manner with her hands folded on the table before her." —*Oliver Twist.*

Maylie, Rose.—Whose real name was Rose Fleming, and who was a sister of Oliver's mother, Agnes Fleming. Passed as Mrs. Maylie's niece.—"She was not past seventeen . . . the changing expression of seventeen and good humour; the thousand lights that played about the face, and left no shadow there; above all the smile, the cheerful happy smile, were made for home, and fireside peace, and happiness."—*Oliver Twist.*

Maylie, Harry.—Son of Mrs. Maylie.—"He seemed about five-and-twenty years of age, and was of the middle height; his countenance was frank and handsome; and his demeanour easy and prepossessing."—*Oliver Twist.*

Maypole Inn.—An old mansion-house which had been converted into an inn, the landlord of which was John Willet.—" In the year 1775, there stood upon the borders of Epping Forest, at a distance of about twelve miles from London, a house of public entertainment called the 'Maypole.' . . . It was no longer a home; children were never born and bred there; the fireside had become mercenary, a something to be bought and sold, a very courtesan; let who would die, or sit beside, or leave it, it was still the same—it missed nobody; cared for nobody; had equal warmth and smiles for all. God help the man whose heart ever changes with the world, as an old mansion when it becomes an Inn."—*Barnaby Rudge.*

Meagles, Mr.—A retired banker, given to travel.—" As I have no need to stick at a bank desk now (though I have been poor enough in my time I assure you, or I should have married Mrs. Meagles long before) we go trotting about the world."—*Little Dorrit.*

Meagles, Mrs.—Wife of Meagles.—" Mrs. Meagles was like Mr. Meagles, comely and healthy, with a pleasant English face, which had been looking at homely things for five-and-fifty years or more, and shone with a bright reflection of them."—*Little Dorrit.*

Meagles, Minnie (Pet).—Daughter of Mr. and Mrs. Meagles.—(*See* **Pet.**)—*Little Dorrit.*

Meagles, Lillie.—Daughter of Mr. and Mrs. Meagles—twin sister of Pet—who died young.—" Pet and her baby sister were exactly alike and so completely one that in our thoughts we have never been able to separate them since."—*Little Dorrit.*

Mealy Potatoes.—The nickname of one of the boys employed at Murdstone and Grinby's.—" He also informed me that our principal associate would be another boy, whom he introduced by the—to me—extraordinary name of Mealy Potatoes. I discovered however that this youth had not been christened by that name, but that it had been bestowed upon him in the warehouse, on account of his complexion which was pale or mealy."—*David Copperfield.*

Meek, Augustus George.—Infant son of Mr. and Mrs. Meek.—*Births—Mrs. Meek of a Son* (Reprinted Pieces).

Meek, Mr. George.—The father of Augustus George Meek.—"Births—Mrs. Meek of a Son. My name is Meek; I am in fact Mr. Meek; that son is mine and Mrs. Meek's. When I saw the announcement in the *Times*, I dropped the paper. I had put it in myself, and paid for it, but it looked so noble that it overpowered me."—*Births—Mrs. Meek of a Son* (Reprinted Pieces).

Meek, Mrs. Mark Jane.—Mother of Augustus George. —*Births—Mrs. Meek of a Son* (Reprinted Pieces).

Meggisson's.—One of the Liverpool sailors' lodging-houses visited by the Uncommercial Traveller.—"Not one of the whole number we visited was without its show of prints and ornamental crockery; the quantity of the latter, set forth on little shelves, and in little cases, in otherwise wretched rooms, indicating that Mercantile Jack must have an extraordinary fondness for crockery, to necessitate so much of that bait in his traps."—*The Uncommercial Traveller* (Poor Mercantile Jack).

Melchisedech.—A solicitor in Clifford's Inn to whom Mr. Tulkinghorn referred George.—*Bleak House.*

Mell, Mr. Charles.—Second assistant at Salem House (afterwards master of a school at Port Middleby in Australia, and president at a dinner given there to Micawber).—"He was a gaunt, sallow, young man, with hollow cheeks, and a chin almost as black as Mr. Murdstone's; but there the likeness ended, for his whiskers were shaved off, and his hair instead of being glossy, was rusty and dry. He was dressed in a suit of black clothes which were rather rusty and dry too, and rather short in the sleeves and legs, and he had a white neckerchief on that was not over clean. I did not and do not suppose that this neckerchief was all the linen he wore, but it was all he showed, or gave any hint of."—*David Copperfield.*

Mell, Mrs.—Mother of Mr. Mell, the assistant master at Salem House. A resident in an almshouse, which fact Steerforth disclosed to Mr. Creakle and brought about Mr. Mell's dismissal from Salem House.—*David Copperfield.*

Mell, Helena.—The daughter of Mr. Mell, present at the Micawber dinner at Port Middleby.—*David Copperfield.*

Mellows.—The landlord of the Dolphin's Head.—"The signboard chafed its rusty hooks, outside the bow window of my room, and was shabby work. No visitor could have denied that the Dolphin was dying by inches, but he showed no bright colours. He had once served another master; there was a newer streak of paint below him, displaying, with inconsistent freshness, the legend By J. Mellows. . . . In the gateway I found J. Mellows, looking at nothing, and apparently experiencing that it failed to raise his spirits."—*The Uncommercial Traveller* (An Old Stage Coaching House).

Melluka, Miss.—The name Polly Tresham gave to the doll presented to her by Jackson.—"There came the agreeable fever of getting Miss Melluka and all her wardrobe and rich possessions into a fly to be taken home with Polly."—Mugby Junction (*Christmas Stories*).

Meltham.—The man who trapped Slinkton.—*Hunted Down.*

Melvilleson, Miss.—A singer at the Sols Arms Harmonic Meetings.—"Mrs. Perkins and Mrs. Piper compare opinions on the subject of the young lady of professional celebrity who assists at the Harmonic Meetings, and who has a space to herself in the manuscript announcement in the window, Mrs. Perkins possessing information that she has been married a year and a half, though announced as Miss Melvilleson, the noted syren, and that her baby is clandestinely conveyed to the 'Sols Arms' every night, to receive its natural nourishment during the entertainments; sooner than which myself, says Mrs. Perkins, I would get my living by selling matches; Mrs. Piper as in duty bound is of the same opinion, holding that a private station is better than public applause."—*Bleak House.*

Mercantile Jack.—"Ever more when on a breezy day I see poor Mercantile Jack running into port with a fair wind under all sail I shall think of the unsleeping host of devourers who never go to bed and are always in their set traps waiting for him."—*The Uncommercial Traveller* (Poor Mercantile Jack).

Mercy.—A nurse to the Uncommercial Traveller, who told him tales, which frightened him in his childhood, of "impossible places and people, but none the less alarmingly real, that I found I had been introduced to by my nurse, before I was six years old, and used to be forced to go back to at night without at all wanting to go. If we all knew our own minds (in a more enlarged sense than the popular acceptation of that phrase) I suspect we should find our nurses responsible for most of the dark corners we are forced to go back to, against our wills."—*The Uncommercial Traveller* (Nurse's Stories).

Merdle, Mr., M.P.—" Mr. Merdle was immensely rich; a man of prodigious enterprise; a Midas without the ears, who turned all he touched to gold. He was in everything good, from banking to building; he was in Parliament of course; he was in the city necessarily. He did not shine in company; he had not very much to say for himself; he was a reserved man, with a broad overhanging watchful head, that particular kind of dull red colour in his cheeks which is rather stale than fresh, and a somewhat uneasy expression about his coat cuffs, as if they were in his confidence, and had reasons for being anxious to hide his hands. In the little he said he was a pleasant man enough, plain, emphatic about public and private confidence, and tenacious of the utmost deference being shown by every one in all things to Society.—*Little Dorrit.*

Merdle, Mrs.—Wife of Mr. Merdle, M.P.—" The lady was not young and fresh from the hand of Nature: but was young and fresh from the hand of her maid. She had large unfeeling handsome eyes; and dark unfeeling handsome hair; and a broad unfeeling handsome bosom; and was made the most of in every particular."—*Little Dorrit.*

Meriton, Henry.—The second mate of the *Haleswell* East Indiaman.—*The Long Voyage* (Reprinted Pieces).

Merrylegs.—A performing dog in Sleary's Circus.—" Signor Jupe was that afternoon to elucidate the diverting accomplishments of his highly trained performing dog Merrylegs."—*Hard Times.*

Merrywinkle, Mr. and Mrs.—The couple who coddle themselves.—" Mr. Merrywinkle is a rather lean and long-necked gentleman, middle-aged, and middle-sized, and usually troubled with a cold in the head. Mrs. Merrywinkle is a delicate-looking lady; with very light hair, and is exceedingly subject to the same unpleasant disorder."—*Sketches of Young Couples.*

Mesheck, Aaron.—A Jew criminal.—*The Detective Police* (Reprinted Pieces).

Mesrour.—The name given to Tabby, Miss Griffin's servant in the Seraglio.—(*See* **Tabby.**)—The Haunted House (*Christmas Stories*).

Micawber, Wilkins, Senior.—A sanguine but easily depressed gentleman in a chronic state of impecuniosity, with whom David lodged when a boy at Murdstone and Grinby's, who became his lifelong friend, and who after exposing the villainy of Uriah Heep emigrated to Australia.—" I went in and found there a stoutish middle-aged person, in a brown surtout and black tights, and shoes; with no more hair upon his head (which was a large one and very shining) than there is upon an egg, and with a very extensive face which he turned full upon me. His clothes were shabby, but he had an imposing shirt collar on. He carried a jaunty sort of a stick, with a large pair of rusty tassels to it, and a quizzing glass hung outside his coat,—for ornament I afterwards found, as he very seldom looked through it, and couldn't see anything when he did. . . . My other piece of advice, Copperfield, said Mr. Micawber, you know. Annual income Twenty pounds, annual expenditure Nineteen, nineteen six, result happiness. Annual income Twenty pounds, annual expenditure Twenty pounds ought and six, result misery."—*David Copperfield.*

Micawber, Mrs. Emma.—Wife of Wilkins Micawber. —" Arrived at his house in Windsor Terrace (which I noticed was shabby like himself but also like himself made all the show it could) he presented me to Mrs. Micawber, a thin and faded lady not at all young. . . . Mr. Micawber (said his wife) has his faults. I do not deny that he is improvident. I do not deny that he has kept me in the dark as to his resources and his liabilities both, but I will never desert Mr. Micawber."—*David Copperfield.*

Micawber, Miss Emma.—Daughter of Mr. Micawber. After the family emigrated she became Mrs. Ridger Begs of Port Middleby, Australia.—*David Copperfield.*

Micawber, Wilkins, Junior.—Musical son of Mr. Micawber; chorister at Canterbury.—*David Copperfield.*

Michael.—The Poor Relation, nephew of Mr. Chill, the miser.—*The Poor Relation's Story* (Reprinted Pieces).

Miff, Mrs.—Pew-opener at the church where Paul Dombey was christened, and where Mr. Dombey was married.—" Mrs. Miff, the wheezy little pew-opener—a mighty dry old lady, sparely dressed, with not an inch of fulness anywhere about her. . . . A vinegary face has Mrs. Miff, and a mortified bonnet, and eke a thirsty soul for sixpences and shillings. Beckoning to stray people to come into pews has given Mrs. Miff an air of mystery, and there is a reservation in the eye of Mrs. Miff, as always knowing of a softer seat, but having her suspicions of the fee."—*Dombey and Son.*

Miff, Mr.—The deceased husband of Mrs. Miff.—" There is no such fact as Mr. Miff, nor has there been these twenty years, and Mrs. Miff would rather not allude to him. He held some bad opinions, it would seem, about free seats, and, though Mrs. Miff hopes he may be gone upwards, she couldn't positively undertake to say so."—*Dombey and Son.*

Miggot.—The laundress of chambers in Gray's Inn, occupied by Mr. Parkle.—" At one period of my uncommercial career, I much frequented another set of chambers in Gray's Inn Square. They were what is familiarly called a top set, and all the eatables and drinkables introduced into them acquired a flavour of cockloft. . . . This however was not the most curious feature of these chambers; that consisted in the profound conviction, entertained by my esteemed friend Parkle (their tenant), that they were clean. Whether it was an inborn hallucination, or whether it was imparted to him by Mrs. Miggot, the laundress, I never could ascertain."—*The Uncommercial Traveller* (Chambers).

Miggs, Miss.—Servant of Mrs. Varden. In love with Simon Tappertit.—" Mrs. Varden's chief aider and abettor, and at the same time her principal victim and object of wrath, was her single domestic servant, one Miss Miggs, or as she was called, in conformity with those prejudices of society which lop and top from poor handmaidens all such genteel excrescences,—Miggs. This Miggs was a tall young lady, very much addicted to pattens in private life, slender and shrewish, of a rather uncomfortable figure, and, though not absolutely ill-looking, of a sharp and acid visage."—*Barnaby Rudge.*

Mike.—A client of Mr. Jaggers.—" A gentleman with one eye, in a velveteen suit and knee breeches."—*Great Expectations.*

Miles, Bob.—A London thief.—*On Duty with Inspector Field* (Reprinted Pieces).

Miles, Owen.—A friend of Master Humphrey.—" An excellent man, of thoroughly sterling character, not of quick apprehension, and not without some amusing prejudices."—*Master Humphrey's Clock.*

Milkwash, Mr.—The poetical young gentleman.—" We do not mean to say that he is troubled with the gift of poesy in any remarkable degree, but his countenance is of a plaintive and melancholy cast; his manner is abstracted, and bespeaks affliction of the soul; he seldom has his hair cut, and often talks about being an outcast, and wanting a kindred spirit."—*Sketches of Young Gentlemen.*

Miller, Mr.—A guest at Manor Farm.—" A little, hard, pipstone, pippin-faced man."—*Pickwick Papers.*

Miller, Mrs.—Sister of Mrs. Vendale.—No Thoroughfare (*Christmas Stories*).

Millers.—One of the two nurses at Matthew Pocket's.—*Great Expectations.*

Mills, Julia.—A sentimental friend of Dora Spenlow; ultimately married an elderly wealthy East India merchant. —" There was a young lady with her—comparatively stricken in years—almost twenty I should say. Her name was Miss Mills, and Dora called her Julia. She was the bosom friend of Dora. . . . I learnt that Miss Mills had had her trials in the course of a chequered existence, and that to these perhaps I might refer that wise benignity of manner which I had already noticed. I found in the course of the day that this was the case, Miss Mills having been unhappy in a misplaced affection, and being understood to have retired from the world, on her awful stock of experience, but still able to take a calm interest in the unblighted hopes and loves of youth."—*David Copperfield.*

Mills, Mr.—Father of Julia Mills.—" Mr. Mills who was always doing something or other to annoy me—or I felt as if he were, which was the same thing—had brought his conduct to a climax by taking it into his head that he would go to India . . . and Julia with him."—*David Copperfield.*

Milly.—Wife of William Swidgers. Matron of the Institution where Mr. Redlaw lectured.—" Mrs. William, like Mr. William, was a simply innocent-looking person, in whose smooth cheeks the cheerful red of her husband's official waistcoat was very pleasantly repeated. But whereas Mr. William's light hair stood on end all over his head, and seemed to draw his eyes up with it, in an excess of bustling readiness for anything; the dark brown hair of Mrs. William was carefully smoothed down, and waved away, under a trim tidy cap, in the most exact and quiet manner imaginable; whereas Mr William's very trousers hitched themselves up at the ankles, as if it were not in their iron-grey nature to rest without looking about them. Mrs. William's neatly-flowered skirts—red and white like her own pretty face—were as composed and orderly as if the very wind that blew so hard out of doors could not disturb one of their folds; whereas his coat had something of a fly-away and half-off appearance about the collar and breast, her little bodice was so placid and neat, that there should have been protection for her in it had she needed any with the roughest people."—*The Haunted Man.*

Milvey, Rev. Frank.—A curate, to whom Mr. and Mrs. Boffin applied to find them a boy to adopt.—" The Reverend Frank Milvey's abode was a very modest abode, because his income was a very modest income. He was quite a young man, expensively educated, and wretchedly paid, with a quite young wife, and half-a-dozen quite young children."—*Our Mutual Friend.*

Milvey, Mrs.—Wife of the Rev. Frank.—" A pretty bright little woman, something worn by anxiety, who had repressed many pretty tastes and bright fancies, and substituted in their stead schools, soup, flannel, coals, and all the week-day cares and Sunday coughs of a large population, young and old."—*Our Mutual Friend.*

Mim, Mr.—Proprietor of a travelling show.—" His master's name was Mim, a wery hoarse man. . . . Mim was a most ferocious swearer."—Doctor Marigold (*Christmas Stories*).

Mincin, Mr.—The very friendly young gentleman.—" If anybody's self-love is to be flattered, Mr. Mincin is at hand; if anybody's overweening vanity is to be pampered, Mr. Mincin will surfeit it. What wonder that people of all stations and ages recognize Mr. Mincin's friendliness." —*Sketches of Young Gentlemen.*

Minerva House.—A ladies' seminary, conducted by the Misses Crumpton.—" Minerva House, conducted under the auspices of the two sisters, was a finishing establishment for young ladies, where some twenty girls, of the ages of from thirteen to nineteen inclusive, acquired a smattering of everything and a knowledge of nothing."—*Sketches by Boz* (Sentiment).

Minns, Augustus.—Cousin of Mr. Budden.—" Mr. Augustus Minns was a bachelor,—of about forty as he said, of about eight-and-forty as his friends said. He was always exceedingly clean, precise, and tidy, perhaps somewhat priggish, and the most retiring man in the world. He usually wore a brown frock coat without a wrinkle; light inexplicables without a spot; a neat neckerchief, with a remarkably neat tie; and boots without a fault; moreover he always carried a brown silk umbrella with an ivory handle. He was a clerk in Somerset House, or as he said himself, he held a responsible situation under Government."—*Sketches by Boz* (Mr. Minns and His Cousin).

Missis, Our.—The manageress of Mugby Junction Refreshment Room.—" We are the Model Establishment, we are at Mugby. Other Refreshment Rooms send their imperfect young ladies up to be finished off by our Missis; for some of the young ladies, when they're new to the business, come into it mild; ah! our Missis she soon takes that out of 'em."—Mugby Junction (*Christmas Stories*).

Misty, Mr.—A member of the Zoology and Botany Section of the Mudfog Association.—" Mr. X. X. Misty communicated some remarks on the disappearance of dancing bears from the streets of London, with observations on the exhibition of monkeys, as connected with barrel organs."—*The Mudfog Sketches.*

Mith, Sergeant.—A London police officer.—" A smooth-faced man, with a fresh bright complexion, and a strange air of simplicity."—*The Detective Police* (Reprinted Pieces).

Mithers, Lady.—A client of Miss Mowcher's.—" *There's* a woman; how *she* wears."—*David Copperfield.*

Mithers.—Husband of Lady Mithers, a client of Miss Mowcher's.—" There's a man. How *he* wears, and his wig too, for he's had it these ten years."—*David Copperfield.*

Mitts, Mrs.—A resident in Titbull's almshouses, who created a sensation in the houses by marrying a Greenwich pensioner.—" Before another week was out, Titbull's was startled by another phenomenon. At ten o'clock in the forenoon, appeared a cab, containing not only the Greenwich pensioner with one arm, but to boot a Chelsea pensioner with one leg. Both dismounting to assist Mrs. Mitts into the cab, the Greenwich pensioner bore her company inside, and the Chelsea pensioner mounted the box by the driver, his wooden leg sticking out after the manner of a bowsprit, as if in jocular homage to his friend's sea-going career. Thus the equipage drove away. No Mrs. Mitts returned."—*The Uncommercial Traveller* (Titbull's Almshouses).

Mivins, Mr.—A prisoner for debt in The Fleet.—" A man in a broad-skirted green coat, with corduroy knee smalls, and grey cotton stockings."—*Pickwick Papers.*

Mobbs, Master.—A pupil at Dotheboys Hall.—*Nicholas Nickleby.*

Moddle, Augustus.—A sentimental boarder at Todgers' who admired Mercy Pecksniff, and ultimately proposed to her sister Charity, but sailed abroad on the eve of the wedding.—*Martin Chuzzlewit.*

Model, The Artist's.—" A shabby man in threadbare black, and with his hands in his pockets."—*The Ghost of Art* (Reprinted Pieces).

Molly.—Housekeeper to Mr. Jaggers. Mother of Estella. —" She was a woman of about forty, I supposed, but I may have thought her younger than she was. Rather tall, of a lithe nimble figure, extremely pale, with large faded eyes and a quantity of streaming hair."—*Great Expectations.*

Monflathers, Miss.—Matron of a boarding-school which visited Jarley's Waxworks.—" Mrs. Jarley had been at great pains to conciliate, by altering the face and costume of Mr. Grimaldi as clown, to represent Mr. Lindley Murray, as he appeared when engaged in the composition of his English Grammar; and turning a murderess of great renown into Mrs. Hannah More; both of which likenesses were admitted by Miss Monflathers (who was at the head of the head boarding and day establishment in the town, and who condescended to take a private view with eight chosen young ladies) to be quite startling from their extreme correctness."—*The Old Curiosity Shop*.

Monks, Mr.—The name assumed by Edward Leeford, the half-brother of Oliver Twist. Employed Fagin to make a criminal of Oliver in the hope of his being sent out of the country, and so the discovery should not be made that Leeford's mother had destroyed a will of her husband which had provided for Oliver.—*Oliver Twist*.

Montague, Julia.—A singer who assisted Mr. Henry Taplin at his benefit.—" Solo, Miss Julia Montague (positively on this occasion only)."—*Sketches by Boz* (The Mistaken Milliner).

Moon, Doctor.—A medical man consulted by Our Bore. —" Moon was interested in the case; to do him justice he was very much interested in the case; and he said kidneys. He altered the whole treatment, gave strong acids, cupped and blistered."—*Our Bore* (Reprinted Pieces).

Mooney, Mr.—Assistant to Mr. Flamstead the scientific old gentleman.—" This Mooney was even more scientific in appearance than his friend, and had, as Tom often declared upon his word of honour, the dirtiest face we can possibly know of in this imperfect state of existence."—*The Lamplighter* (Reprinted Pieces).

Mooney.—The parish beadle who made the arrangements for the inquest on Mr. Nemo's death.—" The beadle is very careful that two gentlemen, not very neat about the cuffs and buttons (for whose accommodation he has provided a special little table near the Coroner), should see all that is to be seen; for they are the public chroniclers of such inquiries by the line, and he is not superior to the universal human infirmity, but hopes to read in print what Mooney the active and intelligent beadle of the district said and did."—*Bleak House*.

Mopes.—The hermit owner of Tom Tiddler's Ground.— " Mr. Mopes, by suffering everything about him to go to ruin; and by dressing himself in a blanket and skewer; and by steeping himself in soot and grease and other nastiness; had acquired great renown in all that country side. . . . He was represented as being all the ages between five-and-twenty and sixty; and as having been a hermit seven years, twelve, twenty, thirty,—though twenty on the whole appeared the favourite term."—Tom Tiddler's Ground (*Christmas Stories*).

Mordlin, Mr.—A musical member of the Brick Lane Branch of the United Grand Junction Ebenezer Temperance Association.—"Brother Mordlin had adapted the beautiful words of 'Who hasn't heard of a Jolly Young Waterman' to the tune of the Old Hundredth."—*Pickwick Papers.*

Morfin, Mr.—Assistant-manager in Dombey and Son's counting-house.—"A cheerful-looking, hazel-eyed, elderly bachelor, gravely attired as to his upper man in black, and as to his legs in pepper-and-salt colour. His dark hair was just touched here and there with specks of grey, as though the tread of time had splashed it; and his whiskers were already white. . . . He was a great musical amateur in his way, after business, and had a paternal affection for his violoncello, which was once in every week transported from Islington, his place of abode, to a certain club room hard by the Bank, where quartettes of a most tormenting and excruciating nature were executed every Wednesday evening by a private party."—*Dombey and Son.*

Morgan, Becky.—An old woman who died, and was buried by old David, the sexton.—*The Old Curiosity Shop.*

Mormon Agent.—The emigration agent on board the *Amazon.*—"A compactly-made handsome man in black, rather short, with rich brown hair and beard, and clear bright eyes; from his speech I shall set him down as American—probably a man who had touched about the world pretty much."—*The Uncommercial Traveller* (Bound for the Great Salt Lake).

Mortair, Mr.—A Vice-President of the Medical Section of the Mudfog Association.—*The Mudfog Sketches.*

Mortimer, Mr.—An alias assumed by Mr. Micawber.—"You see, the truth is—said Traddles in a whisper—he has changed his name to Mortimer, in consequence of his temporary embarrassments, and he don't come out till after dark, and then in spectacles."—*David Copperfield.*

Mould, Mr.—A London undertaker.—"A little elderly gentleman; bald, and in a suit of black; with a note-book in his hand, a massive gold watch-chain dangling from his fob, and a face in which a queer attempt at melancholy was at odds with a smirk of satisfaction; so that he looked as a man might who, in the very act of smacking his lips over choice old wine, tried to make believe it was physic."—*Martin Chuzzlewit.*

Mould, Mrs.—Wife of Mr. Mould, the undertaker.—*Martin Chuzzlewit.*

Mould, The Misses.—Daughters of Mr. Mould.—"Plump as any partridge was each Miss Mould; so round and chubby were their fair proportions, that they might have been the bodies once belonging to the angels' faces in the shop below, grown up, with other heads attached to make them mortal."—*Martin Chuzzlewit.*

Mowcher, Miss.—A dwarf skilled as an improver.—"There came waddling round a sofa a fussy dwarf, of about forty or forty-five, with a very large head and face, a pair of roguish grey eyes, and such extremely little arms that, to enable herself to lay a finger archly against her snub nose, as she ogled Steerforth, she was obliged to meet the finger half-way, and lay her nose against it. . . . He told me that Miss Mowcher had quite an extensive connection, and made herself useful to a variety of people in a variety of ways."—*David Copperfield.*

Muddlebrains, Mr.—A Vice-President of the Zoology and Botany Section of the Mudfog Association.—*The Mudfog Sketches.*

Mudfog.—The town of which Mr. Tulrumble was mayor.—"Mudfog is a pleasant town—a remarkably pleasant town—situated in a charming hollow, by the side of a river, from which river Mudfog derives an agreeable scent of pitch tar, coals, and rope yarn, a roving population in oilskin hats, a pretty steady influx of drunken bargemen, and a great many other maritime advantages."—*The Mudfog Sketches.*

Mudge, Jonas.—Secretary of the Brick Lane Branch of the United Grand Junction Ebenezer Temperance Association.—"The Secretary was Mr. Jonas Mudge, Chandlers' shop-keeper, an enthusiastic and disinterested vessel, who sold tea to the members."—*Pickwick Papers.*

Muff, Professor.—A Vice-President of the Medical Section of the Mudfog Association.—*The Mudfog Sketches.*

Mugby Junction.—A railway station where Jackson alighted at three o'clock in the morning.—"A place replete with shadowy shapes this Mugby Junction, in the black hours of the twenty-four. Mysterious goods trains, covered with palls, and gliding on like vast weird funerals, conveying themselves quietly away from the presence of the few lighted lamps, as if their freight had come to a secret and unlawful end. . . . An earthquake, accompanied with thunder and lightning, going up express to London; now all quiet; all rusty; wind and rain in possession; lamps extinguished; Mugby Junction, dead and indistinct, with its robe drawn over its head, like Cæsar."—Mugby Junction (*Christmas Stories*).

Mull, Professor.—A member of the Mudfog Association.—*The Mudfog Sketches.*

Mullins, Jack.—A customer at the Fellowship Porters tavern.—*Our Mutual Friend.*

Mullion, John.—One of the crew of the *Golden Mary*. —"The man who had kept on burning the blue lights, and who had lighted every new one at every old one before it went out, as quietly as if he had been at an illumination."—The Wreck of the *Golden Mary* (*Christmas Stories*).

Mullit, Professor.—A New York politician.—*Martin Chuzzlewit.*

Murderer, Captain.—The hero of one of the tales told to the Uncommercial Traveller in childhood.—"The first diabolical character, who intruded himself in my peaceful youth, was a certain Captain Murderer. His warning name would seem to have awakened no general prejudice against him, for he was admitted into the best society, and possessed immense wealth. Captain Murderer's mission was matrimony, and the gratification of a cannibal appetite with tender brides. . . . The young woman who brought me acquainted with Captain Murderer had a fiendish enjoyment of my terrors, and used to begin I remember—as a sort of introductory overture—by clawing the air with both hands and uttering a long low hollow groan."—*The Uncommercial Traveller* (Nurse's Stories).

Murdstone, Edward.—A man of a handsome appearance, but a hard stern nature, who married the widow Copperfield, the mother of David, and treated her cruelly. —"He had that kind of shallow black eye—I want a better word to express an eye that has no depths in it to be looked into—which, when it is abstracted, seems, from some peculiarity of light, to be disfigured for a moment at a time by a cast . . . his regular eyebrows, and the rich white and black and brown of his complexion—confound his complexion and his memory—made me think him in spite of my misgivings a very handsome man. I have no doubt that my poor dear mother thought him so too."—*David Copperfield.*

Murdstone, Mrs., the Second.—A lively young woman whose spirit Mr. Murdstone and his sister broke.—"Tyranny, gloom and worry had made Mrs. Murdstone nearly imbecile. She was a lively young woman, sir, before her marriage and their gloom and austerity destroyed her."—*David Copperfield.*

Murdstone, Miss Jane.—A sister of Mr. Murdstone, who resided with him and his wife, and made the wife's life miserable; afterwards companion to Miss Dora Spenlow.—"It was Miss Murdstone who was arrived, and a gloomy-looking lady she was; dark like her brother, whom she greatly resembled in face and voice, and with very heavy eyebrows nearly meeting over her large nose, as if, being disabled by the wrongs of her sex from wearing whiskers, she had carried them to that account. She brought with her two uncompromising hard black boxes, with her initials on the lids in hard brass nails. When she paid the coachman, she took her money out of a hard steel purse, and she kept the purse in a very jail of a bag, which hung upon her arm by a heavy chain, and shut up like a bite. I had never at that time seen such a metallic lady altogether as Miss Murdstone was."—*David Copperfield.*

Murdstone and Grinby.—Wine-merchants in London; the firm of which Mr. Murdstone was a partner, and Mr. Quinion was manager, where David was employed to wash bottles and whence he ran away to his aunt.—"I became, at ten years old, a little labouring hind in the service of Murdstone and Grinby. . . . My working place was established in a corner of the warehouse where Mr. Quinion could see me.—Mr. Quinion formally engaged me to be as useful as I could in the warehouse of Murdstone and Grinby at a salary I think of six shillings a week."—*David Copperfield.*

Mutanhed, Lord.—A visitor at Bath.—"You see the splendidly dressed young man coming this way. The one with the long hair and particularly small forehead, inquired Mr. Pickwick. The same—the richest man in Bath at this moment—young Lord Mutanhed."—*Pickwick Papers.*

Mutual, Monsieur.—A resident at Madam Bouclet's lodgings.—" A spectacled, stuffy, stooping old gentleman; in carpet shoes, and a cloth cap, with a peaked shade, a loose blue frock-coat reaching to his heels, a large limp white shirt frill, and cravat to correspond—that is to say white was the natural colour of his linen on Sundays, but it toned down with the week."—Somebody's Luggage (*Christmas Stories*).

Muzzle.—Footman to Mr. Nupkins at Ipswich.—" Muzzle was an undersized footman, with a long body, and short legs."—*Pickwick Papers.*

Nadgett.—The inquiry agent of the Anglo-Bengalee Company.—" He was the man, at a pound a week, who made all the inquiries. He was a short, dried-up, withered old man, who seemed to have secreted his very blood, for nobody would have given him credit for the possession of six ounces of it in his whole body. How he lived was a secret; where he lived was a secret; and even what he was was a secret. He was mildewed, threadbare, shabby; always had flue upon his legs and back; and kept his linen so secret, by buttoning up and wrapping up, that he might have had none—perhaps he hadn't. He belonged to a class; a race peculiar to the city; who are secrets as profound to one another as they are to the rest of mankind."—*Martin Chuzzlewit.*

Namby.—A sheriff's officer who arrested Mr. Pickwick. —" A man of about forty; with black hair, and carefully combed whiskers. He was dressed in a particularly gorgeous manner, with plenty of articles of jewellery about him—all about three sizes larger than are usually worn by gentlemen—and a rough great coat to crown the whole."—*Pickwick Papers.*

Nancy.—(*See* **Bet.**)—Murdered by Bill Sikes in a fit of anger.—*Oliver Twist.*

Nandy, John Edward.—Father of Mrs. Plornish.—" A poor little reedy, piping old gentleman, like a worn-out bird, who had been in what he called the music-binding business, and met with great misfortunes, and who had seldom been able to make his way; or to see it; or to pay it; or to do anything at all with it, but find it no thoroughfare; had retired of his own accord to the Workhouse, which was appointed by law to be the Good Samaritan of his district."—*Little Dorrit.*

Nathan, Mr.—The dresser at a private theatre.—"A red-headed and red-whiskered Jew."—*Sketches by Boz* (Private Theatres).

Native, The.—Major Bagstock's servant.—*Dombey and Son.*

Neckett.—A bailiff.—"A person in a great white great-coat, with smooth hair upon his head, and not much of it, which he was wiping smoother, and making less of, with a pocket-handkerchief."—*Bleak House.*

Neckett, Charlotte (Charley).—Aged thirteen, daughter of and housekeeper to Neckett; supported his family after his death.—"There came into the room a very little girl, childish in figure, but shrewd and older-looking in the face—pretty-faced too—wearing a womanly sort of bonnet much too large for her, and drying her bare arms upon a womanly sort of apron; her fingers were white and wrinkled with washing, and the soap suds were yet smoking which she wiped off her arms; but for this she might have been a child playing at washing, and imitating a poor working woman with a quick observation of the truth."—*Bleak House.*

Neckett, Tom.—Brother of Charley.—"A mite of a boy, some five or six years old, nursing and hushing a heavy child of eighteen months."—*Bleak House.*

Neckett, Emma.—Sister of Charley—a child of eighteen months.—*Bleak House.*

Neeshawts, Doctor.—A member of the Medical Section of the Mudfog Association.—*The Mudfog Sketches.*

Nemo, Mr.—The name under which Captain Hawdon in his poverty obtained employment as a law writer for Mr. Snagsby.—"Our law writers (said Mr. Snagsby) who live by job work are a queer lot, and this may not be his name but it's the name he goes by."—*Bleak House.*

Nettingall, The Misses.—Principals of girls' boarding-school at Canterbury, where Miss Shepherd was a pupil.—"One day I meet the Misses Nettingall's establishment out walking. Miss Shepherd makes a face as she goes by and laughs to her companion. All is over. . . . I am not at all polite now to the Misses Nettingall's young ladies, and shouldn't dote on any of them if they were twice as many, and twenty times as beautiful. I think the dancing school a tiresome affair, and wonder why the girls can't dance by themselves and leave us alone."—*David Copperfield.*

Newcome, Clemency.—Dr. Jeddler's maid, afterwards Mrs. Britain.—" She was about thirty years old, and had a sufficiently plump and cheerful face, though it was twisted up into an odd expression of tightness, that made it comical. . . . She always wore short sleeves, and always had by some accident grazed elbows, in which she took so lively an interest that she was continually trying to turn them round and get impossible views of them. In general a little cap placed somewhere on her head, though it was rarely to be met with in the place usually occupied in other subjects by that article of dress; but from head to foot she was scrupulously clean, and maintained a kind of dislocated tidiness. Indeed her laudable anxiety to be tidy and compact, in her own conscience as well as in the public eye, gave rise to one of her most startling evolutions, which was to grasp herself sometimes by a sort of wooden handle (part of her clothing and familiarly called a busk) and wrestle as it were with her garments, until they fell into a symmetrical arrangement."—*The Battle of Life.*

Nicholas.—Butler of Bellamy's.—" Nicholas is the butler of Bellamy's, and has held the same place, dressed exactly in the same manner, and said precisely the same things, ever since the oldest of its present visitors can remember. An excellent servant Nicholas is—an unrivalled compounder of salad dressing; an admirable preparer of soda water and lemon; a special mixer of cold grog and punch; and above all an unequalled judge of cheese."—*Sketches by Boz* (A Parliamentary Sketch).

Nickits.—The improvident owner of an estate of which Bounderby became the owner by the bank foreclosing on a mortgage.—" Nickits (as a man came into my office and told me yesterday) who used to act in Latin in the Westminster School plays, with the Chief Justices and nobility of this country applauding him till they were blue in the face, is drivelling at this minute in a fifth floor up a narrow back street in Antwerp."--*Hard Times.*

Nickleby, Godfrey.—The paternal grandfather of young Nicholas and Kate.—"There once lived in a sequestered part of the County of Devon, one Mr. Godfrey Nickleby, a worthy gentleman. At length, after five years, when Mrs. Nickleby had presented her husband with a couple of sons, and that embarrassed gentleman, impressed with the necessity of making some provision for his family, was seriously revolving in his mind a little commercial speculation, of insuring his life next quarter day, and then falling from the monument by accident, there came one morning by the general post, a black-bordered letter, to inform him how his uncle Mr. Ralph Nickleby was dead, and had left him the bulk of his little property, amounting in all to five thousand pounds. When he died some fifteen years after this period, and some five after his wife, he was enabled to leave to his eldest son Ralph three thousand pounds in cash, and to his youngest son Nicholas one thousand and the farm, which was as small a landed estate as one would desire to see."—*Nicholas Nickleby.*

Nickleby, Ralph, the Elder.—Grand-uncle of Ralph Nickleby, the Younger, and of his brother Nicholas.—*Nicholas Nickleby.*

Nickleby, Ralph, the Younger.—Uncle of young Nicholas and Kate Nickleby; a moneylender, a hard, sour man, with whom his nephew Nicholas quarrelled.—"Mr. Ralph Nickleby was not strictly speaking what you would call a merchant; neither was he a banker; nor an attorney; nor a Special Pleader; nor a notary. He was certainly not a tradesman, and still less could he lay claim to the title of a professional gentleman, for it would have been impossible to mention any recognized profession to which he belonged. He appeared to have a very extraordinary and miscellaneous connection, and very odd calls he made, some at great rich houses, and some at small poor houses, but all upon one subject,—money."—*Nicholas Nickleby.*

Nickleby, Nicholas, The Elder.—The father of young Nicholas and Kate, a country gentleman of limited means who was ruined by speculation.—"Mr. Nickleby looked about him for the means of repairing his capital, now sadly reduced by this increase in his family, and the expenses of their education. The run of luck went against

Mr. Nickleby, a mania prevailed; a bubble burst; four stockbrokers took villa residences at Florence; four hundred nobodies were ruined; and among them Mr. Nickleby. His reason went astray after this. . . . This fit of wandering past, he solemnly commended them to One Who never deserted the widow or her fatherless children, and, smiling gently on them, turned upon his face and observed that he thought he could fall asleep."—*Nicholas Nickleby*.

Nickleby, Nicholas, The Younger.—Nephew of Ralph Nickleby who disliked him, and sent him to teach at Dotheboys Hall, whence he ran away, and became a strolling player; afterwards a clerk, and ultimately a partner in the firm of Cheeryble Brothers.—" The uncle and nephew looked at each other for some seconds, without speaking,—the face of the old man was stern, hard-featured and forbidding, that of the young one open, handsome and ingenuous. The old man's eye was keen with the twinklings of avarice and cunning; the young man's bright with the light of intelligence and spirit. His figure was somewhat slight, but manly, and well-formed, and, apart from all the grace of youth and comeliness, there was an emanation from the warm young heart in his look and bearing which kept the old man down. It galled Ralph to the heart's core, and he hated Nicholas from that hour."—*Nicholas Nickleby*.

Nickleby, Mrs.—Mother of young Nicholas and Kate, a lady of trying temper, given to be irrelevant in her remarks and anecdotes, and whose attitude when her observations were not regarded was—" Never mind, wait and see. You won't believe anything I say of course. It's much better to wait; a great deal better; it's satisfactory to all parties, and there can be no disputing; all I say is remember what I say now; and when I say I said so, don't say I didn't."—*Nicholas Nickleby*.

Nickleby, Kate.—Sister of Nicholas Nickleby, the Younger, and niece of Ralph Nickleby; married Frank Cheeryble.—*Nicholas Nickleby*.

Niner, Miss Margaret.—Niece of Slinkton, whom he tried to poison.—*Hunted Down*.

Nipper, Susan.—Florence Dombey's maid and her devoted friend.—A young lady sharp of tongue but warm of heart, who ultimately married Mr. Toots.—"A short brown womanly girl, with a little snub nose, and black eyes like jet beads . . . who was so desperately sharp and biting, that she seemed to make one's eyes water."—*Dombey and Son.*

Nixon, Mr. Felix.—The domestic young gentleman.—"Felix is a young gentleman who lives at home with his mother . . . the two chief subjects of Felix's discourse are himself and his mother, both of whom would appear to be very wonderful and interesting persons."—*Sketches of Young Gentlemen.*

Nixon, Mrs.—Mother of the domestic young gentleman.—"Mrs. Nixon has a tolerably extensive circle of female acquaintance, being a good-humoured, talkative, bustling little body, and to the unmarried girls among them she is constantly vaunting the virtues of her son."—*Sketches of Young Gentlemen.*

Nixons, The.—In the audience at the private theatricals at Rose Villa.—(*See* **Glumper.**)—*Sketches by Boz* (Mrs. Joseph Porter).

Noakes, Mr.—A Vice-President of the Statistical Section of the Mudfog Association.—*The Mudfog Sketches.*

Noakes, Percy.—The originator of the Steam Excursion.—"Mr. Percy Noakes was a law student, inhabiting a set of chambers on the fourth floor. Mr. Percy Noakes was what is generally termed a devilish good fellow. He had a large circle of acquaintance, and seldom dined at his own expense. He used to talk politics to papa; flatter the vanity of mamma; do the amiable to their daughters; make pleasure engagements with their sons; and romp with the younger branches. He was always making something for somebody, or planning some party of pleasure, which was his great forte. He invariably spoke with astonishing rapidity; was smart, spoffish, and eight-and-twenty."—*Sketches by Boz* (The Steam Excursion).

Nobody.—The subject of Nobody's Story.—"He lived in a busy place, and he worked very hard to live. He had no hope of ever being rich enough to live a month without hard work; but he was quite content, God knows, to labour with a cheerful will. He was one of an immense family, all of whose sons and daughters gained their daily bread by daily work."—*Nobody's Story* (Reprinted Pieces).

Nockemorf, Dr.—A Bristol surgeon whose practice Bob Sawyer bought.—"I wonder you didn't see the name, said Bob Sawyer, calling his friend's attention to the outer door, on which, in the same white paint, were traced the words 'Sawyer late Nockemorf.'"—*Pickwick Papers.*

Noddy.—A friend of Bob Sawyer.—"A scorbutic youth, in a long stock."—*Pickwick Papers.*

Noggs, Newman.—Ralph Nickleby's clerk.—"It was clear that Mr. Ralph Nickleby did, or pretended to do, business of some kind, and the fact, if it required any further circumstantial evidence, was abundantly demonstrated by the diurnal attendance, between the hours of half-past nine and five, of a sallow-faced man in rusty brown who sat upon an uncommonly hard stool, in a species of butler's pantry, at the end of the passage, and always had a pen behind his ear when he answered the bell. The expression of a man's face is commonly a help to his thoughts, or glossary on his speech, but the countenance of Newman Noggs in his ordinary moods was a problem which no stretch of ingenuity could solve."—*Nicholas Nickleby.*

Nogo, Professor.—A Vice-President of the Medical Section of the Mudfog Association.—*The Mudfog Sketches.*

Noland, Sir Thomas.—Mentioned by Mr. Malderton at the dinner-party to Horatio Sparkins.—"Have you seen your friend Sir Thomas Noland lately, Flamwell, inquired Mr. Malderton,—casting a sidelong look at Horatio, to see what effect the mention of so great a man had upon him."—*Sketches by Boz* (Horatio Sparkins).

Norah.—(Aged seven.)—The little girl with whom Master Harry Walmer (aged eight) ran away to Gretna Green, and whose story Boots at the Holly Tree inn told to Charley.—"Boots could assure me that it was better than a picter and equal to a play to see them babies with their long bright curling hair, their sparkling eyes, and their beautiful light tread rambling about the garden deep in love. Boots was of opinion that the birds believed they was birds and kept up with them singing to please 'em."—The Holly Tree (*Christmas Stories*).

Normandy, Mr.—The friend with whom Chops the Dwarf went into society, when he won a lottery prize.—" He then sent for a young man he knowed, as had a very genteel appearance, and was a Bonnet at a gaming booth (most respectable brought up father having been imminent in the livery stable line, but unfortunate in a commercial crisis, through paintin' an old grey ginger bay, and sellin' him with a Pedigree) and Mr. Chops said to this Bonnet, who said his name was Normandy, which it wasn't,—Normandy, I'm a goin' into Society,—will you go with me."—Going into Society (*Christmas Stories*).

Norris Family.—Relatives of Mr. Bevan, to whom he introduced Martin.—"There were two ladies, one eighteen the other twenty; both very slender and very pretty; their mother, who looked, as Martin thought, much older and more faded than she ought to have looked; and their grandmother, a little sharp-eyed quick old woman, who seemed to have got past that stage, and to have come all right again. Besides these, there were the young ladies' father, and the young ladies' brother; the first engaged in mercantile affairs, the second a student at college."—*Martin Chuzzlewit.*

Nubbles, Christopher.—The full name of Kit.—(*See* **Kit.**)—*The Old Curiosity Shop.*

Nubbles, Mrs.—Mother of Kit.—" The room in which Kit sat himself down was an extremely poor and homely place, but with that air of comfort about it, nevertheless, which—or the spot must be a wretched one indeed—cleanliness and order can always impart in some degree. Late as the Dutch clock showed it to be, the poor woman was still hard at work at an ironing table."—*The Old Curiosity Shop.*

Nubbles, Jacob.—Brother of Kit.—" A sturdy boy of two or three years old, very wide awake, with a very tight nightcap on his head, and a nightgown very much too small for his body, was sitting bolt upright in a clothes basket, staring over the rim with his great round eyes, and looking as if he had thoroughly made up his mind never to go to sleep any more."—*The Old Curiosity Shop.*

Nubbles, Abel.—Child of Kit and Barbara.—" Of course there was an Abel; own godson to the Mr. Garland of that name."—*The Old Curiosity Shop.*

Nubbles, Dick.—Child of Kit and Barbara.—" There was a Dick whom Mr. Swiveller did especially favour."—*The Old Curiosity Shop.*

Nubbles, Jacob, the Second.—Child of Kit and Barbara.—" Nor was there wanting an exact facsimile and copy of little Jacob, as he appeared in those remote times when they taught him what oysters meant."—*The Old Curiosity Shop.*

Nupkins, George.—Mayor of Ipswich.—" George Nupkins, Esquire, the principal magistrate aforesaid, was as grand a personage as the fastest walker would find out between sunrise and sunset. In front of a big book-case; in a big chair; behind a big table; and before a big volume; sat Mr. Nupkins, looking a full size larger than any one of them, big as they were."—*Pickwick Papers.*

Nupkins, Mrs.—Wife of Mr. Nupkins.—" A majestic female, in a pink gauze turban, and a light brown wig."—*Pickwick Papers.*

Nupkins, Miss Henrietta.—Daughter of Mr. Nupkins. —" Miss Nupkins possessed all her mamma's haughtiness without the turban; and all her ill nature without the wig."—*Pickwick Papers.*

Nutmeg Grater.—The name of the village inn kept by Britain and Clemency.—" This village inn had assumed on being established an uncommon sign. It was called the ' Nutmeg Grater '; and, underneath that household word was inscribed, up in the tree on the same flaming board, and in the like golden characters, By Benjamin Britain."—*The Battle of Life.*

Oakum Head.—The name given to the leader of the refractories in Wapping Workhouse.—" Refractories led by Oakum Head with folded arms."—*The Uncommercial Traveller* (Wapping Workhouse).

Obenreizer, Mr.—A wine-merchant's agent in London —discovered identity of Vendale with Wilding.—" A black-haired young man, of a dark complexion, through whose swarthy skin no red glow ever shone; when colour would have come into another cheek, a hardly discernible heat would come into his, as if the machinery for bringing up the ardent blood were there, but the machinery were dry."—No Thoroughfare (*Christmas Stories*).

O'Bleary, Frederick.—A boarder at Mrs. Tibbs'.—" Mr. O'Bleary was an Irishman, recently imported; he was in a perfectly wild state and had come over to England to be an apothecary, a clerk in a Government Office, an actor, a reporter, or anything else that turned up—he was not particular."—*Sketches by Boz* (The Boarding House).

O'Brien, Mr.—A passenger on a Thames steamer.—(*See* **Brown, Mr.**)—*Sketches by Boz* (The River).

Odd Girl, The.—A town-bred maid at the Haunted House.—" We took with us a deaf stable man, my bloodhound Turk, two women servants, and a young person called an Odd Girl. . . . The odd girl, who had never been in the country, alone was pleased, and made arrangements for sowing an acorn in the garden, outside the scullery window, and rearing an oak."—The Haunted House (*Christmas Stories*).

Old Gruffandgrim.—(*See* **Bill Barley.**)—*Great Expectations.*

Omer, Mr.—" We walked away to a shop in a narrow street, on which was written Omer, Draper, Tailor, Haberdasher, Funeral Furnisher, &c. It was a close and stifling little shop full of all sorts of clothing made and unmade."—*David Copperfield.*

Omer, Minnie.—Daughter of Mr. Omer. Married Joram, her father's assistant, and afterwards his partner in the firm of Omer and Joram.—*David Copperfield.*

Onowenever, Mrs.—The mother of " Her," an early love of the Uncommercial Traveller.—" It is unnecessary to name Her more particularly; she was older than I, and had pervaded every chink and crevice of my mind for three or four years. I had held volumes of imaginary conversations with her mother, on the subject of our union, and I had written letters, more in number than Horace Walpole's, to that discreet woman, soliciting her daughter's hand in marriage. I had never had the remotest intention of sending any of these letters; but to write them, and, after a few days, to tear them up, had been a sublime occupation."—*The Uncommercial Traveller* (Birthday Celebrations).

Orange, Mrs.—A friend of Mrs. Lemon.—" One of the inhabitants of this country, a truly sweet young creature of the name of Mrs. Orange. Mrs. Orange took off her pinafore, and dressed herself very nicely, and took up her baby, and went out to call upon another lady of the name of Mrs. Lemon."—*Holiday Romance.*

Orange, James.—Husband of Mrs. Orange.—*Holiday Romance.*

Orlick.—Joe Gargery, the blacksmith's journeyman. Pip's enemy. — " A broad-shouldered, loose-limbed, swarthy fellow, of great strength, never in a hurry, and always slouching."—*Great Expectations.*

Overs, John.—A miser whose biography Mr. Boffin pretended to be interested in.—*Our Mutual Friend.*

Overton, Joseph.—The Mayor of Great Winglebury. —" A sleek man, in drab shorts and continuations, black coat, neckcloth and gloves. . . . Mr. Joseph Overton was a man of the world, and an Attorney."—*Sketches by Boz* (The Great Winglebury Duel).

Owen, John.—A pupil at Mr. Marton's school.—" A lad of good parts, and frank and honest temper; but too thoughtless, too playful; too light-headed by far."—*The Old Curiosity Shop.*

Packer, Tom.—A private of marines in the Silver Store Colony Expedition.—The Perils of Certain English Travellers (*Christmas Stories*).

Packlemerton, Jasper.—A character in Jarley's Waxworks.—" That, ladies and gentlemen, said Mrs. Jarley, is Jasper Packlemerton of atrocious memory; who courted and married fourteen wives, and destroyed them all, by tickling the soles of their feet, when they were sleeping in the consciousness of innocence and virtue."—*The Old Curiosity Shop.*

Palmer, Mr.—A frequenter of Doncaster races.—The Lazy Tour of Two Idle Apprentices (*Christmas Stories*).

Pancks, Mr.—Factor to Mr. Casby.—" A quick and eager short dark man came into the room with so much way upon him that he was within a foot of Clennam before he could stop. He was dressed in black and rusty iron grey, had jet black beads of eyes, a scrubby little black chin, wiry black hair, striking out from his head in prongs, like forks or hair-pins, and a complexion that was very dingy by nature, or very dirty by art, or a compound of nature and art. He had dirty hands, and dirty, broken nails, and looked as if he had been in the coals; he was in a perspiration, and snorted, and sniffed, and puffed, and blew like a little labouring steam engine. . . . It may be all extraordinary together, returned Pancks; it may be out of the ordinary course and yet be business; in short, it is business; I am a man of business; what business have I got in this present world except to stick to business? No business."—*Little Dorrit.*

Pangloss.—A Liverpool official who accompanied the Uncommercial Traveller to see discharged troops come home from India.—"My official friend Pangloss is lineally descended from a learned doctor of that name, who was once tutor to Candide, an ingenious young gentleman of some celebrity. In his personal character he is as humane and worthy a gentleman as any I know; in his official capacity he unfortunately preaches the doctrines of his renowned ancestor, by demonstrating on all occasions that we live in the best of all possible worlds."—*The Uncommercial Traveller* (The Great Tasmania's Cargo).

Pankey, Miss.—A boarder at Mrs. Pipchin's at Brighton.—"A mild little blue-eyed morsel of a child, who was shampooed every morning, and seemed in danger of being rubbed away altogether."—*Dombey and Son.*

Papers.—The bookstall-boy at Mugby Junction.—"There's Papers for instance . . . him as belongs to Smith's bookstall."—Mugby Junction (*Christmas Stories*).

Paragon, Mary Anne.—The first servant David and Dora had.—"I doubt whether two young birds could have known less about keeping house than I and my pretty Dora did. We had a servant of course. . . . Her name was Paragon. Her nature was represented to us as being feebly expressed in her name. She had a written character as large as a proclamation. . . . Our treasure was warranted sober and honest. I am therefore willing to believe that she was in a fit when we found her under the boiler; and that the deficient teaspoons were attributable to the dustman."—*David Copperfield.*

Pardiggle, Mrs.—One of the philanthropic ladies of Mrs. Jellyby's circle.—"She was a formidable style of lady, with spectacles, a prominent nose, and a loud voice, who had the effect of wanting a great deal of room; and she really did, for she knocked down little chairs with her skirts that were quite a great way off. She seemed to come in like cold weather."—*Bleak House.*

Pardiggle, Mr.—Husband of Mrs. Pardiggle.—"An obstinate-looking man, with a large waistcoat and stubbly hair."—*Bleak House.*

Pardiggle Boys.—Sons of Mrs. Pardiggle.—"These, said Mrs. Pardiggle, with great volubility, are my five boys; Egbert, my eldest (twelve), is the boy who sent out his pocket money to the amount of five and threepence, to the Tockahoopo Indians; Oswald, my second (ten and a half), is the child who contributed two and ninepence to the Great National Smithers Testimonial; Francis, my third (nine), one and sixpence halfpenny; Felix, my fourth (seven), eightpence to the Superannuated Widows; Alfred, my youngest (five), has voluntarily enrolled himself in the Infant Bands of Joy, and is pledged never through life to use tobacco in any form. My young family are not frivolous."—*Bleak House.*

Parker.—A London constable.—*On Duty with Inspector Field* (Reprinted Pieces).

Parker, Mrs. Johnson.—"The mother of seven extremely find girls—all unmarried."—*Sketches by Boz* (Our Parish).

Parker, Uncle.—The name given by Silas Wegg to a gentleman who regularly passed his stall.—"Mr. Wegg was an observant person, or, as he himself said, took a powerful sight of notice. He saluted all his regular passers-by every day . . . for Uncle Parker, who was in the army (at least so he had settled it), he put his open hand to the side of his hat, in a military manner, which that angry-eyed, buttoned-up, inflammatory-faced, old gentleman appeared but imperfectly to appreciate."—*Our Mutual Friend.*

Parkes, Phil.—A forest ranger, one of John Willet's three cronies.—*Barnaby Rudge.*

Parkins.—A friend of Our Bore.—*Our Bore* (Reprinted Pieces).

Parkins, Mrs.—A Temple laundress.—" Mrs. Parkins, my laundress, wife of Parkins, the porter, then newly dead of a dropsy."—*The Ghost of Art* (Reprinted Pieces).

Parkle, Mr.—A friend of the Uncommercial Traveller who resided in chambers in Gray's Inn Square.—" Parkle lived in that top set years bound body and soul to the superstition that they were clean."—*The Uncommercial Traveller* (Chambers).

Parksop, Mr.—Grandfather of George Silverman.—*George Silverman's Explanation.*

Parsnidge, Mr.—A friend of Mr. Murdstone whom David met on board the *Skylark.*—*David Copperfield.*

Parsons, Gabriel.—A friend of Mr. Watkins Tottle.—" A short elderly gentleman, with a gruffish voice. He was a rich sugar-baker, who mistook rudeness for honesty, and abrupt bluntness for an open and candid manner; many besides Gabriel mistake bluntness for sincerity."—*Sketches by Boz* (A Passage in the Life of Mr. Watkins Tottle).

Parsons, Mrs. Fanny.—Wife of Gabriel Parsons.—*Sketches by Boz* (A Passage in the Life of Mr. Watkins Tottle).

Parsons, John.—Son of Mr. Gabriel Parsons.—*Sketches by Boz* (A Passage in the Life of Mr. Watkins Tottle).

Parsons, Miss Laetitia.—A musical lady—a guest at the school ball at Minerva House.—" The brilliant execution of Miss Laetitia Parsons, whose performance of 'The Recollections of Ireland' was universally declared to be almost equal to that of Moscheles himself."—*Sketches by Boz* (Sentiment).

Parvis, Arson.—One of the old residents at the village of Laureau.—A Message from the Sea (*Christmas Stories*).

Patty.—Sister of the tenant of the Haunted House.—" I moved in with my maiden sister. I venture to call her eight-and-thirty, she is so very handsome, sensible and engaging."—The Haunted House (*Christmas Stories*).

Pawkins, Major.—An American to whom Martin was introduced at New York.—" Major Pawkins (a gentleman of Pennsylvanian origin) was distinguished by a very large skull, and a great mass of yellow forehead; in deference to which commodities it was currently held, in bar-rooms and other such places of resort, that the Major was a man of huge sagacity."—*Martin Chuzzlewit.*

Pawkins, Mrs.—Wife of Major Pawkins.—"Among the ladies was Mrs. Pawkins, who was very straight, bony, and silent."—*Martin Chuzzlewit.*

Payne, Doctor.—An army surgeon present at the proposed duel between Dr. Slammer and Mr. Winkle.—" A little fat man with black hair."—*Pickwick Papers.*

Peak.—Sir John Chester's man, who was in his service at the time he was killed, in a duel, by Mr. Haredale.—" Two days elapsed before the body of Sir John was found; as soon at it was recognized, and carried home, the faithful valet, true to his master's creed, eloped with all the cash and movables he could lay his hands on and started as a finished gentleman upon his own account. In this career he met with great success, and would certainly have married an heiress in the end, but for an unlucky check which led to his premature decease. He sank under a contagious disorder, very prevalent at that time, and vulgarly termed the jail fever."—*Barnaby Rudge.*

Peaks, The.—The original name of Bleak House, so re-named by Tom Jarndyce.—*Bleak House.*

Peal of Bells, The.—A village inn.—" The traveller sat at his breakfast in the little sanded parlour of the 'Peal of Bells' village alehouse . . . the village street was like most other village streets, wide for its height; silent for its size; and drowsy in the dullest degree."—Tom Tiddler's Ground (*Christmas Stories*).

Pebbleson Nephew.—The original name of the wine-merchant's business acquired by Wilding and Co.—No Thoroughfare (*Christmas Stories*).

Pecksniff, Seth.—A hypocrite—an architect in Salisbury.—" The brazen plate upon the door (which being Mr. Pecksniff's could not lie) bore this inscription —Pecksniff Architect—to which Mr. Pecksniff on his card of business added—and Land Surveyor. In one sense, and one only, he may be said to have been a Land Surveyor on a pretty large scale, as an extensive prospect lay stretched out before the windows of his house. Of his architectural doings nothing was clearly known, except that he had never designed or built anything; but it was generally understood that his knowledge of the science was almost awful in its profundity. He was a most exemplary man; fuller of virtuous precept than a copy-book; some people likened him to a direction post, which is always telling the way to a place but never goes there."—*Martin Chuzzlewit.*

Pecksniff, Charity.—Elder daughter of Mr. Pecksniff. —*Martin Chuzzlewit.*

Pecksniff, Mercy.—Younger daughter of Mr. Pecksniff, married Jonas Chuzzlewit.—"She was the most arch, and at the same time the most artless, creature was the youngest Miss Pecksniff, that you can possibly imagine."—*Martin Chuzzlewit.*

Peddle and Pool.—Solicitors; of Monument Yard, London.—*Little Dorrit.*

Pedro.—One of Jerry's performing dogs.—"One of the dogs had a cap upon his head, tied very carefully under his chin, which had fallen down upon his nose, and completely obscured one eye . . . being a new member of the Company, and not quite certain of his duty, he kept his unobscured eye anxiously upon his master."—*The Old Curiosity Shop.*

Peecher, Miss.—School-mistress at Bradley Headstone's school; in love with Bradley.—"Small, shining, neat, methodical, and buxom was Miss Peecher, cherry-cheeked and tuneful of voice; a little pin-cushion; a little housewife; a little book; a little workbox; a little set of tables and weights and measures and a little woman all in one."—*Our Mutual Friend.*

Peepy.—Youngest child of Mrs. Jellyby.—"One of the dirtiest little unfortunates I ever saw. Peepy (so self-named) was the unfortunate child."—*Bleak House.*

Peepy, the Hon. Miss.—A former resident at the Watering Place.—"Some few seasons since, an ancient little gentleman came down and stayed at the hotel, who said he had danced there in bygone ages with the Honorable Miss Peepy, well known to have been the beauty of her day, and the cruel occasion of innumerable duels."—*Our English Watering Place* (Reprinted Pieces).

Peerybingle, John.—A carrier; husband of Dot.—" This John, so heavy, but so light of spirit; so rough upon the surface, but so gentle at the core; so dull without, so quick within; so stolid, but so good."—*The Cricket on the Hearth.*

Peerybingle, Mrs. (Dot).—Wife of John Peerybingle the carrier.—" It was pleasant to see Dot, with her little figure, and her baby in her arms; a very doll of a baby; glancing with a coquettish thoughtfulness at the fire, and inclining her delicate little head just enough on one side to let it rest in an odd, half natural, half affected, wholly nestling, and agreeable manner, on the great rugged figure of the Carrier."—*The Cricket on the Hearth.*

Peffer and Snagsby.—The name of Mr. Snagsby's firm.—*Bleak House.*

Peffer, Mr.—The deceased partner of Mr. Snagsby.—" Peffer is never seen in Cook's Court now; he is not expected there, for he has been recumbent this quarter of a century in the churchyard of St. Andrew's, Holborn."—*Bleak House.*

Pegg.—A crimp.—" Sharpeye turns to Mr. Superintendent, and says, as if the subject of his remarks were wax-work, this man's a regular bad one likewise; his real name is Pegg; gives himself out as Waterhouse."—*The Uncommercial Traveller* (Poor Mercantile Jack).

Peggotty, Daniel.—A Yarmouth fisherman and dealer in shellfish. Owner of a house constructed out of a turned-up boat. A kind-hearted bachelor with whom resided his nephew Ham, and his niece Little Emily.—" A hairy man with a very good-natured face."—*David Copperfield.*

Peggotty, Clara.—Sister of Daniel Peggotty. Mrs. Copperfield's servant, David's early nurse, and his lifelong friend. Ultimately responded to the repeated intimation of the Yarmouth carrier that " Barkis is willin' " and became Mrs. Barkis.—" Peggotty! repeated Miss Betsy with some indignation. Do you mean to say, child, that any human being has gone into a Christian church, and got himself named Peggotty? It's her surname, said my mother faintly. Mr. Copperfield called her by it, because her Christian name was the same as mine."—*David Copperfield.*

Peggotty, Joe.—A deceased brother of Daniel Peggotty, father of Ham.—*David Copperfield.*

Peggotty, Ham.—A young fisherman, afterwards a boat-builder, at Yarmouth. Affianced to Little Emily.—"He was now a huge strong fellow of six feet high, broad in proportion, and round shouldered; but with a simpering boy's face and curly light hair, that gave him quite a sheepish look. He was dressed in a canvas jacket, and a pair of such very stiff trousers, that they would have stood quite as well alone without any legs in them, and you couldn't so properly have said he wore a hat, as that he was covered in atop, like an old building, with something pitchy."—*David Copperfield.*

Peggy.—A housemaid.—Going into Society (*Christmas Stories*).

Peggy.—Chamberlain to King Watkins.—*Holiday Romance.*

Pegler, Mrs.—The name assumed by Bounderby's mother.—"It was an old woman, tall and shapely still, though withered by time, on whom his eyes fell when he stopped and turned. She was very cleanly and plainly dressed; had country mud upon her shoes; and was newly come from a journey. The flutter of her manner in the unwonted noise of the streets; the spare shawl, carried unfolded on her arm; the heavy umbrella and the little basket; the long-fingered gloves to which her hands were unused; all bespoke an old woman from the country."—*Hard Times.*

Pell, Solomon.—An insolvent-court attorney employed by Mr. Weller.—"The Attorneys who sit at a large bare table below the Commissioners are after all the greatest curiosities. The professional establishment of the more opulent of these gentlemen consists of a blue bag and a boy, generally a youth of the Jewish persuasion. They have no fixed offices; their legal business being transacted in the parlours of public-houses, or the yards of prisons . . . their looks are not prepossessing and their manners are peculiar. Mr. Solomon Pell, one of this learned body, was a fat, flabby, pale man, in a surtout which looked green one minute and brown the next, with a velvet collar of the same chameleon tints. His forehead was narrow; his face wide; his head large; and his nose all on one side; as if Nature, indignant with the propensities she observed in him in his birth, had given it an angry tweak which it had never recovered. Being short-necked and asthmatic, however, he respired principally through this feature, so perhaps what it wanted in ornament, it made up in usefulness."—*Pickwick Papers.*

Pell, Mrs.—The deceased wife of Solomon Pell.—"Now it's curious, said Pell, looking round with a sorrowful smile, Mrs. Pell was a widow; that's very extraordinary, said a mottlefaced man; it's a curious coincidence, said Pell; not at all, gruffly remarked the elder Mr. Weller, more widders is married than single wimmin."—*Pickwick Papers.*

Peltirogus, Horatio.—Hinted at by Mrs. Nickleby as an aspirant for Kate's hand.—"She even went so far as to hint, obscurely, at an attachment entertained for her daughter by the son of an old neighbour of theirs, one Horatio Peltirogus (a young gentleman who might have been at the time four years old or thereabouts), and to represent it indeed as almost a settled thing between the families."—*Nicholas Nickleby.*

Penwren, Mr.—One of the old residents in the village of Laureau.—A Message from the Sea (*Christmas Stories*).

Peploe, Mrs.—A neighbour of Mrs. Macklin.—(*See* **Macklin.**)—*Sketches by Boz* (The Streets—Night).

Peploe, Master.—A neighbour of Mrs. Macklin.—(*See* **Macklin.**)—*Sketches by Boz* (The Streets—Night).

Pepper (The Avenger).—Pip's page-boy.—"I had got on so fast of late that I had even started a boy in boots,—top boots,—in bondage and slavery to whom I might be said to pass my days. For, after I had made this monster (out of the refuse of my washerwoman's family) and had clothed him, with a blue coat, canary waistcoat, white cravat, creamy breeches, and the boots already mentioned, I had to find him a little to do, and a great deal to eat; and with both of these horrible requirements he haunted my existence."—*Great Expectations.*

Peps, Doctor.—The medical man who attended Mrs. Dombey at the birth of Paul.—"Doctor Parker Peps, one of the Court Physicians, and a man of immense reputation for assisting at the increase of great families."—*Dombey and Son.*

Perch.—Messenger at Dombey and Son's counting-house.—"Perch, the Messenger, whose place was on a little bracket, like a time-piece."—*Dombey and Son.*

Perch, Mrs.—Wife of Mr. Perch.—*Dombey and Son.*

Percy, Lord Algernon.—The commander of the Militia called out to quell the rioters.—" In Lincoln's Inn they gave up the hall and commons to the Northumberland Militia under the command of Lord Algernon Percy."—*Barnaby Rudge.*

Perker, Mr.—Solicitor to Mr. Wardle and Mr. Pickwick. —" He was a little high-dried man, with a dark squeezed-up face, and small restless black eyes, that kept winking and twinkling on each side of his little inquisitive nose, as if they were playing a perpetual game of peep-bo with that feature. He was dressed all in black; with boots as shiny as his eyes; a low white neckcloth; and a clean shirt with a frill to it. A gold watch-chain and seals depended from his fob; he carried his black kid gloves *in* his hands not *on* them; and as he spoke thrust his wrists beneath his coat tails, with the air of a man who was in the habit of propounding some regular posers."—*Pickwick Papers.*

Perkins.—A general dealer in the village near the Haunted House.—" Perkins (said Ikey),—Bless you, Perkins wouldn't go a-nigh the place;—No, observed the young man with considerable feeling, he an't overwise an't Perkins, but he an't such a fool as that."—The Haunted House (*Christmas Stories*).

Perkins.—A neighbour of Mrs. Piper.—" Mrs. Perkins, who has not been for some weeks on speaking terms with Mrs. Piper, in consequence of an unpleasantness originating in young Perkins having 'fetched' young Piper 'a crack,' renews her friendly intercourse on this auspicious occasion."—*Bleak House.*

Perkins Institution.—A Boston asylum for the blind. —*American Notes.*

Perkinsoff, Mary Anne.—A maid at Mrs. Lirriper's.—" Mary Anne Perkinsoff, although I behaved handsomely to her, and she behaved unhandsomely to me, was worth her weight in gold, as overawing lodgers without driving them away; for lodgers would be far more sparing of their bells with Mary Anne than ever I knew them to be with maid or mistress."—Mrs. Lirriper's Lodgers (*Christmas Stories*).

Perrin Brothers.—Makers of a clocklock in Maître Voigt's office at Neuchâtel.—No Thoroughfare (*Christmas Stories*).

Pessell, Mr.—A Vice-President of the Medical Section of the Mudfog Association.—*The Mudfog Sketches.*

Pet.—The family name of Minnie Meagles.—" Pet was about twenty; a fair girl with rich brown hair, hanging free in natural ringlets; a lovely girl with a frank face, and wonderful eyes, so large, so soft, so bright, set to such perfection in her kind good head. She was round, and fresh, and dimpled, and spoilt, and there was in Pet an air of timidity and dependence which was the best weakness in the world."—*Little Dorrit.*

Petowker, Miss Henrietta.—An actress of the Theatre Royal, afterwards in Mr. Crummles' company. A guest at the Kenwigs' supper-party; ultimately married Mr. Lillyvick.—" There was one more young lady, who, next to the collector, was the great lion of the party, being the daughter of a theatrical fireman, who went on in the pantomime, and had the greatest turn for the stage that was ever known, being able to sing and recite in a manner that brought the tears into Mrs. Kenwigs' eyes."—*Nicholas Nickleby.*

Pettifer, Tom.—Steward to Captain Jorgan.—" Mr. Pettifer—a man of a certain plump neatness, with a curly whisker, and elaborately nautical in a jacket and shoes, and all things correspondent—looked no more like a seaman beside Captain Jorgan, than he looked like a Sea Serpent." —A Message from the Sea (*Christmas Stories*).

Phibbs, Mr.—A Cheapside haberdasher.—*Three Detective Anecdotes* (Reprinted Pieces).

Phil.—The janitor at our school.—" He was an impenetrable man, who waited at table between whiles, and throughout the half kept the boxes in severe custody. He was morose even to the chief; and never smiled, except at breaking up, when, in acknowledgment of the toast—Success to Phil, Hooray—he would slowly carve a grin out of his wooden face, where it would remain till we were all gone. Nevertheless, one time when we had the scarlet fever in the School, Phil nursed all the sick boys of his own accord, and was like a mother to them."—*Our School* (Reprinted Pieces).

Phoebe.—The lame daughter of Lamps the Mugby Junction porter.—" The room upstairs was a very clean white room, with a low roof. Its only inmate lay on a couch that brought her face to a level with the window. The couch was white too, and her simple dress or wrapper being light blue, like the band around her hair, she had an ethereal look, and a fanciful appearance of lying among clouds. She was engaged in very nimbly and dexterously making lace. The charm of her transparent face, and large bright brown eyes, was not that they were passively resigned, but that they were actively and thoroughly cheerful."—Mugby Junction (*Christmas Stories*).

Phoebe.—Mrs. Squeers' maid.—" For which name Phib was used as a patronizing abbreviation. . . . A small servant girl with a hungry eye."—*Nicholas Nickleby.*

Phunky, Mr.—Junior counsel for Mr. Pickwick.—" Although an infant barrister, he was a full-grown man. He had a nervous manner, and a painful hesitation in his speech; it did not appear to be a natural defect, but seemed rather the result of timidity, arising from the consciousness of being kept down by want of means, or interest, or connection, or impudence, as the case might be; he was overawed by the Sergeant, and profoundly courteous to the Attorney."—*Pickwick Papers.*

Pickle, Mr.—One of a party climbing Vesuvius.—" The head guide looks oddly about him, when one of the Company—not an Italian though an habitué of the mountain, whom we will call for our present purpose Mr. Pickle of Portici,—suggests that, as it is freezing hard, and the usual footing of ashes is covered by the snow and ice, it will surely be difficult to descend."—*Pictures from Italy.*

Pickles, Mr.—A fishmonger.—*Holiday Romance.*

Pickleson.—A giant in Mr. Mim's travelling show.—" He was a languid young man, which I attribute to the distance betwixt his extremities; he had a little head, and less in it; he had weak eyes and weak knees; and altogether you couldn't look at him without feeling that there was greatly too much of him, both for his joints and his mind. . . . He was called Rinaldo di Velasco, his name being Pickleson."—Doctor Marigold (*Christmas Stories*).

Pickwick, Samuel.—The founder and general chairman of the Pickwick Club.—" A casual observer might possibly have remarked nothing extraordinary in the bald head and circular spectacles . . . to those who knew that the gigantic brain of Pickwick was working beneath that forehead, and that the beaming eyes of Pickwick were twinkling behind these glasses, the sight was indeed an interesting one . . . and how much more interesting did the spectacle become when, starting into full life and animation, as a simultaneous call for Pickwick burst from his followers, that illustrious man slowly mounted into the Windsor chair on which he had been previously seated, and addressed the Club himself had founded. What a study for an artist did that exciting scene present. The eloquent Pickwick, with one hand gracefully concealed behind his coat tails, and the other waving in air to assist his glowing declamation; his elevated position revealing these tights and gaiters which, had they clothed an ordinary man, might have passed without observation, but which, when Pickwick clothed them—if we may use the expression —inspired voluntary awe and respect."—*Pickwick Papers.*

Pidger, Mr.—A friend of Miss Lavinia Spenlow.—" I discovered afterwards that Miss Lavinia was an authority in affairs of the heart, by reason of there having anciently existed a certain Mr. Pidger, who played short whist, and was supposed to have been enamoured of her."—*David Copperfield.*

Pierce, Captain.—The Master of the *Haleswell* East Indiaman.—*The Long Voyage* (Reprinted Pieces).

Pierce, Miss Mary.—Daughter of Captain Pierce.—*The Long Voyage* (Reprinted Pieces).

Piff, Miss.—An assistant at Mugby Junction Refreshment Room.—Mugby Junction (*Christmas Stories*).

Pilkins, Doctor.—Mr. Dombey's family physician.—" On the motion—made in dumb show—of Dr. Parker Peps, they went upstairs, the family practitioner opening the room-door for that distinguished professional, and following him out with most obsequious politeness."—*Dombey and Son.*

Pinch, Tom.—Assistant to Mr. Pecksniff.—" An ungainly, awkward-looking, extremely short-sighted man, and prematurely bald. He was perhaps about thirty; but he might have been almost any age between sixteen and sixty, being one of those strange creatures who never decline into an ancient appearance, but look their oldest when they are very young, and get over it at once."—*Martin Chuzzlewit.*

Pinch, Ruth.—Sister of Tom Pinch—married John Westlock.—" She had a good face; a very mild and prepossessing face; and a pretty little figure, slight and short, but remarkable for its neatness; there was something of her brother, much of him indeed, in a certain gentleness of manner, and in her look of timid trustfulness."—*Martin Chuzzlewit.*

Pip, Mr.—A theatre manager whom Jonas Chuzzlewit met at dinner at Mr. Montague Tigg's.—*Martin Chuzzlewit.*

Pip.—An orphan boy, brought up by his sister, Mrs. Joe Gargery.—" My father's family name being Pirrip, and my Christian name Philip, my infant tongue could make of both names nothing larger or more explicit than Pip; so I called myself Pip, and came to be called Pip."—*Great Expectations.*

Pipchin, Mrs.—Keeper of a boarding-house at Brighton where little Paul was sent to recruit; afterwards housekeeper at Mr. Dombey's London residence.—" This celebrated Mrs. Pipchin was a marvellous ill-favoured, ill-conditioned old lady, of a stooping figure, with a mottled face like bad marble, a hook nose, and a hard grey eye, that looked as if it might have been hammered at on an anvil without sustaining any injury."—*Dombey and Son.*

Piper, Professor.—One of the interviewers of Elijah Pogram.—*Martin Chuzzlewit.*

Piper, Mrs. Anastasia.—A witness called at the inquest on Mr. Nemo's death.—" Mrs. Piper has a good deal to say, chiefly in parentheses, and without punctuation, but not much to tell."—*Bleak House.*

Piper, Young.—Son of Mrs. Piper.—" In the first outcry, young Piper dashed off for the fire engines, and returned in triumph, at a jolting gallop, perched up aloft at the Phœnix, and holding on to that fabulous creature with all his might, in the midst of helmets and torches."—*Bleak House.*

Pipkin, Doctor.—A member of the Medical Section of the Mudfog Association.—*The Mudfog Sketches.*

Pipkin, Nathaniel.—The hero of Sam Weller's tale of the parish clerk.—" A harmless, inoffensive, good-natured being; with a turned-up nose; and rather turned-in legs; a cast in his eye; and a halt in his gait."—*Pickwick Papers.*

Pipson, Miss.—One of the pupils at Miss Griffin's school.—" Miss Pipson having curly light hair, and blue eyes (which was my idea of anything mortal and feminine that was called Fair), I promptly replied that I regarded Miss Pipson in the light of a Fair Circassian."—The Haunted House (*Christmas Stories*).

Pirrip, Philip.—The father of Pip, but of whom, or of the members of his family, Pip's only knowledge was derived from the inscription on the tombstone in the churchyard on the marshes.—" I found out for certain that this bleak place overgrown with nettles was the churchyard; and that Philip Pirrip late of this parish, and also Georgiana, wife of the above, were dead and buried; and that Alexander, Bartholomew, Abraham, Tobias, and Roger, infant children of the aforesaid, were also dead and buried."—*Great Expectations.*

Pitt, Jane.—A maidservant at the grammar school.—" Jane was a sort of wardrobe woman to our fellows, and took care of the boxes. She was a very nice young woman; she was not quite pretty, but she had a very frank, honest, bright face, and all our fellows were fond of her. She was uncommonly neat and cheerful, and uncommonly comfortable and kind; and if anything was the matter with a fellow's mother, he always went and showed the letter to Jane."—*The Schoolboy's Story* (Reprinted Pieces).

Planters' House, The.—An hotel at St. Louis.—" Built like an English Hospital, with long passages and bare walls, and skylights above the room-doors for the free circulation of air."—*American Notes* (Reprinted Pieces).

Plornish.—A plasterer of Bleeding Heart Yard, imprisoned for debt in the Marshalsea.—" He was one of those many wayfarers on the road of life, who seem to be afflicted with supernatural corns, rendering it impossible for them to keep up even with their lame competitors; a willing, working, soft-hearted, not hard-headed, fellow, Plornish took his fortune as smoothly as could be expected, but it was a rough one. He tumbled into all kinds of difficulties, and tumbled out of them, and by tumbling through life got himself considerably bruised."—*Little Dorrit.*

Plornish, Mrs.—Wife of Mr. Plornish.—"Clennam went alone into the entry, and knocked at the parlour door. It was opened presently by a woman with a child in her arms, whose unoccupied hand was hastily rearranging the upper part of her dress. This was Mrs. Plornish, and this maternal action was the action of Mrs. Plornish during a large part of her waking existence. Mrs. Plornish was a young woman, made somewhat slatternly in herself and her belongings by poverty, and so dragged at, by poverty and the children together, that their united forces had already dragged her face into wrinkles."—*Little Dorrit.*

Pluck, Mr.—A toady of Sir Mulberry Hawk, introduced to Kate at Ralph Nickleby's dinner-party.—"A gentleman with a flushed face and a flash air."—*Nicholas Nickleby.*

Plummer, Caleb.—A poor toymaker who worked for Gruff and Tackleton.—"Caleb Plummer and his blind daughter lived all alone by themselves, in a little cracked nutshell of a wooden house, which was in truth no better than a pimple on the prominent red-brick nose of Gruff and Tackleton. The premises of Gruff and Tackleton were the great feature of the street, but you might have knocked down Caleb Plummer's dwelling with a hammer or two, and carried off the pieces in a cart."—*The Cricket on the Hearth.*

Plummer, Bertha.—The blind daughter of Caleb Plummer, whom he kept in ignorance of his poverty.—"I have said that Caleb and his poor blind daughter lived here; I should have said that Caleb lived here, and his poor blind daughter somewhere else—in an enchanted home of Caleb's furnishing, where scarcity and shabbiness were not, and trouble never entered."—*The Cricket on the Hearth.*

Plummer, Edward.—Son of Caleb, who had gone abroad and not been heard of for a long time, but returned in time to prevent the marriage of his sweetheart, May Fielding, to Tackleton, and to marry her himself.—*The Cricket on the Hearth.*

Pocket, Matthew.—Cousin of Miss Havisham. A Cambridge graduate, who had become a tutor, and had married a pretty but useless wife.—" Mr. Pocket had been educated at Harrow and Cambridge, where he had distinguished himself; but, when he had the happiness of marrying Mrs. Pocket, he had impaired his prospects, and taken up the calling of a grinder. After grinding a number of dull blades—of whom it was remarkable that their fathers when influential were always going to help him to preferment, but always forgot to do it when the blades had left the grindstone—he had wearied of that poor work and had come to London. Here, after gradually failing in loftier hopes, he had read with divers who had lacked opportunities, or neglected them; and had refurbished divers others for special occasions; and had turned his acquirements to the account of literary compilation and correction; and on such means, added to some very moderate private resources, he maintained his family."—*Great Expectations.*

Pocket, Mrs. Belinda.—Wife of Matthew Pocket.—" Mrs. Pocket was the only daughter of a certain quite accidental deceased Knight, who had invented for himself a conviction that his deceased father would have been made a Baronet, but for Somebody's determined opposition, arising out of entirely personal motives. This imaginative parent had directed Mrs. Pocket to be brought up from her cradle as one who in the nature of things must marry a title, and who was to be guarded from the acquisition of plebeian domestic knowledge. So successful a watch and ward had been established over the young lady by this judicious parent, that she had grown up highly ornamental but perfectly helpless and useless. . . . Mrs. Pocket was in general the object of a queer sort of respectful pity, because she had not married a title; while Mr. Pocket was the object of a queer sort of forgiving reproach, because he had never got one."—*Great Expectations.*

Pocket, Herbert.—Pip's lifelong friend and companion—married Clara Barley.—" Herbert Pocket had a frank and easy way with him, that was very taking. I had never seen any one then, and I have never seen any one since, who more strongly expressed to me, in every look and tone, a natural incapacity to do anything secret or mean. There was something wonderfully hopeful about his general air, and something that at the same time whispered to me that he would never be very successful or rich."—*Great Expectations.*

Pocket, Georgina.—Cousin of Matthew Pocket and toady to Miss Havisham.—" An indigestive single woman who called her rigidity religion, and her liver love."—*Great Expectations.*

Pocket, Sarah.—Cousin of Miss Havisham.—" A little dry brown corrugated old woman, with a small face that might have been made of walnut shells, and a large mouth like a cat's without the whiskers."—*Great Expectations.*

Pocket, Master Alick, and Miss Jane.—Two of the seven young children of Mr. and Mrs. Matthew Pocket.—" They were brought in by Flopsom and Millers, much as though these two non-commissioned officers had been recruiting somewhere for children, and had enlisted these. . . . There were four little girls and two little boys, besides the baby who might have been either, and the baby's next successor who was as yet neither."—*Great Expectations.*

Podder, Mr.—A member of the All Muggleton Cricket Club.—*Pickwick Papers.*

Podgers, John.—A citizen of Windsor.—" A man of strong sound sense; not what is called smart perhaps, and it might be of a rather lazy and apoplectic turn, but still a man of solid parts, and one who meant much more than he cared to show."—*Master Humphrey's Clock.*

Podgers, Reverend Mr.—A divine whose portrait the idle apprentices found on sale at Carlisle.—The Lazy Tour of Two Idle Apprentices (*Christmas Stories*).

Podsnap, Mr. John.—A self-sufficient man, who toadied to the great.—" A too smiling large man, with a fatal freshness on him, two little light-coloured wiry wings one on either side of his else bald head, looking as like his hair brushes as his hair; dissolving red beads on his forehead; large allowance of crumpled shirt collar up behind. It was a trait in Mr. Podsnap's character (and in one form or other it will be generally seen to pervade the depths and shallows of Podsnappery) that he could not endure a hint of disparagement of any friend or acquaintance of his. How dare you, he would seem to say in such a case—I have licensed this person; this person has taken out my certificate; through this person you strike at me, Podsnap the Great. Podsnap always talks Britain, and talks as if he were a sort of private watchman, employed in the British interests against the rest of the world."—*Our Mutual Friend.*

Podsnap, Mrs.—Wife of Mr. John Podsnap.—" Fine woman for Professor Owen, quantity of bare neck and nostrils, like a rocking horse; hard features, majestic head-dress; on which Podsnap has hung golden offerings."—*Our Mutual Friend.*

Podsnap, Georgiana.—Daughter of Mr. Podsnap.—" A certain institution in Mr. Podsnap's mind, which he called 'the young person' may be considered to have been embodied in Miss Podsnap, his daughter . . . an undersized damsel, with high shoulders, low spirits, chilled elbows, and a rasped surface of nose; who seemed to take occasional frosty peeps out of childhood into womanhood, and to shrink back again, overcome by her mother's head-dress, and her father from head to foot—crushed by the mere dead weight of Podsnappery."—*Our Mutual Friend.*

Pogram, The Hon. Elijah.—A fellow-traveller of Martin's when he left Eden.—" He had straight black hair, parted up the middle of his head, and hanging down upon his coat; a little fringe of hair upon his chin; wore no neck-cloth; a white hat; a suit of black, long in the sleeves and short in the legs; soiled brown stockings, and laced shoes. His complexion, naturally muddy, was rendered muddier by too strict an economy of soap and water."—*Martin Chuzzlewit.*

Polly.—A waitress at a restaurant where Guppy entertained his friends to dinner and Smallweed settled the bill. —" Mr. Smallweed, compelling the attendance of the waitress with one hitch of his eyelash, instantly replies as follows: Four Veals and Hams is three; and four potatoes is three and four; and one summer cabbage is three and six; and three marrows is four and six; and six breads is five; and three Cheshires is five and three; and four half-pints of half-and-half is six and three; and four small rums is eight and three; and three Pollys is eight and six—eight and six in half a sovereign, Polly, and eighteenpence out." —*Bleak House.*

Polreath, David.—One of the old residents in the village of Laureau.—A Message from the Sea (*Christmas Stories*).

Poplars, The.—The name of the Haunted House.—" It was a solitary house, standing in a sadly neglected garden; a pretty even square of some two acres. It was easy to see that it was an avoided house—a house that was shunned by the village, to which my eye was guided by a church spire some half a mile off—a house that nobody would take, and the natural inference was that it had the reputation of being a haunted house."—The Haunted House (*Christmas Stories*).

Pordage, Mr. Commissioner.—The resident British official at Silver Store Colony.—" Mr. Commissioner Pordage kept, in a red and black japanned box, like a family lump-sugar box, some document or other, which some Sambo Chief or other had got drunk and spilt ink over (as well as I could understand the matter), and by that means had given up lawful possession of the island. Through having hold of this box, Mr. Pordage got his title of Commissioner. He was styled Consul too, and spoke of himself as 'Government.' "—The Perils of Certain English Travellers (*Christmas Stories*).

Pordage, Mrs.—Wife of the commissioner of Silver Store Colony.—" Mr. Commissioner Pordage was a stiff-jointed, high-nosed old gentleman, without an ounce of fat on him, of a very angry temper, and a very yellow complexion. Mrs. Commissioner Pordage, making allowance for difference of sex, was much the same."—The Perils of Certain English Travellers (*Christmas Stories*).

Porkenham.—A magistrate at Ipswich.—*Pickwick Papers.*

Porkenham, Mrs.—His wife.—*Pickwick Papers.*

Porkenham, Miss.—His daughter.—*Pickwick Papers.*

Porkenham, Sidney.—His son.—*Pickwick Papers.*

Porter.—A Kentucky giant.—" He had a weakness in the region of the knees, and a trustfulness in his long face, which appealed even to five feet nine for encouragement and support."—*American Notes.*

Porter, Mrs. Joseph.—A scandalmonger.—" The good folks of Clapham and its vicinity stood very much in awe of scandal and sarcasm; and thus Mrs. Joseph Porter was courted, and flattered, and caressed, and invited, for much the same reason that induces a poor author, without a farthing in his pocket, to behave with extraordinary civility to a two-penny postman."—*Sketches by Boz* (Mrs. Joseph Porter).

Porter, Miss Emma.—Daughter of Mrs. Porter.—*Sketches by Boz* (Mrs. Joseph Porter).

Porters, Mr.—An admirer of Miss Twinkleton in her younger days.—"Every night, at the same hour, does Miss Twinkleton resume the topics of the previous night, comprehending the tender scandal of Cloisterham, of which she has no knowledge whatever by day, and references to a certain season at Tunbridge Wells (airily called by Miss Twinkleton in this state of her existence The Wells) notably the season wherein a certain finished gentleman (compassionately called by Miss Twinkleton in this stage of her existence Foolish Mr. Porters) revealed a homage of the heart, whereof Miss Twinkleton, in her scholastic state of existence, is as ignorant as a granite pillar."—*Edwin Drood.*

Potkins, William.—A waiter at the Blue Boar.—*Great Expectations.*

Pott, Mr.—The editor of the *Eatanswill Gazette.*—"A tall thin man, with a sandy-coloured head inclined to baldness, and a face in which solemn importance was blended with a look of unfathomable profundity."—*Pickwick Papers.*

Pott, Mrs.—Wife of Mr. Pott.—"Mr. Pott's domestic circle was limited to himself and his wife. If Mr. Pott had a weakness it was perhaps that he was *rather* too submissive to the somewhat contemptuous control and sway of his wife."—*Pickwick Papers.*

Potter, Thomas.—A city clerk; friend of Smithers.—"Mr. Thomas Potter then was a clerk in the city, and Mr. Robert Smithers was a ditto in the same; their incomes were limited, but their friendship was unbounded; they lived in the same street, walked into town every morning at the same hour, dined at the same slap-bang every day, and revelled in each other's company every night; they were knit together by the closest ties of intimacy and friendship, or, as Mr. Thomas Potter touchingly observed, they were thick and thin pals and nothing but it."—*Sketches by Boz* (Making a Night of It).

Potterson, Miss Abbey.—" Sole proprietor and manager of the 'Fellowship Porters,' reigned supreme on her throne the bar; and a man must have drunk himself mad drunk indeed, if he thought he could contest a point with her. Being known, on her own authority, as Miss Abbey Potterson, some waterside heads, which (like the water) were none of the clearest, harboured muddled notions that, because of her dignity and firmness, she was named after, or in some sort related to, the Abbey at Westminster. But Abbey was only short for Abigail, by which name Miss Potterson had been christened at Limehouse Church, some sixty and odd years before. She was a tall, upright, well-favoured woman, though severe of countenance, and had more the air of a school-mistress, than mistress of the 'Six Jolly Fellowship Porters.' "—*Our Mutual Friend.*

Potterson, Job.—A ship steward who identified the body supposed to be Harmon's; brother of Miss Abbey Potterson.—" Lord bless my soul and body, Miss Abbey, cried Mr. Inspector, talk of trades, Miss Abbey, and the way they set their marks on men, who wouldn't know your brother to be a steward. There's a bright and ready twinkle in his eye; there's a neatness in his actions; there's a smartness in his figure; there's an air of reliability about him in case you wanted a basin; that points out the steward."—*Our Mutual Friend.*

Pouch, Mrs. Joe.—A widow whom Mrs. Bagnet regretted George did not marry.—" There was something in her, and something of her."—*Bleak House.*

Powler.—The family name of Mrs. Sparsit's mother.—" The better class of minds did not need to be informed that the Powlers were an ancient stock, who could trace themselves so exceedingly far back that it was not surprising if they sometimes lost themselves,—which they had rather frequently done as respected horseflesh, blind hookey, Hebrew monetary transactions, and the Insolvent Debtors Court."—*Hard Times.*

Pratchett, Mrs.—A head chambermaid.—"Let not inconsistency be suspected, on account of my mentioning Mrs. Pratchett as 'Mrs.,' and having formerly remarked that a waitress must not be married. Readers are respectfully requested to notice that Mrs. Pratchett was not a waitress, but a chambermaid. And a chambermaid *may* be married—if Head generally is married—or says so;—it comes to the same thing, as expressing what is customary."—Somebody's Luggage (*Christmas Stories*).

Pratchett, Mr.—Husband of Mrs. Pratchett the head chambermaid.—"Mr. Pratchett is in Australia and his address there is 'The Bush.' "—Somebody's Luggage (*Christmas Stories*).

Price, Mr.—A prisoner for debt.—"A coarse vulgar young man, of about thirty, with a sallow face and a harsh voice; evidently possessed of that knowledge of the world, and captivating freedom of manner, which is to be acquired in public-house parlours, and at low billiard tables."—*Pickwick Papers*.

Price, Matilda.—Friend of Fanny Squeers; married John Browdie.—"A Miller's daughter of only eighteen who had contracted herself unto the son of a small corn factor resident in the nearest market town."—*Nicholas Nickleby*.

Prig, Mrs. Betsy.—A nurse friend of Mrs. Gamp.—"Mrs. Prig was of the Gamp build, but not so fat; and her voice was deeper and more like a man's; she had also a beard."—*Martin Chuzzlewit*.

Priscilla.—Mrs. Jellyby's housemaid.—*Bleak House*.

Prodgit, Mrs.—Nurse to Mrs. Meek.—"She wore a black bonnet of large dimensions, and was copious in figure; the expression of her countenance was severe and discontented."—*Births—Mrs. Meek of a Son* (Reprinted Pieces).

Prosee, Mr.—A member of the Mechanical Science Section of the Mudfog Association.—*The Mudfog Sketches*.

Pross, Solomon.—Known by the name of Barsad. Brother of Miss Pross.—"A heartless scoundrel, who had stripped her of everything she possessed, as a stake to speculate with, and had abandoned her in her poverty for evermore, with no touch of compunction."—(*See* **Barsad, John.**)—*A Tale of Two Cities.*

Pross, Miss.—A strong-minded woman, the companion and friend of Lucie Manette.—" A wild-looking woman, whom, even in his agitation, Mr. Lorry observed to be all of a red colour, and to have red hair, and to be dressed in some extraordinary tight-fitting fashion, and to have on her head a most wonderful bonnet, like a grenadier wooden measure, and good measure too, or a great stilton cheese, came running into the room."—*A Tale of Two Cities.*

Provis.—The name assumed by Magwitch when he returned home, after making his fortune in New South Wales, under which name he passed as Pip's uncle.—*Great Expectations.*

Pruffle.—Manservant to a scientific gentleman at Bristol.—*Pickwick Papers.*

Pubsey and Co.—The name under which Fascination Fledgeby's money-lending business was conducted by Mr. Riah.—*Our Mutual Friend.*

Puffer, Princess.—The name bestowed by Deputy upon the old woman who kept an opium den visited by Jasper.—*Edwin Drood.*

Pugstyles, Mr.—A constituent of Mr. Gregsbury, M.P., who headed a deputation to the member to complain of his conduct.—" A plump old gentleman in a violent heat. Mr. Pugstyles put on his spectacles, and referred to a written paper, which he drew from his pocket; whereupon nearly every other member of the deputation pulled a written paper from his pocket, to check Mr. Pugstyles off as he read the questions."—*Nicholas Nickleby.*

Pumblechook.—The much flattered and consequential bachelor—uncle of Joe Gargery.—" Was a well-to-do corn chandler in the nearest town and drove his own chaise cart. . . . He was a large, hard-breathing, middle-aged, slow man, with a mouth like a fish, dull staring eyes, and sandy hair standing upright on his head, so that he looked as if he had just been all but choked, and had that moment come to."—*Great Expectations*.

Pumpkinskull, Professor.—A member of the Mudfog Association.—*The Mudfog Sketches*.

Pupford, Miss Euphemia.—Principal of the Lilliputian College.—"Miss Pupford is one of the most amiable of her sex; it necessarily follows that she possesses a sweet temper, and would own to the possession of a great deal of sentiment, if she considered it quite reconcilable with her duty to parents; deeming it not in the bond, Miss Pupford keeps it as far out of sight as she can—which (God bless her) is not very far."—Tom Tiddler's Ground (*Christmas Stories*).

Pupker, Sir Matthew.—Chairman of meeting of promoters of the United Metropolitan Muffin Company.—*Nicholas Nickleby*.

Purblind, Mr.—A member of the Mudfog Association.—*The Mudfog Sketches*.

Purday, Captain.—A resident in our parish.—"An old naval officer on half-pay. He attends every vestry meeting that is held; always opposes the constituted authorities of the parish; denounces the profligacy of the churchwardens; contests legal points against the vestry clerk; *will* make the tax-gatherer call for his money till he won't call any longer, and then he sends it; finds fault with the sermon every Sunday; says that the organist ought to be ashamed of himself; offers to back himself for any amount to sing the psalms better than all the children put together, male and female; and in short conducts himself in the most turbulent and uproarious manner."—*Sketches by Boz* (Our Parish).

Pussy.—The pet name which Edwin Drood bestowed on Rosa Bud.—*Edwin Drood*.

Pyegrave.—A client of Miss Mowcher's.—"There's Charlie Pyegrave, the Duke's son, she said . . . what a man he is. There's a whisker; as to Charlie's legs, if they were only a pair (which they ain't) they'd defy competition."—*David Copperfield*.

Pyke, Mr.—A toady to Sir Mulberry Hawk, introduced to Kate at Ralph Nickleby's dinner-party.—" A sharp-faced gentleman, who was sitting on a low chair with a high back reading the paper."—*Nicholas Nickleby.*

Quale, Mr.—An admirer of Caddy Jellyby.—" A loquacious young man called Mr. Quale, with large shining knobs for temples, and his hair all brushed to the back of his head. He seemed to project those two shining knobs of temples of his into everything that went on, and to brush his hair farther and farther back, until the very roots were almost ready to fly out of his head."—*Bleak House.*

Quanko Samba.—Mentioned by Jingle as taking part in a cricket match in the West Indies.—*Pickwick Papers.*

Queerspeck, Professor.—A member of the Mechanical Science Section of the Mudfog Association.—" Professor Queerspeck exhibited an elegant model of a portable railway, neatly mounted in a green case, for the waistcoat pocket."—*The Mudfog Sketches.*

Quick Ear.—One of the three police officers who accompanied the Police Superintendent and the Uncommercial Traveller to the haunts of Jack ashore.—" We began by diving into the obscurest streets and lanes of the port. Suddenly, pausing, in a flow of cheerful discourse, before a dead wall apparently some ten miles long, Mr. Superintendent struck upon the ground, and the wall opened and shot out, with military salute of hand to temple, two policemen—not in the least surprised themselves, not in the least surprising Mr. Superintendent."—*The Uncommercial Traveller* (Poor Mercantile Jack).

Quilp, Daniel.—A cruel man, who had lent money to Mr. Trent, and turned him out of the Old Curiosity Shop. Drowned in the Thames whilst escaping from the officers of the law.—" An elderly man, of remarkably hard features, and forbidding aspect; and so low in stature as to be quite a dwarf, though his head and face were large enough for the body of a giant. His black eyes were restless, sly, and cunning, his mouth and chin bristly with the stubble of a coarse hard beard, and his complexion was one of that kind which never looks clean or wholesome. But what added most to the grotesque expression of his face was a ghastly smile, which, appearing to be the result of habit, and to have no connection with any mirthful or complacent feeling, constantly revealed the few discoloured fangs that were yet scattered in his mouth, and gave him the aspect of a panting dog. The ugly creature contrived by some means or other,—whether by his ugliness, or his ferocity, or his natural cunning is no great matter—to impress with a wholesome fear of his anger most of those with whom he was brought into daily contact."—*The Old Curiosity Shop*.

Quilp, Mrs. Betsy.—Wife of Daniel Quilp.—"A pretty, little, mild-spoken, blue-eyed woman; who, having allied herself in wedlock to the dwarf, in one of those strange infatuations of which examples are by no means scarce, performed a sound practical penance for her folly every day of her life."—*The Old Curiosity Shop*.

Quilp's Wharf.—Daniel Quilp's place of business.—"On the Surrey side of the river was a small rat-infested, dreary yard, called Quilp's Wharf, in which were a little wooden counting-house, burrowing all awry in the dust, as if it had fallen from the clouds and ploughed into the ground; a few fragments of rusty anchors; several large iron rings; some piles of rotten wood; and two or three heaps of old sheet copper, crumpled, cracked, and battered. On Quilp's Wharf Daniel Quilp was a shipbreaker; yet, to judge from these appearances, he must either have been a shipbreaker on a very small scale, or broken his ships up very small indeed."—*The Old Curiosity Shop*.

Quinch, Mrs.—The senior female resident in Titbull's almshouses.—"Mrs. Quinch being the oldest and have totally lost her head."—*The Uncommercial Traveller* (Titbull's Almshouses).

Quinion, Mr.—Manager for Murdstone and Grinby.—*David Copperfield*.

Rachael.—A factory worker at Coketown.—"She turned, being then in the brightness of a lamp; and, raising her hood a little, showed a quiet oval face, dark and rather delicate, irradiated by a pair of very gentle eyes, and further set off by the perfect order of her shining black hair. It was not a face in its first bloom. She was a woman of five-and-thirty years of age."—*Hard Times*.

Rachael, Mrs. (afterwards Mrs. Chadband).—Miss Barbary's maid, and nurse of Esther Summerson in her childhood.—" Mrs Rachael, our only servant, who took my light away when I was in bed; another very good woman but austere to me."—*Bleak House.*

Raddle, Mrs.—Bob Sawyer's landlady.—" A little fierce woman bounced into the room, all in a tremble with passion, and pale with rage."—*Pickwick Papers.*

Raddle, Mr.—The husband of Mrs. Raddle.—*Pickwick Papers.*

Radfoot, George.—A seaman who had changed clothes with John Harmon, and whose body being found in the river was supposed to be that of Harmon.—*Our Mutual Friend.*

Radley, Mr.—A London hotel-keeper.—" My faultless friend Mr. Radley, of the 'Adelphi Hotel.' "—*American Notes.*

Rainbird, Alice. (aged seven).—Bride of Bob Redforth. —*Holiday Romance.*

Rairyganoo, Sally.—A maid of Mrs. Lirriper's who eloped.—" One of my girls, Sally Rairyganoo, which I still suspect of Irish extraction, though family represented Cambridge, else why abscond with a bricklayer of the Limerick persuasion, and be married in pattens, not waiting till his black eye was decently got round."—Mrs. Lirriper's Legacy (*Christmas Stories*).

Ram Chowdar Doss Asuph al Bowlar.—An East India potentate of whom Captain Helves told a story at the Steam Excursion.—*Sketches by Boz* (The Steam Excursion).

Rames, William.—Second mate of the *Golden Mary*, who took command of a boat after the wreck.—" I leave you, says I, under the command and guidance of Mr. William Rames, as good a sailor as I am, and as trusty and kind a man as ever stepped."—The Wreck of the *Golden Mary* (*Christmas Stories*).

Ramsey.—The defendant in the suit of Ballman and Ramsey.—*Pickwick Papers.*

Rarx, Mr.—A passenger on the *Golden Mary*.—" An old gentleman, a good deal like a hawk, if his eyes had been better, and not so red; who was always talking, morning, noon and night, about the gold discovery; but whether he was making the voyage thinking his old arms could dig for gold; or whether his speculation was to buy it, or to barter it, or to cheat for it, or to snatch it anyhow from other people, was his secret; he kept his secret."—The Wreck of the *Golden Mary* (*Christmas Stories*).

Ravender, William George.—The captain of the *Golden Mary*, an emigrant ship.—" I was apprenticed to the sea when I was twelve years old; and I have encountered a great deal of rough weather, both literal and metaphorical." —The Wreck of the *Golden Mary* (*Christmas Stories*).

Raybrock, Mrs.—The postmistress of Steepways Village.—" A comely elderly woman; short of stature, plump of form; sparkling and dark of eye; who, perfectly clean and neat herself, stood in the midst of her perfectly clean and neat arrangements, and surveyed Captain Jorgan with smiling curiosity."—A Message from the Sea (*Christmas Stories*).

Raybrock, Alfred.—A fisherman. Son of Mrs. Raybrock of Steepways Village; married Kitty Tregarthen.—" A young fisherman of two or three-and-twenty, in the rough sea dress of his craft, with a brown face, dark curling hair and bright modest eyes under his sou'wester hat, and with a frank but simple and retiring manner."—A Message from the Sea (*Christmas Stories*).

Raybrock, Jorgan.—The infant son of Alfred Raybrock and Kitty Tregarthen.—" A rosy little boy took his first unsteady run to a fair young mother's breast; and the name of that infant fisherman was Jorgan Raybrock."—A Message from the Sea (*Christmas Stories*).

Raybrock, Mrs. Hugh.—Wife of Hugh Raybrock, a sailor, whose message Captain Jorgan found in a bottle at sea. Supposed to have been lost at sea, but who returned. —" The Captain, looking in that direction, saw a young widow sitting at a neighbouring window, across a little garden, engaged in needlework, with a young child sleeping on her bosom."—A Message from the Sea (*Christmas Stories*).

Redburn, Jack.—Master Humphrey's companion.— " He is my librarian, secretary, steward, and first minister; director-general of all my affairs, and inspector-general of my household. I should be puzzled to say how old he is;

his health is none of the best, and he wears a quantity of iron-grey hair, which shades his face and gives it rather a worn appearance; but we consider him quite a young fellow notwithstanding; and if a youthful spirit, surviving the roughest contact with the world, confers upon its possessor any title to be considered young, then he is a mere child." —*Master Humphrey's Clock.*

Redforth, Bob.—Cousin of William Tinkling.—*Holiday Romance.*

Redlaw, Mr.—A chemist-lecturer at The Institution.—" Who could have seen his hollow cheek, his sunken, brilliant eye, his black-attired figure indefinably grim although well-knit and well-proportioned; his grizzled hair hanging like tangled seaweed about his face—as if he had been through his whole life a lonely mark for the chafing and beating of the great deep of humanity—but might have said he looked like a haunted man."—*The Haunted Man.*

Refractories, The.—Badly behaved inmates of Wapping Workhouse.—" The oldest Refractory was say twenty; youngest Refractory say sixteen. I have never yet ascertained, in the course of my uncommercial travels, why a refractory habit should affect the tonsils and the uvula; but I have always observed that Refractories of both sexes, and every grade, between a ragged school and the old Bailey, have one voice, in which the tonsils and the uvula gain a diseased ascendency."—*The Uncommercial Traveller.*

Reynolds, Miss.—A pupil at Nuns' House.—*Edwin Drood.*

Riah, Mr.—A poor Jew, who conducted the business of Pubsey and Co., under direction of Fascination Fledgeby. —" An old Jewish man, in an ancient coat, long of skirt and wide of pocket; a venerable man, bald and shining at the top of his head, and with long grey hair flowing down at its sides, and mingling with his beard."—*Our Mutual Friend.*

Richard.—Meg Veck's lover.—" A handsome well-made powerful youngster he was; with eyes that sparkled like the red-hot droppings from a furnace fire, black hair that curled about his swarthy temples rarely, and a smile—a smile that bore out Meg's eulogium on his style of conversation."—*The Chimes.*

Richards, Mrs.—The name which, by Mr. Dombey's desire, Mrs. Toodle, Paul's foster-mother, was to be called in the family.—*Dombey and Son.*

Rickitts, Miss.—A pupil at Nuns' House.—*Edwin Drood.*

Riderhood, Roger.—A riverside character, sometime partner with Hexam, afterwards his enemy.—" Mortimer lighted the candles. They showed the visitor to be an ill-looking visitor with a squinting leer, who as he spoke fumbled at an old sodden fur cap, formless and mangey, that looked like a furry animal, dog or cat, puppy or kitten drowned and decaying.—Lawyer Lightwood (said Riderhood) ducking at him with a servile air—I am a man as gets my living and seeks to get my living by the sweat of my brow."—*Our Mutual Friend.*

Riderhood, Miss Pleasant.—Daughter of Roger Riderhood; ultimately married Mr. Venus.—" Miss Pleasant Riderhood had some little position and connection in Limehouse Hole. Upon the smallest of small scales she was an unlicensed pawnbroker keeping what was popularly called a Leaving Shop by lending insignificant sums on unimportant articles of property deposited with her as security. . . . Pleasant Riderhood shared with most of the lady inhabitants of the Hole the peculiarity that her hair was a ragged knot constantly coming down behind, and that she never could enter upon any undertaking without first twisting it into place."—*Our Mutual Friend.*

Rigaud.—Alias Blandois, alias Lagnier. An unscrupulous adventurer of polished manners, who blackmailed Mrs. Clennam.—" I am—Monsieur Rigaud stood up to say it—I am a cosmopolitan gentleman; I own no particular country; my father was a Swiss—Canton de Vaud; my mother was French by blood, English by birth; I myself was born in Belgium; I am a citizen of the world; call me five-and-thirty years of age; I have seen the world; I have lived here, and lived there, and lived like a gentleman everywhere. . . . He had a certain air of being a handsome man, which he was not; and a certain air of being a well-bred man, which he was not; it was mere swagger and challenge, but in this particular, as in many others, blustering assertion goes for proof half over the world."—*Little Dorrit.*

Rinaldo di Velasco.—The professional name of Pickleson, the giant.—(*See* **Pickleson.**)—Doctor Marigold (*Christmas Stories*).

Robert, Uncle.—A guest at the Christmas family party.—Husband of Aunt Jane.—(*See* **Jane.**)—*Sketches by Boz* (A Christmas Dinner).

Robins, Mr.—An auctioneer who conducted the sale of effects at Mrs. Tibbs' boarding-house.—" Mr. Robins has been applied to to conduct the sale, and the transcendent abilities of the literary gentlemen connected with his establishment are now devoted to the task of drawing up the preliminary advertisement."—*Sketches by Boz* (The Boarding House).

Robinson, Mr.—The gentleman who married the youngest Miss Willis.—" A gentleman in a public office, with a good salary, and a little property of his own beside." —*Sketches by Boz* (Our Parish).

Robinson.—Maidservant at Mrs. Tibbs'.—" Robinson, what *do* you want, said Mrs. Tibbs to the servant, who by way of making her presence known to her mistress, had been giving sundry hems and sniffs outside the door during the preceding five minutes."—*Sketches by Boz* (The Boarding House).

Rodolph, Mr. and Mrs.—Musical friends of the journeyman painter.—" All these were as nothing when compared with his musical friends, Mr. and Mrs. Jennings Rodolph from White Conduit, with whom the ornamental painter's journeyman had been fortunate enough to contract an intimacy, while engaged in decorating the concert room of that noble institution. To hear them sing separately was divine; but when they went through the tragic duet of ' Red Ruffian, retire,' it was, as Miss Martin afterwards remarked, thrilling."—*Sketches by Boz* (The Mistaken Milliner).

Rogers.—A London constable.—*On Duty with Inspector Field* (Reprinted Pieces).

Rogers, Mr.—The third mate of the *Haleswell* East Indiaman.—*The Long Voyage* (Reprinted Pieces).

Rogers, Mr.—A bar parlour orator.—" A stoutish man of about forty, whose short stiff black hair curled closely round a broad high forehead, and a face to which something besides water and exercise had communicated a rather inflamed appearance."—*Sketches by Boz* (The Parlour Orator).

Rogers, Mrs.—A friend of Mrs. Bardell's.—*Pickwick Papers.*

Roker, Tom.—The tipstaff who conveyed Mr. Pickwick to the Fleet prison.—"The hackney coach jolted along Fleet Street as hackney coaches usually do. Mr. Pickwick sat opposite the tipstaff; and the tipstaff sat with his hat between his knees, whistling a tune and looking out of the coach window."—*Pickwick Papers.*

Rokesmith, John.—The name under which John Harmon became Mrs. Wilfer's lodger, Mr. Boffin's secretary, and Bella Wilfer's husband.—"A dark gentleman—thirty at the utmost—an expressive, one might say handsome, face, a very bad manner, in the last degree constrained, reserved, diffident, troubled."—*Our Mutual Friend.*

Roland.—A clerk authorized to sign letters for Defresnier and Co., of Neuchâtel.—No Thoroughfare (*Christmas Stories*).

Rookery, The.—The name of Mrs. Copperfield's cottage.—"Why Rookery, said Miss Betsy—Cookery would have been more to the purpose, if you had had any practical ideas of life either of you. The name was Mr. Copperfield's choice, returned my mother. We thought—Mr. Copperfield thought—it was quite a large rookery, but the nests were very old ones, and the birds have deserted them a long while. David Copperfield all over, cried Miss Betsy—David Copperfield from head to foot. Calls a house a rookery when there's not a rook near it, and takes the birds on trust because he sees the nests."—*David Copperfield.*

Rosa.—Mrs. Rouncewell's maid; married Walter Rouncewell.—"A dark-eyed, dark-haired, shy village beauty comes in—so fresh in her rosy and yet delicate bloom, that the drops of rain which have beaten on her hair look like the dew upon a flower fresh gathered."—*Bleak House.*

Rose.—The sweetheart of the young surgeon who was called to see the body of a criminal who had been hanged.

—" A young medical practitioner, recently established in business, was seated by a cheerful fire in his little parlour . . . his mind reverted to his annual Christmas visit to his native place and dearest friends; he thought how glad they would all be to see him; and how happy it would make Rose, if he could only tell her he had found a patient at last, and hoped to have more, and to come down again in a few months' time and marry her, and take her home to gladden his lonely fireside, and stimulate him to fresh exertions."—*Sketches by Boz* (The Black Veil).

Ross, Frank.—A friend of Mr. Gabriel Parsons.—*Sketches by Boz* (A Passage in the Life of Mr. Watkins Tottle).

Rouncewell, Mrs.—Housekeeper to Sir Leicester Dedlock at Chesney Wold.—" She is a fine old lady, handsome, stately, wonderfully neat, and has such a back, and such a stomacher, that if her stays should turn out when she dies to have been a broad, old-fashioned, family fire-grate, nobody who knows her would have cause to be surprised. It is the next difficult thing to an impossibility to imagine Chesney Wold without Mrs. Rouncewell, but she has only been here fifty years."—*Bleak House*.

Rouncewell, Mr.—An ironmaster; the elder son of Mrs. Rouncewell.—" He is a little over fifty perhaps, of a good figure, like his mother, and has a clear voice, a broad forehead from which his dark hair has retired, and a shrewd though open face. He is a responsible-looking gentleman, dressed in black, portly enough, but strong and active."—*Bleak House*.

Rouncewell, Walter.—Son of Mr. Rouncewell, the ironmaster.—" Out of his apprenticeship, and home from a journey in far countries, whither he was sent to enlarge his knowledge and complete his preparation for the venture of this life."—*Bleak House*.

Rouncewell, Mr., The Elder.—The deceased husband of Mrs. Rouncewell.—" Mr. Rouncewell died some time before the decease of the pretty fashion of pig-tails, and modestly hid his own (if he took it with him) in a corner of the churchyard in the park, near the mouldy porch."—*Bleak House*.

Rouncewell, George.—Younger son of Mrs. Rouncewell. —" Mrs. Rouncewell has known trouble. She has had two sons, of whom the younger ran wild and went for a soldier, and never came back."—*Bleak House.*

" Royal Charter," The.—A ship which drove ashore at Llanallgo.—" That slight obstruction was the uppermost fragment of the wreck of the *Royal Charter*, Australian trader and passenger ship, homeward bound, that struck here, broke into three parts, went down with her treasure of at least five hundred human lives, and has never stirred since."—*The Uncommercial Traveller* (The Shipwreck).

Royal East London Volunteers.—The corps in which Gabriel Varden became an officer.—" As there was to be a grand parade of the Royal East London Volunteers that afternoon, the locksmith did no more work . . . and to be sure, when it was time to dress him in his regimentals, and Dolly, hanging about him in all kinds of graceful winning ways, helped to button and buckle, and brush him up, and get him into one of the tightest coats that ever was made by martial tailor, he was the proudest father in all England." —*Barnaby Rudge.*

Rudge.—Father of Barnaby Rudge. Steward to Mr. Reuben Haredale. Murdered his master. To avert suspicion from himself murdered the gardener, exchanged clothes with him, and cast the body into a pond; which, being found, was supposed to be that of Rudge, who disappeared with a large sum of money he had obtained; but his crime was ultimately traced to him and he suffered the penalty.—*Barnaby Rudge.*

Rudge, Mrs. Mary.—Mother of Barnaby, whose life was embittered by the knowledge that her guilty husband, supposed dead, was still alive.—" She was about forty—perhaps two or three years older—with a cheerful aspect, and a face that had once been pretty. Any one who had bestowed but a casual glance on Barnaby, might have known that this was his mother, from the stray resemblance between them; but where, in his face, there was wildness and vacancy, in hers there was the quiet composure of long effort and quiet resignation."—*Barnaby Rudge.*

Rudge, Barnaby.—Son of Rudge, the murderer of Mr. Reuben Haredale. A young man of weak intellect, who became embroiled in the Gordon riots, and was condemned to death, but at the last moment was pardoned.—" He was about three-and-twenty years old; and, though rather spare, of a fair height, and strong make. His hair, of which he had a great profusion, was red, and hanging in disorder about his face and shoulders, gave to his restless looks an expression quite unearthly. . . . His dress was of green, clumsily trimmed here and there—apparently by his own hands—with gaudy lace . . . the fluttered and confused disposition of all the motley scraps that formed his dress, bespoke, in a scarcely less degree than his eager and unsettled manner, the disorder of his mind, and by a grotesque contrast set off and heightened the more impressive wildness of his face."—*Barnaby Rudge.*

Ruffin, Mr.—A travelling showman.—"Proprietor of a giant and a little lady without legs or arms."—*The Old Curiosity Shop.*

Rugg, Mr.—Mr. Pancks' landlord.—"The private residence of Mr. Pancks was in Pentonville, where he lodged on the second floor of a professional gentleman in an extremely small way; who had an inner-door within the street-door, poised on a spring, and starting open with a click like a trap; and who wrote up in the fanlight Rugg—General Agent—Accountant—Debts Recovered."—*Little Dorrit.*

Rugg, Miss Anastatia.—Daughter of Mr. Rugg, of Pentonville.—"Miss Rugg was a lady of a little property, which she had acquired, together with much distinction in the neighbourhood, by having her heart severely lacerated, and her feelings mangled, by a middle-aged baker resident in the vicinity, against whom she had, by the agency of Mr. Rugg, found it necessary to proceed at law to recover damages for a breach of promise of marriage. Miss Rugg, environed by the majesty of the law, and having her damages invested in the public securities, was regarded with consideration."—*Little Dorrit.*

Rummun, Professor.—A member of the Mudfog Association.—*The Mudfog Sketches.*

Saggers, Mrs.—The second senior resident in Titbull's almshouses.—"Mrs. Saggers has her celebrated palpitations of the heart, for the most part on Saturday nights."—*The Uncommercial Traveller* (Titbull's Almshouses).

Salem House.—The school where David was educated. —" Salem House was a square brick building with wings of a bare and unfurnished appearance."—*David Copperfield.*

Saley, Monsieur P.—The head of a dramatic company, performing in a Flemish town.—" Monsieur P. Saley privileged director of such theatre, situate in the first theatrical arrondissement of the department of the North, invited French-Flemish mankind to come and partake of the intellectual banquet, provided by his family of dramatic artists, fifteen subjects in number."—*The Uncommercial Traveller* (In the French-Flemish Country).

Sally, Old.—A pauper woman who attended Oliver's mother at his birth, who stole from her a locket and ring which afterwards led to the discovery of his parentage.— " There was considerable difficulty in inducing Oliver to take upon himself the office of respiration,—a troublesome practice, but one which custom has rendered necessary to an easy existence. . . . There being nobody by but a pauper old woman, who was rendered rather misty by an unwonted allowance of beer, and a parish surgeon who did such matters by contract, Oliver and Nature fought out the point between them."—*Oliver Twist.*

Sally.—Niece of Uncle Bill.—*Sketches by Boz* (London Recreations).

Sally.—A popular nurse at the Foundling Hospital where William Wilding was boarded.—" There is neither grown person nor child in all the large establishment that I belong to, who hasn't a good word for Sally."—No Thoroughfare (*Christmas Stories*).

Salvatore.—Head guide to Vesuvius.—" Signor Salvatore the head guide with a gold band round his cap."—*Pictures from Italy.*

Sam.—The hostler at the Blue Dragon.—*Martin Chuzzlewit.*

Sam.—A cab-driver who assaulted Mr. Pickwick.—*Pickwick Papers.*

Sampson, Mr.—An insurance manager.—" Most of us see some romances in life. In my capacity as chief manager of a Life Assurance Office, I think I have, within the last thirty years, seen more romances than the generality of men, however unpromising the opportunity may at first sight seem."—*Hunted Down.*

Sampson, George.—A soft youth.—At first an admirer of Bella Wilfer, but transferred his devotion to her sister Lavinia.—*Our Mutual Friend.*

Sanders, Mrs.—A friend of Mrs. Bardell's.—" Mrs. Sanders was a big, fat, heavy-faced personage."—*Pickwick Papers.*

Santeuse, Madame.—A dancing mistress who taught Miss Podsnap.—" No one knows what I suffered at Madame Santeuse's, where I learnt to dance, and make presentation curtseys, and other dreadful things,—or at least where they tried to teach me."—*Our Mutual Friend.*

Sapsea, Thomas.—An auctioneer. Mayor of Cloisterham.—" Accepting the Jackass as the type of self-sufficient stupidity and conceit—a custom perhaps, like some few other customs, more conventional than fair—then the purest Jackass in Cloisterham is Mr. Thomas Sapsea, Auctioneer. He possesses the great qualities of being portentous and dull, and of having a roll in his speech, and another in his gait; not to mention a certain gravely flowing action with his hands, as if he were presently going to confirm the individual with whom he holds discourse. Much nearer sixty years of age than fifty, with a flowing outline of stomach, and horizontal creases in his waistcoat; reputed to be rich; voting at elections in the strictly respectable interest; morally satisfied that nothing but he himself has grown since he was a baby; how can dunder-headed Mr. Sapsea be otherwise than a credit to Cloisterham and Society."—*Edwin Drood.*

Sapsea, Mrs. Ethelinda.—The deceased wife of Mr. Sapsea.—*Edwin Drood.*

Sarah.—A servant at a girls' school at Bury St. Edmunds.—*Pickwick Papers.*

Sarah.—A resident of Seven Dials, who quarrelled with Mrs. Sullivan.—" Vy don't you pitch into her, Sarah, exclaims one half-dressed matron, by way of encouragement. . . . She accordingly complies with the urgent request of the bystanders to pitch in, with considerable alacrity."—*Sketches by Boz* (The Streets—Night).

Sarah.—Maid to an old lady in Our Parish.—"The best known, and most respected, amongst our parishioners, is an old lady, who resided in our parish long before our name was registered in the list of baptisms. The little front parlour, which is the old lady's ordinary sitting-room, is a perfect picture of quiet neatness; the carpet is covered with brown holland, the glass and picture frames are carefully enveloped in muslin. Here the old lady sits, with her spectacles on, busily engaged in needlework; if you call in the evening you will find her cheerful, but rather more serious than usual, with an open Bible on the table before her, of which Sarah, who is just as neat and methodical as her mistress, regularly reads two or three chapters in the parlour aloud."—*Sketches by Boz* (Our Parish).

"Sarah Jane."—The name of a boat, a picture of which hung in Daniel Peggotty's boat-house at Yarmouth.—"Over the little mantel shelf was a picture of the *Sarah Jane* lugger, built at Sunderland, with a real little wooden stern stuck on to it (a work of art, combining composition with carpentry, which I considered to be one of the most enviable possessions that the world could afford)."—*David Copperfield.*

Saville, Sir George.—The Member of Parliament who introduced the Catholic Bill which led to the Gordon riots.—*Barnaby Rudge.*

Sawyer, Bob.—A medical student.—"Mr. Bob Sawyer, who was habited in a coarse blue coat, which, without being either a great-coat or a surtout, partook of the nature and qualities of both, had about him that sort of slovenly smartness and swaggering gait, which is peculiar to young gentlemen who smoke in the streets by day, shout and scream in the same by night, call waiters by their Christian names, and do various other acts and deeds of an equally facetious description. He wore a pair of plaid trousers, and a large rough double-breasted waistcoat; out of doors he carried a thick stick with a big top.

He eschewed gloves, and looked upon the whole something like a dissipated Robinson Crusoe."—*Pickwick Papers.*

Saxby, Long.—An acquaintance of Lord Feenix.—*Dombey and Son.*

Scadder, Mr. Zephaniah.—Agent of the Eden Land Corporation.—" He was a gaunt man, in a huge straw hat, and had a coat of green stuff. The weather being hot, he had no cravat, and wore his shirt collar wide open, so that, every time he spoke, something was seen to twitch and jerk up in his throat, like the little hammers in a harpsicord when the notes are struck. Perhaps it was the truth feebly endeavouring to leap to his lips. If so, it never reached them."—*Martin Chuzzlewit.*

Scadgers, Lady.—Mrs. Sparsit's great aunt.—" An immensely fat old woman, with an inordinate appetite for butcher's meat, and a mysterious leg, which had now refused to get out of bed for fourteen years."—*Hard Times.*

Scaley, Mr.—An officer of the law who served an execution upon Madame Mantalini, and put his man Tom Tix in possession.—" Kate was silently arranging the various articles of decoration, in the best taste she could display, when she started to hear a strange man's voice in the room; and started again to observe on looking round that a white hat, and a red neckerchief, and a broad round face, and a large head, and a part of a green coat, were in the room too."—*Nicholas Nickleby.*

Schutz, Mr.—A passenger on the *Haleswell* East Indiaman.—*The Long Voyage* (Reprinted Pieces).

" Scorpion," The.—The ship of the Latin master sunk by Captain Boldheart.—" The *Scorpion* (so was the bark of the Latin Grammar Master appropriately called) was not slow to return her fire; and a terrific cannonading ensued; in which the guns of *The Beauty* did tremendous execution."—*Holiday Romance.*

Scott, Tom.—The boy who took charge of Quilp's Wharf.—" An amphibious boy in a canvas suit, whose sole change of occupation was from sitting on the head of a pile and throwing stones into the mud, when the tide was out; to standing with his hands in his pockets gazing listlessly on the motion and on the bustle of the river at high water."—*The Old Curiosity Shop.*

Screwzer.—An acquaintance of Lord Feenix.—" A man of an extremely bilious habit."—*Dombey and Son.*

Scroggins, Giles.—The hero of a ballad.—" Everybody said so. Far be it from me to assert that what everybody says must be true. Everybody is often as likely to be wrong as right. In the general experience everybody has been wrong so often and it has taken, in most instances, such a weary while to find out how wrong, that the authority is proved to be fallible. Everybody may sometimes be right—but that's no rule, as the Ghost of Giles Scroggins says in the ballad."—*The Haunted Man.*

Scroo, Mr.—A Vice-President of the Mechanical Science Section of the Mudfog Association.—*The Mudfog Sketches.*

Scrooge, Ebenezer.—Surviving partner of Scrooge and Marley.—" Scrooge and he were partners for I don't know how many years. Scrooge was his sole executor. Scrooge never painted out old Marley's name. There it stood years afterwards above the warehouse door—Scrooge and Marley. The firm was known as Scrooge and Marley. Sometimes people new to the business called Scrooge Scrooge, and sometimes Marley, but he answered to both names. It was all the same to him. Oh but he was a tight-fisted hand at the grindstone, Scrooge; a squeezing, grasping, scraping, clutching, covetous old sinner; hard and sharp as flint from which no steel had ever struck out generous fire; secret and self-contained; and solitary as an oyster. The cold within him froze his old features, nipped his pointed nose, shrivelled his cheek, stiffened his gait, made his eyes red, his thin lips blue, and spoke out shrewdly in his grating voice; a frosty rime was on his head, and on his eyebrows, and his wiry chin. He carried his own low temperature always about with him; he iced his coffee in the dog days; and didn't thaw it one degree at Christmas."—*A Christmas Carol.*

Scrooge, Fred.—Nephew of Scrooge, son of his sister Fan.—" If you should happen by any unlikely chance to know a man more blest in a laugh than Scrooge's nephew, all I can say is I should like to know him too. There is nothing in the world so irresistibly contagious as laughter and good humour."—*A Christmas Carol.*

Scrooge, Mrs. Fred.—Wife of Scrooge's nephew.—"She was very pretty—exceedingly pretty—with a dimpled, surprised-looking, capital face; a ripe little mouth that seemed made to be kissed, as no doubt it was; all kinds of good little dots about her chin, that melted into one another when she laughed; and the sunniest pair of eyes you ever saw in any little creature's head."—*A Christmas Carol.*

Seraphina.—The heroine of a tale told to Mrs. Lirriper by Jemmy Edson.—Mrs. Lirriper's Lodgings (*Christmas Stories*).

Sergeant of Marines.—Who, in command of a search-party out after escaped convicts, interrupted the Christmas dinner-party at Joe Gargery's to get handcuffs repaired. Having made himself agreeable all round, and flattered Uncle Pumblechook into liberality with the wine decanter, "the sergeant took a polite leave of the ladies, and parted from Mr. Pumblechook as from a comrade; though I doubt if he were quite as fully sensible of that gentleman's merits under arid conditions, as when something moist was going."—*Great Expectations.*

Sharp, Mr.—Assistant master at Salem House.—"He was a limp delicate-looking gentleman I thought, with a good deal of nose, and a way of carrying his head on one side, as if it were a little too heavy for him."—*David Copperfield.*

Sharpeye.—One of the three police officers who accompanied the police superintendent and the Uncommercial Traveller, in visiting the haunts of Jack ashore.—"Sharpeye, I soon had occasion to remark, had a skilful and quite professional way of opening doors,—touched catches delicately as if they were keys of musical instruments; opened every door he touched as if he were perfectly confident that there was stolen property behind it; instantly insinuated himself to prevent its being shut."—*The Uncommercial Traveller* (Poor Mercantile Jack).

Sheen and Gloss.—Fashionable London silk mercers.—"To make this article go down, gentlemen, say Sheen and

Gloss, the mercers, to their friends the manufacturers, you must come to us, because we know where to have the fashionable people, and we can make it fashionable."—*Bleak House.*

Shepherd, Miss.—An early love of David's.—" Miss Shepherd is a boarder at the Misses Nettingall's. I adore Miss Shepherd. She is a little girl in a spencer with a round face and curly flaxen hair."—*David Copperfield.*

Sherman, Captain.—The master of a steamer on Lake Champlain.—" He and his vessel are held in universal respect, and no man ever enjoyed the popular esteem, who, in his sphere of action, won and wore it better than this gentleman."—*American Notes.*

Short, Thomas.—Partner with Codlin in Punch and Judy show business.—" A little merry-faced man, with a twinkling eye, and a red nose . . . the real name of the little man was Harris, but it had gradually merged into the less euphonious one of Trotters, which, with the prefatory adjective short, had been conferred upon him by reason of the small size of his legs. Short Trotters, however, being a compound name, inconvenient of use in friendly dialogue, the gentleman upon whom it had been bestowed was known among his intimates as Short."—*The Old Curiosity Shop.*

Sikes, Bill.—A housebreaker of a desperate and brutal character—ultimately hanged for the murder of Nancy.—" A stoutly built fellow, of about five-and-thirty, in a black velveteen coat, very soiled drab breeches, lace-up half boots, and grey cotton stockings, which inclosed a bulky pair of legs with large swelling calves; the kind of legs which, in such costume, always look in an unfinished and incomplete state, without a set of fetters to garnish them." —*Oliver Twist.*

Silver Store.—A small British Colony on an island in the West Indies.—" It had been given the name of Silver Store. The reason of its being so called, was that the English colony owned and worked a silver mine, over on the mainland in Honduras, and used this island as a safe and convenient place to store their silver in, until it was annually fetched away by the sloop."—The Perils of Certain English Travellers (*Christmas Stories*).

Silverman, George.—A child of poor parents.—" My parents were in a miserable condition of life, and my infant home was a cellar in Preston."—*George Silverman's Explanation.*

Silverman, Mr.—The father of George.—" Father, with his shoulders rounded, would sit quiet on a three-legged stool, looking at the empty grate, until she would pluck the stool from under him, and bid him go bring some money home."—*George Silverman's Explanation.*

Silverman, Mrs.—Mother of George.—" Mother had the gripe and clutch of poverty upon her face; upon her figure; and not least of all upon her voice. Her sharp and high-pitched words were squeezed out of her, as by the compression of bony fingers on the leathern bag; and she had a way of rolling her eyes about, and about the cellar, as she scolded, that was gaunt and hungry."—*George Silverman's Explanation.*

Silverstone, Mr. and Mrs.—The egotistical couple.—" They may be young, old, middle-aged, well-to-do, or ill-to-do; they may have a small family, a large family, or no family at all; there is no outward sign by which an egotistical couple may be known and avoided; they come upon you unawares."—*Sketches of Young Couples.*

Simmery, Mr.—A friend of Mr. Wilkins Flasher.—" A very smart young gentleman, who wore his hat on his right whisker . . . both gentlemen had very open waistcoats; and very rolling collars; and very small boots; and very big rings; and very little watches; and very large guard chains; and symmetrical inexpressibles; and scented pocket handkerchiefs."—*Pickwick Papers.*

Simmons.—The beadle of our parish.—" The parish beadle is one of the most, perhaps *the* most, important member of the local administration. He is not so well off as the churchwarden certainly; nor is he so learned as the vestry clerk; nor does he order things quite so much his own way as either of them. But his power is very great notwithstanding, and the dignity of his office is never impaired by the absence of efforts on his part to maintain it."—*Sketches by Boz* (Our Parish).

Simmons, Mrs. Henrietta.—A guest at Mrs. Quilp's tea-party.—" Mrs. George remarked that people would talk;

that people had often said this to her before; that Mrs. Simmons, then and there present, had told her so twenty times."—*The Old Curiosity Shop.*

Simmons, Miss.—An assistant at Madame Mantalini's. —*Nicholas Nickleby.*

Simmons, William.—The driver of a van, who gave Martin a lift.—"The driver's name, as he soon informed Martin, was William Simmons; better known as Bill; and his spruce appearance was sufficiently explained by his connection with a large stage-coaching establishment at Hounslow. He aspired to the dignity of the regular box; and expected an appointment on the first vacancy. He was married besides, and had a little key bugle in his pocket, on which, whenever the conversation flagged, he played the first part of a great many tunes, and regularly broke down in the second."—*Martin Chuzzlewit.*

Simpson, Mr.—A prisoner in the Fleet.—*Pickwick Papers.*

Simpson, Mr.—A boarder at Mrs. Tibbs'; married Julia Maplesone.—"Mr. Simpson was one of these young men who are, in society, what walking gentlemen are on the stage, only infinitely worse skilled in his vocation than the most indifferent artist; he was as empty headed as the great bell of St. Paul's; always dressed according to the caricatures published in the monthly fashions; and spelt character with a k."—*Sketches by Boz* (The Boarding House).

Simson, Mr.—A guest at the Steam Excursion.—*Sketches by Boz* (The Steam Excursion).

Six Jolly Fellowship Porters (The Porters).—A riverside public-house, kept by Miss Abbey Potterson.—"A tavern of a dropsical appearance. The bar of the 'Six Jolly Fellowship Porters' was a bar to soften the human breast. The available space in it was not much larger than a hackney coach; but no one could have wished the bar bigger, that space was so girt in by corpulent little casks, and by cordial bottles radiant with fictitious grapes in bunches, and by lemons in nets, and by biscuits in baskets, and by the polite beer pulls, that made low bows when customers were served with beer, and by the cheese in a snug corner, and by the landlady's own small table in a snugger corner near the fire, with the cloth everlastingly laid."—*Our Mutual Friend.*

Skettles, Sir Barnet, M.P.—Present at the breaking-up party of Doctor Blimber's.—"It was Sir Barnet Skettles, Lady Skettles, and Master Skettles. Master Skettles was to be a new boy after the vacation, and Fame had been busy, in Mr. Feeder's room, with his father, who was in the House of Commons, and of whom Mr. Feeder had said that, when he *did* catch the Speaker's eye (which he had expected to do for three or four years) it was anticipated that he would rather touch up the Radicals."—*Dombey and Son.*

Skettles, Lady.—Wife of Sir Barnet Skettles.—*Dombey and Son.*

Skettles, Master Barnet.—Son of Sir Barnet Skettles. A prospective pupil, present at the breaking-up party at Dr. Blimber's.—"Master Skettles was revenging himself for the studies to come on the plum cake."—*Dombey and Son.*

Skewton, The Hon. Mrs.—The mother of Edith Grainger.—An old lady, who affected a youthful manner. —"The discrepancy between Mrs. Skewton's fresh enthusiasm of words, and forlornly faded manner, was hardly less observable than that between her age, which was about seventy, and her dress, which would have been youthful for twenty-seven."—*Dombey and Son.*

Skiffins, Miss.—The lady who married Mr. Wemmick. —"She might have been some two or three years younger than Wemmick, and I judged her to stand possessed of portable property. The cut of her dress upward, both before and behind, made her figure very like a boy's kite; and I might have pronounced her gown a little too decidedly orange, and her gloves a little too intensely green. But she seemed to be a good sort of fellow, and showed a high regard for the aged P."—*Great Expectations.*

Skimpin, Mr.—Junior counsel for Mrs. Bardell.—"Mr. Skimpin proceeded to open the case, and the case appeared to have very little inside it when he had opened it."—*Pickwick Papers.*

Skimpole, Harold.—A selfish, crafty man, who professed to be a simpleton.—"He was a little, bright creature, with a rather large head, but a delicate face and a sweet voice, and there was a perfect charm in him. He had more the appearance in all respects of a damaged young man than a well-preserved elderly one; there was an easy negligence in his manner, and even in his dress (his hair carelessly disposed and his neckerchief loose and flowing as I have seen artists paint their own portraits) which I could not separate from the idea of a romantic youth who had undergone some unique process of depreciation; it struck me as being not at all like the manner or appearance of a man who had advanced in life by the usual road of years, cares and experiences."—*Bleak House.*

Skimpole, Mrs.—Wife of Harold.—" Mrs. Skimpole had once been a beauty, but was now a delicate, high-nosed invalid, suffering under a complication of disorders."—*Bleak House.*

Skimpole, The Misses.—Daughters of Harold.—" This, said Mr. Skimpole, is my beauty daughter Arethusa—plays and sings odds and ends like her father; this is my sentiment daughter Laura—plays a little but don't sing; this is my comedy daughter Kitty—sings a little but don't play; we all draw a little, and compose a little, and none of us have any idea of time or money."—*Bleak House.*

" Skylark."—The name of Mr. Murdstone's yacht.—" They left me during this time with a very nice man, with a very large head of red hair, and a very small shiny hat upon it, who had got a cross-barred shirt or waistcoat on with ' Skylark ' in capital letters across the chest. I thought it was his name; and that as he lived on board ship, and hadn't a street door to put his name on, he put it there instead; but when I called him Mr. Skylark he said it meant the vessel."—*David Copperfield.*

Slackbridge.—A Socialist orator who addressed the electors.—" The orator, perched on a stage, delivered himself of this and what other froth and fume he had in him. He had declaimed himself into a violent heat, and was as hoarse as he was hot. By dint of roaring at the top of his voice, under a flaring gas light, clenching his fists, knitting his brows, setting his teeth, and pounding with his arms, he had taken so much out of himself by this time that he was brought to a stop, and called for a glass of water."—*Hard Times.*

Sladdery, Mr.—A fashionable London bookseller.—" If you want to get this print upon the tables of my high connection, sir, says Mr. Sladdery, the Librarian; or if you want to get this dwarf or giant into the houses of my high connection, sir; or if you want to secure to this entertainment the patronage of my high connection, sir; you must leave it if you please to me, for I have been accustomed to study the leaders of my high connection, sir, and I may tell you without vanity that I can turn them round my finger, in which Mr. Sladdery, who is an honest man, does not exaggerate at all."—*Bleak House.*

Slammer, Doctor.—A guest at the Rochester Charity Ball.—" One of the most popular personages, in his own circle, present was a little fat man, with a ring of upright black hair round his head, and an extensive bald plain on the top of it,—Doctor Slammer, surgeon to the 97th."—*Pickwick Papers.*

Slasher, Doctor.—A surgeon at Bartholomew's Hospital.—" You consider Mr. Slasher a good operator, said Mr. Pickwick. Best alive, replied Hopkins. Took a boy's leg out of the socket last week—boy ate five apples and a ginger cake—exactly two minutes after it was all over, boy said he wouldn't lie there to be made game of, and he'd tell his mother if they didn't begin."—*Pickwick Papers.*

Slaughter, Lieutenant.—A friend of Captain Waters.—*Sketches by Boz* (The Tuggses at Ramsgate).

Sleary, Mr.—Proprietor of a circus.—" Last of all appeared Mr. Sleary, a stout man as already mentioned, with one eye fixed and one loose eye; a voice (if it can be called so) like the efforts of a broken old pair of bellows; a flabby surface, and a muddled head, which was never sober and never drunk."—*Hard Times.*

Sleary, Josephine.—Daughter of Mr. Sleary, an equestrienne in the circus.—" A pretty fair-haired girl of eighteen, who had been tied on a horse at two years old, and had made a will at twelve, which she always carried about with her, expressive of her dying desire to be drawn to the grave by the two piebald ponies."—*Hard Times.*

Sliderskew, Peg.—Housekeeper to Arthur Gride.—" A short, thin, weasen, blear-eyed old woman; palsy stricken and hideously ugly."—*Nicholas Nickleby.*

Slinkton Mr. Julius.—A rogue who traded in life insurance.—" He was about forty or so, dark, exceedingly well dressed in black, being in mourning."—*Hunted Down.*

Slithers, Mr.—Master Humphrey's barber.—" My barber is at all times a very brisk, bustling, active little man; for he is, as it were, chubby all over, without being stout or unwieldy."—*Master Humphrey's Clock.*

Sloppy.—A foundling kept by Betty Higden, who turned the mangle for her; afterwards employed by Mr. Boffin to remove the dust heaps.—" Mrs. Betty Higden's home was then perceived to be a small home with a large mangle in it; at the handle of which machine stood a very long boy, with a very little head, and an open mouth of disproportionate capacity, that seemed to assist his eyes in staring at the visitors. . . . Why you see, speaking quite correctly, he has no right name. I always understood he took his name from being found on a sloppy night."—*Our Mutual Friend.*

Slout, Mr.—The master of the workhouse who punished Oliver because he asked for more gruel.—" Boys have generally excellent appetites. Oliver Twist and his companions suffered the tortures of slow starvation for three months . . . a council was held; lots were cast who should walk up to the Master after supper that evening and ask for more; and it fell to Oliver Twist."—*Oliver Twist.*

Slowboy, Tilly.—Mrs. Peerybingle's maid.—" She was of a spare and straight shape this young lady, insomuch that her garments appeared to be in constant danger of sliding off those sharp pegs her shoulders, on which they were loosely hung. . . . The maternal and paternal Slowboy were alike unknown to fame, and Tilly had been bred by public charity a foundling."—*The Cricket on the Hearth.*

Sludberry, Thomas.—The defendant in a suit at Doctors' Commons.—" The gentleman in the spectacles having concluded his judgment, and a few minutes having been allowed to elapse to afford time for the buzz in the court to subside, the Registrar called on the next cause, which was the office of the Judge promoted by Bumple against Sludberry. A general movement was visible in the court at this announcement, and the obliging functionary with silver staff whispered us that there would be some fun now, for this was a brawling case."—*Sketches by Boz* (Doctors' Commons).

Sluffen, Mr.—A master chimney-sweep, of Adam-and-Eve Court. Chairman of the Chimney Sweeps' Dinner.—"The Master Sweeps, influenced by the restless spirit of innovation, actually interposed their authority, in opposition to the dancing, and substituted a dinner—an anniversary dinner at White Conduit House—where clean faces appeared in lieu of black ones, smeared with rose pink; and knee tops and cords superseded nankeen drawers and rosetted shoes."—*Sketches by Boz* (The First of May).

Slug, Mr.—President of the Statistical Section of the Mudfog Association.—"His complexion is a dark purple, and he has a habit of sighing constantly."—*The Mudfog Sketches.*

Slum, Mr.—A friend of Mrs. Jarley's.—"A tallish gentleman, with a hook nose and black hair; dressed in a military surtout, very short and tight in the sleeves, and which once had been frogged and braided all over, but was now sadly shorn of its garniture, and quite threadbare; dressed too in ancient grey pantaloons, fitting tight to the leg, and a pair of pumps in the winter of their existence." —*The Old Curiosity Shop.*

Slumkey, Hon. Samuel.—The successful candidate in the Eatanswill election.—"A small body of electors remained unpolled on the very last day. They were calculating and reflecting persons, who had not yet been convinced by the arguments of either party, although they had had frequent conferences with each. One hour before the poll, Mr. Perker solicited the honour of a private interview with these intelligent, these noble, these patriotic men. It was granted. His arguments were brief but satisfactory. They went in a body to the Poll; and when they returned the Honourable Samuel Slumkey of Slumkey Hall was returned also."—*Pickwick Papers.*

Slummintowkens, The.—A family at Ipswich in the social circle of Mr. Nupkins.—*Pickwick Papers.*

Slurk, Mr.—Editor of the *Eatanswill Independent.*—"A shortish gentleman, with very stiff black hair, cut in the porcupine or blacking-brush style, and standing stiff and straight all over his head; his aspect was pompous and threatening; his manner was peremptory; his eyes were sharp and restless; and his whole bearing bespoke a feeling of great confidence in himself, and a consciousness of immeasurable superiority over all other people."—*Pickwick Papers*.

Sly, Mr.—Landlord of the King's Arms Hotel at Lancaster.—Doctor Marigold (*Christmas Stories*).

Slyme, Chevy.—A degenerate nephew of old Martin Chuzzlewit.—" Mr. Slyme had once been, in his way, the choicest of swaggerers, but in an evil hour this off-shoot of the Chuzzlewit trunk, being lazy and ill-qualified for any regular pursuit, and having dissipated such means as he ever possessed, had formally established himself as a Professor of Taste."—*Martin Chuzzlewit.*

Smalder Girls, The.—(*See* **Johnson, Tom.**)

Smallweed, Bart.—A junior law clerk, the friend and admirer of Mr. William Guppy.—" Whether Smallweed (metaphorically called Small, and eke Chickweed, as it were jocularly to express a fledgling) was ever a boy is much doubted in Lincoln's Inn; he is now something under fifteen, and an old limb of the law. He is a town-made article, of small stature and weazen features; but may be perceived from a considerable distance by means of his very tall hat. He is a weird changeling, to whom years are nothing; he stands precociously possessed of centuries of owlish wisdom; and if ever he lay in a cradle, it seems as if he must have lain there in a tail coat; he has an old, old eye has Smallweed, and he drinks and smokes in a monkeyish way, and his neck is stiff in his collar, and he is never to be taken in, and he knows all about it, whatever it is."—*Bleak House.*

Smallweed, Mr.—Bart's paralyzed grandfather.—" Mr. Smallweed's grandfather is likewise of the party. He is in a helpless condition as to his lower, and nearly so as to his upper limbs, but his mind is unimpaired; it holds as well as it ever held the first four rules of arithmetic, and a certain small collection of the hardest facts; in respect of ideality, reverence, wonder, and such other phrenological attributes, it is no worse off than it used to be; everything that Mr. Smallweed's grandfather ever put away in his mind was a grub at first, and is a grub at last; in all his life he has never bred a single butterfly."—*Bleak House.*

Smallweed, Mrs.—Grandmother of Bart; sister of Krook; an imbecile.—" With such infantine graces as a total want of observation, memory, understanding, and interest; and an eternal disposition to fall asleep over the fire, and into it."—*Bleak House.*

Smallweed, Mr., the elder.—The deceased great-grandfather of Bart.—" A horny-skinned, two-legged, money-getting species of spider, who spun webs to catch unwary flies, and retired into holes until they were entrapped. The name of this old pagan's god was compound interest; he lived for it, married it, died of it. Meeting with a heavy loss, in an honest little enterprise, in which all the loss was intended to have been on the other side, he broke something,—something necessary to his existence, therefore it couldn't have been his heart,—and made an end of his career."—*Bleak House.*

Smallweed, Judith.—The twin sister of Bart.—" Judy never owned a doll, never heard of Cinderella, never played at any game; it is doubtful whether Judy knows how to laugh. She has so rarely seen the thing done that the probabilities are strong the other way; of anything like a youthful laugh she certainly can have no conception. One might infer from Judy's appearance that her business rather lay with the thorns than the flowers, but she had in her time been apprenticed to the art and mystery of artificial flower making."—*Bleak House.*

Smangle, Mr.—A prisoner for debt in the Fleet.—" An admirable specimen of a class of gentry which can never be seen in full perfection but in such places. He was a tall fellow, with an olive complexion, long dark hair, and very thick bushy whiskers meeting under his chin; there was a rakish vagabond smartness, and a kind of boastful rascality about the whole man, that was worth a mine of gold."—*Pickwick Papers.*

Smart, Tom.—A commercial traveller; the hero of The Bagman's Story.—" If any bagman of that day could have caught sight of the little neck-or-nothing sort of gig, with a clay-coloured body and red wheels, and the vixenish, ill-tempered, fast-going bay mare, that looked like a cross between a butcher's horse and a twopenny post-office pony, he would have known at once that this traveller could have been no other than Tom Smart, of the great house of Bilson and Slum, Cateaton Street, City."—*Pickwick Papers* (The Bagman's Story).

Smauker, Mr.—A footman at Bath who introduced Sam Weller to the Footmen's Club.—" With a very grave face, Mr. Weller slowly read as follows—A select company of the Bath footmen presents their compliments to Mr. Weller, and requests the pleasure of his company this evening, to a friendly swarry, consisting of boiled leg of mutton with the usual trimmings; the swarry to be on the table at half-past nine o'clock punctually. This was inclosed in another note, which ran thus—Mr. John Smauker, the gentleman who had the pleasure of meeting Mr. Weller at the house of their mutual acquaintance Mr. Bantam a few days since, begs to enclose Mr. Weller the herewith invitation."—*Pickwick Papers.*

Smif, Putnam.—A New York clerk who wrote to Martin asking assistance to visit England.—*Martin Chuzzlewit.*

Smiggers, Joseph.—The Vice-President of the Pickwick Club.—*Pickwick Papers.*

Smike.—A boy who was left at Dotheboys Hall and forgotten, afterwards discovered to be the son of Ralph Nickleby. Ran away with Nicholas and became a strolling player.—" Although he could not have been less than eighteen or nineteen years old, and was tall for that age, he wore a skeleton suit, such as is usually put upon very little boys, and which, though most absurdly short in the arms and legs, was quite wide enough for his attenuated frame."—*Nicholas Nickleby.*

Smith, Mr.—A London clerk.—" He was a tall, thin, pale person, in a black coat, scanty grey trousers, little pinched-up gaiters, and brown beaver gloves. He had an umbrella in his hand—not for use, for the day was fine—but evidently because he always carried one to the office in the morning."—*Sketches by Boz* (Thoughts About People).

Smith, Mr.—A Member of Parliament who meets a constituent at the House of Commons.—" Mr. Smith stops; turns round with an air of enchanting urbanity (for the rumour of an intended dissolution has been very extensively circulated this morning); seizes both the hands of his gratified constituent; and, after greeting him with the most enthusiastic warmth, darts into the lobby, with an extraordinary display of ardour in the public cause, leaving an immense impression in his favour on the mind of his fellow-townsman."—*Sketches by Boz* (A Parliamentary Sketch).

Smith, Samuel.—A draper's assistant who posed as a person of consequence under the name of Horatio Sparkins.—(*See* **Sparkins, Horatio.**)—*Sketches by Boz* (Horatio Sparkins).

Smithers, Robert.—A city clerk, friend of Mr. Thomas Potter.—" There was a spice of romance in Mr. Smithers' disposition, a ray of poetry, a gleam of misery; a sort of consciousness of he didn't exactly know what, coming across him he didn't precisely know why—which stood out in fine relief against the off-hand, dashing, amateur-pickpocket-sort-of-manner, which distinguished Mr. Potter in an eminent degree."—*Sketches by Boz* (Making a Night of It).

Smithers, Miss Emily.—The belle of the school at Minerva House.—" How do I look, dear, inquired Miss Emily Smithers, the belle of the house, of Miss Caroline Wilson, who was her bosom friend, because she was the ugliest girl in Hammersmith, or out of it."—*Sketches by Boz* (Sentiment).

Smithers, Miss.—A pupil at the Bury St. Edmunds girls' school.—*Pickwick Papers.*

Smithick and Watersby.—The owners of the ship *Golden Mary.*—" It is personally neither Smithick nor Watersby that I here mention, nor was I ever acquainted with any man of either of these names; nor do I think that there has been any one of these names in that Liverpool house for years back; but it is in reality the House itself that I refer to, and a wiser merchant and a truer gentleman never stepped."—The Wreck of the *Golden Mary* (*Christmas Stories*).

Smithie Family.—Guests at the Rochester Charity Ball.—" Mr. Smithie, Mrs. Smithie, and the Misses Smithie was the next announcement."—*Pickwick Papers.*

Smiths, The.—In the audience at the private theatricals at Rose Villa.—(*See* **Glumper.**)—*Sketches by Boz* (Mrs. Joseph Porter).

Smivey.—The name Mr. Montague Tigg invented for Martin, when he pledged his watch.—"The name of my friend is Smivey—Chicken Smivey of Holborn; Twenty six and a half B; Lodger. Here he winked at Martin again, to apprise him that all the forms and ceremonies prescribed by law were now complied with."—*Martin Chuzzlewit.*

Smorltork, Count.—A guest at Mrs. Leo Hunter's garden-party.—*Pickwick Papers.*

Smouch.—Assistant to Namby, the sheriff's officer.—"A shabby-looking man in a brown great-coat shorn of divers buttons."—*Pickwick Papers.*

Smuggins.—A comic singer at a Harmony Meeting.—"That little round-faced man, with the small brown surtout, white stockings, and shoes, is in the comic line; the mixed air of self-denial, and mental consciousness of his own powers, with which he acknowledges the call of the chair, is particularly gratifying."—*Sketches by Boz* (The Streets—Night).

Smugglewood, Doctor.—A medical man consulted by Our Bore.—*Our Bore* (Reprinted Pieces).

Snaffletoffle, Mr.—A member of the Mudfog Association.—*The Mudfog Sketches.*

Snagsby, Mr.—A law stationer.—"On the eastern borders of Chancery Lane, that is to say, more particularly in Cook's Court, Cursitor Street, Mr. Snagsby, Law Stationer, pursues his lawful calling. He is a mild, bald, timid man, with a shining head, and a scrubby clump of black hair sticking out at the back. He tends to meekness and obesity. He is emphatically a retiring and unassuming man."—*Bleak House.*

Snagsby, Mrs.—Wife of Mr. Snagsby, niece of Mr. Peffer.—"A short shrewd niece, something too violently compressed about the waist, and with a sharp nose, like a sharp autumn evening, inclining to be frosty towards the end. Mr. Snagsby refers everything not in the practical mysteries of the business to Mrs. Snagsby. She manages the money; reproaches the tax-gatherers; appoints the times and places of devotion on Sundays; licenses Mr. Snagsby's entertainments; and acknowledges no responsibility as to what she thinks fit to provide for dinner. Rumour, always flying bat-like about Cook's Court, and skimming in and out of everybody's windows, does say that Mrs. Snagsby is jealous and inquisitive, and that Mr. Snagsby is sometimes worried out of house and home, and that if he had the spirit of a mouse he wouldn't stand it."—*Bleak House.*

Snap, Betsy.—Housekeeper to Mr. Chill, the miser.—" Betsy Snap was a withered, hard-favoured, yellow old woman—our only domestic."—*The Poor Relation's Story* (Reprinted Pieces).

Snawley.—A canting hypocrite, who placed his two stepsons at Dotheboys Hall.—" Snawley was a sleek, flat-nosed man, clad in sombre garments, and long black gaiters, and bearing in his countenance an expression of much mortification and sanctity."—*Nicholas Nickleby.*

Snawley, Mrs.—Wife of Mr. Snawley.—*Nicholas Nickleby.*

Snevellicci, Miss.—An actress in Mr. Crummles' company.—" There was Miss Snevellicci, who could do anything, from a medley dance to Lady Macbeth; and also always played some part in blue silk knee-smalls at her benefit. Miss Snevellicci was happily married to an affluent young wax-chandler, who had supplied the theatre with candles."—*Nicholas Nickleby.*

Snevellicci, Mr.—An actor, father of Miss Snevellicci.—" An uncommonly fine man Miss Snevellicci's papa was . . . who had been in the profession ever since he had first played the ten-year-old imps in the Christmas pantomimes; who could sing a little; dance a little; fence a little; act a little; and do everything a little, but not much . . . who was always selected, in virtue of his figure, to play the military visitors, and the speechless noblemen; who always wore a smart dress, and came on arm in arm with a smart lady in short petticoats; and always did it too with such an air, that people in the pit had been several times known to cry out Bravo, under the impression that he was somebody."—*Nicholas Nickleby.*

Snevellicci, Mrs.—Miss Snevellicci's mother.—" Who was still a dancer, with a neat little figure, and some remains of good looks, and who now sat, as she danced—being rather too old for the full glare of the footlights—in the background."—*Nicholas Nickleby.*

Snewkes, Mr.—An admirer of Mrs. Kenwigs' sister, and a guest at the Kenwigs' supper-party.—" To these were added a sister of Mrs. Kenwigs who was quite a beauty; besides whom there was another young man supposed to entertain honourable designs upon the lady last mentioned."—*Nicholas Nickleby.*

Sniff, Mrs.—An assistant at Mugby Junction Refreshment Room.—" She's the one as you'll notice to be always looking another way from you when you look at her. She's the one with the small waist, buckled in tight in front, and with the lace cuffs at her wrists, which she puts on the edge of the counter before her, and stands a smoothing, while the public foams."—Mugby Junction (*Christmas Stories*).

Sniff, Mr.—An assistant at Mugby Junction Refreshment Room.—" Sniff is husband to Mrs. Sniff; and is a regular insignificant cove; he looks arter the sawdust department in a back room, and is sometimes, when we are very hard put to it, let behind the counter with a corkscrew, but never when it can be helped, his demeanour towards the public being disgustingly servile."—Mugby Junction (*Christmas Stories*).

Sniggs, Mr.—Mayor of Mudfog before Mr. Tulrumble.—*The Mudfog Sketches.*

Snigsworth, Lord.—Cousin of Mr. Twemlow.—" Revived by soup, Twemlow discourses mildly of the Court Circular with Boots and Brewer; is appealed to at the first stage of the banquet by Veneering, on the disputed question whether his cousin Lord Snigsworth is in or out of town."—*Our Mutual Friend.*

Snipe, Hon. Wilmot.—A guest at the Rochester Charity Ball.—" Who's that little boy with the light hair and pink eyes, in a fancy dress, inquired Mr. Tupman of Mr. Jingle. Hush, pray—pink eyes—fancy dress—little boy—nonsense—Ensign 97th—Honourable Wilmot Snipe—great family Snipes—very."—*Pickwick Papers.*

Snitchey and Craggs.—A firm of solicitors.—" The offices of Messrs. Snitchey and Craggs stood convenient, with an open door, down two smooth steps, in the market place; so that any angry farmer inclining towards hot water might tumble into it at once. Their special council chamber and hall of conference was an old back room upstairs, with a low dark ceiling, which seemed to be knitting its brows gloomily in the consideration of points of law. . . . Round the wainscot there were tiers of boxes, padlocked and fireproof, with people's names painted outside, which anxious visitors felt themselves by a cruel enchantment obliged to spell backwards and forwards, and to make anagrams of, while they sat seeming to listen to Snitchey and Craggs, without comprehending one word of what they said."—*The Battle of Life.*

Snitchey, Jonathan.—The speaking partner of Snitchey and Craggs, Dr. Jeddler's solicitors.—" Snitchey was like a magpie or raven, only not so sleek. . . . We in our profession are little else than mirrors after all, Mr. Alfred, but we are generally consulted by angry and quarrelsome people, who are not in their best looks, and it's rather hard to quarrel with us if we reflect unpleasant aspects. I think, said Mr. Snitchey, that I speak for self and Craggs."—*The Battle of Life.*

Snitchey, Mrs.—Wife of Mr. Snitchey.—" Snitchey and Craggs had each in private life, as in professional existence, a partner of his own. Mrs. Snitchey by a dispensation not uncommon in the affairs of life was on principle suspicious of Mr. Craggs, and Mrs. Craggs was on principle suspicious of Mr. Snitchey."—*The Battle of Life.*

Snivey, Sir Hookham.—A member of the Mudfog Association.—*The Mudfog Sketches.*

Snobb, Hon. Mr.—Introduced to Kate at Ralph Nickleby's dinner-party.—" Wheeling about again, towards a gentleman with the neck of a stork and the legs of no animal in particular, Ralph introduced him as the Honourable Mr. Snobb."—*Nicholas Nickleby.*

Snodgrass, Augustus.—Member of the Pickwick Club.—" On the left of his great leader sat the poetic Snodgrass poetically enveloped in a mysterious blue cloak with a canine skin collar."—*Pickwick Papers.*

Snore, Professor.—President of the Zoology and Botany Section of the Mudfog Association.—*The Mudfog Sketches.*

Snubbin, Serjeant.—Counsel for Mr. Pickwick.—" Mr. Serjeant Snubbin was a lantern-faced, sallow-complexioned man of about five-and-forty; or, as the novels say, he might be fifty. He had that dull-looking boiled eye, which is often to be seen in the heads of people who have applied themselves, during many years, to a weary and laborious course of study. Books of practice, heaps of papers, and opened letters were scattered over the table, without any attempt at order or arrangement; the furniture of the room was old and rickety; the doors of the book-case were rotting on their hinges; the dust flew out from the carpet at every step; the blinds were yellow with age and dirt; the state of everything in the room showed, with a clearness not to be mistaken, that Mr. Serjeant Snubbin was far too much occupied with his professional pursuits, to take any great heed or regard of his personal comforts."—*Pickwick Papers.*

Snuffin, Sir Tumley.—The medical attendant of Mrs. Wititterly.—*Nicholas Nickleby.*

Snuphanuph, Lady.—A visitor at Bath.—" Mr. Pickwick, do you see the lady in the gauze turban? The fat old lady, inquired Mr. Pickwick innocently. Hush, my dear sir, nobody's fat or old in Bath; that's the Dowager Lady Snuphanuph."—*Pickwick Papers.*

Soemup, Doctor.—President of the Medical Section of of the Mudfog Association.—*The Mudfog Sketches.*

Sophia.—The young lady to whom Ruth Pinch was governess.—" A premature little woman, of thirteen years old, who had already arrived at such a pitch of whalebone and education, that she had nothing girlish about her."—*Martin Chuzzlewit.*

Sophia.—One of the maids at Matthew Pocket's who controlled the household.—" Both Mr. and Mrs. Pocket had such a noticeable air of being in somebody else's hands, that I wondered who really was in possession of the house, and let them live there, until I found this unknown power to be the servants."—*Great Expectations.*

Sophronia Sphinx.—The name Dick Swiveller gave the Marchioness, when he sent her to be educated.—"After casting about for some time for a name which should be worthy of her, he decided in favour of Sophronia Sphinx, as being euphonious and genteel, and furthermore indicative of mystery; under this title the Marchioness repaired in tears to the school of his selection."—*The Old Curiosity Shop.*

Sophy.—A maid at Mrs. Lirriper's.—"The willingest girl that ever came into a house, half starved, poor thing, —a girl so willing that I called her willing Sophy; down upon her knees scrubbing early and late, and ever cheerful but always smiling, with a black face."—Mrs. Lirriper's Lodgings (*Christmas Stories*).

Sophy (The Second).—Step-daughter of Mr. Mim, the showman, a deaf and dumb girl whom Doctor Marigold adopted and called by the name of his dead daughter.—"She had a pretty face; and, now that there was no one to drag at her bright dark hair, and it was all in order, there was something touching in her looks, that made the cast most peaceful and quiet, though not at all melancholy."—Doctor Marigold (*Christmas Stories*).

Southcote, Mr.—A swindler.—"Introduced himself as a literary gentleman in the last extremity of distress."—*The Begging-Letter Writer* (Reprinted Pieces).

Southcote, Mrs.—Wife of Mr. Southcote.—*The Begging-Letter Writer* (Reprinted Pieces).

Southcott, Mrs.—A spiritualist of the year 1775.—"Spiritual revelations were conceded to England at that favoured period as at this. Mrs. Southcott had recently attained her five-and-twentieth blessed birthday."—*A Tale of Two Cities.*

Sowerby, Mr.—An undertaker to whom Oliver was apprenticed.—"Mr. Sowerby was a tall, gaunt, large-jointed man, attired in a suit of threadbare black, with darned cotton stockings of the same colour, and shoes to answer. His features were not naturally intended to wear a smiling aspect, but he was in general rather given to professional jocosity."—*Oliver Twist.*

Sowerby, Mrs.—Wife of Mr. Sowerby.—"A short, thin, squeezed-up woman, with a vixenish countenance."—*Oliver Twist.*

Sownds.—The beadle at the church where Mr. Dombey was married.—"Mr. Sownds, the beadle, who is sitting in the sun upon the church steps all this time (and seldom does anything else except in cold weather sitting by the fire), approves of Mrs. Miff's discourses."—*Dombey and Son.*

Sowster, Mr.—The Beadle of the town of Oldcastle.—"Sowster is a fat man, with a more enlarged development of that peculiar conformation of countenance which is vulgarly termed a double chin than I remember to have ever seen before. He has also a very red nose, which he attributes to early rising."—*The Mudfog Sketches.*

Sparkins, Horatio.—The name assumed by Mr. Smith, a draper's assistant who, posing as a person of consequence, made the acquaintance of the Malderton family.—"The first object that met the anxious eyes of the expectant family, on their entrance into the ballroom, was the interesting Horatio, with his hair brushed off his forehead, and his eyes fixed on the ceiling, reclining in a contemplative attitude on one of the seats. . . . We will draw a veil, as novel-writers say, over the scene that ensued. The mysterious, philosophical, romantic, metaphysical Sparkins, he who, to the interesting Teresa, seemed like the embodied idea of the young dukes and poetical exquisites in blue silk dressing-gowns, and ditto ditto slippers, of whom she had read and dreamed, but had never expected to behold, was suddenly converted into Mr. Samuel Smith, the assistant at a cheap shop, the junior partner in a slippery firm of some three weeks' existence."—*Sketches by Boz* (Horatio Sparkins).

Sparkler, Edmund.—Son of Mrs. Merdle by her first marriage.—"The Colonel's son was Mrs. Merdle's only child. He was of a chuckle-headed, high-shouldered make, with a general appearance of being not so much a young man as a swelled boy."—*Little Dorrit.*

Sparks, Timothy.—The writer of the pamphlet on Sunday dedicated to the Bishop of London.—*Sunday under Three Heads* (Reprinted Pieces).

Sparsit, Mrs.—Mr. Josiah Bounderby's housekeeper.—"Mrs. Sparsit had not only seen different days, but was highly connected. She had a great aunt living in these very times called Lady Scadgers. Mr. Sparsit deceased, of whom she was the relict, had been by the mother's side what Mrs. Sparsit still called a Powler. If Bounderby had been a Conqueror, and Mrs. Sparsit a captive princess, whom he took about as a feature in his State processions, he could not have made a greater flourish with her than he habitually did."—*Hard Times*.

Sparsit, Mr.—The deceased husband of Mrs. Sparsit. —"He inherited a fair fortune from his uncle, but owed it all before he came into it, and spent it twice over immediately afterwards. Thus, when he died at twenty-four (the scene of his decease Calais, and the cause brandy) he did not leave his widow, from whom he had been separated soon after the honeymoon, in affluent circumstances."—*Hard Times*.

Spatter, John.—Clerk to Michael the Poor Relation.—*The Poor Relation's Story* (Reprinted Pieces).

Specks, Dr. Joe.—A boyhood companion of the Uncommercial Traveller, whom he met in later years.—"I was suddenly brought up by the sight of a man, who got out of a little phaeton at the doctor's door, and went into the doctor's house. Immediately the air was filled with the scent of trodden grass, and the perspective of years opened, and at the end of it was a little likeness of this man keeping a wicket, and I said God bless my soul, Joe Specks."—*The Uncommercial Traveller* (Dullborough Town).

Specks Junior.—Son of Dr. and Mrs. Specks of Dullborough.—"I dined with them, and we had no other company than Specks Junior, barrister-at-law, who went away as soon as the cloth was removed, to look after the young lady to whom he was going to be married."—*The Uncommercial Traveller* (Dullborough Town).

Speedie, Doctor.—A Cumberland village doctor.—"He was a tall, thin, large-boned old gentleman, with an appearance at first sight of being hard-featured, but, at a second glance, the mild expression of his face, and some particular touches of sweetness and patience about his mouth, corrected this impression, and assigned his long professional rides by day and night, in the bleak hill weather, as the true cause of that appearance."—The Lazy Tour of Two Idle Apprentices (*Christmas Stories*).

Spenlow and Jorkins.—The firm of proctors to whom David was articled.—" Doctors' Commons was approached by a little low archway. Before we had taken many paces down the street beyond it, the noise of the city seemed to melt as if by magic into a softened distance. A few dull courts and narrow ways brought us to the sky-lighted offices of Spenlow and Jorkins."—*David Copperfield.*

Spenlow, Mr. Francis.—A proctor, senior partner of Spenlow and Jorkins.—" Hasty footsteps were heard in the room outside, and Mr. Spenlow, in a black gown trimmed with white fur, came hurrying in, taking off his hat as he came. He was a little light-haired gentleman, with undeniable boots, and the stiffest of white cravats and shirt collars. . . . He was got up with such care, and was so stiff, that he could hardly bend himself, being obliged, when he glanced at some papers on his desk after sitting down in his chair, to move his whole body from the bottom of his spine, like Punch."—*David Copperfield.*

Spenlow, Dora.—Daughter of Mr. Spenlow, whom David married.—" I don't remember who was there except Dora. I have not the least idea what we had for dinner besides Dora. My impression is that I dined off Dora entirely, and sent away half a dozen plates untouched. I sat next to her. I talked to her. She had the most delightful little voice; the gayest little laugh; the pleasantest and most fascinating little ways that ever led a lost youth into hopeless slavery. She was rather diminutive altogether—so much the more precious I thought."—*David Copperfield.*

Spenlow, The Misses Lavinia and Clarissa.—The maiden sisters of Mr. Spenlow, with whom after her father's death Dora went to reside.—" Two dry little elderly ladies, dressed in black, and each looking wonderfully like a preparation in chip or tan of the late Mr. Spenlow. . . . They both had little bright round twinkling eyes, by the way, which were like bird's eyes; they were not unlike birds altogether; having a sharp brisk sudden manner, and a little short spruce way of adjusting themselves, like canaries."—*David Copperfield.*

Spider, The.—Mr. Jaggers' name for Bentley Drummle. —*Great Expectations.*

Spiker, Mrs. Henry.—A lady whom David met at dinner at Mr. Waterbrook's.—"He presented me, with much ceremony, to a very awful lady in a black velvet dress, and a great black velvet hat, whom I remember as looking like a near relation of Hamlet's,—say his aunt." —*David Copperfield.*

Spiker, Mr. Henry.—Husband of Mrs. Spiker.—"Her husband was there too; so cold a man that his head, instead of being grey, seemed to be sprinkled with hoar frost."—*David Copperfield.*

Spine, John.—A novelist.—*Our Bore* (Reprinted Pieces).

Spottletoe, Mr.—A relation of old Martin Chuzzlewit. —"First there was Mr. Spottletoe, who was so bald, and had such big whiskers, that he seemed to have stopped his hair, by the sudden application of some powerful remedy, in the very act of falling off his head, and to have fastened it irrevocably on his face."—*Martin Chuzzlewit.*

Spottletoe, Mrs.—Wife of Mr. Spottletoe.—"Then there was Mrs. Spottletoe, who, being much too slim for her years, and of a poetical constitution, could now, by reason of her strong affection for her uncle Chuzzlewit, and the shock it gave her to be suspected of testamentary designs upon him, do nothing but cry—except moan."—*Martin Chuzzlewit.*

Sprodgkin, Mrs.—A troublesome parishioner of the Rev. Frank Milvey.—"That worthy couple were delayed by a portentous old parishioner of the female gender, who was one of the plagues of their lives. However, beyond themselves, the Reverend Frank Milvey and Mrs. Milvey seldom hinted that Mrs. Sprodgkin was hardly worth the trouble she gave; but both made the best of her, as they did of all their troubles."—*Our Mutual Friend.*

Spruggins, Thomas.—A candidate for the office of Beadle; defeated by Bung.—"The ex-churchwarden rose to propose Thomas Spruggins for Beadle. He had had his eye upon him for years; and this he would say, that a more well-conducted, a more well-behaved, a more sober, a more quiet man, with a more well-regulated mind, he had never met with; a man with a larger family he had never known; the parish required a man who could be depended on; such a man he now proposed."—*Sketches by Boz* (Our Parish).

Spyers, Jem.—The Bow Street officer who detected Conkey Chickweed's fraud.—*Oliver Twist.*

Squeers, Mr. Wackford.—Proprietor of Dotheboys Hall.—"Mr. Squeers' appearance was not prepossessing. He had but one eye, and the popular prejudice runs in favour of two. The eye he had was unquestionably useful, but decidedly not ornamental, being of a greenish grey, and in shape resembling the fan-light of a street door. The blank side of his face was much wrinkled and puckered up, which gave him a very sinister appearance, especially when he smiled, at which times his expression bordered closely on the villainous."—*Nicholas Nickleby.*

Squeers, Mrs.—Wife of Wackford Squeers.—"A female bounced into the room, and seizing Mr. Squeers by the throat, gave him two loud kisses, one close after the other, like a postman's knock. The lady, who was of a large raw-boned figure, was about half a head taller than Mr. Squeers, and was dressed in a dimity night-jacket; with her hair in papers; she had also a dirty night-cap on, relieved by a yellow cotton handkerchief, which tied it under the chin."—*Nicholas Nickleby.*

Squeers, Miss Fanny.—Daughter of Mr. and Mrs. Squeers.—"Miss Fanny Squeers was in her three-and-twentieth year. If there be any one grace or loveliness inseparable from that particular period of life, Miss Squeers may be presumed to have been possessed of it, as there is no reason to suppose that she was a solitary exception to a universal rule. She was not tall like her mother, but short like her father; from the former she inherited a voice of harsh quality; from the latter a remarkable expression of the right eye, something akin to having none at all."—*Nicholas Nickleby.*

Squeers, Master Wackford.—Son of Mr. and Mrs. Squeers.—"The only pupil who evinced the slightest tendency towards locomotion, or playfulness, was Master Squeers; and as his chief amusement was to tread upon the other boys' toes in his new boots, his flow of spirits was rather disagreeable than otherwise."—*Nicholas Nickleby*.

Squires, Olympia.—The Uncommercial Traveller's first love.—" Then came the time when, inseparable from one's own birthday, was a certain sense of merit; a consciousness of well-earned distinction; when I regarded my birthday as a graceful achievement of my own, a monument of my perseverance, independence, and good sense, redounding greatly to my honour. This was about the period when Olympia Squires became involved in the anniversary. Olympia was most beautiful (of course) and I loved her to that degree that I used to be obliged to get out of my little bed in the night expressly to exclaim to solitude—Oh Olympia Squires."—*The Uncommercial Traveller* (Birthday Celebrations).

Squires.—The landlord of The Blue Boar, and friend of Uncle Pumblechook.—*Great Expectations*.

Squod, Phil.—An attendant at George's shooting gallery.—" A little grotesque man with a large head. . . . He is a little man, with a face all crushed together, who appears, from a certain blue and speckled appearance that one of his cheeks presents, to have been blown up in the way of business at some odd time or times. He has a curious way of limping round the gallery with his shoulder against the wall, and tacking off at objects he wants to lay hold of instead of going straight to them, which has left a smear all round the four walls, conventionally called Phil's mark."—*Bleak House*.

Stables, The Hon. Bob.—A guest at Chesney Wold.—" There is the Honourable Bob Stables, who can make warm mashes with the skill of a veterinary surgeon, and is a better shot than most gamekeepers. He has been for some time particularly desirous to serve his country, in a post of good emoluments, unaccompanied by any trouble or responsibility."—*Bleak House*.

Stagg.—A blind man, keeper of the rooms where the 'Prentice Knights held their meetings. Friend of Rudge, who aided him to blackmail his wife.—" He wore an old tie wig, as bare and frowzy as a stunted hearth broom. His eyes were closed, but, had they been wide open, it would have been easy to tell, from the attentive expression of the face he turned towards them, and from a certain anxious raising and quivering of the lids, that he was blind."—*Barnaby Rudge*.

Stalker, Inspector.—A London police officer.—"Inspector Stalker is a shrewd hard-headed Scotchman—in appearance not at all unlike a very acute, thoroughly-trained schoolmaster from the Normal Establishment at Glasgow."—*The Detective Police* (Reprinted Pieces).

Staple, Mr.—A guest at the Cricket Club Dinner at Dingley Dell.—"A little man, with a puffy say-nothing-to-me-or-I'll-contradict-you sort of countenance."—*Pickwick Papers*.

Stareleigh, Mr. Justice.—The judge who presided at the Bardell and Pickwick Trial.—"Mr. Justice Stareleigh was a most particularly short man, and so fat that he seemed all face and waistcoat. He rolled in upon two little turned legs; and having bobbed gravely to the Bar, who bobbed gravely to him, put his little legs underneath his table, and his little three-cornered hat upon it; and when Mr. Justice Stareleigh had done this, all you could see of him was two queer little eyes, one broad pink face, and somewhere about half of a big and very comical-looking wig."—*Pickwick Papers*.

Starling, Alfred.—One of the guests at the Haunted House.—"Alfred is a young fellow who pretends to be fast (another word for loose as I understand the term); but who is much too good and sensible for that nonsense, and who would have distinguished himself before now, if his father had not unfortunately left him a small independence of two hundred a year, on the strength of which his only occupation in life has been to spend six."—The Haunted House (*Christmas Stories*).

Starling, Mrs.—A friend of Mr. and Mrs. Leaver, the loving couple.—"A widow lady, who lost her husband when she was young, and lost herself about the same time,—for by her own count she has never grown five years older."—*Sketches of Young Couples*.

Startop.—One of the students who boarded at Matthew Pocket's.—"Startop had been spoiled by a weak mother and kept at home when he ought to have been at school. . . . He was reading and holding his head as if he thought himself in danger of exploding it with too strong a charge of knowledge."—*Great Expectations.*

Steadman, John.—Mate of the *Golden Mary.*—" A brisk, bright, blue-eyed fellow; a very neat figure, and rather under the middle size; never out of the way, and never in it; a face that pleased everybody, and that all children took to, a habit of going about singing as cheerily as a blackbird; and a perfect sailor."—The Wreck of the *Golden Mary* (*Christmas Stories*).

Steele, Tom.—A Waterloo Bridge suicide.—*Down with the Tide* (Reprinted Pieces).

Steepways.—A fishing village in Devonshire.—" The village was built sheer up the face of a steep and lofty cliff; there was no trade in it; there was no wheeled vehicle in it; there was not a level yard in it."—A Message from the Sea (*Christmas Stories*).

Steerforth, James.—The senior boy at Salem House. A selfish youth of charming manners. Became friendly with David and was introduced to the Peggotty household at Yarmouth. Induced Little Emily to run away with him on the eve of her marriage to Ham. Led an aimless life of pleasure, and ultimately was drowned by the wreck of his yacht off Yarmouth.—*David Copperfield.*

Steerforth, Mrs.—The mother of James Steerforth.—" An elderly lady, though not very far advanced in years, with a proud carriage and a handsome face."—*David Copperfield.*

Stiggins, Mr.—A preacher friend of Mrs. Weller's.—" Sitting bolt upright in a high-backed chair was a man in threadbare black clothes, with a back almost as long and stiff as that of the chair itself, who caught Sam's most particular and special attention at once. He was a prim-faced, red-nosed man, with a long thin countenance, and a semi-rattlesnake sort of eye—rather sharp, but decidedly bad."—*Pickwick Papers.*

Stiltstalking, Lord Lancaster.—A guest at Mrs. Gowan's dinner.—" A grey old gentleman, of dignified and sullen appearance, turned out to be Lord Lancaster Stiltstalking, who had been maintained by the Circumlocution Office for many years, as a representative of the

Britannic Majesty abroad. This noble refrigerator had iced several European Courts in his time, and done it with complete success."—*Little Dorrit.*

Strandenheim.—A shopkeeper in Strasbourg.—" The owner was a shopkeeper, by name Strandenheim,—by trade —I couldn't make out what by trade, for he had forborne to write that up and his shop was shut. He wore a black velvet skull cap and looked usurious and rich; a large-lipped, pear-nosed, old man, with white hair, and keen eyes, though near sighted."—*The Uncommercial Traveller* (Travelling Abroad).

Straw, Sergeant.—A London police officer.—" A little, wiry Sergeant of meek demeanour and strong sense."—*The Detective Police* (Reprinted Pieces).

Streaker.—Housemaid at the Haunted House.—" The Cook (an amiable woman but of a weak turn of intellect) burst into tears on beholding the kitchen . . . Streaker, the housemaid, feigned cheerfulness, but was the greater martyr."—The Haunted House (*Christmas Stories*).

Strong, Doctor.—The master of the school at Canterbury where David was educated.—" Doctor Strong looked almost as rusty to my thinking as the tall iron rails and gates outside the house, and almost as stiff and heavy as the great stone urns that flanked them, and were set up on the top of the red brick wall at regular distances all round the house, like sublimated skittles for Time to play at. He was in his library (I mean Dr. Strong was) with his clothes not particularly well brushed; and his hair not particularly well combed; his knee-smalls unbraced; his long black gaiters unbuttoned; and his shoes yawning like two caverns on the hearth-rug. Turning upon me a lustreless eye, that reminded me of a long forgotten blind old horse, who once used to crop the grass and tumble over the graves in Blunderstone churchyard, he said he was glad to see me; and then he gave me his hand; which I didn't know what to do with, as it did nothing for itself. . . . The Doctor himself was the idol of the whole school; and it must have been a badly composed school if he had been anything else, for he was the kindest of men; with a simple faith in him that might have touched the stone hearts of the very urns upon the wall."—*David Copperfield.*

Strong, Mrs. Annie.—The young wife of Dr. Strong.—"Sitting at work not far off from Dr. Strong was a very pretty young lady, whom he called Annie, and who was his daughter I supposed. . . . I was much surprised to hear Mr. Wickfield in bidding her good morning address her as Mrs. Strong. . . . Some of the higher scholars boarded in the Doctor's house, and through them I learned at second hand some particulars of the Doctor's history, as how he had not yet been married twelve months to the beautiful young lady I had seen in the study, whom he married for love, for she had not a sixpence, and had a world of poor relations (so our fellows said) ready to swarm the Doctor out of house and home."—*David Copperfield.*

Struggles, Mr.—A Dingley Dell cricketer.—*Pickwick Papers.*

Stryver, Mr.—A London barrister who defended Darnay.—"Mr. Stryver, a man of little more than thirty, but looking twenty years older than he was, stout, loud, red, bluff, and free from any drawback of delicacy, had a pushing way of shouldering himself (morally and physically) with companies and conversations, that argued well for his shouldering his way up in life."—*A Tale of Two Cities.*

Stubbs, Mrs.—The laundress of Mr. Percy Noakes' chambers in Gray's Inn Square.—"A dirty old woman with an inflamed countenance."—*Sketches by Boz* (The Steam Excursion).

Styles, Mr.—A Vice-President of the Statistical Section of the Mudfog Association.—*The Mudfog Sketches.*

St. Evremonde, The Marquis.—Uncle of Charles Darnay—French nobleman, killed by Gaspard, a peasant, whose child he had driven over and killed.—"He was a man about sixty, handsomely dressed, haughty in manner, and with a face like a fine mask; a face of transparent paleness, every feature in it clearly defined, one set expression on it."—*A Tale of Two Cities.*

St. Evremonde, The Marquis (deceased).—Father of Charles Darnay. Twin-brother of the Marquis who was killed by Gaspard.—*A Tale of Two Cities.*

St. Evremonde, Marquise.—Mother of Charles Darnay.—*A Tale of Two Cities.*

St. Julien, Horatio.—The stage name of Jem Larkins. —" With the double view of guarding against the discovery of friends or employers, and enhancing the interest of an assumed character, by attaching a high-sounding name to its representative, these geniuses assume fictitious names which are not the least amusing part of the play-bill of a private theartre."—(*See* **Larkins, Jem.**)—*Sketches by Boz* (Private Theatres).

Sullivan, Mrs.—A resident of Seven Dials. Quarrelled with Sarah.—*Sketches by Boz* (The Streets—Night).

Summerson, Esther.—The daughter of Lady Dedlock, but who was unaware of her parentage.—" I was brought up from my earliest remembrance—like some of the princesses in the fairy stories, only I was not charming—by my godmother."—*Bleak House.*

Superintendent, Mr.—A police official who accompanied the Uncommercial Traveller to the haunts of Jack ashore.—" In Mr. Superintendent I saw, as anybody might, a tall, well-looking, well-set-up man, of a soldierly bearing, with a cavalry air, a good chest, and a resolute, but not by any means ungentle face."—*The Uncommercial Traveller* (Poor Mercantile Jack).

Susan.—Servant to Mrs. Mann, the workhouse matron. —*Oliver Twist.*

Sweedlepipe, Paul.—A barber and bird-fancier.—" He was a little elderly man, with a clammy cold right hand, from which even rabbits and birds could not remove the smell of shaving soap. He wore in his sporting character a velveteen coat, a great deal of blue stocking, ankle boots, a neckerchief of some bright colour, and a very tall hat. Pursuing his more quiet occupation of a barber, he generally subsided into an apron, not over clean; a flannel jacket; and corduroy knee-shorts."—*Martin Chuzzlewit.*

Sweeney, Mrs.—A laundress of Gray's Inn.—" The genuine laundress is an institution, not to be had in its entirety out of and away from the genuine chambers. Again, it is not to be denied that you may be robbed elsewhere. Elsewhere you may have—for money—dishonesty, drunkenness, dirt, laziness and profound incapacity. But the veritable, shining red-faced, shameless laundress; the true Mrs. Sweeney; in figure, colour, texture, and smell, like the old damp family umbrella; the tip-top complicated abomination of stockings, spirits, bonnet, limpness, looseness and larceny, is only to be drawn at the fountain-head. Mrs. Sweeney is beyond the reach of individual art. It requires the united efforts of several men to ensure that great result, and it is only developed in perfection under an Honourable Society and in an Inn of Court."—*The Uncommercial Traveller* (Chambers).

Sweet William.—A travelling showman.—"A silent gentleman, who earned his living by showing tricks upon the cards; and who had rather deranged the natural expression of his countenance by putting small leaden lozenges into his eyes, and bringing them out by his mouth, which was one of his professional accomplishments; probably as a pleasant satire upon his ugliness, was called Sweet William."—*The Old Curiosity Shop*.

Swidger, William.—The keeper of the institution where Mr. Redlaw, the haunted man, lectured.—"A fresh-coloured busy man."—(*See* **Milly.**)—*The Haunted Man.*

Swidger, Philip.—Father of William.—"Such a many of us Swidgers—why there's my father, sir, superannuated Keeper and Custodian of this Institution—eighty-seven year old—He's a Swidger."—*The Haunted Man.*

Swidger, Mrs. (deceased).—Wife of old Philip.—*The Haunted Man.*

Swidger, George.—A ne'er-do-well brother of William.—"Redlaw paused at his bedside, and looked down on the figure that was stretched upon the mattress. It was that of a man who should have been in the vigour of his life, but on whom it was not likely the sun would ever shine again."—*The Haunted Man.*

Swidger, Charley, Junior.—Nephew of Mrs. William Swidger.—"Mrs. William may be taken off her balance by water; as at Battersea, when rowed into the piers by her young nephew Charley Swidger, Junior, aged twelve, which had no idea of boats whatever."—*The Haunted Man.*

Swillenhausen, Baron von.—The father of the lady of Grogzwig.—*Nicholas Nickleby.*

Swillenhausen, Baroness von.—The mother of the lady of Grogzwig.—*Nicholas Nickleby.*

Swills, Little.—A comic vocalist at the Sols Arms Harmonic Meetings.—" A chubby little man, in a large shirt-collar, with a moist eye and an inflamed nose."—*Bleak House.*

Swiveller, Dick.—The friend and tool of Fred Trent. —" His attire consisted of a brown body coat, with a great many brass buttons up the front, and only one behind; a bright check neckerchief; a plaid waistcoat; soiled white trousers; and a very limp hat, worn with the wrong side foremost to hide a hole in the brim."—*The Old Curiosity Shop.*

Swiveller, Rebecca.—Aunt of Dick Swiveller, who left him an annuity.—" If you had been another sort of nephew, you would have come into possession (so says the Will and I see no reason to doubt it) of five-and-twenty thousand pounds; as it is, you have fallen into an annuity of one hundred and fifty pounds a year, but I think I may congratulate you even upon that."—*The Old Curiosity Shop.*

Swosser, Captain.—The first husband of Mrs. Bayham Badger.—*Bleak House.*

Sylvia.—A girl who lived at Hoghton Towers.—*George Silverman's Explanation.*

Tabby.—Servant at Miss Griffin's school, called Mesrour in the Seraglio.—" We knew we could trust a grinning and good-natured soul called Tabby, who was the serving drudge of the house, and had no more figure than one of the beds; and upon whose face there was always more or less black lead. I slipped into Miss Bates' hand after supper a little note to that effect; dwelling on the black lead, as being in a manner deposited by the finger of Providence, pointing Tabby out for Mesrour, the celebrated chief of the Blacks of the Harem."—The Haunted House (*Christmas Stories*).

Tacker, Mr.—Chief assistant to Mr. Mould, the undertaker.—" An obese person; with his waistcoat in closer connection with his legs than is quite reconcilable with the established idea of grace; with that cast of feature which is figuratively called the bottle-nose; and with a face covered all over with pimples. He had been a tender plant once upon a time; but from constant blowing in the fat atmosphere of funerals, had run to seed."—*Martin Chuzzlewit.*

Tackleton.—A toy merchant.—" Tackleton the toy merchant, pretty generally known as Gruff and Tackleton —for that was the firm, though Gruff had been bought out long ago, only leaving his name, and as some said his nature according to its dictionary meaning, in the business —Tackleton the toy merchant was a man whose vocation had been quite misunderstood by his parents and guardians."—*The Cricket on the Hearth.*

Tadger, Mr.—A member of the Brick Lane Branch of the United Grand Junction Ebenezer Temperance Association.—" A little emphatic man with a bald head and drab shorts who answered to the name of Brother Tadger."—*Pickwick Papers.*

Tamaroo.—The name the boarders gave to an old woman engaged as a maid-of-all work at Todgers' boarding-house.—" She was a very little old woman, and always wore a very coarse apron, with a bib before and a loop behind; together with bandages on her wrists, which appeared to be afflicted with an everlasting sprain. She was on all occasions chary of opening the street-door; and ardent to shut it again; and she waited at table in a bonnet." —*Martin Chuzzlewit.*

Tangle, Mr., K.C.—One of the counsel in the Jarndyce Chancery suit.—" A large advocate with great whiskers; a little voice; and an interminable brief. Mr. Tangle knows more of Jarndyce and Jarndyce than anybody. He is famous for it,—supposed never to have read anything else since he left school."—*Bleak House.*

Tape.—The fairy godmother of Prince Bull.—" She was a fairy this Tape, and was a bright red all over; she was disgustingly prim and formal, and could never bend herself a hair's breadth this way or that way out of her naturally crooked shape; but she was very potent in her wicked art."—*Prince Bull* (A Fairy Tale) (Reprinted Pieces).

Tapkins, Mrs.—One of the callers at Mr. Boffin's new house.—" All the world and his wife and daughters leave cards. Sometimes the world's wife has so many daughters, that her card reads rather like a miscellaneous lot at an auction, comprising Mrs. Tapkins, Miss Tapkins, Miss Frederica Tapkins, Miss Antonia Tapkins, Miss Malvina Tapkins, and Miss Euphemia Tapkins; at the same time, the same lady leaves a card of Mrs. Henry George Alfred Swoshle *née* Tapkins; also a card Mrs. Tapkins at Home Wednesdays, Music, Portland Place."—*Our Mutual Friend.*

Tapley, Mark.—The jovial chief hostler at the Blue Dragon.—" He was a young fellow of some five or six-and-twenty perhaps, and was dressed in such a free and fly-away fashion, that the ends of his loose red neckcloth were streaming out behind him quite as often as before. He turned a whimsical face and a very merry pair of blue eyes on Mr. Pinch. Lord bless you, sir, said Mark, you don't half know me though. I don't believe there ever was a man as could come out so strong under circumstances that would make other men miserable, as I could if I could only get a chance."—*Martin Chuzzlewit.*

Taplin, Harry.—A singer with whom Miss Martin, the ambitious milliner, attempted to sing a duet called " The Time of Day."—" The comic gentleman was all smiles and blandness; he had composed a duet expressly for the occasion, and Miss Martin should sing it with him."—*Sketches by Boz* (The Mistaken Milliner).

Tappertit, Simon.—Apprentice to Gabriel Varden, locksmith. His vanity and conceit led him into bad company, and he took a leading part in the Gordon riots. —" Sim, as he was called in the locksmith's family, or Mr. Simon Tappertit, as he called himself, and required all men to style him out of doors, on holidays, and Sundays out, was an old-fashioned, thin-faced, sleek-haired, sharp-nosed, small-eyed, little fellow; very little, not more than five feet high, and thoroughly convinced in his own mind that he was above the middle size, rather tall in fact than otherwise . . . he had also some majestic shadowy ideas, which had never been fathomed by his intimate friends, concerning the power of his eye, indeed he had been known to go so far as to boast that he could utterly quell and subdue the haughtiest beauty by a simple process, which he termed 'eyeing her over.' . . . It may be inferred from these premises that in the small body of Mr. Tappertit there was locked up an ambitious and aspiring soul. . . . He was in years just twenty, in his looks much older; and in conceit at least two hundred."—*Barnaby Rudge.*

Tappleton, Lieutenant.—Dr. Slammer's second, in proposed duel with Mr. Winkle.—" A portly personage in a braided surtout."—*Pickwick Papers.*

Tartar, Bob.—The head boy at the grammar school. —" His father was in the West Indies, and he owned himself that his father was worth millions."—*The Schoolboy's Story* (Reprinted Pieces).

Tartar, Lieutenant.—A neighbour of Neville Landless in Staple Inn.—" A handsome gentleman, with a young face, but with an older figure in its robustness and its breadth of shoulder; say a man of eight-and-twenty, or at the most thirty; so extremely sunburnt, that the contrast between his brown visage and the white forehead, shaded out of doors by his hat, and the glimpses of white throat below the neckerchief, would have been almost ludicrous, but for his broad temples, bright blue eyes, clustering brown hair, and laughing teeth."—*Edwin Drood.*

Tatham, Mrs.—A pawnbroker's customer.—" An old sallow-looking woman, who has been leaning, with both arms on the counter, with a small bundle before her, for half an hour."—*Sketches by Boz* (The Pawnbroker's Shop).

Tatt, Mr.—A friend of Inspector Wield.—" A gentleman formerly in the public line, quite an amateur detective in his way, and very much respected."—*Three Detective Anecdotes* (Reprinted Pieces).

Tattycoram.—A foundling named Harriet Beadle (Pet's maid) known in the Meagles' household as Tattycoram.—" A handsome girl, with lustrous dark hair and eyes, and very neatly dressed. . . . Harriet we changed into Hattey, and then into Tatty. . . . The originator of the Institution for these poor foundlings having been a blessed creature of the name of Coram, we gave that name to Pet's little maid. At one time she was Tatty, and at one time she was Coram, until we got into a way of mixing the two names together, and now she is always Tattycoram."—*Little Dorrit.*

Taunton, Captain.—An army officer who took an interest in Richard Doubledick.—" The Captain of Richard

Doubledick's Company was a young gentleman not above five years his senior, whose eyes had an expression in them which affected Private Richard Doubledick in a very remarkable way. They were bright, handsome, dark eyes —what are called laughing eyes generally; and when serious rather steady than severe—but they were the only eyes now left in this narrowed world that Private Richard Doubledick could not stand. Unabashed by evil report and punishment, defiant of everything else and everybody else, he had but to know that those eyes looked at him for a moment, and he felt ashamed."—The Seven Poor Travellers (*Christmas Stories*).

Taunton, Mrs.—Mother of Captain Taunton.—" It was a Sunday evening and the lady sat at her quiet garden window reading the Bible."—The Seven Poor Travellers (*Christmas Stories*).

Taunton, Mrs.—One of the party on the Steam Excursion.—" A good-looking widow of fifty, with the form of a giantess and the mind of a child. The pursuit of pleasure; and some means of killing time, were the sole end of her existence."—*Sketches by Boz* (The Steam Excursion).

Taunton, The Misses Emily and Sophia.—Daughters of Mrs. Taunton.—" She doted on her daughters, who were as frivolous as herself."—*Sketches by Boz* (The Steam Excursion).

Taylor, Jemmy, of Southwark.—A miser whose biography Mr. Boffin pretended to be interested in.—*Our Mutual Friend.*

Taylor, Mr.—A Boston seamen's missionary.—" Mr. Taylor addresses himself peculiarly to seamen, and was once a mariner himself. He looked a weather-beaten, hard-featured man, of about six or eight-and-fifty, with deep lines graven as it were into his face, dark hair, and a stern keen eye."—*American Notes.*

Tellson and Company.—A banking house in London with French connections.—" Tellson's Bank of Temple Bar was an old-fashioned place, even in the year one thousand seven hundred and eighty. . . . Cramped in all kinds of dim cupboards and hutches at Tellson's, the oldest of men carried on the business gravely. When they took a young man into Tellson's London House, they hid him somewhere till he was old. They kept him in a dark place, like a cheese, till he had the full Tellson flavour and blue mould upon him. Then only was he permitted to be seen, spectacularly poring over large books, and casting his breeches and gaiters into the general weight of the establishment."—*A Tale of Two Cities.*

Testator, Mr.—The tenant of a set of London chambers.—"This was a man who, though not more than thirty, had seen the world in divers irreconcilable capacities; had been an officer in a South American regiment among other odd things; but had not achieved much in any way of life, and was in debt and in hiding."—*The Uncommercial Traveller* (Chambers).

Tetterby, Adolphus.—A struggling newsvendor—father of a large family.—"The small man who sat in the small parlour, making fruitless attempts to read his newspaper peaceably in the midst of this disturbance, was the father of the family, and the chief of the firm described in the inscription over the little shop front by the name and title of—A. Tetterby and Co., Newsmen—indeed, strictly speaking, he was the only personage answering to that designation, as Co. was a mere poetical abstraction altogether baseless and impersonal."—*The Haunted Man.*

Tetterby, Mrs. Sophia.—Wife of Adolphus Tetterby, whom he referred to as "my little woman."—"The process of induction by which Mr. Tetterby had come to the conclusion that his wife was a little woman, was his own secret. She would have made two editions of himself very easily, considered as an individual. She was rather remarkable for being robust and portly, but considered with reference to her husband, her dimensions became magnificent."—*The Haunted Man.*

Tetterby and Co.—The firm name under which Adolphus Tetterby carried on business.—"Tetterby's was the corner shop in Jerusalem Buildings; Tetterby's had tried its hand at several things; it had once made a feeble little dart at the toy business . . . it had made a move in the millinery direction . . . it had fancied that a living might be hidden in the tobacco trade . . . time had been when it put a forlorn trust in imitative jewellery . . . in short Tetterby's had tried so hard to get a livelihood out of Jerusalem Buildings in one way or other, and appeared to have done so indifferently in all, that the best position in the firm was too evidently Co.'s; Co. as a bloodless creation being untroubled with the vulgar inconveniences of hunger and thirst; being chargeable neither to the poor rates nor the assessed taxes; and having no young family to provide for."—*The Haunted Man.*

Tetterby, Johnny.—One of the seven sons of Adolphus Tetterby.—"Another little boy—the biggest there but still little—was tottering to and fro, bent on one side, and considerably affected in his knees, by the weight of a large baby, which he was supposed, by a fiction that obtains sometimes in sanguine families, to be hushing to sleep."—*The Haunted Man.*

Tetterby, Sally.—Youngest child of Adolphus Tetterby.—"Tetterby's baby was as well known in the neighbourhood as the postman or the pot boy. It roved from door-step to door-step in the arms of little Johnny Tetterby, and lagged heavily at the rear of troops of juveniles, who followed the tumblers or the monkey, and came up all on one side a little too late for everything that was attractive, from Monday morning till Saturday night."—*The Haunted Man.*

Tetterby, Adolphus, Junior.—Son of Mr. Tetterby.—"Master Adolphus was also in the newspaper line of life, being employed, by a more thriving firm than his father and Co., to vend newspapers at a railway station, where his chubby little person, like a shabbily disguised cupid, and his shrill little voice (he was not much more than ten years old) were as well known as the hoarse panting of the locomotives."—*The Haunted Man.*

Theophile, Corporal.—A soldier billeted in a French town—"A smart figure of a man of thirty, perhaps, a thought under the middle size, but very neatly made—a sunburnt Corporal with a brown peaked beard—faced about at the moment, addressing voluble words of instruction to the squad on hand. Nothing was amiss or awry about the Corporal, a lithe and nimble Corporal quite complete from the sparkling dark eyes under his knowing uniform cap to his sparkling white gaiters."—Somebody's Luggage (*Christmas Stories*).

Thingummy.—The doctor's name for old Sally who was present when Oliver's mother died.—"The pale face of a young woman was raised feebly from the pillow, and a faint voice imperfectly articulated the words, Let me see the child and die. . . . The surgeon deposited it in her arms. . . . They talked of hope and comfort; they had been strangers too long. It's all over, Mrs. Thingummy, said the surgeon at last. Ah, poor dear, so it is, said the nurse."—*Oliver Twist.*

Thomas.—A groom in Sir Leicester Dedlock's service. —*Bleak House.*

Thomas.—Mr. Mortimer Knag's shop-boy.—" Past ten, said Mr. Knags; Thomas, close the warehouse, Thomas was a boy nearly half as tall as a shutter, and the warehouse was a shop about the size of three hackney coaches." —*Nicholas Nickleby.*

Thomas.—A waiter at the Winglebury Arms.—" The waiter pulled down the window-blind and then pulled it up again—for a regular waiter must do something before he leaves a room—adjusted the glasses on the sideboard, brushed a place that was not dusty, rubbed his hands very hard, walked stealthily to the door, and evaporated."—*Sketches by Boz* (The Great Winglebury Duel).

Thomas.—The pastry-cook who supplied refreshments for the private theatrical party at Rose Villa.—*Sketches by Boz* (Mrs. Joseph Porter).

Thomson, Harry.—A friend whom Captain Waters recognised amongst the bathers at Ramsgate.—*Sketches by Boz* (The Tuggses at Ramsgate).

Thomson, Tally-ho.—A criminal.—" Tally-ho Thomson was a famous horse-stealer, couper, and magsman."—*The Detective Police* (Reprinted Pieces).

Thurtell, Mr.—A frequenter of Doncaster races.—The Lazy Tour of Two Idle Apprentices (*Christmas Stories*).

Tibbs, Mrs.—A London boarding-house keeper.—" Mrs. Tibbs was, beyond all dispute, the most tidy, fidgety, thrifty little personage that ever inhaled the smoke of London; and the house of Mrs. Tibbs was decidedly the neatest in all Great Coram Street. . . . There were meat-safe-looking blinds in the parlour windows; blue and gold curtains in the drawing-room, and spring-roller blinds, as Mrs. Tibbs was wont in the pride of her heart to boast, 'all the way up'; the bell lamp in the passage looked as clear as a soap bubble; you could see yourself in all the tables and French polish yourself in any one of the chairs; the banisters were beeswaxed, and the very stair wires made your eyes wink, they were so glittering."—*Sketches by Boz* (The Boarding House).

Tibbs, Mr.—Husband of Mrs. Tibbs.—" Mrs. Tibbs was somewhat short of stature; and Mr. Tibbs was by no means a large man. He had moreover very short legs; but, by way of indemnification, his face was peculiarly long; he was to his wife what the 0 is in 90—he was of some importance with her, he was nothing without her. Mrs. Tibbs was always talking; Mr. Tibbs rarely spoke; but if it were at any time possible to put in a word when he should have said nothing at all, he had that talent."—*Sketches by Boz* (The Boarding House).

Tickit, Mrs.—Housekeeper at Mr. Meagles' cottage.—" A certain Mrs. Tickit, who was cook and housekeeper when the family were at home, and housekeeper only when the family were away, completed the establishment."—*Little Dorrit.*

Tickle, Mr.—A member of the Mudfog Association.—*The Mudfog Sketches.*

Tiddypot, Mr.—A vestryman.—" Mr. Tiddypot of Gumtion House."—*Our Vestry* (Reprinted Pieces).

Tiffey.—A clerk with Spenlow and Jorkins.—" A little dry man, who wore a stiff brown wig, that looked as if it were made of gingerbread."—*David Copperfield.*

Tigg, Montague.—An adventurer.—" The gentleman was of that order of appearance which is currently termed shabby-genteel, though in respect of his dress he can hardly be said to have been in any extremities, as his fingers were a long way out of his gloves, and the soles of his feet were at an inconvenient distance from the upper leather of his boots. He was very dirty, and very jaunty; very bold, and very mean; very swaggering, and very slinking; very much like a man who might have been something better, and unspeakably like a man who deserved to be something worse."—*Martin Chuzzlewit.*

Tiggin and Whelps.—The employers of the Bagman's uncle.—" Tiggin and Whelps were in the printed calico and waistcoat piece line."—*Pickwick Papers.*

Timberhed, Mr.—A Vice-President of the Statistical Section of the Mudfog Association.—*The Mudfog Sketches.*

Timberry, Mr. Snittle.—An actor who presided at the farewell stage dinner to Mr. and Mrs. Crummles, on the eve of their emigrating.—" At length Mr. Snittle Timberry rose, in the most approved attitude, with one hand in the breast of his waistcoat, and the other on the nearest snuff-box, and having been received with great enthusiasm, proposed, with abundance of quotations, his friend Mr. Vincent Crummles."—*Nicholas Nickleby.*

Timkins.—A candidate for the office of Beadle.—" Timkins' success was considered certain; several mothers of families half promised their votes, and the nine small children would have run over the course, but for the production of another placard announcing the appearance of a still more meritorious candidate—Spruggins for Beadle—ten small children (two of them twins) *and* a wife. There was no resisting this. The other candidates, Bung alone excepted, resigned in despair."—*Sketches by Boz* (Our Parish).

Timson, Rev. Charles.—A friend of Mr. Parsons, introduced to Mr. Tottle.—" Here, I hate ceremony, you know—Timson, that's Tottle; Tottle, that's Timson; bred for the church, which I fear will never be bread for him, and he chuckled at the old joke."—*Sketches by Boz* (A Passage in the Life of Mr. Watkins Tottle).

Tinker.—A tramp, who visited the hermit at Tom Tiddler's Ground, along with Mr. Traveller.—" The moral with which the Tinker dismissed the subject was that he said, in his trade, that metal that rotted for want of use had better be left to rot, and couldn't rot too soon, considering how much true metal rotted from over use and hard service."—Tom Tiddler's Ground (*Christmas Stories*).

Tinker, Mr.—Valet to Mr. Dorrit.—*Little Dorrit.*

Tinkling, William.—(aged eight).—The Editor of the *Holiday Romance* (Holiday Romance).

Tiny Tim.—Cripple child of Bob Cratchit.—" Alas for Tiny Tim, he bore a little crutch, and had his limbs supported by an iron frame . . . as good as gold, said Bob. Somehow he gets thoughtful, sitting by himself so much, and thinks the strangest things you ever heard. He told me coming home that he hoped the people saw him in the church, because he was a cripple, and it might be pleasant to them to remember upon Christmas day, Who made lame beggars walk, and blind men to see."—*A Christmas Carol.*

Tip.—The Marshalsea name of Edward Dorrit, Amy's brother.—" His name was Edward, and Ted had been transformed into Tip within the walls. Tip tired of everything. Whatever Tip went into, he came out tired, announcing that he had cut it. Wherever he went, this foredoomed Tip appeared to take the prison walls with him, and to set them up in such trade or calling; and to growl about within their narrow limits, in the old slip-shod, purposeless, down-at-heel way; until the real immovable Marshalsea walls asserted their fascination over him, and brought him back."—*Little Dorrit.*

Tipkisson.—An elector.—" Our honourable friend being come into the presence of his constituents, and having professed with great suavity that he was delighted to see his good friend Tipkisson there in his working dress—his good friend Tipkisson being an inveterate saddler, who alway opposes him, and for whom he has a mortal hatred." —*Our Honourable Friend* (Reprinted Pieces).

Tipp.—The carman at Murdstone and Grinby's.—(*See* **Gregory.**)—*David Copperfield.*

Tippin Family.—Musicians at Ramsgate concert-room. —" The talented Mrs. Tippin, having condescendingly acknowledged the clapping of hands and shouts of bravo which greeted her appearance, proceeded to sing the popular cavatina of ' Bid me Discourse '—accompanied on the piano by Mr. Tippin; after which Mr. Tippin sang a comic song, accompanied on the piano by Mrs. Tippin; the applause consequent upon which was only to be exceeded by the enthusiastic approbation bestowed upon an air with variations on the guitar by Miss Tippin, accompanied on the chin by Master Tippin."—*Sketches by Boz* (The Tuggses at Ramsgate).

Tippins, Lady.—A frequent guest at Veneering's dinner-parties.—" Charming old Lady Tippins on Veneering's right; with an immense, obtuse, drab, oblong face, like a face in a table-spoon, and a dyed Long Walk up the top of her head, as a convenient public approach to the bunch of false hair behind."—*Our Mutual Friend.*

Tisher, Mrs.—Companion and assistant of Miss Twinkleton at the Nuns' House.—" A deferential widow, with a weak back, a chronic sigh, and a suppressed voice; who looks after the young ladies' wardrobes, and leads them to infer that she has seen better days."—*Edwin Drood.*

Titbull, Sampson.—The founder of almshouses in the east of London.—" Of Titbull I know no more than that he deceased in 1723; that his Christian name was Sampson; and his social designation esquire; and that he founded these almshouses, as dwellings for nine poor women and six poor men, by his will and testament."—*The Uncommercial Traveller* (Titbull's Almshouses).

Tix, Tom.—A broker's man who was put in possession at Madame Mantalini's.—" A little man in brown very much the worse for wear, who brought with him a mingled fumigation of stale tobacco and fresh onions."—*Nicholas Nickleby.*

Toby.—Gabriel Varden's beer jug.—" There was also a goodly jug of well-browned clay, fashioned into the form of an old gentleman, not by any means unlike the locksmith, atop of whose bald head was a fine white froth, answering to his wig, indicative beyond dispute of sparkling home brewed ale. . . . This Toby was the brown jug of which previous mention has been made. Applying his lips to the worthy old gentleman's benevolent forehead, the locksmith, who had all this time been ravaging among the eatables, kept them there so long, at the same time raising the vessel slowly in the air, that at length Toby stood on his head upon his nose, when he smacked his lips and set him on the table again with fond reluctance."—*Barnaby Rudge.*

Toby.—One of Jerry's dogs who had once been Short's. —" I've got an animal here, said Jerry,—putting his hand into the capacious pocket of his coat, and diving into one corner as if he were feeling for a small orange or an apple, or some such article—a animal here wot I think you know something of, Short. Ah, cried Short, let's have a look at him. Here he is, said Jerry, producing a little terrier from his pocket. He was once a Toby of yours."—*The Old Curiosity Shop*.

Toddles and Poddles.—Two of the three minders kept by Miss Betty Higden.—" Toddles was the pet name of the boy, Poddles of the girl. At their little unsteady pace, they came across the floor hand in hand, as if they were traversing an extremely difficult road, intersected by brooks."—*Our Mutual Friend*.

Todd's Young Man.—An assistant shopkeeper who conversed with the maids in the early morning.—" Mr Todd's young man tries to whistle coolly, as he goes back to his shop much faster than he came from it; and the two girls run back to their respective places, and shut their street doors with surprising softness, each of them poking heads out of the front parlour window a minute afterwards, however, ostensibly with the view of looking at the mail which just then passes by, but really for the purpose of catching another glimpse of Mr. Todd's young man, who being fond of mails, but more of females, takes a short look at the mail, and a long look at the girls, much to the satisfaction of all parties concerned."—*Sketches by Boz* (The Streets—Morning).

Toddyhigh, Joe.—A boyhood's friend of the Lord Mayor elect.—" The strange man was not over and above well dressed, and was very far from being fat or rich looking, in any sense of the word; yet he spoke with a kind of modest confidence, and assumed an easy gentlemanly sort of an air, to which nobody but a rich man can lawfully presume."—*Master Humphrey's Clock*.

Todgers.—A boarding-house in London where Mr. Pecksniff and his daughters resided.—" Mrs. Todgers' commercial boarding-house was a house of that sort which is likely to be dark at any time; but that morning it was especially dark. There was an odd smell in the passage, as if the concentrated essence of all the dinners that had been cooked in the kitchen since the house was built lingered at the top of the kitchen stairs; in particular there was a sensation of cabbage, as if all the greens that had ever been boiled there were evergreens, and flourished in immortal strength."—*Martin Chuzzlewit*.

Todgers, Mrs.—Proprietrix of the Commercial Boarding-house.—" Mrs. Todgers was a lady, rather a bony and hard-featured lady, with a row of curls in front of her head, shaped like little barrels of beer, and on the top of it something made of net—you couldn't call it a cap exactly—which looked like a black cobweb. She had a little basket on her arm, and in it a bunch of keys jingled as she came." —*Martin Chuzzlewit.*

Tollimglower, Lady.—A friend of her youth referred to by old Mrs. Wardle at Bella Wardle's wedding.—" The worthy old soul launched forth into a minute and particular account of her own wedding, with a dissertation on the fashion of wearing high-heeled shoes, and some particulars concerning the life and adventures of the beautiful Lady Tollimglower deceased."—*Pickwick Papers.*

Tom.—Husband of the sister of Daniel Peggotty. Father of Little Emily.—*David Copperfield.*

Tom.—A police officer who arrested William Warden. —*Sketches by Boz* (The Drunkard's Death).

Tom.—Serving-man at Mr. Gattleton's, who assisted at the private theatricals.—" When the revolt takes place Tom must keep rushing in on one side and out on the other, with a pickaxe, as fast as he can; the effect will be electrical; it will look exactly as if there were an immense number of 'em.—*Sketches by Boz* (Mrs. Joseph Porter).

Tom.—The clerk at the general agency office where Nicholas sought a situation.—" He found himself in a little floorclothed room, with a high desk railed off in one corner, behind which sat a lean youth with cunning eyes and a protruding chin."—*Nicholas Nickleby.*

Tom.—The young surgeon's message-boy.—" A corpulent round-headed boy who, in consideration of the sum of one shilling per week and his food, was let out by the parish to carry medicine and messages."—*Sketches by Boz* (The Black Veil).

Tom.—An assistant to Mr. Mould, the undertaker.—*Martin Chuzzlewit.*

Tom.—A lazy artist.—" My words are well known. I am a young man in the art line. I am a young man of that easy disposition that I lie abed till it's absolutely necessary to get up and earn something, and then I lie abed again till I have spent it."—Somebody's Luggage (*Christmas Stories*).

Tom.—The engine-driver of a train which ran over and killed a signalman.—The Signalman (*Christmas Stories*).

Tom.—Mr. Wardle's coachman.—*Pickwick Papers.*

Tom.—The driver of the Dover mail.—"The Dover mail was in its usual genial position, that the guard suspected the passengers, the passengers suspected one another and the guard, they all suspected everybody else, and the coachman was sure of nothing but the horses."—*A Tale of Two Cities.*

Tom.—Cousin of Captain Boldheart.—"Only one disagreeable incident occurred. Captain Boldheart found himself obliged to put his cousin Tom in irons for being disrespectful. On the boy's promising amendment, however, he was humanely released after a few hours' close confinement."—*Holiday Romance.*

Tom, Captain.—One of Mr. Jaggers' clients, whom Pip met when he visited Newgate with Wemmick.—*Great Expectations.*

Tomkinley, Mr.—A teacher who took Abel Garland to Margate.—"He went to Margate one Saturday, with Mr. Tomkinley, that had been a teacher at the school he went to, and came back upon the Monday; but he was very ill after that."—*The Old Curiosity Shop.*

Tomkins, Miss.—A pupil at the Bury St. Edmunds girls' school.—*Pickwick Papers.*

Tomlinson, Mrs.—A guest at the Rochester Charity Ball.—"Mrs. Tomlinson, the post-office keeper, seemed by mutual consent to have been chosen the leader of the trade party."—*Pickwick Papers.*

Tommy.—A waterman.—"A strange specimen of the human race, in a sackcloth coat, and apron of the same, who, with a brass label and number round his neck, looked as if he were catalogued in some collection of rarities. This was the waterman."—*Pickwick Papers.*

Tommy.—One of the company present in the bar parlour frequented by Mr. Rogers.—" A little greengrocer, with a chubby face."—*Sketches by Boz* (The Parlour Orator).

Tompkins.—A pupil at Dotheboys Hall.—*Nicholas Nickleby.*

Tompkins, Mr. Alfred.—" Mr. Tompkins was a clerk in a wine house; he was a connoisseur in paintings, and had a wonderful eye for the picturesque."—*Sketches by Boz* (The Boarding House).

Toodle, Mrs. Polly.—Wife of an engine-driver, who, after Mrs. Dombey's death, became foster-mother to Paul.—" A plump, rosy-cheeked, wholesome apple-faced young woman."—*Dombey and Son.*

Toodle, Mr.—The husband of Polly (Mrs. Richards), Paul Dombey's foster-mother.—*Dombey and Son.*

Toodle, Robin.—The eldest boy of Polly Toodle. Nominated by Mr. Dombey as a foundationer in the school by the Charitable Grinders and afterwards referred to as Rob the Grinder. Ran away from school. Employed by Carker as a spy upon Florence Dombey; ultimately became a page to Miss Tox.—*Dombey and Son.*

Toogellem, The Hon. Clementina.—Second wife of the fifteenth Earl of Stiltstalking.—*Little Dorrit.*

Toorell, Doctor.—President of the Medical Section of the Mudfog Association.—*The Mudfog Sketches.*

Tootle, Tom.—A customer at the Fellowship Porters tavern.—*Our Mutual Friend.*

Tootleum Boots.—Mrs. Lemon's baby.—*Holiday Romance.*

Toots, Mr.—A pupil at Dr. Blimber's. The friend of Paul Dombey, and admirer of his sister Florence; a kind-hearted youth of independent means, who ultimately married Susan Nipper.—"One young gentleman, with a swollen nose and an excessively large head (the oldest of the ten who had gone through everything) suddenly left off blowing one day, and remained in the establishment a mere stalk; and people did say that the Doctor had rather overdone it with young Toots, and that, when he began to have whiskers, he left off having brains." —*Dombey and Son.*

Tope, Mr.—Verger at Cloisterham Cathedral.—"Mr. Tope, chief verger and showman, and accustomed to be high with excursion parties."—*Edwin Drood.*

Tope, Mrs.—Wife of Mr. Tope.—"Christmas Eve in Cloisterham. . . Mr. and Mrs. Tope are daintily sticking sprigs of holly into the carvings and sconces of the Cathedral stalls, as if they were sticking them into the coat-buttonholes of the dean and the chapter."—*Edwin Drood.*

Topper, Mr.—A guest at Fred Scrooge's Christmas dinner.—"Topper had clearly got his eye upon one of Scrooge's niece's sisters, for he answered that a bachelor was a wretched outcast."—*A Christmas Carol.*

Toppit, Miss.—A literary lady introduced to Elijah Pogram by Mrs. Hominy.—"Wore a brown wig of uncommon size."—*Martin Chuzzlewit.*

Topsawyer, Mr.—A mythical personage whom a waiter at the Yarmouth inn mentioned to David when he dined there on his way to school in order to induce him to hand over his tankard of ale.—"There was a gentleman here yesterday, he said, a stout gentleman of the name of Topsawyer. . . . He came in here, said the waiter,—looking at the light through the tumbler,—ordered a glass of this ale,—*would* order it. I told him not—drank it—and fell dead. It was too old for him. It oughtn't to be drawn, that's the fact."—*David Copperfield.*

Tott.—A non-commissioned officer, whose widow (known as Mrs. Belltott) was Miss Maryon's maid at Silver Store. —The Perils of Certain English Travellers (*Christmas Stories*).

Tottle, Watkins.—An impecunious bachelor.—"Mr. Watkins Tottle was a rather uncommon compound of strong uxorious inclinations, and an unparalleled degree of anteconnubial timidity. He was about fifty years of age; stood four feet six inches and three-quarters in his socks—for he never stood in stockings at all—plump, clean, and rosy. He lived on an annuity, which was well adapted to the individual who received it in one respect —it was rather small. He received it in periodical payments, on every alternate Monday; but he ran himself out about a day after the expiration of the first week, as regularly as an eight-day clock, and then, to make the comparison complete, his landlady wound him up, and he went on with a regular tick."—*Sketches by Boz* (A Passage in the Life of Mr. Watkins Tottle).

Towlinson.—Footman at Mr. Dombey's town house. Married Anne, the housemaid.—*Dombey and Son.*

Tox, Miss Lucretia.—The particular friend of Mrs. Chick, and a devoted admirer of Mr. Dombey.—"The lady thus specially presented was a long lean figure, wearing such a faded air, that she seemed not to have been made in what linen-drapers call fast colours originally; and to have, by little and little, washed out. But for this she might have been described as the very pink of general propitiation and politeness."—*Dombey and Son.*

Tox, Mrs.—Mother of Miss Tox.—"Sitting on the window seat, and looking out upon the sparrows and the blink of sun, Miss Tox thought likewise of her good mamma deceased . . . of her virtues and her rheumatism."—*Dombey and Son.*

Tox, Mr.—"Miss Tox sat down upon the window seat, and thought of her good papa deceased,—Mr. Tox of the Customs Department of the public service."—*Dombey and Son.*

Tozer.—A pupil at Dr. Blimber's.—"A solemn young gentleman, whose shirt collar curled up the lobes of his ears."—*Dombey and Son.*

Tozer, Mrs.—Mother of Tozer, one of Dr. Blimber's pupils.—"Tozer was constantly galled and tormented by a starched white cambric neckerchief, which he wore at the express desire of Mrs. Tozer, his parent, who, designing him for the church, was of opinion that he couldn't be in that forward state of preparation too soon."—*Dombey and Son.*

Trabb.—A master tailor.—"He was a prosperous old bachelor, and his open window looked into a prosperous little garden and orchard, and there was a prosperous iron safe let into the wall at the side of his fireplace, and I did not doubt that heaps of his prosperity were put away in it in bags."—*Great Expectations.*

Trabb's Boy.—The shop-boy of Mr. Trabb, the tailor. —" Mr. Trabb's boy was the most audacious boy in all that country side."—*Great Expectations.*

Traddles, Thomas.—A pupil at Salem House (afterwards a barrister, and ultimately a judge). The lifelong friend of David.—" Poor Traddles. In a tight sky-blue suit that made his arms and legs like German sausages or roly-poly puddings, he was the merriest and most miserable of all the boys. He was always being caned . . . and was always going to write to his uncle about it and never did. After laying his head on the desk for a little while, he would cheer up somehow, begin to laugh again, and draw skeletons all over his slate, before his eyes were dry. I used at first to wonder what comfort Traddles found in drawing skeletons, and for some time looked upon him as a sort of hermit, who reminded himself by those symbols of mortality that caning couldn't last for ever. But I believe he only did it because they were easy, and didn't want any features."—*David Copperfield.*

Trampfoot.—One of the three police officers who accompanied the police superintendent and the Uncommercial Traveller to the haunts of Jack ashore.—(*See* **Quickear.**) —*The Uncommercial Traveller* (Poor Mercantile Jack).

Traveller, Mr.—A visitor to Mopes the hermit.—" Mr. Traveller, having finished his breakfast, and paid his moderate score, walked out to the threshold of the ' Peal of Bells ' (inn), and, thence directed by the pointing finger of his host, he took himself toward the ruined hermitage of Mr. Mopes the hermit."—Tom Tiddler's Ground (*Christmas Stories*).

Travellers, The.—Passengers on board ship with Mr. Meagles and Arthur Clennam.—" The rest of the party were of the usual materials; travellers on business, and travellers for pleasure; officers from India on leave; merchants in the Greek and Turkey trades; a clerical English husband, in a meek strait-waistcoat, on a wedding trip with his young wife; a majestic English mamma and papa, of the patrician order, with a family of three growing-up daughters, who were keeping a journal for the confusion of their fellow-travellers; and a deaf old English mother, tough in travel, with a very decidedly grown-up daughter indeed, which daughter went sketching about the universe, in the expectation of ultimately toning herself off into the married state."—*Little Dorrit.*

Travellers, The Seven Poor.—The Watts Charity guests who dined at the Rochester Inn on Christmas Eve.—" Strictly speaking, there were only six poor travellers; but being a traveller myself, though an idle one, and being withal as poor as I hope to be, I brought the number up to seven."—The Seven Poor Travellers (*Christmas Stories*).

Traveller, The Second.—One of the Seven Poor Travellers.—" Secondly, a very decent man indeed, with his right arm in a sling, who had a certain clean agreeable smell of wood about him, from which I judged him to have something to do with shipbuilding."—The Seven Poor Travellers (*Christmas Stories*).

Traveller, The Third.—One of the Seven Poor Travellers.—" Thirdly, a little sailor-boy, a mere child, with a profusion of rich dark brown hair, and deep womanly-looking eyes."—The Seven Poor Travellers (*Christmas Stories*).

Traveller, The Fourth.—One of the Seven Poor Travellers.—" Fourthly, a shabby-genteel personage, in a threadbare black suit, and apparently in very bad circumstances; with a dry suspicious look; the absent buttons on his waistcoat eked out with red tape; and a bundle of extraordinarily tattered papers sticking out of an inner breast pocket."—The Seven Poor Travellers (*Christmas Stories*).

Traveller, The Fifth.—One of the Seven Poor Travellers.—" Fifthly, a foreigner by birth, but an Englishman in speech; who carried his pipe in the band of his hat, and lost no time in telling me, in an easy, simple engaging way, that he was a watchmaker from Geneva, and travelled all about the Continent, mostly on foot, working as a journeyman and seeing new countries—possibly (I thought) also smuggling a watch or so now and then."—The Seven Poor Travellers (*Christmas Stories*).

Traveller, The Sixth.—One of the Seven Poor Travellers.—" Sixthly, a little widow, who had been very pretty, and was still very young; but whose beauty had been wrecked in some great misfortune, and whose manner was remarkedly timid, scared, and solitary."—The Seven Poor Travellers (*Christmas Stories*).

Traveller, The Seventh.—One of the Seven Poor Travellers.—" Seventhly and lastly, a traveller of a kind familiar to my boyhood, but now almost obsolete—a book-pedlar, who had a quantity of pamphlets and numbers with him, and who presently boasted that he could repeat more verses in an evening than he could sell in a twelvemonth." —The Seven Poor Travellers (*Christmas Stories*).

Tredegar, John.—One of the old residents at the village of Laureau.—A Message from the Sea (*Christmas Stories*).

Tregarthen, Kitty.—Sweetheart of Alfred Raybrock.—" A prettier sweetheart the sun could not have shone upon, that shining day. . . . She wore neither hat nor bonnet, but merely a scarf or kerchief, folded squarely back over the head to keep the sun off—according to a fashion that may be sometimes seen in the more genial parts of England, as well as of Italy, and which is probably the first fashion of head-dress that came into the world, when grasses and leaves went out."—A Message from the Sea (*Christmas Stories*).

Tregarthen, Mr.—Father of Kitty.—" He was rather an infirm man, but could scarcely be called old yet; with an agreeable face, and a promising air of making the best of things."—A Message from the Sea (*Christmas Stories*).

Tremont House.—A Boston hotel.—" The hotel (a very excellent one) is called the Tremont House. It has more galleries, colonnades, piazzas, and passages than I can remember or the reader would believe."—*American Notes.*

Trent, Mr.—Grandfather of Little Nell, keeper of the Old Curiosity Shop.—" He was a little old man, with long grey hair. The haggard aspect of the little old man was wonderfully suited to the place; he might have groped among old churches, and tombs, and deserted houses, and gathered all the spoils with his own hands; there was nothing in the whole collection but was in keeping with himself—nothing that looked older or more worn than he." —*The Old Curiosity Shop.*

Trent, Fred.—Brother of Little Nell.—" He was a young man, of one-and-twenty or thereabouts, well made, and certainly handsome, though the expression of his face was far from prepossessing, having, in common with his manner and even his dress, a dissipated, insolent air which repelled one."—*The Old Curiosity Shop*.

Trent, Nelly.—Granddaughter of Mr. Trent.—(*See* **Little Nell.**)

Trent, Master Humphrey.—Younger brother of Little Nell's grandfather; known as the single gentleman.—"That friend,—single gentleman or younger brother, which you will,—had at his heart a heavy sorrow, but it bred in him no misanthropy or monastic gloom; he went forth into the world a lover of his kind."—*The Old Curiosity Shop*.

Tresham, Mrs. Beatrice.—Wife of Mr. Tresham, an early lover of Jackson's.—"A careworn woman like this, with her hair turned grey. Before him were the ashes of a dead fire that had once burned bright. This was the woman he had loved. This was the woman he had lost."—Mugby Junction (*Christmas Stories*).

Tresham, Mr.—The invalid husband of Beatrice, and father of Polly.—"There, stretched on a sofa, lay a sick man, sorely wasted, who covered his eyes with his emaciated hands."—Mugby Junction (*Christmas Stories*).

Tresham, Polly.—Child of Mr. and Mrs. Tresham.—Mugby Junction (*Christmas Stories*).

Trinkle, Mr.—An upholsterer in Cheapside.—*Three Detective Anecdotes* (Reprinted Pieces).

Trott, Alexander.—A young man who went to Winglebury to visit Emily Brown but eloped to Gretna Green with Julia Manners.—"Mr. Trott was a young man; had highly promising whiskers, an undeniable tailor, and an insinuating address."—*Sketches by Boz* (The Great Winglebury Duel).

Trotter, Job.—The accomplice of Jingle, who posed as his valet.—"A young fellow in mulberry-coloured livery."—*Pickwick Papers*.

Trottle.—The man who listened to Jarber's tale of the House to Let.—Going into Society (*Christmas Stories*).

Trotwood, Betsy.—Great-aunt of David Copperfield the younger. A strong-minded but kind-hearted lady who adopted David after he ran away from home upon his mother's second marriage to Mr. Murdstone.—" An aunt of my father's, and consequently a great aunt of mine, of whom I shall have more to relate by and by, was the principal magnate of our family. Miss Trotwood, or Miss Betsy, as my poor mother always called her, when she sufficiently overcame her dread of this formidable personage to mention her at all (which was seldom), had been married to a husband younger than herself, who was very handsome, except in the sense of the homely adage handsome is that handsome does . . . immediately upon the separation she took her maiden name again, bought a cottage in a hamlet on the sea-coast a long way off, established herself there as a single woman with one servant, and was understood to live secluded ever afterwards in an inflexible retirement."—*David Copperfield.*

Truck, Mr.—A Vice-President of the Mechanical Science Section of the Mudfog Association.—*The Mudfog Sketches.*

Truefitt.—A London hairdresser in the holiday season. —" At Mr. Truefitt's, the excellent hairdresser's, they are learning French to beguile the time."—*The Uncommercial Traveller* (Arcadian London).

Trundle, Mr.—A young man who married Isabella Wardle.—*Pickwick Papers.*

Tuckle, Mr.—Chairman at the Bath Footmen's Swarry. —" A stoutish gentleman, in a bright crimson coat with long tails, vividly red breeches, and a cocked hat."—*Pickwick Papers.*

Tugby.—The porter at Sir Joseph Bowley's. Married Mrs. Chickenstalker.—" Trotty had small difficulty in recognizing in the stout old lady Mrs. Chickenstalker, always inclined to corpulency even in the days when he had known her as established in the general line and having a small balance against him in her books. . . . The firm was Tugby late Chickenstalker."—*The Chimes.*

Tuggs, Joseph.—A London grocer who was left a fortune.—" Once upon a time there dwelt in a narrow street, on the Surrey side of the water, within three minutes' walk of

Old London Bridge, Mr. Joseph Tuggs,—a little dark-faced man, with shiny hair, twinkling eyes, short legs, and a body of very considerable thickness, measuring from the centre button of his waistcoat in front to the ornamental buttons of his coat behind. Mr. Joseph Tuggs was a grocer; it might be supposed that a grocer was beyond the reach of calumny; but no—the neighbours stigmatized him as a chandler; and the poisonous voice of envy distinctly asserted that he dispensed tea and coffee by the quartern, retailed sugar by the ounce; cheese by the slice; tobacco by the screw; and butter by the pat."—*Sketches by Boz* (The Tuggses at Ramsgate).

Tuggs, Mrs.—Wife of Joseph Tuggs.—"The figure of the amiable Mrs. Tuggs, if not perfectly symmetrical was decidedly comfortable."—*Sketches by Boz* (The Tuggses at Ramsgate).

Tuggs, Miss Charlotte.—Who called herself Charlotta. Daughter of Joseph Tuggs.—"The form of her only daughter Miss Charlotta Tuggs was fast ripening into that state of luxuriant plumpness which had enchanted the eyes, and captivated the heart, of Mr. Joseph Tuggs in his earlier days."—*Sketches by Boz* (The Tuggses at Ramsgate).

Tuggs, Simon.—Who called himself Cymon. Son of Joseph.—"Mr. Simon Tuggs, his only son, and Miss Charlotte Tuggs's only brother, was as differently formed in body, as he was differently constituted in mind, from the remainder of his family. Mr. Simon Tuggs kept his father's books and his own counsel."—*Sketches by Boz* (The Tuggses at Ramsgate).

Tulkinghorn, Mr.—The family lawyer of Sir Leicester Dedlock.—"An oyster of the old school, whom nobody can open. The old gentleman is rusty to look at, but is reputed to have made good thrift out of aristocratic marriage settlements, and aristocratic wills, and to be very rich. He is surrounded by a mysterious halo of family confidences, of which he is known to be the silent depository."—*Bleak House.*

Tulrumble, Nicholas.—A successful coal merchant; afterwards Mayor of Mudfog.—"Nicholas began life in a wooden tenement of four feet square, with a capital of two and ninepence, and a stock-in-trade of three bushels and a half of coals, exclusive of the large lump which hung by way of signboard outside; then he enlarged the shed and kept a truck; then he left the shed, and the truck too, and started a donkey, and a Mrs. Tulrumble; then he moved again and set up a cart; the cart was soon afterwards exchanged for a wagon; and so he went on—like his great predecessor, Whittington, only without a cat for a partner—increasing in wealth and fame, until at last he gave up business altogether, and retired with Mrs. Tulrumble and family to Mudfog Hall."—*The Mudfog Sketches.*

Tulrumble, Mrs.—Wife of the Mayor of Mudfog.—*The Mudfog Sketches.*

Tulrumble, Mr., Junior.—Son of the Mayor of Mudfog. —" Mr. Tulrumble junior took to smoking cigars and calling the footman a feller."—*The Mudfog Sketches.*

Tungay.—The porter at Salem House.—" A stout man with a bull neck, a wooden leg, overhanging temples, and his hair cut close all round his head. . . . I heard that, with the single exception of Mr. Creakle, Tungay considered the whole establishment, masters and boys, as his natural enemies, and that the only delight of his life was to be sour and malicious."—*David Copperfield.*

Tupman, Tracy.—Member of Pickwick Club.—" The too susceptible Tupman who, to the wisdom and experience of maturer years, superadded the enthusiasm and ardour of a boy, in the most interesting and pardonable of human weaknesses—love. Time and feeding had expanded that once romantic form; the black silk waistcoat had become more and more developed; inch by inch had the gold watch-chain beneath it disappeared from within the range of Tupman's vision, and gradually had the capacious chin encroached upon the borders of the white cravat; but the soul of Tupman had known no change—admiration of the fair sex was still its ruling passion."—*Pickwick Papers.*

Tupple, Mr.—A guest at Dobble's New Year Party.— " A junior clerk in the same office; a tidy sort of young man, with a tendency to cold and corns, who comes in a pair of boots with black cloth fronts, and brings his shoes in his coat pocket, which shoes he is at this very moment putting on in the hall."—*Sketches by Boz* (The New Year).

Turnstile.—The tailor of whom Mr. Augustus Cooper ordered a coat for the assembly.—" Mr. Augustus Cooper had ordered a new coat for the occasion,—a two pound tenner from Turnstile. It was his first appearance in public. As to Mr. Augustus Cooper's share in the quadrille, he got through it admirably; he was missing from his partner now and then certainly, and discovered on such occasions to be either dancing with laudable perseverance in another set, or sliding about in perspective without any definite object; but, generally speaking, they managed to shove him through the figure, until he turned up in the right place."—*Sketches by Boz* (The Dancing Academy).

Turveydrop, Mr. Prince.—A dancing master—married Caddy Jellyby.—" A little, blue-eyed, fair man, of youthful appearance, with flaxen hair parted in the middle, and curling at the ends all round his head; he had a little fiddle, which we used to call at school a kit, under his left arm, and its little bow in the same hand; his little dancing shoes were particularly diminutive, and he had a little innocent feminine manner. Young Mr. Turveydrop's name (said Caddy) is Prince; I wish it wasn't, because it sounds like a dog, but of course he didn't christen himself."—*Bleak House.*

Turveydrop, Mr.—The vain and selfish father of Prince. —" He was a fat old gentleman, with a false complexion, false teeth, false whiskers, and a wig. He was pinched in and swelled out, and got up and strapped down, as much as he could possibly bear. He had a cane; he had an eye-glass; he had a snuff-box; he had rings; he had wristbands; he had everything but any touch of nature; he was not like youth; he was not like age; he was not like anything in the world but a model of deportment."—*Bleak House.*

Turveydrop, Mrs.—The deceased wife of Mr. Turveydrop.—" He had married a meek little dancing mistress, with a tolerable connection (having never in his life before done anything but deport himself); and had worked her to death, or had at the best suffered her to work herself to death, to maintain him in those expenses which were indispensable to his position."—*Bleak House.*

Twemlow, Mr. Melvin.—A mild-mannered gentleman who lived upon an annuity allowed him by his cousin Lord Snigsworth; and whom the Veneerings cultivated.—

"Grey, dry, polite, susceptible to east wind, First-Gentleman-in-Europe collar and cravat, cheeks drawn in, as if he had made a great effort to retire into himself some years ago, and had got so far and had never got any further."—*Our Mutual Friend.*

Twigger, Edward.—A resident in Mudfog.—"A merry-tempered, pleasant-faced, good-for-nothing sort of vagabond, with an invincible dislike to manual labour, and an unconquerable attachment to strong beer and spirits; whom everybody knew, and nobody except his wife took the trouble to quarrel with, who inherited from his ancestors the appellation of Edward Twigger, and rejoiced in the sobriquet of Bottle-nosed Ned."—*The Mudfog Sketches.*

Twinkleton, Miss.—Principal of Nuns' House Ladies Seminary at Cloisterham.—"Miss Twinkleton has two distinct and separate phases of being. Every night at the same hour does Miss Twinkleton smarten up her curls a little, brighten up her eyes a little, and become a sprightlier Miss Twinkleton than the young ladies have ever seen."—*Edwin Drood.*

Twist, Oliver.—A parish foundling. Born in a workhouse where his mother died at his birth, afterwards found to be the illegitimate son of Edward Leeford and Agnes Fleming. Named Oliver Twist by Mr. Bumble the Parish Beadle.—"We name our foundlings in alphabetical order. The last was a S.—Swabble I named him. This was a T.—Twist I named him. The next one as comes will be Unwin, and the next Vilkins. I have got names ready made to the end of the alphabet, and all the way through it again when we come to Z."—*Oliver Twist.*

Twopence, Thomas.—A hero of a school book used at the night school where Charley Hexam taught.—"Unwieldy young dredgers, and hulking mudlarks, were referred to the experiences of Thomas Twopence, who having resolved not to rob (under circumstances of uncommon atrocity) his particular friend and benefactor of eighteenpence, presently came into supernatural possession of three-and-sixpence, and lived a shining light ever afterwards."—*Our Mutual Friend.*

Uncommercial Traveller, The.—"Allow me to introduce myself, first negatively. No landlord is my friend and brother; no chambermaid loves me; no waiter worships me; no boots admires and envies me; when I go upon my journeys I am not usually rated at a low figure in the bill; when I come home from my journeys I never get any commission . . . and yet—proceeding now to introduce myself positively—I am both a town traveller and a country traveller, and am always on the road. Figuratively speaking, I travel for the great house of Human Interest Brothers, and have rather a large connection in the fancy goods way."—*The Uncommercial Traveller.*

Underry, Mr.—One of the guests at the Haunted House. —" Mr. Underry, my friend and solicitor; who came down, in an amateur capacity, to go through with it, as he said—and who plays whist better than the whole Law List, from the red cover at the beginning to the red cover at the end."—The Haunted House (*Christmas Stories*).

Upwitch, Mr. Richard.—A juror in the Bardell and Pickwick Trial.—*Pickwick Papers.*

Valentine.—Orderly to Captain de la Cour.—" Was there not Private Valentine in that very house, acting as sole housemaid, valet, cook, steward, and nurse in the family of his Captain, Monsieur le Capitaine de la Cour; cleaning the floors; making the beds; doing the marketing; dressing the Captain; dressing the dinners; dressing the salads; and dressing the baby, all with equal readiness."—Somebody's Luggage (*Christmas Stories*).

Valiant Soldier, The.—A public-house where Nell and her grandfather sheltered in a storm.—*The Old Curiosity Shop.*

Varden, Gabriel.—A London locksmith; father of Dolly Varden.—" A round, red-faced, sturdy yeoman, with a double chin and a voice husky with good living, good sleeping, good humour, and good health. . . . Bluff, hale, hearty, and in a green old age; at peace with himself, and disposed to be so with all the world."—*Barnaby Rudge.*

Varden, Mrs.—Wife of Gabriel Varden, and mother of Dolly.—" Mrs. Varden was a lady of what is commonly called an uncertain temper,—a phrase which, being interpreted, signifies a temper tolerably certain to make everybody more or less uncomfortable. Thus it generally happened that, when other people were merry, Mrs. Varden was dull; and that when other people were dull,

Mrs. Varden was disposed to be amazingly cheerful. . . . Like some other ladies who in remote ages flourished upon this globe, Mrs. Varden was most devout when most ill-tempered. Whenever she and her husband were at unusual variance, then the Protestant Manual was in high feather."—*Barnaby Rudge.*

Varden, Dolly.—Daughter of Gabriel Varden, the locksmith; a pretty flirt, who ultimately married Joe Willet after his return from the wars, and settled down with him at the Maypole inn.—"Gabriel stepped into the road, and stole a look at the upper windows. One of them chanced to be thrown open at the moment, and a roguish face met his; a face lighted up by the loveliest pair of sparkling eyes that ever locksmith looked upon; the face of a pretty laughing girl, dimpled, and fresh, and healthful, the very impersonation of good humour and blooming beauty."—*Barnaby Rudge.*

Vaubon.—The engineer of the fortification of an old French town.—"Vaubon engineered it to that perplexing extent that to look at it was like being knocked on the head with it; the stranger becoming stunned and sterterous under the shock of its incomprehensibility."—Somebody's Luggage (*Christmas Stories*).

Veck, Toby (Trotty).—A London ticket-porter who heard voices in the Chimes.—"They called him Trotty from his pace, which meant speed if he didn't make it. . . . A weak, small spare old man, he was a very Hercules this Toby in his good intentions. He loved to earn his money. He delighted to believe—Toby was very poor and couldn't well afford to part with a delight—that he was worth his salt."—*The Chimes.*

Veck, Meg.—Veck's daughter.—"Toby found himself face to face with his own child, and looking close into her eyes—bright eyes they were—eyes that were beautiful and true, and beaming with hope—with hope so young and fresh; with hope so buoyant, vigorous, and bright, despite the twenty years of work and poverty on which they had looked that they became a voice to Trotty and said I think we have some business here—a little."—*The Chimes.*

Vendale, George.—A foundling known at the hospital as Walter Wilding, adopted by Mrs. Vendale.—No Thoroughfare (*Christmas Stories*).

Veneering, Hamilton, M.P.—A purse-proud upstart, who cultivates society, but ultimately becomes bankrupt. Sole partner in the drug store of Chicksey, Veneering and Stobbles.—" Mr. and Mrs. Veneering were bran new people in a bran new house in a bran new quarter of London."—*Our Mutual Friend.*

Veneering, Mrs. Anastasia.—Wife of Hamilton Veneering, M.P.—*Our Mutual Friend.*

Vengeance, The.—A woman of the company of female patriots led by Madame Defarge.—" The short, rather plump, wife of a starved grocer, and the mother of two children withal, this lieutenant had already earned the complimentary name of The Vengeance."—*A Tale of Two Cities.*

Venning, Mrs.—One of the British residents at Silver Store Colony.—" There was one handsome elderly lady, with very dark eyes and grey hair, that I inquired about. I was told that her name was Mrs. Venning."—The Perils of Certain English Travellers (*Christmas Stories*).

Ventriloquist, The.—A performer at a fair in a Flemish town.—" The Proprietor is replaced behind the table by the Ventriloquist, who is thin and sallow and of a weakly aspect."—*The Uncommercial Traveller* (In the French-Flemish Country).

Venus, Mr.—A taxidermist and articulator of human bones. A friend of Silas Wegg.—" Not to name myself as a workman without an equal, I've gone on improving myself in my knowledge of anatomy, till, both by sight and by name, I'm perfect. Mr. Wegg, if you was brought here loose in a bag, to be articulated, I'd name your smallest bones blindfold, equally with your largest, as fast as I could pick 'em, and I'd sort 'em all, and sort your wertebrae, in a manner that would equally surprise and charm you."—*Our Mutual Friend.*

Verisopht, Lord Frederick.—A dupe of Ralph Nickleby, and a guest at his dinner-party. Fell in love with Kate; killed in a duel with Sir Mulberry Hawk.—" The gentleman addressed, turning round, exhibited a suit of clothes of the most superlative cut; a pair of whiskers of similar quality; a moustache; a head of hair; and a young face. It was not difficult to see that the majority of the company preyed upon the unfortunate young Lord, who, weak and silly as he was, appeared by far the least vicious of the party."—*Nicholas Nickleby.*

Vestry Clerk.—" The vestry clerk, as everybody knows, is a short pudgy little man in black, with a thick gold watch-chain, of considerable length, terminating in two large seals and a key. He is an attorney, and generally in a bustle; at no time more so than when he is hurrying to some parochial meeting, with his gloves crumpled up in one hand, and a large red book in the other."—*Sketches by Boz* (Our Parish).

Vholes, Mr.—Richard Carstone's Chancery solicitor.—" A sallow man, with pinched lips that looked as if they were cold; a red eruption here and there upon his face; tall and thin; about fifty years of age; high-shouldered and stooping. Dressed in black, black-gloved, and buttoned to the chin, there was nothing so remarkable in him as a lifeless manner, and a slow, fixed way he had of looking at Richard. He was further remarkable for an inward manner of speaking."—*Bleak House.*

Vholes, The Misses.—Daughters of Mr. Vholes.—" I am (said Mr. Vholes) a widower with three daughters, Emma, Jane, and Caroline; and my desire is so to discharge the duties of life as to leave them a good name."—*Bleak House.*

Vizier, The Grand.—Of the Seraglio at Miss Griffin's school.—" We were out walking, two and two, on which occasion the Grand Vizier had his usual instruction to take note of the boy at the turnpike, and if he profanely gazed (which he always did) at the beauties of the Harem, to have him bowstrung in the course of the night."—The Haunted House (*Christmas Stories*).

Voigt, Maître.—A notary in Neuchâtel.—" A rosy, hearty, handsome old man; chief notary of Neuchâtel; known far and wide in the canton as Maître Voigt. His long brown frock-coat, and his black skull cap, were among the institutions of the place; and he carried a snuff-box, which in point of size, was popularly believed to be without parallel in Europe."—No Thoroughfare (*Christmas Stories*).

Wackles, Miss Sophy.—A young lady admired by Dick Swiveller.—" Miss Sophy was a fresh, good-humoured buxom girl of twenty."—*The Old Curiosity Shop.*

Wackles, Miss Melissa.—Sister of Sophy.—" Miss Melissa might have seen five-and-thirty summers or thereabouts and verged on the autumnal."—*The Old Curiosity Shop.*

Wackles, Miss Jane.—Younger sister of Sophy.—" Miss Jane numbered scarcely sixteen years."—*The Old Curiosity Shop.*

Wackles, Mrs.—Mother of Sophy.—" Mrs. Wackles was an excellent, but rather venomous, old lady of three score." —*The Old Curiosity Shop.*

Wackles' Seminary.—A girls' school at Chelsea.— " There Miss Sophia Wackles resided with her widowed mother, and two sisters, in conjunction with whom she maintained a very small day school, for young ladies of proportionate dimensions; a circumstance which was made known to the neighbourhood by an oval board over the front first floor window, whereon appeared in circumambient flourishes the words Ladies' Seminary. The several duties of instruction in this establishment were thus discharged—English grammar, composition, geography, and the use of the dumb-bells, by Miss Melissa Wackles; writing, arithmetic, dancing, music, and general fascination by Miss Sophy Wackles; the art of needlework, marking and samplery, by Miss Jane Wackles; corporal punishment, fasting and other tortures and terrors, by Mrs. Wackles." —*The Old Curiosity Shop.*

Wade, Miss.—A fellow-traveller with Mr. and Mrs. Meagles.—" A handsome young Englishwoman, travelling quite alone, who had a proud, observant face, and had either withdrawn herself from the rest, or been avoided by the rest—nobody, herself excepted perhaps, could have quite decided which."—*Little Dorrit.*

Waghorn, Mr.—A Vice-President of the Mechanical Science Section of the Mudfog Association.—*The Mudfog Sketches.*

Wakefield, Mr. and Mrs.—Guests at the Steam Excursion.—*Sketches by Boz* (The Steam Excursion).

Wakefield, Miss.—A guest at the Steam Excursion. Daughter of Mr. and Mrs. Wakefield.—" The girl was about six years old; dressed in a white frock, with a pink sash, and dog's-eared-looking little spencer."—*Sketches by Boz* (The Steam Excursion).

Wakeley.—The coroner who presided at an inquest on which the Uncommercial Traveller was a juror.—" The Coroner, who was nobly patient and humane (he was the late Mr. Wakeley), cast a look of strong encouragement in my direction."—*The Uncommercial Traveller* (Recollections of Mortality).

Waldengraver.—The stage name adopted by Mr. Wopsle.—*Great Expectations.*

Walker, H.—A case mentioned in the report upon converts by the Committee of the Brick Lane Branch of the United Grand Junction Ebenezer Temperance Association. —" H. Walker; tailor, wife and two children. When in better circumstances, owns to having been in the constant habit of drinking ale and beer; says he is not certain whether he did not, twice a week for twenty years, taste dog's nose, which your Committee find upon inquiry to be compounded of warm porter, moist sugar, gin and nutmeg (a groan—and ' So it is ' from an elderly female); is now out of work and penniless; thinks it must be the porter (cheers); or the loss of the use of his right hand; is not certain which, but thinks it very likely that, if he had drank nothing but water all his life, his fellow-workman would never have stuck a rusty needle in him, and thereby occasioned his accident (tremendous cheering); has nothing but cold water to drink; and never feels thirsty (great applause)."—*Pickwick Papers.*

Walker, Mick.—One of the boys employed at Murdstone and Grinby's.—" On the first morning of my so auspiciously beginning life on my own account, the oldest of the regular boys was summoned to show me my business. His name was Mick Walker, and he wore a ragged apron and a paper cap. He informed me that his father was a bargeman, and walked, in a black velvet head-dress, in the Lord Mayor's Show."—*David Copperfield.*

Walker, Mr.—A debtor detained in Solomon Jacobs' sponging-house.—" A horse-dealer from Islington."—*Sketches by Boz* (A Passage in the Life of Mr. Watkins Tottle).

Walker, Mr.—A neighbour of Mrs. Macklin.—(*See* **Macklin.**)—*Sketches by Boz* (The Streets—Night).

Walker, Mrs.—A neighbour of Mrs. Macklin.—(*See* **Macklin.**)—*Sketches by Boz* (The Streets—Night).

Walmer, Mr.—Father of Harry, a child of whom Cobbs, the boots of the Holly Tree inn, told Charley tales.—"Master Harry Walmer's father, you see, he lived at the Elmses, down away at Shooter's Hill there, six or seven miles from London. He was a gentleman of spirit, and good-looking, and held his head up when he walked, and had what you may call fire about him. He wrote poetry, and he rode, and he ran, and he cricketed, and he danced, and he acted, and he done it all equally beautiful. He was uncommon proud of Master Harry, as was his only child, but he didn't spoil him neither."—The Holly Tree (*Christmas Stories*).

Walmer, Master Harry (aged eight).—Only son of Mr. Walmer of the Elmses.—(*See* **Walmer, Mr.**)—The Holly Tree (*Christmas Stories*).

Walter, Edward McNeville.—The assumed name under which Theodosius Butler courted Miss Brooks Dingwall. —*Sketches by Boz* (Sentiment).

Warden, William, Senior.—A drunkard.—"There is scarcely a man, in the constant habit of walking day after day through any of the crowded thoroughfares of London, who cannot recollect, among the people whom he 'knows by sight,' to use a familiar phrase, some being of abject and wretched appearance, whom he remembers to have seen in a very different condition, whom he has observed sinking lower and lower, by almost imperceptible degrees, and the shabbiness and utter destitution of whose appearance at last, strike forcibly upon him as he passes by. Alas! such cases are of too frequent occurrence to be rare items in any man's experience; and but too often arise from one cause—drunkenness—that fierce rage for the slow, sure poison, that oversteps every other consideration; that casts aside wife, children, friends, happiness, and station; and hurries its victims madly on to degradation and death."—*Sketches by Boz* (The Drunkard's Death).

Warden, Mrs.—Wife of Warden, the drunkard.—"They listened for her breath, but no sound came; they felt for the palpitation of the heart, but no faint throb responded to the touch; that heart was broken, and she was dead. The time had been when many a friend would have crowded round him in his affliction, and many a heartfelt condolence would have met him in his grief. Where were they now? One by one, friends, relations, the commonest acquaintance even, had fallen off from and deserted the drunkard. His wife alone had clung to him, in good and evil, in sickness and poverty, and how had he rewarded her,—he had reeled from the tavern to her bed-side, in time to see her die."—*Sketches by Boz* (The Drunkard's Death).

Warden, William, Junior.—Son of Warden, the drunkard, whom, for drink, his father betrayed to the police.—"Sitting on an old box, with his head resting on his hand, and his eyes fixed on a wretched cinder fire that was smouldering on the hearth, was a young man of about two-and-twenty, miserably clad in an old coarse jacket and trousers."—*Sketches by Boz* (The Drunkard's Death).

Warden, John.—Son of Warden, the drunkard; emigrated to America.—*Sketches by Boz* (The Drunkard's Death).

Warden, Mary.—Daughter of Warden, the drunkard.—"The father remained the same; poorer, shabbier, and more dissolute looking; but the same confirmed and irreclaimable drunkard; the boys had long ago run wild in the streets, and left him; the girl alone remained; but she worked hard, and words or blows could always procure him something for the tavern."—*Sketches by Boz* (The Drunkard's Death).

Warden, Henry.—Youngest son of Warden, the drunkard—shot in a poaching affray.—*Sketches by Boz* (The Drunkard's Death).

Warden, Michael.—A spendthrift client of Snitchey and Craggs.—"A man of thirty or about that time of life, negligently dressed, and somewhat haggard in the face, but well made, well attired, and well looking."—*The Battle of Life.*

Wardle, Mr.—Of Manor Farm, Dingley Dell. A friend of Mr. Pickwick.—"A stout old gentleman in a blue coat and bright buttons, corduroy breeches and top boots."—*Pickwick Papers.*

Wardle, Mrs.—Mother of Mr. Wardle.—" A very old lady in a lofty cap and faded silk gown.—No less a personage than Mr. Wardle's mother occupied the post of honour on the right-hand corner of the chimney-piece; and various certificates of her having been brought up in the way she should go when young, and of her not having departed from it when old, ornamented the walls, in the form of samplers of ancient date, worsted landscapes of equal antiquity, and crimson silk tea-kettle holders of a more modern period."—*Pickwick Papers.*

Wardle, Miss Emily.—Daughter of Mr. Wardle, married Mr. Snodgrass.—*Pickwick Papers.*

Wardle, Isabella.—Daughter of Mr. Wardle, married Mr. Trundle.—*Pickwick Papers.*

Wardle, Miss Rachel.—Sister of Mr. Wardle. Eloped with Jingle.—" A lady of uncertain age."—*Pickwick Papers.*

Warren, The.—Mr. Haredale's house, which was burnt down by the Gordon rioters.—" It was a dreary, silent building, with echoing courtyards, desolated turret chambers, and whole suites of rooms shut up and mouldering to ruin . . . it would have been difficult to imagine a bright fire blazing in the dull and darkened rooms; or to picture any gaiety of heart or revelry that the frowning walls shut in. It seemed a place where such things had been, but could be no more; the very ghost of a house, haunting the old spot in its outward form, and that was all."—*Barnaby Rudge.*

Waterbrook, Mr.—A London solicitor, a friend of Mr. Wickfield.—" I found Mr. Waterbrook to be a middle-aged gentleman, with a short throat and a good deal of shirt collar, who only wanted a black nose to be the portrait of a pug dog."—*David Copperfield.*

Waterbrook, Mrs.—Wife of Mr. Waterbrook.—" The room door opened, and Mrs. Waterbrook, who was a large lady—or who wore a large dress—I don't exactly know which, for I don't know which was dress and which was lady—came sailing in."—*David Copperfield.*

Waterhouse.—An alias of Pegg the crimp.—(*See* **Pegg.**) —*The Uncommercial Traveller* (Poor Mercantile Jack).

Waters, Captain Walter.—An adventurer who met the Tuggs family on the Ramsgate boat.—" A stoutish military-looking gentleman, in a blue surtout buttoned up to his chin, and white trousers chained down to the soles of his boots."—*Sketches by Boz* (The Tuggses at Ramsgate).

Waters, Mrs. Belinda.—Wife of Captain Waters.—" A young lady in a puce-coloured silk cloak, and boots of the same, with long black ringlets, large black eyes, brief petticoats, and unexceptionable ankles."—*Sketches by Boz* (The Tuggses at Ramsgate).

Watkins, Mr.—Godfather to Kate Nickleby.—" Mr. Watkins, you know Kate, my dear, that your poor papa went bail for, who afterwards ran away to the United States, and sent us a pair of snow-shoes, with such an affectionate letter that it made your poor dear father cry for a week. You remember, the letter in which he said that he was sorry he couldn't repay the fifty pounds just then, because his capital was all out at interest, and he was very busy making his fortune; but that he didn't forget you were his god-daughter, and he should take it very unkind if we didn't buy you a silver coral, and put it down to his old account."—*Nicholas Nickleby.*

Watkins, King.—Father of Alicia.—" There was once a King; and he had a Queen; and he was the manliest of his sex; and she was the loveliest of hers. The King was, in his private profession, under Government; the Queen's father had been a medical man."—*Holiday Romance.*

Watts, Richard.—The founder of a Rochester Charity for poor travellers.—" What says the inscription over the quaint old door—Richard Watts, Esq., by his Will dated 22 Aug., 1579, founded this charity for six poor travellers, who, not being rogues or Proctors, may receive gratis for one night lodging, entertainment and fourpence each."—The Seven Poor Travellers (*Christmas Stories*).

Watty, Mr.—A bankrupt client of Mr. Perker's.—" There never was such a pestering bankrupt as that since the world began, I do believe, said Lowton, throwing down his pen with the air of an injured man; his affairs haven't been in Chancery quite four years yet, and I'm d——d if he don't come worrying here twice a week."—*Pickwick Papers.*

Wedgington, Mr.—A variety artiste.—" Mrs. B. Wedgington sang to a grand piano, Mr. B. Wedgington did the like, and also took off his coat, tucked up his trousers, and danced in clogs."—*Out of the Season* (Reprinted Pieces).

Wedgington, Mrs.—Wife of Mr. Wedgington.—*Out of the Season* (Reprinted Pieces).

Wedgington, Master B.—Son of Mr. and Mrs. Wedgington.—*Out of the Season* (Reprinted Pieces).

Weedle, Anastasia.—An emigrant on board the *Amazon.* —" A pretty girl in a bright Garibaldi this morning elected by universal suffrage the beauty of the ship."—*The Uncommercial Traveller* (Bound for the Great Salt Lake).

Weeks, Mr.—Clerk to Dodson and Fogg.—" A gentleman in a brown coat and brass buttons, inky drabs, and bluchers."—*Pickwick Papers.*

Weevle.—The name assumed by Jobbling when he resided at Krook's.—*Bleak House.*

Wegg, Silas.—A balladmonger and street vendor with a wooden leg, who was taken up by Mr. Boffin, and who repaid his kindness by prying around his premises, and having found a Harmon will of later date than that under which Mr. Boffin took the Harmon estate, hoped to blackmail Boffin, but was checkmated by the production of a will of a still later date.—" Assuredly this stall of Silas Wegg's was the hardest little stall of all the sterile little stalls in London. It gave you the face-ache to look at his apples; the stomach-ache to look at his oranges; the toothache to look at his nuts. . . . Wegg was a knotty man, and a close-grained, with a face carved out of very hard material, that had just as much play of expression as a watchman's rattle. When he laughed certain jerks occurred in it, and the rattle sprung. Sooth to say he was so wooden a man that he seemed to have taken his wooden leg naturally, and rather suggested to the fanciful observer that he might be expected—if his development received no untimely check—to be completely set up with a pair of wooden legs in about six months."—*Our Mutual Friend.*

Wegg, Thomas.—Father of Silas Wegg.—" Mr. Boffin, don't allow yourself to be made uncomfortable by the pang it gives me to part from my stock and stall. Similar emotion was undergone by my own father, when promoted, for his merits, from his occupation as a waterman to a situation under Government. His Christian name was Thomas."—*Our Mutual Friend.*

Weller, Tony.—A coachman; father of Sam Weller.—" It is very possible that at some earlier period of his career, Mr. Weller's profile might have presented a bold and determined outline. His face however had expanded, under the influence of good living, and a disposition remarkable for resignation; and its bold fleshy curves had so far extended beyond the limits originally assigned to them, that, unless you took a full view of his countenance in front, it was difficult to distinguish more than the extreme tip of a very rubicund nose. His chin, from the same cause, had acquired the grave and imposing form which is generally described by prefixing the word double to that expressive feature; and his complexion exhibited that peculiarly mottled combination of colours which is only seen in gentlemen of his profession, and in underdone roast beef."—*Pickwick Papers.*

Weller, Mrs.—Wife of Tony Weller, landlady of the Marquis of Granby public-house.—" A rather stout lady of comfortable appearance."—*Pickwick Papers.*

Weller, Sam.—Boots at the White Hart inn, afterwards valet to Mr. Pickwick.—" He was habited in a coarse striped waistcoat, with black calico sleeves, and blue glass buttons, drab breeches, and leggings, a bright red handkerchief was wound in a very loose and unstudied style round his neck; and an old white hat was carelessly thrown on his head. . . . Mr. Pickwick led his new attendant to one of these convenient emporiums, where gentlemen's new and second-hand clothes are provided, and the troublesome and inconvenient formality of measurement dispensed with; and, before night had closed in, Mr. Weller was furnished with a grey coat with the P.C. button; a black hat with a cockade to it; a pink striped waistcoat; light breeches and gaiters; and a variety of other necessaries too numerous to recapitulate. Well, said that suddenly transformed individual, I wonder whether I'm meant to be a footman; or a groom; or a gamekeeper; or a seedsman; I looks like a compo' of every one of them; never mind—there's a change of air; plenty to see, and little to do; and all this suits my complaint uncommon; so long life to the Pickwicks, says I."—*Pickwick Papers.*

Weller, Tony, Junior.—Son of Sam Weller.—" Mr. Weller introduced a very small boy, firmly set upon a couple of very sturdy legs, who looked as if nothing could ever knock him down. Besides having a very round face, strongly resembling Mr. Weller's, and a stout little body of exactly his build, this young gentleman, standing with his little legs very wide apart, as if the top boots were familiar to them, actually winked upon the housekeeper with his infant eye, in imitation of his grandfather."—*Master Humphrey's Clock.*

Weller, Sam, Junior.—Son of Sam Weller.—" How many brothers and sisters have you, my dear, she asked after a short silence; one brother and no sister at all, replied Tony; Sam his name is, and so's my father's."—*Master Humphrey's Clock.*

Wemmick, John, Junior.—Confidential clerk to Mr. Jaggers, the lawyer.—" Casting my eyes on Mr. Wemmick as he went along, to see what he was like in the light of day, I found him to be a dry man, rather short in stature, with a square, wooden face, whose expression seemed to have been imperfectly chipped out with a dull-edged chisel. There were some marks in it which might have been dimples if the material had been softer, and the instrument finer, but which, as it was, were only dents. He wore his hat on the back of his head, and looked straight before him, walking in a self-contained way, as if there were nothing in the streets to claim his attention. His mouth was such a post office of a mouth that he had a mechanical appearance of smiling."—*Great Expectations.*

Wemmick, John, Senior.—(*See* **Aged P.**)—*Great Expectations.*

West, Dame.—The grandmother of Harry, the pupil of the village school, who died.—*The Old Curiosity Shop.*

Westlock, John.—A pupil of Mr. Pecksniff—married Ruth Pinch.—*Martin Chuzzlewit.*

Westwood, Mr.—Sir Mulberry Hawk's second at the duel with Lord Verisopht.—(*See* **Adams.**)—*Nicholas Nickleby.*

Wharton, Mr. Granville.—A pupil of George Silverman's.—" A young gentleman near coming of age, very well connected, but what is called a poor relation. He was well looking, clever, energetic, enthusiastic, bold; in the best sense of the term a thorough young Anglo-Saxon."—*George Silverman's Explanation.*

Wheezy, Professor.—A Vice-President of the Zoology and Botany Section of the Mudfog Association.—*The Mudfog Sketches.*

Whelp, The.—A name which Harthouse bestowed upon Tom Gradgrind.—"It was very remarkable that a young gentleman, who had been brought up under one continuous system of unnatural restraint, should be a hypocrite, but it was certainly the case with Tom; it was very strange that a young gentleman who had never been left to his own guidance for five consecutive minutes, should be incapable at last of governing himself, but so it was with Tom; it was altogether unaccountable that a young gentleman whose imagination had been strangled in his cradle, should be still inconvenienced by its ghost, in the form of grovelling sensualities, but such a monster beyond all doubt was Tom."—*Hard Times.*

Whiff, Miss.—An assistant at Mugby Junction Refreshment Room.—Mugby Junction (*Christmas Stories*).

Whiffers, Mr.—One of the select company of Bath footmen.—*Pickwick Papers.*

Whiffin, Mr.—The town-crier at Eatanswill.—*Pickwick Papers.*

Whiffler, Mr. and Mrs.—The couple who dote on their children.—"They have usually a great many of them, six or eight at least. The children are either the healthiest in all the world, or the most unfortunate in existence. In either case, they are equally the theme of their doting parents, and a source of mental anguish and irritation to their doting parents' friends."—*Sketches of Young Couples.*

Whimple, Mrs.—The landlady of the house at Millpond Bank, where Magwitch went into hiding.—"An elderly woman of a pleasant and thriving appearance."—*Great Expectations.*

Whisker.—Mr. Garland's pony.—"The pony was coming along, at his own pace, and doing exactly as he pleased with the whole concern. If the old gentleman remonstrated by shaking the reins, the pony replied by shaking his head. It was plain that the utmost the pony would consent to do was to go, in his own way, up any street that the old gentleman particularly wished to traverse; but that it was an understanding between them that he must do this after his own fashion, or not at all. The pony preserved his character for independence and principle down to the last moment of his life, which was an unusually long one, and caused him to be looked upon indeed as the very Old Parr of ponies."—*The Old Curiosity Shop*.

White.—One of Mrs. Lemon's pupils.—*Holiday Romance*.

White.—A London constable.—*On Duty with Inspector Field* (Reprinted Pieces).

White, Mrs.—A New York society lady.—*Martin Chuzzlewit*.

White, Tom.—The name given to Oliver by the officer in Mr. Fang's Court.—" Finding him really incapable of understanding the question, and knowing that his not replying would only infuriate the Magistrate the more, and add to the severity of the sentence, he hazarded a guess—he says his name's Tom White, your worship, said this kind-hearted thief-taker."—*Oliver Twist*.

White, Betsy.—A woman found in the house of Pegg, the crimp, when visited by the police and the Uncommercial Traveller.—" Betsy looks over the banisters, with a forcible expression in her protesting face, of an intention to compensate herself for the present trial, by grinding Jack finer than usual when he does come."—*The Uncommercial Traveller* (Poor Mercantile Jack).

White, Mr.—A gay friend of Mr. Augustus Cooper.—" Whereas young White, at the gasfitter's over the way, three years younger than him, had been flaring away like winkin'—going to the theatre—supping at harmonic meetings—eating oysters by the barrel—drinking stout by the gallon—even stopping out all night, and coming home as cool in the morning as if nothing had happened."—*Sketches by Boz* (The Dancing Academy).

White Hart.—The inn where Sam Weller was boots.—"There are in London several old Inns—great, rambling, queer old places they are, with galleries and passages; and staircases wide enough and antiquated enough to furnish materials for a hundred ghost stories . . . one of these a no less celebrated one than the 'White Hart.'"—*Pickwick Papers.*

Whitrose, Lady Belinda.—One of the models used by the Doll's Dressmaker.—"I squeeze among the crowd, and I look about me. When I see a great lady very suitable for my business, I say, you'll do, my dear, and I take particular notice of her, and run home, and cut out and baste her. There was Lady Belinda Whitrose. I made her do double duty in one night."—*Our Mutual Friend.*

Wickfield, Mr.—A solicitor in Canterbury.—"His hair was quite white now, though his eyebrows were still black. He had a very agreeable face, and I thought was handsome. There was a certain richness too in his complexion, which I had been long accustomed, under Peggotty's tuition, to connect with port wine, and I fancied it was in his voice too, and referred his growing corpulency to the same cause. He was very cleanly dressed, in a blue coat, striped waistcoat, and nankeen trousers, and his fine frilled shirt and cambric neckcloth looked unusually soft and white, reminding my strolling fancy of the plumage on the breast of a swan."—*David Copperfield.*

Wickfield, Agnes.—Daughter of Mr. Wickfield.—"I cannot call to mind where or when in my childhood I had seen a stained glass window in a church. Nor do I recollect its subject. But I know that, when I saw her turn round in the grave light of the old staircase, and wait for us above, I thought of that window, and I associated something of its tranquil brightness with Agnes Wickfield ever afterwards."—*David Copperfield.*

Wickham, Mrs.—Paul Dombey's nurse.—"Mrs. Wickham was a waiter's wife, which would seem equivalent to being any other man's widow. Mrs. Wickham was a meek woman, of a fair complexion, with her eyebrows always elevated, and her head always drooping; who was always ready to pity herself, or to be pitied, or to pity anybody else; and who had a surprising natural gift of viewing all subjects in one utterly forlorn and pitiable light, and bringing dreadful precedents to bear upon them, and deriving the greatest consolation from the exercise of that talent."—*Dombey and Son.*

Wigder, Mr. and Mrs.—The plausible couple.—"The truth is that the plausible couple are people of the world . . . hence it is that plausible couples scarcely ever fail of success on a pretty large scale."—*Sketches of Young Couples.*

Wield, Inspector.—A London police officer.—"Inspector Wield is a middle-aged man, of a portly presence, with a large moist knowing eye, a husky voice, and a habit of emphasizing his conversation by the aid of a corpulent forefinger, which is constantly in juxtaposition with his eyes or nose."—*The Detective Police* (Reprinted Pieces).

Wiglomeration.—Mr. John Jarndyce's name for Chancery Court procedure.—"It's the only name I know for the thing. Counsel will have something to say about it; the Chancellor will have something to say about it; the satellites will have something to say about it; they will all have to be handsomely fee'd all round about it; the whole thing will be vastly ceremonious, wordy, unsatisfactory, and expensive; and I call it in general Wiglomeration."—*Bleak House.*

Wiggs and Co.—The owner of the ship *Polyphemus.*—(*See* **Brown, Captain John.**)—*Dombey and Son.*

Wigsby, Mr.—A member of the Mudfog Association.—*The Mudfog Sketches.*

Wigsby, Mr.—A vestryman.—"Thirty-seven gentlemen, many of them of great eminence, including Mr. Wigsby of Chumbledon Square."—*Our Vestry* (Reprinted Pieces).

Wilcocks, Mrs.—A miser whose biography Mr. Boffin pretended to be interested in.—*Our Mutual Friend.*

Wilding and Co.—A firm of wine merchants in London.—"In a Courtyard in the city of London which was no thoroughfare either for vehicles or foot passengers, a courtyard diverging from a steep, a slippery, and a winding street, connecting Tower Street with the Middlesex shore of the Thames, stood the place of business of Wilding and Co., Wine Merchants."—No Thoroughfare (*Christmas Stories*).

Wilding, Walter.—A wine merchant.—" An innocent, open-speaking, unused-looking man, Mr. Walter Wilding, with a remarkably pink and white complexion, and a figure much too bulky for so young a man, though of good stature; with crispy curling brown hair and amiable bright blue eyes."—No Thoroughfare (*Christmas Stories*).

Wilfer, Bella.—Daughter of Reginald Wilfer, the girl whom John Harmon was to marry as a condition of inheriting his father's wealth, and whom he ultimately did marry under the name of John Rokesmith.—" A girl of about nineteen, with an exceedingly pretty figure and face, but with an impatient and petulant expression both in her face and in her shoulders (which in her sex and at her age are very expressive of discontent)."—*Our Mutual Friend.*

Wilfer, Reginald W.—A clerk in the drug store of Chicksey, Veneering and Stobbles; father of Bella Wilfer. —" The Reginald Wilfer family were of such commonplace extraction and pursuits that their forefathers had for generations modestly subsisted on the docks, the Excise Office, and the Custom House. The existing R. W. Wilfer was a poor clerk, so poor a clerk, through having a limited salary and an unlimited family, that he had never yet attained the modest object of his ambition, which was to wear a complete new suit of clothes, hat and boots included, at one time. . . . He was shy and unwilling to own to the name of Reginald as being too aspiring and self-assertive a name. In his signature he used only the initial R."—*Our Mutual Friend.*

Wilfer, Lavinia.—A younger sister of Bella Wilfer.—*Our Mutual Friend.*

Wilfer, Cecilia.—A married daughter of Mr. and Mrs. Wilfer.—" I have now in my pocket—(said Mrs. Wilfer)—a letter from your sister Cecilia, received this morning—received three months after her marriage, poor child, in which she tells me that her husband must unexpectedly shelter under their roof his reduced aunt. But I will be true to him, mamma, she touchingly writes, I will not leave him, I must not forget that he is my husband—let his Aunt come ! "—*Our Mutual Friend.*

Wilfer, Mrs.—Wife of Reginald Wilfer.—" Mrs. Wilfer was of course a tall woman, and angular. Her lord being cherubic, she was necessarily majestic, according to the principle which matrimonially unites contrasts. She was much given to tying up her head in a pocket handkerchief, knotted under the chin. This headgear, in conjunction with a pair of gloves worn within doors, she seemed to consider as at once a kind of armour against misfortune (invariably assuming it when in low spirits or difficulties) and as a species of full dress."—*Our Mutual Friend.*

Wilhelm.—A German courier at St. Bernard Convent who told the tale of the twin brothers.—*To be Read at Dusk* (Reprinted Pieces).

Wilkins, Mr. Samuel.—The young man who kept company with Miss Jemima Evans.—"Mr. Samuel Wilkins was a carpenter; a journeyman carpenter of small dimensions, decidedly below the middle size—bordering perhaps upon the dwarfish. His face was round and shining, and his hair carefully twisted into the outer corner of each eye, till it formed a variety of that description of semi-curls usually known as 'aggerawators.' His earnings were all-sufficient for his wants, varying from eighteen shillings to one pound five weekly; his manner undeniable; his Sabbath waistcoats dazzling. No wonder that with these qualifications Samuel Wilkins found favour in the eyes of the other sex; many would have been captivated by far less substantial qualifications. But Samuel was proof against their blandishments, until at length his eyes rested on those of a being for whom from that time forth he felt fate had destined him; he came and conquered; proposed and was accepted; loved and was beloved. Mr. Wilkins kept company with Jemima Evans."—*Sketches by Boz* (Miss Evans and The Eagle).

Wilkins, Dick.—A fellow-apprentice with Scrooge at Fezziwig's.—*A Christmas Carol.*

Wilkins.—Under-gardener to Captain Boldwig.—*Pickwick Papers.*

Willet, John.—The landlord of the Maypole inn.—"A burly, large-headed man, with a fat face, which betokened profound obstinacy and slowness of apprehension; combined with a very strong reliance upon his own merits. It was John Willit's ordinary boast, in his more placid moods, that if he were slow he was sure; which assertion could in one sense at least be by no means gainsaid, seeing that he was in everything the reverse of fast, and withal one of the most dogged and positive fellows in existence; always sure that what he thought or said or did was right; and holding it as a thing quite settled and ordained by the laws of nature and Providence, that anybody who said or did or thought otherwise must be inevitably, and of necessity, wrong."—*Barnaby Rudge.*

Willet, Joe.—Son of John Willet; lover of Dolly Varden; enlisted as a soldier, and after five years' absence returned at the time of the Gordon riots; rescued Miss Haredale and Dolly from the hands of the rioters, and ultimately married Dolly and became landlord of the Maypole inn.—"The landlord's son Joe, a broad-shouldered, strapping young fellow of twenty, whom it pleased his father still to consider a little boy, and to treat accordingly."—*Barnaby Rudge.*

William.—Sweetheart of Mary the maid-of-all-work.—*Sunday under Three Heads* (Reprinted Pieces).

William.—A boy who removed from the country to London with his widowed mother, and who died of overwork in London.—"They were a young lad of eighteen or nineteen, and his mother, a lady of about fifty, or it might be less. The mother wore widow's weeds, and the boy was also clothed in deep mourning. They were poor, very poor; for their only means of support arose from the pittance the boy earned by copying writings and translating for booksellers."—*Sketches by Boz* (Our Next-Door Neighbour).

William.—A younger brother of George, present with the family at Astley's.—(*See* **George.**)—*Sketches by Boz* (Astley's).

William.—The driver of the stage coach by which David travelled from Canterbury to London.—"The main object in my mind, I remember, when we got fairly on the road, was to appear as old as possible to the coachman, and to speak extremely gruff. . . . You are going through, sir, said the coachman. Yes, William, I said, condescendingly (I knew him), I am going to London."—*David Copperfield.*

William.—A waiter at the Yarmouth inn where David dined.—*David Copperfield.*

William.—The waiter at the Saracen's Head tavern where Mr. Squeers put up when he visited London.—*Nicholas Nickleby.*

William.—Deputy hostler at the Bull inn, Rochester.—"Shiny Villiam; so called probably from his sleek hair and oily countenance."—*Pickwick Papers.*

Williams.—A London constable.—*On Duty with Inspector Field* (Reprinted Pieces).

Williams, William.—A customer at the Fellowship Porters tavern.—"At half-past ten, on Miss Abbey looking in again, and saying William Williams, Bob Glamour, and Jonathan, you are all due,—William, Bob, and Jonathan, with similar meekness, took their leave and evaporated."—*Our Mutual Friend.*

Williamson, Mrs.—The landlady of the Winglebury Arms.—*Sketches by Boz* (The Great Winglebury Duel).

Willis.—A family of four sisters.—"The four Miss Willises settled in our parish thirteen years ago. The house was the perfection of neatness—so were the four Miss Willises; everything was formal, stiff, and cold—so were the four Miss Willises. Not a single chair of the whole set was ever seen out of its place; not a single Miss Willis of the whole four was ever seen out of hers. There they always sat, in the same places, doing exactly the same things, at the same hour; the eldest Miss Willis used to knit; the second to draw; the two others to play duets on the piano. They seemed to have no separate existence, but to have made up their minds to winter through life together."—*Sketches by Boz* (Our Parish).

Willis, Mr.—A debtor detained in Solomon Jacobs' sponging-house.—"A young fellow of vulgar manners, dressed in the very extreme of the prevailing fashion, was pacing up and down the room, with a lighted cigar in his mouth, and occasionally applying, with much apparent relish, to a pint pot, the contents of which were chilling on the hob."—*Sketches by Boz* (A Passage in the Life of Mr. Watkins Tottle).

Wilson, Mr.—The gentleman who played "Iago" at the private theatricals at Rose Villa.—*Sketches by Boz* (Mrs. Joseph Porter).

Wilson, Mr. and Mrs.—Friends of Mr. and Mrs. Kitterbell.—" Mr. and Mrs. Wilson from over the way —uncommonly nice people."—*Sketches by Boz* (The Bloomsbury Christening).

Wilson, Miss Caroline.—A pupil at Minerva House. —(*See* **Smithers, Miss.**)—*Sketches by Boz* (Sentiment).

Winking Charley.—A vagrant.—" Here is Winking Charley, a sturdy vagrant in one of Her Majesty's jails."—*Lying Awake* (Reprinted Pieces).

Winkle, Nathaniel.—Member of Pickwick Club.—" The sporting Winkle, communicating additional lustre to a new green shooting coat, plaid neckerchief, and closely fitting drabs."—*Pickwick Papers.*

Winkle, Mr., Senior.—Father of Nathaniel Winkle.— " A little old gentleman in a snuff-coloured suit, with a head and face the precise counterpart of those belonging to Mr. Winkle, Junior, excepting that he was rather bald."—*Pickwick Papers.*

Winks.—The nickname given to Deputy.—" The travellers give me the name, on account of my getting no sleep, and being knocked up all night; whereby I get one eye roused open afore I shut the other. That's what Winks means. Deputy's the highest name to indict me by; but you wouldn't catch me pleading to that neither."—*Edwin Drood.*

Wisbottle, Mr.—A boarder at Mrs. Tibbs'.—" Mr. Wisbottle on the other hand was a high Tory. He was a clerk in the Woods and Forests Office, which he considered rather an aristocratic employment; he knew the Peerage by heart, and could tell you off-hand where any illustrious personage lived; he had a good set of teeth and a capital tailor."—*Sketches by Boz* (The Boarding House).

Wisk, Miss.—A lady with a mission, who married Mr. Quale.—" Miss Wisk's Mission, my guardian said, was to show the world that woman's mission was man's mission; and that the only genuine mission of both man and woman was to be always moving declaratory resolutions, about things in general, at public meetings. Miss Wisk informed us with great indignation, before we sat down to breakfast, that the idea of woman's mission lying chiefly in the narrow sphere of Home was an outrageous slander on the part of her tyrant man."—*Bleak House.*

Witchem, Sergeant.—A London police officer.—" Sergeant Witchem, shorter and thicker set, and marked with the smallpox, has something of a reserved and thoughtful air, as if he were engaged in deep arithmetical calculations."—*The Dectective Police* (Reprinted Pieces).

Witherden, Mr.—A solicitor to whom Abel Garland was articled.—" Mr. Witherden was short, chubby, fresh-coloured, brisk, and pompous."—*The Old Curiosity Shop.*

Witherfield, Miss.—The lady whose room at the Ipswich Hotel Mr. Pickwick mistook for his own room.—" Mr. Pickwick almost fainted with horror and dismay; standing before the dressing glass was a middle-aged lady, in yellow curl papers, busily engaged in brushing what ladies call their back hair."—*Pickwick Papers.*

Withers.—Page to the Hon. Mrs. Skewton.—" The chair having stopped, the motive power became visible, in the shape of a flushed page-boy pushing behind, who seemed to have in part outgrown, and in part out-pushed, his strength, for when he stood upright he was tall, and wan, and thin."—*Dombey and Son.*

Withers, Luke.—A gambler discussed at the Valiant Soldier public-house.—" I haven't seen such a storm as this, said a sharp, cracked voice of most disagreeable quality, when a tremendous peal of thunder had died away, since the night when old Luke Withers won thirteen times running on the red."—*The Old Curiosity Shop.*

Wititterly, Mrs. Julia.—The lady to whom Kate Nickleby became companion and secretary, after she left Madame Mantalini.—" The lady had an air of sweet insipidity, and a face of engaging paleness; there was a faded look about her, and about the furniture, and about the house. She was reclining on a sofa, in such a very unstudied attitude, that she might have been taken for an actress, all ready for the first scene in a ballet, and only waiting for the drop curtain to go up."—*Nicholas Nickleby.*

Wititterly, Mr. Henry.—Husband of Mrs. Wititterly.—" An important gentleman of about eight-and-thirty, of rather plebeian countenance, and with a very light head of hair."—*Nicholas Nickleby.*

Wizzle, Mr.—An intended guest at the Steam Excursion. —*Sketches by Boz* (The Steam Excursion).

Wobbler, Mr.—An official of the Circumlocution Office. —*Little Dorrit.*

Wolf, Mr.—A newspaper editor, whom Jonas Chuzzlewit met at dinner at Mr. Montague Tigg's.—*Martin Chuzzlewit.*

Wood, Jemmy, of Gloucester.—A miser whose biography Mr. Boffin pretended to be interested in.—*Our Mutual Friend.*

Woodcourt, Dr. Allan.—A London surgeon who married Esther Summerson.—"He was not rich; all his widowed mother could spare had been spent in qualifying him for his profession; it was not lucrative to a young practitioner with very little influence in London; and, although he was night and day at the service of numbers of poor people, and did wonders of gentleness and skill for them, he gained very little by it in money."—*Bleak House.*

Woodcourt, Mrs.—Mother of Dr. Allan.—"A pretty old lady with bright black eyes."—*Bleak House.*

Woodcourt, Mr.—The deceased husband of Mrs. Woodcourt.—"Poor Mr. Woodcourt, my dear, she would say, was descended from a great Highland family, the MacCourts of MacCourt. He served his King and Country as an officer in the Royal Highlanders, and he died on the field."—*Bleak House.*

Woodensconce, Mr.—President of the Statistical Section of the Mudfog Association.—*The Mudfog Sketches.*

Woolford, Miss.—A circus rider at Astley's.—"Another cut from the whip; a burst from the orchestra; a start from the horse; and round goes Miss Woolford again, on her graceful performance, to the delight of every member of the audience, young or old."—*Sketches by Boz* (Astley's).

Wopsle.—One of the guests at the Christmas dinner at Gargery's, on the day the convicts were captured.—"Mr. Wopsle, united to a Roman nose, and a large shining bald forehead, had a deep voice which he was uncommonly proud of; indeed it was understood among his acquaintance that, if you could only give him his head, he would rend the clergyman into fits; he himself confessed that if the church was thrown open—meaning to competitors—he would not despair of making his mark in it."—*Great Expectations*.

Wopsle's Great Aunt.—Kept a dame school, assisted by Biddy, her granddaughter, which Pip attended. "She was a ridiculous old woman of limited means, and unlimited infirmity, who used to go to sleep from six to seven every evening, in the society of youth who paid twopence per week each for the improving opportunity of seeing her do it." —*Great Expectations*.

Wosky, Doctor.—The medical attendant of Mrs. Bloss. —"He was a little man, with a red face—dressed of course in black, with a stiff white neckerchief. He had a very good practice, and plenty of money, which he had amassed by invariably humouring the worst fancies of all the females of all the families he had ever been introduced into."—*Sketches by Boz* (The Boarding House).

Wozenham, Miss.—Keeper of a rival boarding-house commented on by Mrs. Lirriper.—"Some there are who do not think it lowering themselves to make their names that cheap, and even going the lengths of a portrait of the house not like it, with a blot in every window, and a coach and four at the door, but what will suit Wozenham's lower down on the other side of the way will not suit me, Miss Wozenham having her opinions and me having mine."—Mrs. Lirriper's Lodgings (*Christmas Stories*).

Wrasp and Co.—London solicitors to whom Dick Swiveller carried a message from Sampson Brass.—*The Old Curiosity Shop*.

Wrayburn, Eugene.—A briefless barrister, who disliked his profession, and idled his time away, chiefly in the company of his friend Mortimer Lightwood. By his attentions to Lizzie Hexam he aroused the jealousy of Bradley Headstone, who attacked him murderously and threw him into a river, whence Lizzie rescued him, and he married her.—"And I, said Eugene, have been called seven years and have had no business at all, and if I had I shouldn't know how to do it. It was forced upon me, said the gloomy Eugene, because it was understood that we wanted a barrister in the family."—*Our Mutual Friend.*

Wrayburn, Mr., Senior.—Father of Eugene.—" My respected father having always, in the clearest manner, provided (as he calls it) for his children, by pre-arranging from the hour of the birth of each, what the devoted little victim's calling and course in life should be, pre-arranged for myself that I was to be the barrister I am (with the slight addition of an enormous practice which has not accrued) and also the married man I am not."—*Our Mutual Friend.*

Wren, Jenny.—The business name of Fanny Cleaver, the Doll's Dressmaker.—" Her real name was Fanny Cleaver, but she had long ago chosen to bestow upon herself the appellation of Miss Jenny Wren. Stop a bit, interposed Miss Wren, I'll give the lady my card. She produced it from her pocket with an air, after struggling with the gigantic door key which had got upon the top of it and kept it down. Miss Abbey, with manifest tokens of astonishment, took the diminutive document, and found it to run concisely thus—Miss Jenny Wren, Doll's Dressmaker. Dolls attended at their own residences."—*Our Mutual Friend.*

Wright's.—A Rochester hotel Mr. Jingle disapproved of. —" Wright's next house—dear—very dear—half-a-crown in the bill if you look at the waiter—charge you more if you dine at a friend's house than if you dined in the coffee-room —rum fellows—very."—*Pickwick Papers.*

Wrymug, Mrs.—A client of the General Agency in want of a cook.—" Mrs. Wrymug, said Tom—pleasant place—Finsbury—wages Twelve guineas; no tea; no sugar; serious family."—*Nicholas Nickleby.*

Wugsby, Mrs. Colonel.—One of the party with whom Mr. Pickwick played whist at Bath.—" The Dowager Lady Snuphanuph, and two other ladies of an ancient and whist-like appearance, were hovering over an unoccupied card-table; and they no sooner set eyes upon Mr. Pickwick, under the convoy of Angelo Bantam, than they exchanged glances with each other, seeing that he was precisely the very person they wanted to make up the rubber."— —*Pickwick Papers.*

Wugsby, Miss Jane.—Daughter of Mrs. Col. Wugsby. —*Pickwick Papers.*

Yawler.—A schoolmate of Traddles, who afterwards assisted him when he went to the bar.—" I began with the assistance of the son of a professional man, who had been to Salem House,—Yawler with his nose on one side—do you recollect him? "—*David Copperfield.*

York, The Five Sisters of.—The title of a tale told by one of the passengers to beguile the time when the coach on which Squeers and Nicholas travelled broke down.—*Nicholas Nickleby.*

Zobeide.—The name given to Miss Bule when Miss Griffin's school was supposed to be a Seraglio.—(*See* **Bule, Miss.**)—The Haunted House (*Christmas Stories*).